Proceedings of the Boston Area Colloquium in Ancient Philosophy

Volume VII
1991

Edited by
John J. Cleary

UNIVERSITY
PRESS OF
AMERICA

Lanham • New York • London

Copyright © 1993 by
University Press of America®, Inc.
4720 Boston Way
Lanham, Maryland 20706

3 Henrietta Street
London WC2E 8LU England

Co-published by arrangement with
the Boston Area Colloquium in Ancient Philosophy

ISBN: 0–8191–8560–4 (cloth : alk. paper)
ISBN: 0–8191–8561–2 (paper : alk. paper)
ISSN: 1059–986X
LCN: 90–657386

 The paper used in this publication meets the minimum requirements of
American National Standard for Information Sciences—Permanence
of Paper for Printed Library Materials, ANSI Z39.48–1984.

In Memory of

Gregory Vlastos

1907—1991

Contents

Contents

Preface

Although I am not a number mystic, yet I must admit that in my life some special significance is to be attached to the number 7. For instance, I arrived in the U.S. for the first time on July 7th, 1977 (7/7/'77) when I was 28 years old (7 x 4). This only struck me as being significant when I reflected on the fact that I was producing volume 7 of these *Proceedings* once again as sole editor. Perhaps all of this is sheer coincidence recollected in tranquillity, and thereby fashioned into a poetic symmetry from the haphazard jumble that we call life. Since I am in no position to decide these profound questions about fate and chance, I will take refuge in the ancient custom of reckoning the ages of man in 7 year stages, by simply reporting that I reached 35 (7 x 5) on becoming Director of BACAP and 42 (7 x 6) on editing this volume.

Leaving this as a puzzle for the numerologists, let me reflect on what BACAP has meant both in my own life and in the life of our academic community in Boston over the last decade. Since I have narrated the early history of this organization in the preface to Volume 1, I will focus on its general significance for contemporary university life with its disciplinary and institutional barriers. Within this setting BACAP is a unique structure that crosses these boundaries in a way that may provide a model for other cooperative projects. The Colloquium is not a foundation with money and staff of its own, nor is it a corporate entity separate from the seven universities which are currently participating in it: Boston College, Boston University, Brown University,

John J. Cleary

Clark University, College of The Holy Cross, Harvard University, Wellesley College. Its whole existence and functioning depends on the voluntary work of the BACAP committee, whose members represent each of these participating institutions. This standing committee meets 3-4 times per year to make all major decisions connected with the program, and these are put into effect by the Director or Co-Director, who coordinates the activities of the Colloquium from a home institution. By conventional wisdom such a loose organization cannot survive without some formal foundational basis, but over the last 7 years I have learned that the volunteer spirit is tenacious. I have learned also that no cooperative enterprise can prosper without a supportive community in which individuals are prepared to put the common good above their own selfish interests. BACAP is such a community, and so I wish to pay tribute to all past and present members of the committee, but especially to Hermann Cloeren (College of the Holy Cross) who is its longest-serving member and one of the unsung heroes of the whole enterprise.

Contrary to the growing trend towards narrow expertise, one of the major goals of the Colloquium has been to cross boundaries not only between disciplines like philosophy and classics, but also to break down artificial barriers between expert and amateur within the field of liberal arts education. Thus, for instance, an expert in some relevant field is invited to visit one of the participating universities (some with exclusively undergraduate programs in philosophy and classics) and to make sophisticated material accessible at every level from undergraduates to faculty members. While the visit is organized in the standard format of lectures and seminars, in practice the informal discussion and contact with the visitor often turns out to be more important for participating faculty and students. So one should not take this series of *Proceedings* as being an adequate reflection of the whole BACAP program, though it is published for the express purpose of sharing some aspects of our program with the wider academic community. With some exceptions, what is published is usually a revised version of the lecture delivered by the visitor, along with critical remarks upon the paper made on the same occasion by an invited commentator.

Therefore, except for two chapters that lack commentaries, this volume contains revised versions of papers and commentaries which were read to the Colloquium during the academic year 1990-91. The two notable exceptions are the papers of Richard Kraut and Richard Janko, which were originally given as informal seminars and subsequently written up for this series, since their public lectures had already been committed elsewhere for publication. Although Richard Janko's paper might be more at home in a journal on papyrology, I am very glad that he agreed to publish it here because of its importance for scholars in Hellenistic philosophy and philology.

In addition to the eight colloquia consisting of papers and commentaries, this volume also contains a number of important appendices just like previous volumes in the series. For instance, there are two general indices (names & contents, index locorum) which were collated from particular indices for each contribution compiled by the contributors themselves. I am most grateful to each of the authors for helping to improve the accessibility of the volume by making indices and bibliographies according to the standard formats. Finally, I wish to thank them for providing me with the brief biographical material which constitutes the appendix called "About our Contributors".

Although this series is deliberately named *Proceedings*, the papers published in it are often extensively revised versions of public lectures or seminars originally presented in the Colloquium. For this process of revision, authors are given editorial directives and the reports of independent readers as guidelines for turning their lectures into publishable papers. In addition, this process enables both speaker and commentator to continue their dialogue in the spirit of cooperative inquiry which usually permeates such exchanges. The editor plays an active role in the whole process of revision, which may continue up to and including the proofreading stage, given the flexibility in our method of producing camera-ready copy. For help in this editorial work, I gratefully acknowledge the help of the following colleagues on both sides of the Atlantic: Patrick Byrne (Boston College), John Dillon (Trinity College, Dublin), Thomas Finan & Gerard Watson (St Patrick's College, Maynooth), and Markus Wörner (University College Galway).

I also wish to acknowledge the work of my new editorial assistant, Alfonso Capone, who measured up well to the task of learning a new system while being given work that he couldn't refuse. Despite many difficulties, he successfully produced at Boston College the camera-ready copy of this volume of *Proceedings*, which was sent to our co-publisher, University Press of America. I would like to thank the people in the co-publishing program, including Jonathan Sisk and Maureen Muncaster, for getting the series back on track in their production schedule. Last but not least, I wish to acknowledge the moral and financial support of the academic vice-president at Boston College, William Neenan S.J., who would be my perpetual nomination for 'administrator of the year' if there were such an award.

This volume is dedicated to the memory of the late Gregory Vlastos, who died in November 1991. Prof. Vlastos participated in our BACAP program a number of years ago, and he has always been a steadfast supporter of the Colloquium. It is no exaggeration to say that his death represents a great loss to ancient philosophy, since he was universally recognized as one of the greatest Plato scholars in the field.

Boston College & St Patrick's College, Maynooth

Introduction

Given the loose structure of the BACAP program itself, it is natural to expect that the resulting set of papers and commentaries will contain diverse themes and treatments rather than displaying any overall thematic unity. Indeed, as readers of previous volumes of our *Proceedings* already know, diversity may rightly be seen as the hallmark of every BACAP program since the initial publication of this series in 1985. In those heady days, diversity had not yet become a fad and indeed it was looked at rather askance as being the sign of a certain woollymindedness. But, at the risk of being un-fashionable once again, I must emphasize that the rationale behind the diversity of this volume is perfectly simple; namely, that it reflects the different themes and interests of the speakers who were invited to participate in our series during the last academic year. Since no attempt is ever made to impose uniformity or to specify a particular theme for the year, I will not try to discover any hidden unity that might be mysteriously running through all the contributions to this volume. In fact, there is a wide variety of topics ranging from Aristotle to Gnostic Platonism, though a significant number of papers concentrate on specific problems in the interpretation of Plato and Aristotle. So I will adopt the piecemeal approach of summarizing each chapter as a self-contained unit with its own problems, claims and objections. Of course, the purpose of my introduction is to whet the appetite for reading the highly diverse set of papers contained in the volume, so ideally it should function as a translucent guide that directs the reader to items of interest.

John J. Cleary

In a rich historical paper on "Gnostic Platonism", **Harold Attridge** sets out to map the points of contact between gnosticism and platonism from the second to the fourth centuries C.E. His plan is to trace the two broad streams of gnosticism, the Sethian and the Valentinian, from their sources to their disappearance into the desert of Roman orthodoxy. The high watermark of their confluence with Platonism seems to have been registered by Plotinus who criticized some unnamed Gnostics within his own circle for being confused Platonists. Previously, Hippolytus of Rome had condemned the Valentinian Gnostics as heretics, precisely because of their attachment to pagan philosophies such as Pythagoreanism and Platonism. So it seems that the Gnostics fell between two stools, so to speak.

In exploring the two traditions of Gnosticism that were criticized by Hippolytus and Plotinus, Attridge draws on some new primary sources from the Nag Hammadi library, especially the *Apocryphon of John*, an important Sethian text, and a supposed work of Valentinus called the *Gospel of Truth*. His main historical thesis is that both streams of Gnosticism are being swelled by tributaries from professional Platonic philosophy, so that they eventually overflow their narrow Christian banks. Attridge claims that the negative theology of the *Apocryphon of John* displays a new philosophical sophistication which may reflect some fresh Platonic influences. For instance, he sees structural similarities at the highest levels of reality in both Sethian Gnosticism and Pythagoreanizing Platonism. Just as Numenius posited two levels of Mind, and Plotinus divided the Mind from the Soul; so also the Gnostics split Sophia into two parts, one of which remains above in the Pleroma, while the other descends into the phenomenal world.

But, as **Pheme Perkins** points out in her commentary, it is more controversial to use the *Gospel of Truth* as evidence for Valentinian Gnosticism. Given the lack of sources for Valentinus, however, Attridge may be excused for making a conjectural connection. Although he claims (p. 17) that there is a general similarity of method between this work and Plutarch's

On Isis and Osiris, he is well aware that this is not sufficient to establish a Valentinian connection with the Platonic tradition. Thus he examines a remarkable passage from the *Gospel of Truth*, which meditates on the Son as revealing the Name of the Father. This is part of an epistemological problem generated by Jewish and Christian doctrine that the transcendent God was unknowable, and resolved in Christian circles by saying that Jesus reveals the hidden God. Attridge claims that Valentinus (as putative author of *Gospel of Truth*) is adopting some elements from both the Jewish and Christian traditions, while combining them with quasi-philosophical reflections reminiscent of Plato on the nature of the Name. In the *Seventh Epistle*, for instance, there is a distinction (342A-B) between three classes of object through which knowledge is achieved, i.e. name, definition, and image; which Attridge finds paralleled in an attested fragment of Valentinus where he distinguishes between a face, the portrait of a face, and the name attached to the portrait. Similarly, in the *Gospel of Truth*, it is said that the Son-Name actually provides knowledge of its referent, while the notion of 'image' is absent from the work. Attridge thinks that it has been deliberately excluded, however, since the Son was traditionally called an 'image' of God and so would have an inferior status according to Platonic metaphysics. He claims that Valentinus applied the Platonic conditions for naming at the noumenal level (cf. *Cratylus* 438C ff.) to the single case of the Name of the Unnameable. But, in the absence of firm evidence for a philosophical problem of naming in the *Gospel of Truth*, I find such parallels with Plato to be rather artificial, especially since an acquaintance with Platonic metaphysics would have forced the author to grapple with the problem. It is only in the subsequent Valentinian tradition, as carried on by Ptolemy and Theodetus, that we find clear evidence for the systematizing influence of Platonism.

By contrast, **Richard Kraut** confines himself to a well-attested text and to a difficulty that has engaged modern interpreters of Plato for decades. In a tightly-argued paper entitled "Return to the Cave", he explores an exegetical and philosophical problem

arising from the passage in Plato's *Republic* (519-21) which specifies that, after being educated by the polis, the philosopher ruler
must sacrifice theoretical studies for the sake of political activity.
The general philosophical problem is that this requirement
seems to be unjust to these rulers themselves because it does not
contribute to their happiness, which is best promoted by continuing with theoretical studies. Plato's ostensible solution is that
this requirement is just because the rulers have benefited from
the education provided by the city, and so it is right that they be
required to devote some time to public service. But this solution
raises an exegetical problem by seeming to conflict with Plato's
claim that justice is always in one's best interests, since theoretical study rather than political activity would appear to serve the
best interests of the philosopher guardians. Such an apparent
conflict between justice and self-interest seems to undermine the
whole project of the *Republic*.

Modern scholars have adopted two quite different strategies in
dealing with this exegetical problem: (1) to admit it as an exception to Plato's general defense of justice in terms of self-interest
(e.g. N. White); (2) to find a way in which the requirement does
promote the greatest good of philosophers over the long run
(e.g. D. Reeve). While Kraut generally adopts the second strategy, he executes it rather differently. First, he challenges the putative evidence that Plato believes philosophers to be acting contrary to their best interests by ruling in the ideal city. He
suggests that the apparent failure of Plato to explain how the
philosopher profits from ruling might actually be our failure as
readers to understand how it fits under his general defense of
justice. Besides the argument from silence, however, there
appears to be positive evidence that ruling is contrary to the
philosopher's good in the assertion (521B7) that he will be compelled to rule. But Kraut does not accept that this implies non-
rational coercion, since they may be rationally persuaded to rule
by something like the whole argument laid out in the *Republic*.
In any case, he insists, the point of Plato's talk of compulsion is
rather that the philosopher-rulers are not free to do what they
want because of the benefits they have received from the city. In

order to make his solution more convincing philologically, Kraut might have cited from the *Republic* parallel uses of the language of compulsion with regard to the conversion to theoretical studies brought about through mathematics.

But the strongest argument for a conflict in the *Republic* between justice and self-interest is based on Plato's assertion that the philosophical life is better than the political life, and so the philosopher is reluctant to give up the theoretical life. By way of objection, Kraut claims that the argument runs together two distinct questions: 1) Is philosophical activity better than political activity? 2) Would the philosopher trained by the state be better off to continue philosophizing, and thereby violate the just requirement to rule, or to spend some time ruling and thereby fulfil the requirement? Although Plato answers yes to the first question, Kraut insists that he is not committed to saying that philosophical activity is most advantageous in all circumstances. Yet he concedes that Plato owes us an explanation of why just and unjust circumstances make so much difference, given that the philosopher despises the political life; cf. *Rep.* 521b1 ff.

In proposing his own solution to the exegetical problem, Kraut explicitly assumes that Plato's metaphysics plays a central role in his defense of justice; i.e. that the philosopher is the paradigm of a just person and that the Forms are the most valuable objects one can possess. But the Forms are arranged in a systematic order which it is the task of the philosopher to embody in the political sphere. Indeed, Plato seems to have held that justice in the soul and in the city involve the sort of harmonious relationships that reflect the systematic order of the Forms. If the philosopher were to recognize a political arrangement as just under which he is required to rule, yet refused to rule, he would be undermining his own happiness which involves living the best kind of life in imitation of the Forms.

Thus Kraut takes Plato to be arguing deontologically rather than consequentially; i.e. the injustice in the act of refusal is by itself a decisive objection apart from its consequences. When he

John J. Cleary

is understood in this way, it follows that the justice of requiring philosophers to rule is intimately connected with the advantage of governing in this situation. One cannot profit by dissociating oneself from the Forms, since the best life is achieved by imitating their order; and if we fail to imitate this just order then we are refusing to do what is justly required of us in human relationships. Thus, once the philosopher sees why ruling is just, he will be rationally persuaded that it would be contrary to his best interests to continue his purely philosophical activities, even though in other circumstances such activity would be more advantageous than political activity.

In considering potential objections to his solution, Kraut does take seriously the question of why the philosopher should imitate the Forms in a political manner, especially since he is more suited to a purely contemplative imitation. In the absence of textual evidence, he constructs a hypothetical answer which he holds to be consistent with Plato's view that one should never reject the Forms as models. Such a "principle of purity" Kraut takes to imply that ruling would be better for the philosopher under certain circumstances, since a refusal to rule would involve rejection of the Forms as models. By contrast, there is no such rejection involved in turning from theoretical to practical political activity, since human beings cannot always be contemplating the Forms.

Kraut's interpretation shows that Plato's conception of the human good is not intellectualist in the strong sense; i.e. that in all circumstances one's good is best promoted by intellectual activity, since political activity is appropriate under certain circumstances. It also shows that Plato's belief in the coincidence of the good of the individual with that of the community is based upon the assumption that the individual does best in imitating the Forms, which themselves constitute a kind of moral community. So it can never be in the interest of an individual to subvert a system of distributive justice that is in the best interest of his community. Hence Kraut thinks he has established that Plato is not an egoist in any strict modern sense according to which one's own good always takes precedence over that of the community. When Plato deprives the guardians of private property and requires them to rule, both requirements are justified as promoting the happiness of the community rather than of the philosopher rulers. But, since self-interest is such a powerful motive for action, it is essential to the stability of Plato's ideal polis that its rulers be rationally convinced of the coincidence of their own interests with those of the community. Perhaps the enormous effort which he expends on this argument in the *Republic* is Plato's implicit recognition of the divergence of these interests in the *Realpolitik* of ancient Athens.

With reference to the ancient quarrel between poetry and philosophy, in a fine paper on "Epicurean Poetics" **Elizabeth Asmis** tries to build an explanatory bridge between Epicurus, who seems to have rejected poetry, and Lucretius who chose to write a great poem on the nature of the universe. For a start she claims that the attitude of Epicurus to poetry is connected with his rejection of Plato's intellectual curriculum as something unnecessary for the good life, which he identifies with the life of pleasure. Furthermore, he rejects the traditional educational system based on teaching Homer because it is too philological and intellectual, and so is not conducive to pleasure. Yet Epicurus does approve of enjoying musical and poetical performances, though he insists that intellectual training is unnecessary and may even inhibit enjoyment. Thus he distinguished between poetry as education (which he condemned) and poetry as entertainment (which he welcomed), while assuming that the philosophically trained mind can enjoy a poetic performance without being corrupted by the contents. Unlike Plato, he never proposed that some kind of purified poetry might serve as a way to philosophy because he had complete confidence in the ability of human reason to find a way to the truth through clear (prose) speech.

Asmis takes as a sign of internal tension in this apparently clear-cut position of Epicurus the fact that it was both defended and revised by subsequent generations of followers. Thus, for instance, Cicero taunts Torquatus, a young Epicurean friend, with being unfaithful to his uneducated master because he devotes himself to literature. From Cicero's rather polemical picture Asmis reconstructs a possible Epicurean defense in terms of some definition of education as what contributes to happiness, and which excludes poetry and liberal studies as 'childish'. According to this later interpretation, Epicurus is taken to be proposing a philosophical revision of the common-place notion of education; so that his famous 'hoist sail' motto means that one can enjoy the song of the Sirens without suffering any destructive influence. For instance, Sextus Empiricus (*adv. math.* I.1) reports that Epicurus held that learning makes no contribution to wisdom; whereas philosophy can render poetry harmless and even extract some good from it by supplying proofs which allow listeners to distinguish between good and bad.

Asmis defends her conjectural reconstruction by arguing that it is consistent with the main tenets of Epicureanism as reported, for instance, in Philodemus' *On Music*, which says that poems lack the clarity of philosophical demonstration and hence are of limited use for moral instruction. But Philodemus also thought that the poetry of Homer can provide beneficial moral guidance for rulers, and this looks like an inconsistency. Asmis does not think so, however, because it fits with a tradition of Epicurean interpretation which holds that philosophy may illuminate truths found incidentally in poems. Yet there is the additional problem for Philodemus of justifying his own poetic composition of epigrams in the face of the Epicurean prohibition of poetic composition as unsuitable for the wise man. Asmis suggests that Philodemus may have interpreted this as being directed against professional poetizing, rather than against amateur efforts for the sake of pleasure.

By contrast, Lucretius seems to represent the opposite approach of refurbishing poetry as a suitable vehicle for philosophical instruction. In defense of his new departure, Lucretius proposes to use poetry as a means of attracting the ordinary person to Epicurean philosophy. Appealing to the criterion of clarity, he claims that poetry is a suitable medium for philosophical discourse because it brings clarity to the obscurity of Epicurean discoveries. For example, his *De Rerum Natura* is intended as a demonstrative discourse designed to lead the soul in the direction of truth, and it involves a complete reversal of the usual Epicurean attitude to poetry.

David Sider's commentary offers additional evidence in support of Asmis' general claims about the historical development in Epicurean attitudes to poetry. Consistent with the later friendly attitude, for instance, he names Metrodorus of Lampsakos and Titus Albucius from among a group of obscure Epicureans who clothed their didactic message in poetic garb. With regard to Epicurus' hostility to poetry, Sider makes the interesting suggestion that his attitude might reflect a political intention of breaking down social barriers that were erected on wealth and the associated privilege of a liberal education. Finally, Sider considers the question of what a poetics might mean for Epicurus; i.e. whether he would accept the proselytizing poetry of Lucretius or Philodemus' concept of poetry as light entertainment. Judging by the *Symposium* of Epicurus, Sider concludes that he would have been more at home with Philodemus' notion that poetry can serve only as charming and witty entertainment at an elegant dinner.

In his masterly paper on "The Idea of the Will in Chrysippus, Posidonius, and Galen", **Jaap Mansfeld** argues against the claim of Albrecht Dihle that the ancients had no concept of the will in our modern sense. Noting Dihle's failure to give a clear definition or theory of the will, Mansfeld doubts whether we moderns have any clear-cut concept of the will that is lacking among the ancients. Despite such unclarity about the notion of will, however, Dihle claimed that one can find it in the Old Testament but not in Greek and Roman authors before Augustine of Hippo. Against this claim, Mansfeld argues that one can find a notion of God's will in Stoic philosophy but that it is completely rational (i.e. bound by physical and mathematical laws), in contrast to

Judaic and Christian notions which attribute to God the arbitrary freedom to work miracles. He concedes however that no Greek ever thought of the will as an autonomous mental function which does not depend on reason, and which can also be clearly distinguished from desire and the emotions. In other words, Greek psychology does not treat the idea of the will as an independent topic.

Yet Mansfeld insists that the idea of the will does play an important part in the philosophy of mind of at least some Greek philosophers, contrary to the misleading inference that there is no corresponding concept because the standard philological research can find no exact equivalent to 'will' in ancient Greek. As an alternative approach, Mansfeld takes an intuitively obvious instance of an act of will, like moving one's finger, and looks for conceptual equivalents in the work of Greek thinkers. Since the notion of will is typically associated with power or capacity, he uses the notion of 'strength' as his lode-star for steering towards a theory of will in classical antiquity.

Mansfeld's first port of call is with the Stoics who rejected the standard dualist view of psychic functions by arguing for the so-called ἡγεμονικόν which embraces both reason and the passions. The physical subject for this part is the πνεῦμα, which may have either good or bad tension. When making a wrong judgment, the ἡγεμονικόν weakens its good tension and thereby gives rise to a condition of distress. By contrast, strength seems to be right reason considered in relation to choosing, deciding or acting, and this sinewy character of the soul is like what we might call a "strong will". Psychologically, this ὁρμή is described in terms of reason giving the command to act, following upon a φαντασία in the soul. Chrysippus used the example of the running man, by contrast with one walking calmly, to illustrate how excess of ὁρμή can cause the soul to make wrong decisions. Mansfeld takes the ὁρμή that leads to walking to correspond with what we would call an act of will, just as is the ὁρμή to stop walking. But the running man is not able to stop when he wants, and so his movement is stronger than the wish to stop. Similarly, the irrational ὁρμή is opposed to reason, just as in the case of angry or passionate people. Thus Mansfeld concludes that for Chrysippus the ὁρμή or will to act is a permanent feature of the pneumatic ruling part of the soul as a whole, which is operational not only when the soul is wholly rational but also when it has succumbed to passion.

In his critique of Chrysippus, however, Posidonius returns to the tripartite psychology of Plato when he insists that anger and desire are different psychic functions which may be impervious to reason. Trading on the failure of Chrysippus to explain why some people weep against their will, Posidonius argues that this occurs because the pressure of affective motions is so strong that they cannot be controlled by the will. For him this shows the existence of a conflict between reason and the affections, and hence the existence of opposed functions of the soul. Galen sides with Posidonius against Chrysippus on the tripartition of the soul, since he thinks that he can establish it scientifically through vivisections which show that parts of the soul are in different parts of the body. For instance, since reason is the ruling part of the soul, he claims that it must be located in the head where the nerves have their beginning. *Pace* Aristotle Galen argues that, since the nerves originate in the brain, the commands issued by the regent part of the soul in the brain are transmitted *via* the motor nerves, which use the muscles as levers to move the limbs. Quite unusually for ancient science, these claims are supported by vivisection experiments which showed that touching the brain affected voluntary motions, whereas touching the heart did not. If the motor nerves which transmit the 'psychic power' are cut, then the decision to move or speak is not put into effect; and this is an example of an act of will that fails to yield a result.

In Galen's account, this relation between will and strength in voluntary motion is compatible with a tripartite division of the soul, since that part rules which is the strongest. Thus reason, even if it has the required knowledge, will be unable to hold anger in check as long as it lacks the required strength. Galen thinks that each part of the soul can set a ὁρμή in motion, so that the strongest part will prevail in case of conflict. But Mansfeld notes an apparent inconsistency between Galen's claim that each part of the soul can generate its own ὁρμή, and his thesis that the brain qua location of reason is the source of all the nerves. The latter thesis deprives the other parts of the soul of the means for generating impulses that would move limbs in response to their conations. Thus Mansfeld concludes that Galen's physiology does not cohere with his moral psychology and his philosophy of mind.

By way of commentary, **David Sedley** welcomes Mansfeld's comprehensive treatment of the function of the will in Stoic moral psychology, though he is more inclined to deal with it in terms of separate questions that have diverse histories: (1) what mental power enables us to translate intention into action? (2) what power is more abundant in strong-willed people? With reference to the Stoics, Sedley agrees with Mansfeld that Posidonius sees the battle for psychic domination as being between reason and two irrational forces with the strongest being victorious. But he thinks the crucial question is whether the 'clout' of reason is something independent, as with Plato, or merely a function of reason, as with Posidonius. In the latter case the strength of the reasoning faculty is identical with its degree of understanding, which can in turn be identified with the tensional strength of the πνεῦμα. While it seems clear that Posidonius treated psychic strength as doing the work of will in translating thought into action, it is not so obvious that the same is true for the monistic psychology of Chrysippus, since the degree of understanding of the ruling part seems to be irrelevant to its 'clout' in producing action. Despite such doubts, however, Sedley concludes that for Chrysippus also the soul's weakness of resolve can be identified with pneumatic weakness, which in turn is identical with an inability to stick to its judgements. As a final historical note, he suggests that the idea of the will as a form of mental 'clout' was a popular notion that Chrysippus tried to bring into line with his Socratic intellectualism.

At the beginning of an innovative paper on "Philosophy and Literature", **Christopher Rowe** puts his interpretive cards on the table in announcing his intention to treat the *Phaedo* as a whole by examining the connection of parts. When he insists that Plato can be given a determinate reading, however, he is refusing to play the wild-card poker which is the delight of deconstructionists like Derrida. But, on the other hand, he wants to avoid the excessively analytic game played by interpreters who focus on the arguments in a Platonic dialogue, while neglecting the overall dialogical structure. Along with modern interpreters of Plato such as Burger and Dorter, Rowe insists that the arguments should not be isolated from their dramatic context because they cannot be properly assessed without knowing their purpose, which is indicated by how they are introduced, presented and received. Rowe thinks there is ample evidence that Plato was not interested purely in argument as such, and that he viewed philosophy differently from the way modern analytic philosophers view it.

For instance, Rowe claims that Plato intends the so-called argument from affinity to fail, so as to illustrate the eristic error of claiming an argument to be stronger than it really is. As a complete philosopher, Socrates will only be convinced by arguments that have passed the most stringent objective tests, which go well beyond what is required to persuade an audience. The realization that the argument from affinity is inadequate constitutes an essential step in the movement of the dialogue towards a more ambitious final argument for the immortality of the soul, which is provisionally accepted as trustworthy. Thus, Rowe claims, the failure of the affinity argument shows us that philosophical argument depends on a commitment to finding truth, and not simply on an ability to convince whoever happens to be listening.

But (he argues) the idea of philosophy as mutual interchange is also basic to the *Phaedo* as a whole, since the objection of Simmias and Cebes to the affinity argument is what pushed the discussion into its new phase. Philosophy is not a form of gossip, however, since one must have conversation partners who can spot weaknesses and propose alternative avenues of inquiry. While this is the best test of truth available, it is not a guarantee against error. Although he concedes that Simmias and Cebes are linked with Philolaus, he refuses to accept them as 'mere' Pythagoreans because the dialogue emphasizes their familiarity with Socrates' methods and ideas. He insists that their actual role is that of Socratic partners in the discussion, who are sufficiently intelligent to drive it forward. Thus, according to Rowe, the *Phaedo* reports a conversation between like-thinking but critical minds, which are collaborating in the construction and demolition of arguments.

In defense of his general interpretation, Rowe cites the passage (61C) where Cebes challenges Socrates on his proposal that the philosopher should be striving to die, which appears to contravene a Pythagorean prohibition on suicide. Since neither Simmias nor Cebes appear to be familiar with this rule, Rowe concludes that they are not genuine Pythagoreans, but he seems to overlook the possibility that they might belong to the secular group called μαθηματικοί. In any case, Rowe attaches more importance to the fact that Socrates defends himself against Cebes, not in a set speech but rather in his usual manner. He takes this to show that what distinguishes a philosophical *logos* from a rhetorical *logos*, as from an eristic one, is the purpose for which it is uttered; i.e. that it be received critically and that it be defended in such a way as to persuade both oneself and others.

But cooperation is just as essential as criticism to the dialectical model of philosophy, and Rowe finds this illustrated in the passage where Cebes recollects the theory of Forms from previous conversations with Socrates in order to help support one of the arguments for immortality. Within the overall strategy of the dialogue, Rowe thinks that the form-hypothesis matters as much as the argument from recollection, since it grounds the final and most powerful argument. Thus, from the dramatic perspective, the conversation makes its first solid gain with the help of Cebes, and so Rowe considers him to be a philosopher in the Socratic mould rather than any kind of Pythagorean.

Thomas Tuozzo's incisive commentary takes issue with the description of Simmias and Cebes as perfect Socratic philosophers, since he does not rate their contribution to the discussion any higher than that of gifted neophytes. This may look like an unimportant difference of opinion, but actually it has a considerable bearing on how the argument and the literary context are to be combined in reading the *Phaedo*. While Tuozzo heartily agrees with Rowe's sentiments about putting the two aspects together, in practice he finds that Rowe behaves like a typical analytic philosopher when he treats the arguments in isolation and fails to clarify how they build on each other to form a complete dialogical argument. Tuozzo also accuses Rowe of neglecting their rhetorical function of producing conviction in hearers like Simmias and Cebes, who don't complain about the arguments as long as they help to charm away the fear of death. Furthermore, Socrates' use of myth and other types of incantation seems to be aimed at the emotional side of his audience, which includes Simmias and Cebes who do not appear to be on the same rational level as Socrates. As an alternative interpretation to that of Rowe, therefore, Tuozzo suggests that the various arguments in the *Phaedo* have a dual function; i.e. the rhetorical one of producing conviction in the audience as to the immortality of the soul, and the dialectical one of provoking reflection on immortality that will lead to a better philosophical understanding for those who are able to identify fallacy and ambiguity.

In an elegant paper on "The Ascent in Plato's *Symposium*", Richard Patterson addresses the exegetical question of how, according to Plato, one ascends the ladder of love to reach the vision of Beauty. Patterson's motivation for raising this question is found in his contention that Diotima's account of this ascent is not completely perspicuous and needs to be elaborated in more detail. So his focus is on the famous passage in the *Symposium* (210A4 ff.) which describes the ascent, sometimes as a move from a particular to a general beauty, and sometimes as a transition to a higher level. According to this account, the lover ascends from the love of bodily to spiritual beauty, then to the love of laws, then to the love of understanding, before finally coming to rest in the love of Beauty itself. Patterson concedes that the various stages in the ascent are set out unambiguously, but he insists that the *how* of the ascent is not clearly described. He is particularly interested in the questions of how reason gets involved in the process, what is its special subject-matter, and how does it reveal a new object of ἔρως.

Briefly formulated, Patterson's general answer to these questions goes as follows. At each level of the ascent, the lover is stimulated by the object of ἔρως to bring forth a *logos* which tries to say what makes it so beautiful. However, reflection on this *logos* shows that what the lover found so attractive was really some other beauty, which is inadequately reflected by the first object of ἔρως. So this new beauty is preferred because it is really the reason why one experienced ἔρως on seeing its reflection in a particular body, for instance. Hence no further explanation is needed as to why ἔρως is now transferred to this higher beauty, since the process is both rational and aesthetic. But there is no danger of an infinite regress here, because the process finds its natural completion in Beauty itself, which is beautiful in itself and not by virtue of some other beauty.

This plausible general account of the rational dynamic of ascent is given detailed support with relevant texts. According to the *Symposium* (210B7-8), the 'right' approach to a beautiful body involves not only sexual desire but also fair discourse. Drawing on a parallel with the *Charmides*, Patterson argues that the connection between psychic and bodily beauty is essential to understanding the initial phase of the ascent in the *Symposium*. He takes it to be a well-attested Platonic thesis that all true goods of the body flow from a proper condition of the soul, as illustrated by the person of Socrates in many dialogues. Thus Patterson suggests that it is precisely such facts about bodily beauty as a reflection of inner beauty which the noble *logos* must reveal, with the result that the lover realizes that what he really loves is the beautiful disposition of mind. So the transition from bodily to psychic beauty is not so much a transfer of ἔρως to a new object as an awakening to the fact that it was beauty of soul that attracted one all along. The next step in the ascent is similar in that ἔρως produces an appropriate *logos*, which deals with the origin and nature of beauty in the soul; i.e. that spiritual virtue not only arises from beautiful laws and practices but is actually a kind of law established in the soul. This insight may also be related to the unity of virtue thesis, which the *Republic* elucidates in terms of a constitution founded in the soul.

Once again, at a higher level, the noble *logos* that is stimulated by beautiful laws and practices shows that what makes them desirable is that they are grounded in an objective understanding of the subject-matter in question. So, with the realization that the real reason for the beauty of laws is the wisdom and understanding that underpins them, the lover reaches the penultimate stage in the ascent where he lusts after knowledge. But, when he tries to say what enthralls him about knowledge, he must seek a higher science whose subject-matter is simply Beauty itself. Thus, consistent with both the *Republic* and the *Symposium*, the ultimate goal of all learning will be an understanding of the Good or a love of Beauty itself. In concrete terms this means that there must be a norm of goodness beyond that found directly in any individual science; otherwise goodness and beauty might be completely relative. So the final step in the ascent involves the insight that the beauty of goodness is what constitutes the beauty of the sciences; i.e. the beauty of knowing what is objectively good or beautiful. Furthermore, this is the final step because all the goods of body, soul, laws, and sciences are good only insofar as they embody wisdom or understanding of what is good and beautiful. Any attempt to explain why Beauty itself is beautiful will not lead us higher because we can only give a negative account; e.g. that it is not the beauty of anything else. Therefore the *logos* presents no positive object for which ἔρως might strive, and hence there is no further question as to why we desire Beauty itself.

By way of conclusion, Patterson claims that the general condition for the *Symposium* ascent is the desire for the procreation of *logos* at each stage, which is driven by the natural impulse of the

John J. Cleary

lover to praise the beauty of the beloved. This is illustrated through the party-game in the dialogue, though all the speakers mistakenly assume that ἔρως is itself something beautiful rather than a desire for the beauty that is lacking. This mistake is shown up by means of Socrates' interrogation of Agathon, who admits to not knowing what he is talking about. Patterson suggests that dissatisfaction with such ignorance about the nature of beauty is perhaps the most important thing for the lover who is to approach beauty properly, and this chimes with Plato's constant theme that awareness of one's ignorance is not only a necessary condition for the pursuit of understanding but also a powerful goad to philosophic activity. Finally, the two activities of praising and understanding the object of ἔρως are not distinct for the true lover who gives a genuine encomium based on the truth about the object of praise.

At the outset of his engaging commentary, **Joseph Lawrence** outlines the differences of opinion between himself and Patterson, the most important of which concerns the relationship between the ascent accounts in the *Symposium* and the *Republic*. Whereas Patterson treats them as being so compatible that one may be used to elucidate obscure points in the other, Lawrence finds them to be opposed and to be reflecting the tension between ἔρως and *logos*. Patterson dissolves this tension with his assumption that for Plato there is only erotic passion for form, which directs the lover away from the lower bodily passions. By contrast, Lawrence finds Plato to be insisting upon the descent to base lust so as to emphasize passion rather than calculation as being essential to all kinds of ἔρως. One important implication of this reading is that the *logoi* stimulated by desire cannot be purely logical but must also be poetic, since Plato insists that they must be beautiful. But they are not just exercises in poetic exuberance, so they must be philosophical in the sense that they stimulate desire for further discourse. Of course, as Lawrence argues, these *logoi* are not sophistical either because they are given with humble awareness of ignorance of ultimate things. Indeed, philosophy is closer to poetry because the Beautiful is also the source of truth that is never completely revealed. In this respect Lawrence faults Patterson for making the ascent in the *Symposium* look too much like a passionless exercise in clarifying our desires by resorting to logical reasoning.

In his stimulating paper called "Aristotle on Substance, Essence and Biological Kinds", **David Charles** raises a series of exegetical and philosophical problems by comparing Aristotle's treatment of the problem of definition in logical, metaphysical, and biological writings. Beginning with the account of essential definition given in the *Analytics*, Charles explores the approach to substance made in the *Metaphysics* and to biological kinds in the treatises on animals. His general conclusion is that, while the logical account seems to fit the abstract metaphysical treatment of essence, it does not work so well for the empirical subject-matter of biology.

With regard to the *Analytics* model of definition, Charles raises a question about the type of information involved in the discovery of a complete definition that results from a scientific inquiry into the essence of any object. Aristotle rejects the Platonic method of division as inadequate for discovering definitions because it cannot establish something as an essential attribute, and it also fails to account for the unity of definition. Thus, as Charles points out, we can expect these epistemic and unity conditions for definition to be satisfied by Aristotle's proposed method of getting definitions. The epistemic condition is satisfied by an immediate proposition which has an unmediated causal connection between its terms, whereas the unity condition is satisfied by a single efficient cause that is also a middle term. In cases where such a middle term can be found, the relevant essences are also *made clear* through syllogistic demonstration, even though definitions are strictly speaking indemonstrable first principles. By means of his analysis, therefore, Charles throws a great deal of light on Aristotle's puzzling treatment of definition in *Posterior Analytics* II.

Turning his attention to the central books of the *Metaphysics*, Charles finds Aristotle to be consistent in his treatment of

John J. Cleary

essence as either an efficient or teleological cause, though there is some ambiguity in his references to substances like 'house'; i.e. it could be either the compound house or some formal essence. But it is clear that the teleological cause is explanatorily basic for all the other necessary properties of house, so that an immediate premiss gives the form/matter connection; e.g. being a cover for possessions belongs necessarily to these bricks. Yet there are elements in the definition of a composite substance which go beyond the explanatorily basic phenomenon; i.e. the form is an actuality that requires the presence of some matter as potentiality. Charles finds here the first sign of trouble for the simple *Analytics* model that assumes one essential cause to be basic for every natural kind, though he thinks that this "beautiful picture" is completely upset by Aristotle's research in biology.

It seems that Aristotle may have been aware of such methodological difficulties because in *Parts of Animals* I.4 he deliberates on whether one should follow a piecemeal or universal method in describing the properties of genera and species. Relying on conventional usage, he decides to pursue the approach which identifies genera as having some 'common nature' and as subsuming species that are not far removed from each other. This gives Aristotle a basis for his general classification of animals in *History of Animals* I, where he distinguishes genera on the basis of genuine differences in (a) types of locomotion, (b) methods of breathing, and (c) methods of eating. So the 'common nature' of a single genus means that its members have a distinctive shared way of fulfilling at least some of these basic life-functions. This can be clarified by comparison with a certain grouping, such as wingless quadrupeds, which fails to be a genus because it divides into viviparous and oviparous, and so the means of reproduction are too diverse for them to share a single common nature.

By contrast with the *Posterior Analytics*, the biological research of the *Historia Animalium* suggests a different picture of essential definition, since its notion of a 'common nature' is that of a collection of distinctive ways of performing certain basic soul functions like moving, breathing, and reproducing. Within the resulting genera, more specific common natures are demarcated by distinctive ways of performing these and other soul functions. But, according to Charles, the problem with this picture is that it leaves unclear how the set of soul functions themselves form an *organized* rather than an accidental unity. In the *Analytics* picture, it was necessary to find one property that explained the unity of the kind, but it is difficult to find such a property for the 'common nature' discussed in *Parts of Animals* I. According to Charles, the problem arises because Aristotle's different teleological and causal explanations do not have a common starting-point in one basic property which explains the rest, as in the *Analytics* model. So he concludes that, within the biological domain, Aristotle could not consistently hold his teleological model of explanation together with his favored tree model for establishing the unity of kinds. In other words, he lacked a way of establishing the proper unity of the so-called 'common natures' which biology discovers.

By way of commentary, **Mary Louise Gill** raises doubts about the correctness of the analysis of Aristotle's difficulty offered by Charles in terms of a breakdown of the simple *Analytics* picture of definition in the face of complex biological research. Given that Aristotle raised the issue about unity of definition without giving a satisfactory solution, she concedes that the reconstruction of the unity made by Charles is plausible in the light of *Posterior Analytics* II.8-10. But she is troubled by the fact that this reconstruction does not fit the complex methods of definition used in *Historia Animalium*, and so she proposes an alternative account that would at least make Aristotle consistent in both places. Using a discussion of division from *Metaphysics* VII.12 as a middle grou d, Gill suggests that Aristotle's simple account of the unity of definition might be consistently applied to complex biological research if one does not insist like Charles upon one single feature as the cause of unity. In order to avoid merely accidental unity like that of 'white man', Aristotle might have posited a single cause like soul which is a complex unity because of its hierarchy of functions (e.g. nutrition, reproduction and locomotion). Since none of these functions is reducible to the other nor explanatorily basic, an adequate definition of animal must therefore mention a set of appropriate differentiae without thereby undermining its unity.

Richard Janko's paper, aptly titled "Philodemus Resartus", provides us with a fascinating insight into the difficulties surrounding the deciphering of the Herculaneum papyri, which were discovered over two centuries ago but whose secrets have not yet been fully revealed. With reference to this problem of decipherment, Janko describes a technical breakthrough made independently by D. Obbink and D. Delattre in reconstructing these fragmentary papyri, which promises to supply scholars with the means for reconstructing many important Hellenistic texts, especially in Epicurean philosophy. Janko goes into considerable technical detail with regard to the deciphering of Philodemus' *On Music* and *On Poems*, in order to show what fundamental alterations to our knowledge of Hellenistic philosophy, literary theory and linguistics may result from this papyrological advance.

Along with telling us more about the influential views of Philodemus, it is anticipated that the technical progress will give us a better knowledge of the vocabulary used by Hellenistic critics, grammarians and philosophers of the late Roman *Republic* before the pure Atticists wiped the slate clean, as it were. Janko sees this breakthrough as an opportunity to reverse the general scholarly neglect of the Herculaneum papyri, which he rates as one of the most challenging and exciting treasure-troves for classical philology and ancient philosophy. If anyone should doubt his word, they should consult the contents of his BACAP public lecture which will be published elsewhere, or connect these discoveries with the issues discussed by Elizabeth Asmis in this volume.

Boston College and St Patrick's College, Maynooth

Colloquium 1
Gnostic Platonism
Harold W. Attridge

In the early second century a Samaritan named Justin embarked on a religious quest.[1] Like other intellectuals of his day, he explored the available philosophical options. Before he discovered his true spiritual home, Justin found the solutions of the Platonists most appealing. Philosophy, however, was ultimately unsatisfying, and he eventually joined the Christian community, which he served as a teacher in Rome until his martyrdom around 165.[2]

Approximately two and a half centuries later, another probing soul made his tortuous way to Christian commitment. At a station on the path to his decisive encounter with Romans 12 at Cassiciacum Augustine took a step away from Manichaeism after reading the "libri platonici," translations of neo-Platonic texts, possibly by Marius Victorinus, the story of whose conversion Augustine later relates. From such literature Augustine learned what he came to understand as a proper concept of God and a metaphysics that enabled him to deal with the problem of evil in a new and more satisfying way than the Manichaeans had proposed.[3]

The stories of the encounters with Platonism by Justin Martyr and Augustine are emblematic of a phenomenon some aspects

1. Justin, *Dial.* 2

2. See Andresen (1952/53), pp. 157–95; Grant 1956, pp. 246–48; Barnard 1967, van Winden, 1971, Osborne 1973, and Joly 1973.

3. Augustine, *Confessions* 7.9. On Marius Victorinus, *Conf.* 8.2

of which I wish to explore with you this evening. From the second to the fourth century, and on to the end of antiquity, the foremost component of the Greek intellectual tradition was professedly Platonic. Many of the leading religious thinkers in the Christian tradition, following a path blazed in the first century by the Jewish philosopher and exegete Philo,[4] engaged in dialogue with the Greek intellectual tradition, and that meant Platonism. Such engagement is evident in the leading theologians of the Alexandrian tradition, Clement[5] and Origen,[6] but it is present elsewhere, in apologetic historians such as Eusebius,[7] or even at the fringes of Hellenistic influence, in the Syrian Christian Bar Daisan of Edessa.[8]

It is a truism that there was involvement with Platonism on the part of early Christians. There has, however, been considerable debate in recent years among historians of philosophy and Christian doctrine about the extent and nature of that involvement. The late German historian of Platonism, Heinrich Dörrie, vigorously maintained,[9] that, at least before the wholesale baptism of neo-Platonism in the fourth and fifth century by figures such Marius Victorinus and Pseudo-Dionysius, the engagement with Platonism by most Christian theologians was governed by apologetic concerns. Christians cited Platonists only to prove them wrong or to show the superiority of their own philosophical theology. Dörrie's assessment has not won universal acclaim,[10] but it has forced students of later antiquity to think carefully about what they mean by a Christian (or for that matter Jewish, or Gnostic) Platonism.

4. See Chadwick 1967, pp. 137–92, esp. chap. 9, "The beginnings of "Christian philosophy: Justin: The Gnostics."

5. See Osborne 1957, Lilla 1971, and May 1983, pp. 123–32.

6. See Trigg 1983, and Crouzel 1989.

7. See Ricken 1978, pp. 321–52.

8. On Bar Daisan see esp. Drijvers1970, pp. 190–210; 1975, pp. 109–22; and 1982, pp. 157–75.

9. Dörrie 1971, pp. 15–28; 1976, pp. 166–210; 1981, pp. 1–46;.1987.

10. For critical perspectives see Meijering 1974, pp. 15–28; Aland 1983, pp. 11–30; May 1983, pp. 129; Beyschlag 1988, pp. 107–13, 128–30. For a general review of the earlier phases of the discussion see Ritter 1984, pp. 31–56.

2

The problem of the relationship between Platonism and Christianity is replicated on a somewhat smaller scale in the relationship between Platonism and Gnosticism, our subject this evening. One end of the spectrum of modern scholarly opinion was maintained by Hans Jonas, who argued that both Gnosticism and the Platonism of Plotinus were manifestations of the same "spirit of late antiquity."[11] Hans Joachim Krämer and John Dillon are more reserved. Yet in Krämer's analysis, certain Gnostics were clear representatives of one strand, the quadripartite, of middle Platonic metaphysics.[12] In the vague but suggestive phrase of Dillon, Gnostics, along with Hermetists and others, comprised the "dark underside" of the Platonic tradition.[13] At the other end of the spectrum, Dörrie and A.H. Armstrong see nothing but a superficial appropriation of some Platonic motifs in Gnostic circles.[14]

The contemporary range of opinion about the affiliations of the Gnostics is mirrored in antiquity. Plotinus in *Enneads* 2.9[15] suggested that the Gnostics are Platonists manqué, thinkers who had been inspired by authentic Platonic positions, but who had made fundamental errors and been attracted by some notions that were downright silly.[16] From that critique, by the way, we know at least that there was some actual contact between Platonists and Gnostics. That judgment is supported by the

11. See Jonas 1964 and 1966; 1971, pp. 45–53.

12. Krämer 1964.

13. Dillon 1977.

14. Armstrong 1978, pp. 87–124. This article represents an explicit modification of one earlier position (Armstrong1967a, pp. 195–268, esp. pp. 243–45): "It is easy to attribute the resemblances higher up [scil. the ontological ladder] to Platonic and Neopythagorean influences on Gnosticism, which there undoubtedly were" and "the possibility of some Gnostic influence [scil. on Plotinus]... cannot be absolutely ruled out." Yet he was more reserved in Armstrong 1940, p. 50 (Repr. 1967).

15. Much has been written on *Enn.* 2.9. For the earlier literature see Roloff 1970, Elsas 1975, and Bazan 1974, pp. 463–78; and 1980.

16. Cf. esp. *Enn.* 2.9.6: "Generally speaking, some of these people's doctrines have been taken from Plato, but others, all the new ideas they have brought in to establish a philosophy of their own, are things they have found outside the truth. For the judgements too, and the rivers in Hades and the reincarnations

biography of Plotinus by Porphyry which indicates that the positions criticized were held by personal acquaintances of Plotinus, members of his circle in Rome in the middle of the third century.[17]

Another negative assessment appears in Christian sources somewhat earlier than Plotinus. Hippolytus, the crusty heresiologist and anti-pope of the early third century, made it his business to find Greek philosophical roots for all the heretical positions that he combatted. In his *Refutation of all heresies*, or *Philosophoumena*, he connected Valentinian Gnostics to the Pythagorean and Platonic traditions,[18] claiming not, like Plotinus, that his opponents are not properly Platonic, but that they are much too devoted to their Platonism. Gnostics, then, were too Platonic for a rigorously orthodox bishop, but not Platonic enough for a professional Platonic philosopher, although in each case the critics acknowledged significant contact between Gnostics and the Platonic tradition.

As a way of reflecting on these assessments, I propose to consider some of the primary sources for the phenomenon of Gnosticism that have come to light in recent decades. These discoveries are from the Nag Hammadi library, a collection of some fifty tractates originally written in Greek but preserved in Coptic translation. The library was sequestered in the Upper Egyptian desert in the late fourth century, probably as a result of pressure

---

come from Plato. And the making a plurality in the intelligible world, Being, and Intellect, and the Maker different from Intellect, and Soul, is taken from the words in the *Timaeus*. For Plato says, "The maker of this universe thought that it should contain all the forms that intelligence discerns contained in the Living Being that truly is" (*Tim.* 39E7–9). But they did not understand, and took it to mean that there is one mind which contains in it in repose all realities, and another mind different from it which contemplates them, and another which plans—but often they have soul as the maker instead of the planning mind—and they think that this is the maker according to Plato, being a long way from knowing who the maker is." Note the designation of Gnostic theories at 2.9.6.55 as "delusion" (ἀπατή); or at 2.9.10, the theory of a fallen Sophia as "absurdity" (ἀτοπία).

17. At *Enn.* 2.9.10, Plotinus refers to the Gnostics as his friends. Porphyry's account is in *Life* 16.8–9.

18. Hippolytus, *Ref.* 6.21.1; 6.29.1.

on the monks of the region to conform to stricter standards of orthodoxy.

My strategy will be to explore the two streams of Gnostic tradition involved in the critiques by Hippolytus and Plotinus. Although there is considerable debate among historians of ancient religion about the precise definition and extension of "Gnosticism," these two streams of tradition, the Valentinian[19] and the "Barbeloite" or "Sethian,"[20] are paradigm cases of the religion. Both generally fall within the broader phenomenological definition of Gnosticism championed by many researchers since the influential work of Hans Jonas.[21] Both, that is, tend to be dualist, anticosmic religions of salvation, although, as I will suggest at least for the case of Valentinianism, the dualism is moderated, possibly under Platonic influence. Both streams also fit within the narrower definition of Gnosticism as the religion of a specific group or set of related groups, with a core of definable symbolic expressions about the structure of the world and the source and destiny of the human self within it, although those symbolic systems also undergo significant development.[22] Whoever else may be usefully grouped under the Gnostic umbrella, Valentinians and Sethians certainly belong there.

In speaking of these Gnostic phenomena I use the term "stream" advisedly, because in assessing the relations between Platonism and Gnosticism a diachronic perspective is required. As we know, we cannot step into the same stream twice. Although there are elements of continuity in groups, the streams

19. Older works on Valentinian Gnosticism such as Sagnard 1947 and Orbe 1958–1966 remain valuable, but need to be updated on the basis of the Nag Hammadi evidence.

20. There has been debate about the implications of the designation of some Gnostics as Sethian, a designation originally proposed by Schenke 1974, pp. 165–72. The results of the debate are summarized in Layton 1987.

21. Jonas 1964, 1966. His definition influenced heavily the work of the Messina Conference, Bianchi, ed. 1970, and is enshrined in the widely used survey of Gnosticism by Rudolph, 1977. For further reflections on the problem of definition, see Bianchi 1977, pp. 16–26; Rudolph, 1983, pp. 21–37; and Pearson 1990.

22. Such a perspective informs the useful collection of primary texts by Layton 1987.

do meander across the ancient intellectual landscape, while being fed by various tributaries and intersecting at specific points. For both Sethians and Valentinians I propose to consider three phases, without suggesting that these phases are rigidly distinct or exhaustive of all the developmental stages of the two movements. To anticipate the results of this exploration, I shall suggest that between the early second and mid-third centuries various Gnostics displayed a growing, and increasingly complex, engagement with Platonic philosophical traditions. One stream, the Sethian, moves, in its metaphysics, into closer contact with professional philosophy and may have left a mark upon it.[23] The other stream, the Valentinian, begins as a kind of Platonic-Christian appropriation of the first stream. It moves through two phases of systematization in which it acquires a philosophical structure for its version of Christian systematic theology.

The first phase of both movements can be set in the late first to mid-second century C.E. Developments at this stage remain the most obscure part of the history of the Gnostic phenomenon, although research stimulated by the Nag Hammadi collection continues to shed new light on the period.[24] I agree with those scholars who see the so-called Sethian tradition to be the earlier of the two Gnostic streams.[25] It probably appears first on the fringes of Jewish circles,[26] perhaps among disaffected "god-fearers," in Syria or in Egypt. The movement was apparently characterized by a radical exegesis of the Jewish scriptures, particularly of Genesis, that provided a rationale for sectarian identity by anchoring the alienated baptizing group[27] in the scriptural

23. For an attempt to sketch a history of the Sethian literary corpus, with many useful observations about its philosophical elements, see Turner 1986, pp. 55–86.

24. See, e.g., Stroumsa 1984, and Jackson 1985.

25. A major contemporary exception to the scholarly consensus about the relationship between Sethian and Valentinian Gnosticism, originally propounded by Irenaeus, is Pétrement, 1984.

26. For evidence of the Jewish elements in Gnosticism, see Pearson 1984, and 1990.

27. On the allusions to baptismal practice in the Sethian texts, see now Sevrin 1986.

tradition of Seth, the son of Adam, who, as "another seed," took the place of the righteous Abel. Thinkers in this group, perhaps stimulated by condemnation from official circles,[28] eventually attempted to explain how they could be in the difficult social and general human situation in which they found themselves. Their explanation consisted in a story about the origins of the cosmos and the spiritual entities within it, the current structure of the cosmos, and its ultimate fate. The general contours of the basic Gnostic myth of this tradition are probably familiar, although there is considerable variation in the details of various reports which need not concern us here.

The basic plot of the Sethian cosmogonies revolves around the figure of divine Wisdom, Sophia or Faith-Wisdom (πίστις-σοφία). An element of the supernal world, obviously derived from Jewish sapiential traditions, Sophia commits a primal sin and falls from the Pleroma, the world of divine fullness. She thereby produces the phenomenal, material world and the ignorant and jealous deity who rules over it. Ialdabaoth by name, he is a thinly disguised version of the Old Testament's Yahweh. He heads up a group of astral powers who contribute to the fashioning of the bodily prison in which the human spirit is held captive. Sophia herself or a being produced by her eventually comes to rescue her captive offspring by awakening in them the spark of Gnosis.

The abortive begetting by Wisdom explains the existence of this world and its ersatz deity, but whence came Wisdom herself? Some texts are not concerned to answer that question. The primitive aretalogy describing the descents of Pronoia embedded in the important Sethian text, the *Apocryphon of John* (NHC 2,1:30, 12-31, 31), gives no hints about the origins of the revealer figure. Other accounts are vague, positing Wisdom as a second principle beside a primal spirit.[29] Still other accounts seem to

28. For this hypothesis about the generation of key elements in the Gnostic myths, see Segal 1977.

29. See *Hypostasis of the Archons* NHC 2,4:94, 4ff; *Origin of the World* NHC 2,5:98, 10–23; *The Thunder* NHC 6,2:13, 3–5.

7

presuppose a mythical triad of primal Father, Spirit-Mother, and Child (or children), one of whom is Sophia.[30] Such stories in their various versions enabled their tradents to symbolize the conflicts and pressures that impinged on their lives and to score various points against their opponents, the archons of synagogue, church, or state who served the oppressive ruler of this world. Yet all of this seems to be rather unpromising raw material with which to effect a synthesis with Platonism.

At a second stage of the Sethian tradition, we find the primitive mythological schemes elaborated in various ways. Part of this revision involves not metaphysics or epistemology, but the appropriation of popular Greek psychology or popular physics.[31] The sources of such learning are handbooks of astrology or other occult sciences, such as the nonextant *Book of Zoroaster*, whence the *Apocryphon of John* claims to have garnered its information about the astral powers that shaped the human soul.[32] A similar text was *The Configuration of the Fate of Heaven That is Beneath the Twelve*, cited by the author of the untitled Sethian tractate currently known as *On the Origin of the World*.[33]

It is, however, possible to detect more serious appropriations of philosophical elements in the Sethian cosmogonic myths. An illustration of the growing theological and philosophical sophistication of this stream of the Gnostic movement is evident in the description of the first principle in the *Apocryphon of John*. This Sethian classical text is found in four copies in our ancient sources, and was known in some form to Irenaeus when he composed his massive heresiological work around 180. The *Apocryphon of John* is clearly a composite work which, like the Pentateuch or the Gospels, grew over time, probably as an authoritative statement of Sethian self-understanding. Although literary archaeology can be a precarious business, there are some clear seams in the various versions of the text

30. Such seems to be the most basic structure of the *Apocryphon of John*, the best-attested version of the Gnostic story.

31. See Perkins 1980a, pp. 36–46.

32. *Ap. John* NHC 2,1:19,9–10

33. *Or. World* NHC 2,5:107,15.

and these suggest some of the stages of its redaction. In the version of Nag Hammadi Codex 2 the description of the first and second principles displays similarities to the simple description of a first principle and Sophia in the typologically more primitive accounts in the *Hypostasis of the Archons* and the *Origin of the World*. This description is, however, expanded or interrupted by two elements, an affirmation of the absolute transcendence of the first principle, and a very Christian-sounding notice that the unknown first principle is made manifest only by the Revealer who came from that transcendent monad.

The apparent expansion reads, in part:

He is the invisible Spirit of whom it is not right to think of as a god, or something similar. For he is more than a god, since there is nothing above him, for no one lords it over him. For he does not exist in something inferior to him since everything exists in him. For it is he who establishes himself. He is eternal, since he does not need anything. For he is total perfection. He did not lack anything that he might be completed by it; rather he is always completely perfect in light. He is illimitable, since there is no one prior to him to set limits to him. He is unsearchable, since there exists no one prior to him to examine him. He is immeasurable, since there was no one prior to him to measure him. He is invisible, since no one saw him. He is eternal, since he exists eternally. He is ineffable (ἄρρητος), since no one was able to comprehend him to speak about him. He is unnameable (ἀκατονόμαστος), since there is no one prior to him to give him a name (NHC 2, 1:2, 33-3, 17).

The via negativa of this portion of the *Apocryphon of John* manifests a new sophistication about the transcendence of the first principle in this Gnostic stream.

A second move accompanies the affirmation of the transcendence of the first principle, namely an explanation of the generation of the second principle. The *Apocryphon of John* portrays an

Harold W. Attridge

imaginative version of the Aristotelian (and later Platonic) notion of the prime mover contemplating itself, thereby producing a subject-object duality. *Ap. John* BG 27,1-14 reads:

(The Invisible Spirit) contemplated his own image when he saw it in the pure light-water which surrounds him; and his thought (ἔννοια) performed an act, it appeared, it stood (ⲁⲥⲁⲍⲉⲣⲁⲧⲥ̄) before him out of the brilliance of the light. This is the power which is before the All, which appeared; that is, the perfect Providence (πρόνοια) of the All, the light, the likeness of the light, the image of the Invisible. She is the perfect power, Barbelo, the perfect aeon of glory.

This explanation of the initial development from Unity to Multiplicity in the *Apocryphon of John* is part of the same systematizing phase of the Sethian Gnostic phenomenon. Whether this took place prior to the Christianization of the movement or was part of that process is unclear. The systematizing, in any case, involved an attempt to offer an explanation of the nature of, and relations among first principles.

The roots of that systematization clearly lie in philosophy. The production of a second principle, the feminine dyad, from the masculine One,[34] was a traditional Pythagorean affirmation. The "aggressive," as Merlan called them, Pythagoreans of the first century transformed the numerical emanationist scheme. Moderatus posited a First transcendent One, "beyond being and essence," an echo of the famous line of the *Republic* (509B 6-9) that said that the idea of the Good was "beyond being,"[35] a second One consisting of mathematical ideas, and a third principle, undifferentiated or potential quantity.[36] The affirmation of a transcendent first principle continues, both in moderate

34. For the sexual dichotomy, cf. Hippolytus, *Ref.* 6.29.3–4.

35. On the history of this phrase, see Whittaker 1969, pp. 91–104. Precisely Plato does not say νοῦ καὶ οὐσίας. This is the mystery which Whittaker is addressing.

36. For the text and translation of the report from Simplicius, *In Phys.* 230,34–231,27 Diels, see de Vogel 1959, vol 3, pp. 349–51; and Merlan 1967, pp. 14–132, esp. pp. 91–92. The importance of the text was first indicated by Dodds 1928, pp. 129–42. There is a question as to how much of the text is authentic

Platonists such as Plutarch, in his *On the E at Delphi*, and particularly in the "Pythagoreanizing" wing of the Platonic tradition, particularly in Numenius, perhaps the most interesting Platonist of the mid to late second century. In his view Plato taught a hierarchy at the head of which was "The first Nous called Being itself, utterly unknown to all."[37]

The process by which Numenius explained movement from primal unity to multiplicity is similar to that of the *Apocryphon of John*. This first principle, identified by Numenius with the Idea of the Good in Plato's *Republic*, generates a second principle, the demiurgic Nous, who "produces his own idea," presumably by contemplating the first principle. He also produces the world before returning to contemplation.[38]

The Platonic tradition continues in the same vein through Plotinus. Michael Williams, in his study of the philosophical theme of the "stability" of the spiritual world,[39] notes the interesting parallel between *Ap. John* BG 27,1-14 and Plotinus, *Enn.* 5.2.1,7-13. Plotinus has it that:

(The One), being perfect since it neither seeks nor has nor needs anything, overflowed, as it were, and its "spill-over" made another thing. That which came into being turned back (ἐπεστράφη) toward That one and was filled and became a beholder of That one and thus a Nous. And its stability (στάσις) toward That one created Being (τὸ ὄν), while the vision directed toward That one created the Nous. Therefore, since it stood at rest (ἔστη) before That one in order to behold, it became Nous and Being at the same time.[40]

---

first-century Pythagoreanism and how much is neo-Platonic elaboration. I follow Merlan and Armstrong 1978, p. 116.

37. Frag. 17 des Places (26 Leemans), from Eusebius, *Praeparatio evangelica* 11.18.22–23.

38. Frag. 16 des Places (25 Leemans), from Eusebius, *Praep. evan.* 11.22.3–5.

39. Williams 1985, pp. 104–105.

40. Plotinus, however, in his discussion of the Gnostics is critical of a position like that of Numenius that posited two "minds" in the intelligible world (*Enn.* 2.9.1; 2.9.6).

There are undeniable structural similarities between the structure of the highest levels of reality in the revised Sethianism and the Pythagoreanizing Platonism of the second century. Precisely with the major witness to this strand of the Platonic stream, Numenius, we find yet another important similarity with Sethian theologoumena.

Recall that Numenius posited two levels of Mind, one equated with the Idea of the Good of the *Republic*, the other equated with the Demiurge of the *Timaeus*. Yet this second principle, because involved in matter, is somehow split into two deities that remain somehow one.[41] That move anticipates, on the one hand, the Plotinian division of Mind and Soul, but it also parallels many of the Gnostic explanations of the generation of movement out of the supernal world, according to which the heavenly being Sophia splits into two portions, one of which remains on high in the Pleroma, while the other descends to the phenomenal world.[42] One might debate the direction of dependence here, but it seems to me that the more likely explanation is from philosophers to the Gnostics. The philosophical doctrine affords a way of dealing with two sets of problems. Exegetically, it explains the relationship between the two figures of Demiurge and World Soul or Living Being in the *Timaeus*, both of which are distinct from the first principle, which is rather equated with the Idea of the Good of the *Republic*, or, as in Plotinus, with the One of the *Parmenides*. Ontologically, the split helps to bridge the gap between transcendence and immanence which remained a fundamental issue throughout the history of religious Platonism. The notion of the split mind is then used by Gnostic interpreters as a useful rationalization of the mythical fall of Sophia.

Before we turn to the final and clear phase of the Sethian-Platonist encounter we must turn to the second Gnostic stream

41 Frag. 11 des Places (20 Leemans), from Eusebius, *Praep. evan.* 11.17.11–18. Even Armstrong 1978, pp. 98–99, sees closer connections between Numenius and the Gnostics than with other elements of the Platonic tradition.

42. For examples of the division, cf. the report about the teaching of Valentinus in Irenaeus, *Adv. Haer.* 1.11.1–12.3.

that we shall follow from the first through the third century. Valentinian theology began in Alexandria in the early second century, apparently as an offshoot or interpretation of the Sethian stream, probably when Sethianism had already been given a philosophical veneer. At that time and place several intellectuals found something meaningful in Christian teaching and tried to understand that teaching in conjunction with their philosophical training. The most important examples apart from Valentinus are Basilides and Carpocrates. The precise contours of their synthesis of Christianity and Hellenism remain obscure. The case of Basilides is beset with problems due to the radically divergent reports about his teaching in the heresiologists.[43] Yet if there is any truth to the report that Basilides taught of the radical transcendence of the first principle, of whom not even existence could be predicated,[44] we may hear another echo of Plato's remark about being "beyond being." The reportedly libertine ethics of Carpocrates and Epiphanes led to considerable vilification, but their stance toward the Law could be construed as a consistent application of Pauline principles in the light of a vision of the ideal society akin to that of the *Republic* where all things, including wives, were held in common.[45]

Alexandrian Christianity in the early second century obviously was an environment conducive to intellectual experimentation. Valentinus was part of that environment before migrating to

43. Irenaeus (*Adv. Haer.* 1.24.3–7) presents a rather Platonic/Valentinian Basilides, whose intelligible hierarchy consists of the Unoriginate Father – Nous – Logos – Phronesis – Sophia – Dynamis (the last three perhaps should be understood as aspects or attributes of the level of reality associated with Logos) – the planetary powers. Hippolytus (*Ref.* 7.20.1–27.13) attributes to Basilides a radical negative theology, from whose first principle a series of "Sonships" emanated. If we knew more about the school of Basilides we might be able to fit these divergent accounts, as well as the other fragmentary remains, into some sort of developmental sequence. For the relevant passages, see Foerster 1972, vol 1, pp. 59–83, and Layton 1987, pp. 417-44, who gives preference to the account in Irenaeus.

44. Hippolytus, *Ref.* 7.20.2–21.1.

45. The key text is Clement of Alexandria, *Strom.* 3.2.5,2–9,3. A translation, along with other data on the Carpocratians, may be found in Foerster 1972, vol 1, pp. 38–40. A full dossier on the Carpocratians is assembled by Smith 1973, pp. 295–350.

Rome near mid-century. The scanty fragments of his works preserved in patristic testimonies[46] give evidence of a person with some literary skills, a taste for complex metaphors, and perhaps an ascetical bent. We would be able to say little about his involvement with Platonism, or any other philosophical school, on the basis of these texts alone. One of the tractates from Nag Hammadi, the *Gospel of Truth*,[47] has provided new grist for the mill. A text of Valentinus by this name was known to Irenaeus, and it is likely that the Nag Hammadi tractate is identical with it.

A problem for the identification is the fact that the Gospel of Truth bears little resemblance to the presentations of the Valentinian system reported by the heresiologists of the late second century. I believe that there are enough hints of Valentinian theology in the text to warrant the attribution to Valentinus, and that the discrepancies between the text and later reports can in part be attributed to the genre of the work, a homily designed to appeal to a general Christian audience.[48]

If the *Gospel of Truth* is in fact by Valentinus, and I will assume that attribution here, we may use it to pursue our theme. In the work we find little systematic metaphysics or epistemology. Yet there were professional Platonists in the early second century whose interest and literary products range beyond works of technical philosophy. Although Plutarch lacks the subtlety of a Plotinus, or even the plodding systematizing of an Albinus, he displays a set of interests with interesting parallels to the *Gospel of Truth*. While Plutarch can display his philosophical erudition by refuting the mistakes of Epicureans or Stoics,[49] he is equally content to explore the existential truth hidden in the guise of exotic myths, a pursuit he follows with considerable success in his *On Isis and Osiris*. There Egyptian myth is interpreted not only in terms of metaphysics, but also through another, Persian, mythical tradition. The intricate interweaving of the myth of the

46. See Layton 1987, pp. 217–49.

47. For the critical text, translation, and notes, see Attridge 1985. An alternative translation may be found in Layton 1987, pp. 250–64.

48. See Attridge 1986, pp. 239–56.

49. Particularly in his essays, *Non posse vivere suaviter, De Stoicis repugnandis*.

dominion of Error (Πλάνη) and Gospel traditions in the *Gospel of Truth* exhibits an approach to religious questions and traditions similar to that of Plutarch.[50] A similar interest in and engagement with the wisdom of the orient is also found in the fragments of Numenius.

General similarities of method between the *Gospel of Truth* and *On Isis and Osiris* are perhaps insufficient to demonstrate a Valentinian connection with the Platonic tradition. There are indications of a more important link, although one that displays the particular combination of hermeneutical and metaphysical interests in Valentinus.

One of the most remarkable passages in the *Gospel of Truth* is a meditation on the revealing Son as the Name of the Father (38,8-40,10). This obscure text wrestles with a problem of religious epistemology generated by the assumption that Valentinus shared with the revisers of the Sethian tradition, with Philo before him, and with other Christian teachers of second-century Alexandria, the assumption that the transcendent God was, in essence, unknowable. Christians of course had an answer to the problem of divine transcendence in the person of Jesus, understood as the one who revealed the hidden God. A saying attributed to Jesus himself in Matt 11:27 articulates this perspective. This theology of Jesus as the revealer characterizes the fourth Gospel, which may be in dialogue with some form of Gnosticism. It is evident in the Christian revisers of Sethianism whose hand is felt in the *Apocryphon of John*,[51] where it is affirmed after its emphasis on divine transcendence, that:

> We know not the ineffable things, and we do not understand what is immeasurable, except for him who came forth from him, namely from the Father. For it is he who told it to us alone to say that God was known through his revealing Son.

As a Christian, Valentinus shared this perspective, but as a

50. For similar judgments see Stead 1969, pp. 75–104, esp. 93 and 1980, pp. 75–95.
51. *Ap. John, NHC* 2,1:4,15–19.

15

Harold W. Attridge

reflective Christian, he was interested in explaining how revelation worked. *The Gospel of Truth* in general offers such an explanation and the meditation on the Son as Name is part of that explanation.

The argument in the passage is obscure and convoluted, perhaps in part due to the quality of the Coptic translation.[52] But certain central affirmations stand out.

a. The Father has an ineffable Name, which is revealed through the Son (38,22-24).

b. The Son in fact is the name of the Father, begotten by him (38,7; 38.32-34; 39,19-20; 39,25).

c. The Name that is the Son is no ordinary name. Nor is it a description composed of attributes (39,3-6).

d. The one who (or that which) names in the proper sense is the one who truly and exclusively knows the object of the name (39,7-11).

e. The Proper or True Name that is the Son provides direct and unmediated access to the reality of the Father, i.e., rest or abiding in the Father for those to and over whom the name is uttered (38,20; 38,28-29; 40,30-41,13).

The imagery and conceptuality of the passage have complex roots. The first and last of the points that I have enumerated are clearly traditional Jewish Christian elements. The notion that God has an ineffable name derives from the Jewish tradition that the tetragrammaton, YHWH, was not be pronounced, except, of course, by the high priest in the holy of holies on the Day of Atonement. The second point, the claim that the Son reveals the Father, is familiar from Matthew 11 and John 17, where Jesus thanks the Father for giving him the name to bestow on his disciples.

The last of my five points spells out the practical implications of the reflection on Jesus as Name, apparently alluding to bap-

---

52. Fragments of a different, and apparently clearer, translation are preserved in Codex 13.

16

tismal practices of initiating new members of the community in the Name of Jesus, or in the triple Name of Father, Son, and Spirit, as a result of which the newly "Christened" bore the name of Christ, and did so as a permanent affair, not as a temporary loan.[53]

Within the traditions about the name of the Son, traditions familiar to Valentinus from his religious heritage, appears a more abstract reflection about the nature of the Name. Such reflection is not unparalleled in second-century sources. Valentinus was possibly aware of contemporary theories about the Logos or Word of God that we meet in second-century apologists such as Justin. These theories, as is well known, appropriated the Stoic distinction between thought as λόγος ἐνδιάθετος and speech as the λόγος προφορικός, to suggest how there might be phases in the existence of the Son, while continuity with his source in the Father. Valentinus does not follow this path in treating the Son as the name of the Father. If he knew the Logos theology of the apologists he may well have thought that it addressed the wrong theological problem, that it was, to use modern categories, too much interested in the ontological status of the Son and not enough interested in his soteriological function. Nonetheless, the parallel indicates something of the engagement with philosophical tradition in the environment of the *Gospel of Truth*. This text may display another kind of engagement.

I suggest, in fact, that the notions which Valentinus deploys, with some irony to be sure, are Platonic. They are found in the treatments of names in the *Cratylus* and in the *Seventh Epistle*. The latter, whether or not it is authentic, distinguishes (342A-B):

> for everything that exists ... three classes of objects through which knowledge about it must come; the knowledge itself is a fourth, and we must put as a fifth entity the actual object of knowledge which is the true reality. We have then, first, a name; second, a description; third, an image; and fourth, a knowledge of the object.

53. A similar reflection on permanent vs. borrowed and hence temporary names, associated with baptism, appears in the Valentinian *Gospel of Philip*.

17

Harold W. Attridge

The analysis is exemplified in the case of a circle, of which there is the name circle, the definition of it, "composed of nouns and verbal expressions," the class of objects drawn or worked on a lathe, knowledge, understanding and correct opinion concerning them, found not in sounds but in minds, "whereby it evidently differs in its nature from the real circle and from the aforementioned three."

Valentinus was clearly aware of the distinctions made in this text, since one of his few meager fragments to have survived, in Clement of Alexandria, *Strom.* 4.89.6-4.90.1, makes a point about the relationship between the spiritual and the material by sketching an analogy with a work of art.[54] Valentinus makes a distinction between a face, the portrait of a face, and the name attached to the portrait, and the unclarity which the name rectifies. The function of the terms of the illustration suggests that the epistemological analysis of Plato's *Seventh Epistle* is familiar, but that Valentinus accords a higher epistemic status to names than does Plato. In this regard he may be reacting critically against a position of his older contemporary, Basilides, who seems, if Hippolytus is correct, to have denied the possibility of there being any name for the first principle. Perhaps Basilides accepted the Platonic critique of the possibility of knowledge through names.[55] Confronting the passage on the Son qua name in the *Gospel of Truth* with Plato's reflections on naming suggests why that might be so.

The *Gospel of Truth* recalls the distinctions of the *Seventh Epistle*, in its remark that the Son qua Name is not "composed of appellations" or perhaps better, "predications." It is not a composite explanation, as Plato put it, nor is it, to use Aristotelian terms that may also lurk in the background, a definition combin-

54. See Layton 1987, p. 237.

55. Hippolytus, *Ref.* 7.20.3, "For what is not even inexpressible ... is above every name that is named. For the names do not even suffice, he says, for the world, so multiform is it, but fall short. And I do not have it in me to find correct names for everything; rather it is proper to comprehend ineffably, without using names, the characteristics of the things which are to be named. For (the existence of the) same designation(s for different things) has caused the hearers confusion and error about the things."

18

ing genus and species. It is, like the object it names, simple. So far the distinctions of the *Epistle* are preserved, but the *Gospel of Truth* departs radically from the Platonic text in its affirmations that the Son-Name actually provides knowledge of its referent. On this point the *Gospel of Truth* coheres with the fragment of Valentinus in Clement in its highly positive assessment of the epistemic function of at least one name. Plato's whole point in the *Epistle* is just the opposite, that knowledge comes from studying realities, and not names. Is it the case, then, that Valentinus uses language reminiscent of Plato without comprehension or consistency?

I think not, and I suspect that a reason for his departure from the clear epistemology of the *Epistle* lies in Plato himself, read within Valentinus' Christian framework. Note that the *Gospel of Truth* does not explicitly cite the third of Plato's categories, the "image." As the fragment indicates, Valentinus clearly knows of the distinction of image (εἰκών) from name and reality. He may choose not to make the distinction because Christian tradition emphatically calls the Son an "image" of God.[56] Valentinus had ample warrant for ignoring the distinction between the two terms in the *Cratylus* (439A), where Socrates says "Have we not several times acknowledged that names rightly given are the likenesses and images of the things which they name?" The text obviously suggests that some names are "likenesses and images" of the reality named.

What names are those that are rightly given? The *Cratylus* provides an answer which, I suggest, aided Valentinus, but before we see what the answer is, it may be useful to remember what the *Cratylus* itself was about. Much of the dialogue is a tour de force of etymologizing, as Socrates and his interlocutors explore the problem of whether signifiers, of which common nouns or "names" are the paradigmatic case, have a natural or conventional relationship to what they signify. The final results are rather aporetic.

Contradictions appear in the way various kinds of names are applied (438C) and, as in the *Seventh Epistle*, the one who would

56. Cf. 2 Cor 4:4; Col 1:15.

learn is urged to look for the truth behind the name/images (439A-B). To learn that truth is, by the way, difficult, "beyond you and me," says Socrates to his interlocutor (439B). The problem with names in the phenomenal world is that they are applied to things in a state of flux. They are full of contradictions because their referents are unstable. There may indeed be a natural relationship between signifier and signified, but it is not enough to guarantee any sort of knowledge (439C-E).

The critique of names and their epistemic instability at the phenomenal level suggests a contrast with the noumenal level where objects are stable, and their signifying images, by implication, correctly applied. In that realm, the necessary conditions advanced by Socrates for the existence of knowledge-providing names will obtain: The named will be immutable (439E); the namer will really know the thing named (438A); the namer will be a "power more than human" (438C). These are the conditions which the *Gospel of Truth* seems to invoke, although it does so not for a whole realm of forms, but only for the single case of the Name of the Unnameable.

Some of what Valentinus is doing would have sounded familiar to contemporary Platonists, but some of it would have been quite strange. His rhetoric is more evocative than definitive. He may simply be involved in an elaborate metaphorical play describing rather ordinary Christian experience, or in the articulation of a more mystical position. He could, for instance, be saying that the experience of encounter with the Divine in Christian Baptism or Eucharist, rituals where the Name of Christ is invoked, is the point where the transcendent becomes known. He could also be suggesting that true knowledge of the One/Father only takes place in the position of the Son, where there is direct, non-discursive, grasp of the reality of God.[57]

---

57. Theories about names continue in Valentinian sources. In the *Tri. Trac.*, other aspects of which are to be discussed below, names are inadequate to express the Father, who can name himself (NHC 1,5:55,4–5), who is made known through a Son (65,28–66,5). The name, "Father," awakens the spiritual hypostases (61,14–19), and each of the hypostases or aeons of the spiritual world is a "name" of the Father (73,8–18). In the *Gos. Philip*, worldly names are decep-

We will not tarry on the possible ways in which the imagery of Valentinus might be construed. I hope I have said enough to suggest how at least this one highly creative second-century religious thinker may have utilized one element of his Platonic heritage in order to engage in critical reflection on his Christian religious tradition.

The second stage of the Valentinian tradition may be dealt with more quickly. The disciples of Valentinus operative from the middle to the late second century are perhaps the best known representatives of the Gnostic phenomenon. It was primarily they who stimulated the negative reaction of the anti-Gnostic Fathers, Justin, Clement of Alexandria, Irenaeus, Hippolytus, Tertullian. In those patristic sources we find abundant attestations of the systematizing tendencies of the school. How far back into the teaching of Valentinus himself the structured metaphysics of a Ptolemy or a Theodotus go remains a matter of some debate. My own suspicion is that what Irenaeus reports as the system of Valentinus in *Adv. haer.* 1.11 may well depend on the master's own writing, perhaps in his attempt to sketch the sort of myth that he found useful to exploit for his purposes as Plutarch did the myths of Isis and Osiris. I doubt whether Valentinus accorded as much importance to this "system" as did either his pupils or his detractors.[58]

His pupils, particularly Ptolemaios,[59] conceived of a hierarchi-

tive, while names in the eternal realm would be used correctly; the name that the Father gave the Son is not uttered, but the Son becomes the Father by wearing the name of the Father; those who have the name know it but do not say it (NHC 2,3:53,23–54,13).

58. Note the judgment by Stead 1969, pp. 93: "I think it more likely that Valentinus and Ptolemaeus at least were men of a certain sophistication, who were able to operate with gnostic mythology much as contemporary Platonists dealt with the *Timaeus*, accepting it as an authoritative parable which could nevertheless be reinterpreted, rather than as literally exact." There has been debate about whether the major interests of the Valentinian school were in the ontology implied by the myths they used or the psychological processes they symbolized. The Valentinians themselves claimed that they were primarily interested in the latter (Irenaeus, *Adv. Haer.* 2.15.3; Plotinus, *Enn.* 2.9.16). Their claim has been supported by Koschorke 1975, p. 36, but rejected as apologetics by Abramowski, 1983, pp. 1–10, esp. p. 8.

59. For a collection of the texts see Foerster, *Gnosis*, 121–61.

cally structured universe, that would have paralleled the ontological hierarchy of one strand of middle-, and much of neo-
Platonism. At the apex of the chain of being stands a first principle, either dyadic or, in the account of the Valentinian system
recorded by Hippolytus, monadic, from which emanates a spiritual or noetic world, comprised of what sound like
Christianized versions of Platonic ideas, i.e., abstractions such as
Vitality (Ζωή) and Truth ('Αλήθεια) are paired with Word (Λόγος)
and Church ('Εκκλησία). Beneath this world of spirit or mind
stands a psychic world, generated, as ever, by the waywardness
of an emanation of God who splits into two. The psychic world,
with the Demiurge at its head, stands over the material cosmos
where elements of the divine spirit are entrapped awaiting
release.[60] The cosmic tripartition of all that is other than the first
principle, a tripartition into spirit, soul, and matter, is replicated
at the social and individual levels. The world may be divided
into spiritual Valentinians, ordinary psychic Christians, and
material pagans. The individual soul apparently has the same
trichotomy, apparently with the same three potentialities. Time,
as well as space, is tripartite, being divided among the pagans,
Jews, and Christians. These trichotomies intersect in various
ways and their driving principles stand in some tension, a phenomenon we shall have to explore further. The ontological
structures are certainly influenced by Platonic thinking, as
found in such religiously minded thinkers as Numenius. Yet for
all their ingenuity, the successors of Valentinus, at least as
reported in the church Fathers, do not have quite the master's
creative sparkle.

At this point let me leave the Valentinian tradition and return
for a final visit with the Sethians, in the last phase of the movement that we will consider. One of the remarkable discoveries
resulting from the Nag Hammadi find has been the recovery of
several texts that bear names mentioned by Porphyry in his
account of the Gnostic literature read in Plotinus' circle in Rome.
The contents of those texts provide enough similarities to the

---

60. Parallels between the derivation of matter from soul in Valentinian
Gnosticism and Plotinus have long been observed. Cf., e.g., de Vogel 1953, pp.
43–64, esp. p. 47ff.

criticism of Plotinus to confirm suspicion that they were indeed the texts read in some form by Plotinus' Gnostic friends.[61] Unfortunately, most of these texts are quite fragmentary, but enough of at least one of them, *Allogenes* (NHC 11,3), survives to enable us to explore early third-century philosophical Sethianism.[62]

Allogenes is formally a revelation dialogue,[63] with parallels in in Jewish apocalypses and other revelatory literature such as the Corpus Hermeticum. In it a symbolic figure, Allogenes, the person of "another race," receives revelations from an angelic figure about the structure of the noumenal world and the way in which one may experience a mystical ascent of the soul to encounter the highest principle in that world.[64] The text displays obvious affinities to the Sethian tradition of the second century, affinities most evident in its designation of hypostases in the noumenal world. Yet, like other Sethian texts, *Marsanes*[65] and *Zostrianos*,[66] which stem from the same general phase of the movement, *Allogenes* departs significantly from earlier treatises in its lack of any overt Christian elements. Absent is the identification of the bringer of salvific revelation with Christ; absent too is the polemical exegesis of the Genesis story of creation, which vilified Yahweh as the ignorant or oppressive creator. The lack of such explicitly Christian elements probably represents not a witness to a primitive phase of the Sethian movement, but to its dechristianization in the third century.[67]

What is left when the Christian elements are gone is an ontolo-

61. See Robinson 1977, pp. 132–42.

62. The critical edition of the text is now available in Hedrick, ed., 1990, pp. 173–267.

63. On this genre in gnosticism in general see Perkins, 1980.

64. A fundamental study of the text is Turner 1980, pp. 324-51.

65. For the critical edition, translation, notes and introduction, see Pearson 1981, pp. 229–347. His analysis is also available in his essay "The Tractate Marsanes (NHC X) and the Platonic Tradition," in Bianchi , ed., 1978, pp. 373–84, a revised version of which appears in Pearson 1990, pp. 148–64.

66. On this text (NHC 8,1) see Sieber 1973, pp. 233–40.

67. For this interpretation of the late Sethian texts see, e.g., Abramowski 1983, pp. 1–10.

Harold W. Attridge

gy that supports and fosters a mystical piety, not unlike what emerges later in Platonic circles in, e.g., Iamblichus. The structure of the intelligible world in late Sethianism evidences similarities with the Platonic tradition as it developed from Numenius through Plotinus. At the apex of the hierarchy stands a transcendent first principle treated with the conventional negative theology. The text hovers between a monadic and a dyadic description of this first principle. In any case, it posits a second principle coordinate with the first, described as a triply powered spirit. This triply powered spirit resembles the transcendent water of the *Apocryphon of John*, looking into which the first principle sees itself reflected and hence contemplates itself as object. In fact the triply powered spirit of Allogenes may be an interpretation of precisely that earlier Sethian entity. We shall return to the function of this entity momentarily

At a lower level of reality lies a familiar Gnostic figure, Barbelo, the name of the ancient mother figure in the primitive Father, Mother, Son triad. This version of Barbelo, however, replicates precisely on its level of reality the structure of the highest level. It is comprised of three principles or aspects, the Hidden (Καλυπτός), the noetic First Manifest (Πρώτωφανης), and the Self-generate (Αὐτογενής).

The latter half of the text consists of one lengthy revelation discourse in which the visionary, Allogenes, is told how he must mount up the chain of intelligible being, grasping these aspects of the divine before he can achieve his vision of the primal principle. What he will come to realize and perhaps experience is the utter transcendence of that principle. He will thereby come to a mystical-Gnostic version of realizing the ancient Platonic ideal of escaping the evils of the phenomenal world and becoming "assimilated unto God insofar as is possible."[68]

Much of what we find in this text as I have described it could well fit the description of the Gnostics known by Plotinus, with their multiplication of oddly named spiritual entities.[69] Yet

68. *Theaet.* 176C–E; cf. *Rep.* 9.585; *Timaeus* 90A; *Laws* 4.716A. Plotinus' mystical experiences are well known; cf., e.g., *Enn.* 4.7.10.

69. *Enn.* 2.9.2.

24

Gnostic Platonism

there is one interesting dimension to the analysis of the noumenal world that establishes a connection with third-century Platonism. The constituent elements of the triply powered spirit are designated Existence (ὕπαρξις, οὐσία, Coptic: ⲡⲉⲧϣⲟⲟⲡ = τὸ ὄν); Vitality (ⲱⲛⲍ =ζωή; or more abstractly ⲘⲚⲧⲱⲛⲍ); and Intellection (ⲘⲚⲧⲉⲓⲙⲉ or ⲛⲟⲏⲧⲏⲥ, also called Blessedness, ⲘⲚⲧⲙⲁⲕⲁⲣⲓⲟⲥ). This triad plays a prominent role in neo-Platonism.[70] It appears occasionally in Plotinus, although without a systematic function;[71] in Marius Victorinus, from whom Augustine probably learned of it,[72] and in the fifth century in Proclus, as a set of attributes of all intelligibles.[73] This dual attestation, and the appearance of the triad in the anonymous *Parmenides Commentary* sometimes attributed to Porphyry,[74] has served as the grounds for the suggestion that the triad was introduced by Porphyry.[75] The Nag Hammadi text *Allogenes* now suggests that the triad was known in the third century. It already performs there the function that it will come to have in later neo-Platonism, of bridging the gap between the utterly transcendent One and the subordinate elements of the divine world. Although the Monad is, in the traditional phrase, "beyond mind and being," existence, intelligibility, and vitality are the mirror in which the transcendent is for the Gnostics reflected. Plotinus and his school could not, and in fact did not, find such a doctrine objectionable.

We have followed Sethianism from its rude beginnings in the late first century as a critical religious stance based on a radical exegesis of biblical materials which demonized the creator and his world through its final phase in the sophisticated salons of third-century Rome where the protest has vanished and the myth has come to symbolize a structure for a rational mystical experience.

70. A review of the evidence and the discussion is available in Wire 1990, pp. 173–91, esp. pp. 188–91. See also King 1991.

71. *Enn.* 1.6.7; 3.6.6; 6.6.8. See Hadot 1960, pp. 142–57.

72. *Civ. dei* 10.23.

73. See Dodds 1963, p. 220.

74. Kroll 1892, pp. 599–627; Hadot 1961 pp. 410–38.

75. See. Theiler 1933, p. 4; and Hadot 1966, pp. 127–57, and *idem* 1968, pp. 1.102–43

The last stage of Valentinianism, at least the last stage that I shall treat this evening, shows a slightly different movement. One of the tractates found in the same codex as the *Gospel of Truth* presents a comprehensive review of Valentinian theology. In the comprehensive scope of its systematization this text, the *Tripartite Tractate*,[76] carries to a new level the tendencies of the intermediate phase of the Valentinian school. It also bears formal as well as contentual similarities to third-century works of Christian theology, such as Origen's *De principiis*.[77]

This Valentinian *Summa* is, however, a thorough revision of Valentinian theology. The revision simplifies and rationalizes the description of the Godhead. At the highest level of reality is found a Trinity of a transcendent Father, his Son, and the Spiritual Church. The text also reduces the mythical or dramatic dimensions of the description of the intelligible universe. Gone are the enumerated aeons that make up the earlier Valentinian Ogdoad, Decad, and Duodecad. These are replaced with an indeterminate multitude of spiritual entities. Gone too is the figure of Sophia, replaced by a masculine member of the spiritual world produced from the highest Trinity. The figure, named the Logos, performs many of the same functions of the old fallen feminine Sophia. Gone is the radically negative assessment of the Demiurge who rules over the world of soul and creates the phenomenal world. There is a chief psychic archon but his actions are not malevolent, only ignorant. Consequently the text articulates even more strongly the relatively positive stance toward creation that we can detect behind the late Sethian texts.

The forces that generated this revision of Valentinian theology were complex. The most important were no doubt ecclesiastical. Criticism of Valentinian theology by Irenaeus, Clement, Tertullian and other theologians and bishops of like mind had its impact. The Valentinians always considered themselves Christians and attempted to remain within the Great Church.

76. For the critical text, translation, and notes, see Attridge, Pagels in Attridge, ed., 1985.

77. These parallels are highlighted in the most recent critical edition and commentary, Thomassen and Painchaud 1989.

The *Tripartite Tractate* is an example of their intellectual attempt to do so.

Philosophical criticism does not seem to have been a major independent factor. The dialogue partners of the author of this text were Christians, not professional Platonists. The response that the anonymous Valentinian theologian gives to his critics does, however, involve the use of certain philosophical principles and perspectives that suggest that he or she had at least a passing exposure to professional philosophical discussion. Time constrains me to give but three examples.

First, we find in the *Tripartite Tractate* some technical philosophical jargon. A common way of discussing first principles since the first century had been to use a shorthand of prepositions.[78] The three first principles, God, the Ideas, Matter, common among many middle Platonists, could be referred to as the ὑφ οὗ, the ἐξ οὗ and the πρὸς ὅ, all inspired by passages in the *Timaeus*.[79] A hierarchy of four or more first principles could also be expressed in this way. In its revisionist account of devolution from and reintegration into the Divine, the text assigns one hypostasis a role as the one "from or through whom" everything outside of the Father is produced (NHC 1, 5:65,10). That there is some "prepositional theology" at work here is clear, although precisely what the affirmation is remains ambiguous, since the Coptic phrase ⲉⲧⲉ ⲁⲃⲁⲗ ⲍⲓⲧⲟⲟⲧϥ̄ could translate either ὑφ οὗ, ἐξ οὗ or δι' οὗ.[80] I earlier thought that some sort of instrumental causality was being attributed to the hypostasis in question. The hypostasis would therefore have been best identified as the Logos, the late Valentinian equivalent of Sophia. I now suspect that a different bit of prepositional philosophy is being affirmed, as I shall explain in a moment.

A second and more interesting philosophical element in the text is a careful deployment of the commonplace, but ultimately Aristotelian, categories of act and potency to describe the relationship of hypostases in the intelligible world. One fairly obvi-

78. See Dörrie 1971, pp. 17–33, esp. 21.

79. *Tim.* 28A4, 28A6, 31B7.

80. Cf. Crum 1962, pp. 429b.

ous way, in an emanationist system, to bridge the gap between an ultimately transcendent first principle and the beings that emerge from it is to say that the latter potentially exist as discrete hypostases within the former. The *Tripartite Tractate* takes that path, making its point through a number of images,[81] the most striking of which is that of the spiritual hypostases or aeons in a fetal state in the intellectual womb of the Father.[82]

In making this point the *Tripartite Tractate* used a distinction at home in the Platonic tradition. As far back in the history of the school as Speusippus, the Dyad of Plato's *Philebus* could be viewed as pure potentiality. Even Plotinus can speak of the second hypostasis of his system, Mind or Nous, as potency coming to actuality.[83] This is particularly striking because Plotinus frequently insists on the full actuality of Nous,[84] and one of the major points on which he criticizes the Gnostics known to him is the sort of deployment of categories of act and potency to hypostases of the intelligible world where all is actuality.[85]

Given the sense in which the highest principles have certain potentialities, the prepositional metaphysics applied to the second hypostasis of this system should probably be translated "the one from whom."

Although these and other interesting parallels with philosophical discourse can be catalogued, it is clear that this Valentinian system remains an example of Christian theology. This is evi-

81. In describing the process of emanation the text also uses the utterly conventional images of spring-stream, light-radiance, root-branches, perfume-fragrance, etc. See, e.g., 66,13–29.

82. *Tri. Trac.* NHC 1,5:60,1–62,33, esp. 60,29–33 and 61,20–62,5.

83. *Enn.* 3.8.11,1–2.

84. *Enn.* 2.5.3; 5.9.4,6–14. Armstrong 1967, p. 62, notes that this is a point of serious inconsistency in Plotinus.

85. *Enn.* 2.9.2,23–26: "For they will not assert that there is one principle which exists potentially and another which exists actually; for it would be ridiculous to distinguish things existing actually and potentially, and so multiply natures, in things which exist actually and are without matter." The *Allogenes*, by the way, may offer a response to such a criticism with its suggestion that categories of act and potency should be applied analogously to the highest level of reality. There hyperactuality and hyperpotentiality obtain. Cf. NHC 11,3:48,14–37.

dent in the text's conventional critique of philosophy as epistemologically inferior to revealed religion.[86] In the description of the intelligible world, this is nowhere more apparent than in the attribution of Will and Freedom to all spiritual hypostases. Most strikingly, the transcendent Father wills the process of emanation from himself, including the creation of the Demiurge and the material world, and wills himself to be known.[87] The Logos, responsible for the rupture in the Godhead, acts in freedom,[88] as do all creatures here below.

So much, then, for the final stage of Valentinianism available to us. Let me draw our survey to a close at this point. What I have tried to do for you this evening has been, in effect, to trace a chapter in the intellectual history of late antiquity, or to revert to my earlier metaphor, to follow two speculative streams from the first through the third century. This journey through the bayous of the ancient mind has I hope shown something of the complexity of the relationship of religious and philosophical elements in the period. Plato's heirs were indispensable dialogue partners with Gnostics of various kinds, as they were for Christians. The dialogue produced not simply apologetics, although that was there, but also fusion and synthesis of mystical piety and speculative metaphysics. The foundations for the more complete syntheses of the fourth and fifth centuries were being laid deep in the second.

University of Notre Dame

---

86. *Tri. Trac.* 108,13–114,30.

87. *Tri. Trac.* 55,35; 62,30; 71,36–72,1; on the Demiurge: 100,19–101,5.

88. *Tri. Trac.* 74,21.

Commentary on Attridge

Pheme Perkins

Professor Attridge has situated the quest for "gnostic platonism" between Justin Martyr in the mid-second century C.E. and St. Augustine in the late fourth century. By the end of Augustine's life in the fifth century C.E., that version of gnostic religion, Manichaeism, from which he claimed Platonism had helped to rescue him, was in decline. He has pointed out that for Christian apologists intellectual seriousness required an engagement with Platonic philosophy—though what Platonism was for second and early third century intellectuals remains a matter of debate. Therein lies one difficulty. The "platonism" with which we compare Christian and gnostic writings is the reconstructed Platonism of twentieth century scholars.

Some reconstructions, such as Prof. Armstrong's, rely on general categories derived from Plato's extant works. From that perspective second and third century gnostic—and even Christian—writers do not appear to have taken over any but the most superficial terms, ontological schemata and perhaps a few theological sentences or principles. The gnostics are clearly much more concerned with exegeting (or some might say deconstructing) biblical and apocryphal Jewish legends and the developing Christian traditions.

Other reconstructions, such as Prof. Krämer's or Prof. Dillon's, construct Platonism through sources like Philo, Numenius, the Seventh letter and a strong dose of pythagoreanism. Gnostic and early Christian thinkers, though marginal, share a growing emphasis on divine transcendence, the problem of mediating principles between the One and the world of multiplicity and quest for experiential recognition of the link between the self and the divine not strictly mediated by philosophical dialectic.

Prof. Attridge clearly inclines toward this latter view, though his solution to the methodological quandary has been to construct two rather fragile trajectories in gnostic writings which indicate, as he reads it, a developing tradition of engagement with Platonic philosophy. I concur in general with the broad division of the speculative gnostic religious texts into Sethian and Valentinian streams. However, we know that the Valentinian arises in a speculative milieu shaped by Christianity. Its engagement with Platonism is at least, in part, the desire to play the same role as other Christian teachers like Justin Martyr, to provide a speculative, intellectual (and religious/cultic) interpretation of Christianity for an elite.

Prof. Attridge's best hope for a gnostic engagement with Platonism that is independent of the encounter with Christianity lies in the Sethian stream, which is developing an elaborate mythical scheme that emerged from heterodox, Jewish exegesis. Even here, the case is far from secure. "Platonizing" and "Christianizing" appear in the same texts—or in some texts which appear to represent a later move away from Christianity such as those circulating among Plotinus' acquaintances in Rome, like *Allogenes*. Prof. Attridge also consistently presumes that "Alexandria" is the matrix for these developments. However, the best documented evidence, Justin, Valentinus, Ptolemy and Plotinus, points not to Alexandria but Rome. (Two of the other heresiologists, Irenaeus of Lyons and Hippolytus also had ties to Rome.)

Some of the platonism of Philo or Origen or of Alexandrian gnostics like Basilides might be related to what is found in these works, but methodologically and historically, we should note that the mature intellectual activity of these individuals is related to Rome, not Alexandria. Also on minor historical quibbles, I do not think that we have any evidence at all to justify assuming that Valentinus was the author of *Gospel of Truth*. Nor should *Tripartite Tractate*, Prof. Attridge's third stage Valentinian example, be located in the same context as *Gospel of Truth*. This text has an unusual Logos Christology—which is Alexandrian and speculative, but not that of Justin Martyr, whose Logos doctrine is entirely soteriological: how Christ operates for the salvation of the cosmos throughout its history. Further, elements in the Christology of *Tripartite Tractate*, which I cannot go into here, suggest some concern with the Arian debates of Alexandria in the late third century. Any Platonism in this text is certainly mediated through Christian theological speculation.

You may have noted, that Prof. Attridge's two streams end up in different places with quite different concerns on my hypothesis. The Sethian with *Allogenes* and the other writings circulating among Plotinus' friends in third century C.E. Rome. That stream is dechristianizing, adopting a "rational mysticism" (Prof. Attridge's phrase), a triadic hierarchy leading to the transcendent One and personal contemplation. This move is in part shaped by the pressures of Roman Christianity, which had been consolidating against speculative and deviant teaching since the mid-second century C.E.: Marcion was expelled; Valentinus passed over for bishop, and even Hippolytus a bit too intellectual for official Roman taste. . . Another gnostic teacher in the mid-second century, Ptolemy, whose letter to a wealthy Roman lady explaining the gnostic position on the Old Testament survives, may be the same as the Roman martyr Ptolemy. He died at about the same time as Justin—and for similar reasons, jealousy over the influence of such teachers in the households of prominent Roman matrons!

Tripartite Tractate, on the other hand, shows us a more deeply christianized and monistic rendering of the gnostic view of the world. The female Wisdom or Sophia figure has been replaced by the Logos, Son of God. Prof. Attridge incorrectly states that this third stage moderates the radically negative assessment of the Demiurge found in other gnostic writings. As he knows perfectly well, this radical evaluation of the Demiurge belongs to the Sethian, mythologizing tradition which uses it as an item of revolt against the God of the Old Testament. Valentinianism has always had a moderated view of the ignorance/error of the Demiurge. Prof. Attridge has proposed a "prepositional theology" as evidence that *Tripartite Tractate* was concerned with Platonic speculation. However, this topos had been known in Christian circles since St. Paul used a version of a stoic formula in 1 Cor 8:6. In the passage to which he refers, the translation "by whom" is probably to be preferred, since the image is closer to that of Aristotle's unmoved mover. The entire cosmos seeks this hypostasis. Prof. Attridge's new proposal, a confusing treatment of act and potency does not seem apposite.

Although we can find early evidence for some of the terms in neoplatonic speculation in Nag Hammadi texts, this evidence does not show us a philosophical tradition at work interpreting its own heritage. Plotinus rightly insists that the gnostics do not intend to be "platonists." However, he is too careful a thinker to make the mistake that Prof. Attridge attributes to him. Plotinus does not say that gnostics misuse the categories of act and potency in *Enn.* II 9, 1, 23-24. He says that that is too absurd even for gnostics, who tend to multiply natures. This remark belongs to the rhetorical arsenal of any decent polemicist: find an absurdity which your opponent has not committed, but might as well have done.

Indeed, those Christian thinkers like Justin and Augustine who had been led along toward faith by a "conversion to philosophy," are without any clear gnostic counterparts. *Tripartite Tractate*'s polemical presentation of the relationship between religion and philosophy sees the Greeks as furthest from the truth. The Hebrew prophets know some truth about god and exoteric Christianity truths that will "save" the masses, though not lead them to the highest form of union with God. Prof. Attridge, in the end, admits that *Tripartite Tractate* intends to be theology, not philosophy. He also admits that the author critiques philosophy as inferior to revealed religion—but so do all other gnostic texts which make any reference to philosophy.

The contrast between gnostic and Christian authors like Justin and Augustine on the place of philosophy belongs to the larger question of the genre and rhetoric of the individual writings. Gnostic authors give us revelation dialogues, inspired homilies or revealed treatises. They do not write spiritual biographies or dialogues which engage contemporary persons as fictive speakers in the discussion. Our Christian authors give accounts of the attractiveness, helpfulness and errors engendered by philosophy. Justin Martyr in his quasi-biographical introduction to *Dialogue with Trypho* (chs. 1-9) credits Platonism with drawing his mind toward incorporeal things. However, it also produced in him an inflated claim to wisdom, which he thought could be quickly gained. He expected that he would be able to see God immediately (2,6). This remark is a stock rhetorical topos. Plotinus says the same about the gnostics. The old man challenges Justin the philosopher with being a sophist not a person of action. The Christian, on the other hand, can grasp the Logos, mount it and look down from above on the errors of others (3,2). The polemic goes on to challenge the philosophical presumption of those who think that the human soul can naturally attain knowledge of God (3,4-6, 2).

Insofar as they insist that the only true knowledge about the divine is revealed, the gnostic authors are much closer to their Christian opponents than they are to platonists. (It is no wonder that Celsus did not distinguish gnostic from orthodox Christians.) Like their Christian counterparts, what the gnostics seek to "explain" when they write treatises is not a philosophical system but religious myth and cultic practice. Theurgy, which came to play an important role in neoplatonic circles, can be said to bring some Platonists closer to the gnostic practices of corporate, mystic ascent to contemplation of the One through chanting such as we find in the dechristianized Sethian texts like *Allogenes*. But we do not have in these gnostic writers a desire to exegete, interpret or correct the Platonic tradition as such.

Philosophical terms, slogans, principles and perhaps even summaries of philosophical doctrine can be detected in gnostic

writings. Some of their authors had undoubtedly studied philosophy as Justin had. But it is hard to imagine the gnostic
teacher Ptolemy going to martyrdom wearing a philosopher's
cloak in the name of his new revelation. Gnostic writers polemi-
cize against Jewish Scripture (and its God) and Christian preach-
ing. From the latter, they appear to have taken up both the use
of philosophical material to explicate a mythological tradition
and common anti-philosophical positions on the temporal
beginning of the material world, the knowledge of god, revelation and the human soul. We may learn something of the state
of Platonism in the second and third century from the philosophical commonplaces in gnostic texts as Prof. Attridge has
suggested. Insofar as union with the divine was a widely
shared goal among intellectuals in late antiquity the more speculative and mystical forms of gnosticism might attract Christians
as the Valentinians did or some pagans in the circles around
Plotinus. But in the end gnostics and Platonists seem too far
apart to have been serious enemies, let alone bedfellows.

Boston College

ATTRIDGE/PERKINS BIBLIOGRAPHY

Abramowski, L., 1983: "Nag Hammadi 8,1 'Zostrianus' Das Anonymum Brucianum, Plotin Enn. 2,9 (33)," in Blume and Mann 1983, pp. 1–10.

Aland, B., 1983: "Christentum, Bildung und Römische Oberschicht: Zum 'Octavius' des Minucius Felix," in Blume and Mann 1983, pp. 11–30.

Andresen, C., 1952/53: "Justin und der mittlere Platonismus," *ZNW* 44, pp. 157–95.

Armstrong, A. H., 1940: *The Architecture of the Intelligible Universe in the Philosophy of Plotinus: An Analytical and Historical Study* (Cambridge; reprinted, Amsterdam, 1967).

_____ 1967a: ("Part III. Plotinus," in Armstrong 1967b, pp. 195–268).

_____ ed., 1967b: *The Cambridge History of Later Greek and Early Medieval Philosophy* (Cambridge) .

_____ 1978: "Gnosis and Greek Philosophy," in Bianchi 1978, pp. 87–124.

Attridge, H. W., ed., 1985: *Nag Hammadi Codex I (The Jung Codex)* (2 vols.; Leiden).

_____ 1986: "The Gospel of Truth as an Exoteric Text," in Hedrick and Hodgson 1986, pp. 239–56.

Barnard, L. W., 1967: *Justin Martyr: His Life and Thought* (Cambridge).

Bazan, F. G., 1974: "Gnóstica: El capítulo XVI de la Vida de Plotino de Porfirio," *Salesianum* 36, pp. 463–78.

_____ 1980: *Plotino y la gnosis* (Buenos Aires).

Beyschlag, K., 1988: *Grundriß der Dogmengeschichte. Band I: Gott und Welt* (2d ed; Grundrisse 2; Darmstadt).

Bianchi, U., ed., 1970: *Le Origini dello Gnosticismo: Colloquio di Messina 13–18 Aprile 1966* (Numen Supplement 12; Leiden).

_____ 1977: "A propos de quelques discussions récentes sur la termi-nologie, la définition et la méthode de l'étude du gnosticisme," *Proceedings of the International Colloquium on Gnosticism, Stockholm August 20–25, 1973* (Stockholm), pp. 16–26.

_____ et al., edd., 1978: *Gnosis. Festschrift für Hans Jonas* (Göttingen).

Blume, H.-D., and F. Mann, edd., 1983: *Platonismus und Christentum: Festschrift für Heinrich Dörrie* (JAC Ergänzungsband 10; Münster).

Chadwick, H., 1967: "Part II. Philo and the Beginnings of Christian Thought," in Armstrong, 1967b, pp. 137–92.

Crouzel, H., 1980: Origen: *The Life and Thought of the First Great*

Theologian (San Francisco).

Crum, W. , 1962: *A Coptic Dictionary* (Oxford).

Dietrich, A., ed., 1975: *Synkretismus im syrisch-persischen Kulturgebiet* (Abh. der Akad. der Wiss. in Gött. Philologisch-Hist. Kl. Dritte Folge 96; Göttingen).

Dillon, J., 1977: *The Middle Platonists*, 80 B. C. to A. D. 220 (Ithaca).

Dodds, E. R., 1928: "The Parmenides of Plato and the Origin of the Neo-Platonic One," *Classical Quarterly* 32, pp. 129–42.

_____ ed., 1960: E. R. Dodds, ed., *Les Sources de Plotin: Dix exposés et discussions* (Entretiens sur l'antiquité classique 5; Genève)

_____ 1963: Proclus, the Elements of Theology (2d ed.; Oxford).

Dörrie, H., ed., 1966: *Porphyre: 8 exposés suivis de discussions* (Entretiens sur l'antiquité classique 12; Genève).

_____1971a: "Die Erneuerung des Platonismus im ersten Jahrhundert vor Christus," in Schuhl and Hadot 1971, pp. 17–33.

_____ 1971b: "Was ist 'spätantiker Platonismus'? Überlegungen zur Grenzziehung zwischen Platonismus und Christentum," *Theologische Rundschau* 36, pp. 15–28.

_____ 1976: "Der Platonismus in der Kultur- und Geistesgeschichte der frühen Kaiserzeit," in idem, *Platonica minora* (Studia et testimonia antiqua 8; München), pp. 166–210.

_____ 1981: "Die Andere Theologie, Wie stellten die frühchristlichen Theologen des 2.–4. Jahrh. ihren Lesern die 'griechische Weisheit' (= den Platonismus) dar?" *Theologie und Philosophie* 56, pp. 1–46.

_____ 1987: Die geschichtlichen Wurzeln des Platonismus (Stuttgart-Bad Cannstatt).

Drijvers, H. J. W., 1970: "Bardaisan of Edessa and the Hermetica: The Aramaic Philosopher and the Philosophy of his Time," *Jaarbericht van het Vooraziatisch-Egyptisch Genootschap Ex Oriente Lux* 21, pp. 190–210.

_____ 1975: "Bardaisan von Edessa als Repräsentant des syrischen Synkretismus im 2. Jarhhundert n. Chr." in Dietrich 1975, pp. 109–22.

_____ 1982: "Facts and Problems in Early Syriac-Speaking Christianity," *The Second Century* 2, pp. 157–75.

Elsas, C., 1975: *Neuplatonische und gnostische Weltablehnung in der Schule Plotins* (Berlin/New York).

Foerster, W., 1972: *Gnosis: A Selection of Gnostic Texts* (2 vols.; Oxford).

Grant, R. M., 1956: "Aristotle and the Conversion of Justin," *Journal of Theological Studies* n.s. 7, pp. 246–48.

Hadot, P., 1960: "Etre, Vie, Pensé chez Plotin et avant Plotin," in Dodds, 1960, pp. 142–57.

_____ 1966: "La métaphysique de Porphyre," in Dörrie, 1966, pp. 127–57.

_____ 1968: *Porphyre et Victorinus* (2 vols.; Paris).

Hedrick, C. W., ed., 1990: *Nag Hammadi Codices XI, XII, XII*I (NHS 28; Leiden) 173–267.

_____ and R. Hodgson, Jr., 1986: *Nag Hammadi, Gnosticism and Christianity* (Peabody, MA).

Jackson, H. M., 1985: *The Lion Becomes Man: The Gnostic Leontomorphic Creator and the Platonic Tradition* (SBLDS 81; Atlanta:).

Joly, R., 1973: *Christianisme et Philosophie: Études sur Justin et les Apologistes grecs du deuxième siècle* (Bruxelles).

Jonas, H., 1964, 1966: *Gnosis und spätantiker Geist* (2 vols.; FRLANT 33 and 45; Göttingen).

_____ "The Soul in Gnosticism and Plotinus," in Schuhl and Hadot 1971, pp. 45–53, reprinted in H. Jonas, *Philosophical Essays: From Ancient Creed to Technological Man* (Englewood Cliffs, NJ, 1974).

King, K. L., 1991: *Allogenes: Nag Hammadi Codex XI,3, Introduction, Text, Translation, Notes* (Sonoma, CA).

Koschorke, K., 1975: "Hippolyt's Ketzerbekämpfung und Polemik gegen die Gnostiker," *Göttinger Orientforschungen* 6,4.

Krämer, H. J., 1964: *Der Ursprung der Geistmetaphysik: Untersuchungen zur Geschichte des Platonismus zwischen Platon und Plotin* (Amsterdam).

Kroll, W., 1892: "Ein neuplatonischer Parmenideskommentar in einem Turiner Palimpsest," *Rheinisches Museum* 47, pp. 599–627.

Layton, B., 1987: *The Gnostic Scriptures* (New York).

Lilla, S. R. C., 1971: *Clement of Alexandria: A Study in Christian Platonism and Gnosticism* (New York and London).

May, G., 1983: "Platon und die Auseinandersetzung mit den Häresien bei Klemens von Alexandrien," in Blume and Mann, 1983, pp. 123–32.

Meijering, E. P., 1974: "'Wie platonisierten die Christen?' Zur Grenzziehung zwischen Platonismus, kirchlichem Credo und patristischer Theologie," *Vigiliae Christianae* 28 , pp. 15–28.

Merlan, P., 1967: "Part I. Greek Philosophy from Plato to Plotinos," in Armstrong 1967b, pp. 14–132.

Bibliography

Orbe, A., S.J., 1958–1966: *Estudios Valentinianos* (5 vols.; Rome).

Osborne, E., 1957: *The Philosophy of Clement of Alexandria* (Cambridge).

_____ 1973: *Justin Martyr* (BHTh 47; Tübingen).

Pearson, B. A., 1978: "The Tractate Marsanes (NHC X) and the Platonic Tradition," in Bianchi 1978, pp. 373–84, a revised version of which appears in his *Gnosticism*, 148–64.

_____ 1981: "NHC X,1: Marsanes," in B. A. Pearson, ed., *Nag Hammadi Codices IX and X* (NHS 15; Leiden), pp. 229–347.

_____ 1984: "Jewish Sources in Gnostic Literature," in M. E. Stone, ed., *The Literature of the Jewish People in the Period of the Second Temple* (Assen, Philadelphia) pp. 443–81.

_____ 1990: Gnosticism, Judaism, and Egyptian Christianity (Minneapolis).

Perkins, P., 1980: *The Gnostic Dialogue: The Early Church and the Crisis of Gnosticism* (New York).

_____ 1980: "On the Origin of the World (CG II,5): A Gnostic Physics," *Vigiliae Christianae* 34. pp. 36–46.

Pétrement, S., *1984: Le Dieu séparé: Les origines du gnosticisme* (Paris).

Ricken, F., 1978: "Zur Rezeption der platonischen Ontologie bei Eusebios von Kaisareia, Areios und Athanasios," *Theologie und Philosophie* 53, pp. 321–52.

Ritter, A. M., 1984: "Platonismus und Christentum in der Spätantike," *Theologische Rundschau* 49, pp. 31–56.

Robinson, J. M., 1977: "The Three Steles of Seth and the Gnostics of Plotinus," in *Proceedings of the International Colloquium on Gnosticism, Stockholm, August 20–25, 1973* (Stockholm, Leiden), pp. 132–42.

Roloff, D., 1970: *Plotin, Die Großschrift III,8–V,8–V,5–II,9* (Untersuchungen zur antiken Literatur und Geschichte 8; Berlin).

Rudolph, K., 1977: *Gnosis: The Nature and History of Gnosticism* (San Francisco).

_____ 1983: "'Gnosis' and 'Gnosticism'—the Problems of Their Definition and Their Relation to the Writings of the New Testament," in A. H. B. Logan and A. J. M. Wedderburn, *The New Testament and Gnosis: Essays in honour of Robert McL. Wilson* (Edinburgh, 1983), pp. 21–37.

Sagnard, F., 1947: *La gnose valentinienne et le témoignage de saint Irenée* (Paris).

Schenke, Hans-Martin, 1974: "Das sethianische System nach Nag-Hammadi Handschriften," in P. Nagel, ed., *Studia Coptica* (Berlin, 1974) pp. 165–72.

Schuhl, P. M., and P. Hadot, edd., 1971: *Le néoplatonisme* (Colloques internationaux du centre national de la recherche scientifique; Paris)

Segal, A., 1977: *Two Powers in Heaven: Rabbinic Reports about Christianity and Gnosticism* (Leiden).

Sevrin, J. M, 1986: *Le dossier baptismal séthien: Études sur la sacramentaire gnostique* (Bibliothèque copte de Nag Hammadi, Section "Études" 2; Québec).

Sieber, J. H., 1973: "An Introduction to the Tractate Zostrianus from Nag Hammadi," *Novum Testamentum* 15, pp. 233–40.

Smith, M., 1973: *Clement of Alexandria and a Secret Gospel of Mark* (Cambridge).

Stead, G. S., 1969: "The Valentinian Myth of Sophia," *Journal of Theological Studies* n.s. 20, pp. 75–104, reprinted in *Substance and Illusion in the Christian Fathers* (London, 1985).

_____ 1980: "In Search of Valentinus," in B. Layton, ed., *The Rediscovery of Gnosticism: Proceedings of the International Conference on Gnosticism at Yale, New Haven, Connecticut, March 28–31, 1978*; Vol. 1, *The School of Valentinus (SHR 41; Leiden) pp. 75–95, reprinted in Substance and Illusion in the Christian Fathers* (London: Variorum, 1985).

Stroumsa, G. A., 1984: *Another Seed: Studies in Gnostic Mythology* (NHS 24; Leiden).

Theiler, W., 1933: *Porphyrios und Augustin* (Halle).

Thomassen, E., and L. Painchaud, 1989: *Le Traité Tripartite (NH I,5)* (Bibliothèque copte de Nag Hammadi, Section "Textes" 19; Québec).

Trigg, J. W., 1983: *Origen: The Bible and Philosophy in the Third-century Church* (Atlanta).

Turner, J. D., 1980: "The Gnostic Threefold Path to Enlightenment," *Novum Testamentum* 22, pp. 324–51.

_____ 1986: "Sethian Gnosticism: A Literary History," in Hedrick and Hodgson,1986, pp. 55–86.

Vogel, C. de, 1953: "On the Neoplatonic Character of Platonism and the Platonic Character of Neoplatonism," *Mind* 62, pp. 43–64.

_____ 1959: *Greek Philosophy: A Collection of Texts with Notes and Explanations* (3 vols.; Leiden).

Whittaker, J., 1969: "EPEKEINA NOU KAI OUSIAS," *Vigiliae Christianae* 23, pp. 91–104.

Bibliography

Williams, M. A., 1985: *The Immovable Race: A Gnostic Designation and the Theme of Stability in Late Antiquity* (NHS 29; Leiden).
Winden, J. C. M. van , 1971: *An Early Christian Philosopher: Justin Martyr's Dialogue with Trypho Chapters One to Nine* (Leiden).

Colloquium 2
Return to the Cave: *Republic* 519-521
Richard Kraut

In this paper, I propose a solution to a difficulty in Plato's *Republic* that has long troubled scholars. The problem arises from Socrates' requirement that after the rulers of the ideal city have completed their philosophical education, they must set aside their purely theoretical studies for a while in order to hold political office (519c-d). Immediately after Socrates lays down this requirement, Glaucon asks whether it treats the philosophers unjustly and is contrary to their interest (519e); to which Socrates replies that the laws of the ideal city are not designed to produce the greatest happiness of any one group of individuals, but must instead promote the good of the whole community (519e-520a). He goes on to argue that the requirement is appropriate: since the philosophers have benefitted from the splendid education the city has given them, and since that education makes them more qualified to rule than any other group, it is just that they be asked to devote some of their time to public service (520a-d). Having been properly educated, they will recognize the justice of this arrangement and will accept it, however grudgingly (520e).

The difficulty created by this interchange is that it seems to undermine Plato's attempt to show that justice is always in one's best interests. For the passage insists that although the philosophers will recognize the justice of the requirement and abide by it, they will do so with appropriate reluctance, for they rightly regard purely philosophical activity as better for them than the activity of ruling the city (521a-b). Their reluctance is something Plato even welcomes, because he thinks that a city

43

Richard Kraut

cannot be well ruled if citizens compete for office and regard ruling as something fine (521a; cf. 540b). So, Plato is apparently saying that in this particular case it is contrary to one's interest to act justly. And that seems to conflict with what he had promised to show in Book II.[1] The whole project of the *Republic*, as it is understood by many of its readers, is to argue that there is no conflict between justice and self-interest; and yet in this passage Plato seems to be saying that one of the good features of his ideal city is that there is a *divergence* between one's own good and justice: the fact that ruling, though justly required, is not in the best interests of the philosophers serves as a guarantee to the other citizens that office is not being sought for self-interested reasons. So the passage is puzzling not simply because it apparently provides a counter-example to the dialogue's principal thesis, but also because Plato himself seems to recognize the feature that makes it a counter-example.

Scholars who think the difficulty soluble have pursued one of two strategies. Nicholas White has used the passage to show that, contrary to initial appearances, Plato does not promise to give a completely general defense of justice in terms of self-interest; rather, on this reading, he recognizes that in this one case an exception must be made.[2] Other scholars, most recently, C.D.C. Reeve, have tried to discover a way in which ruling does after all promote the greatest good of the philosophers over the long run.[3] The solution I will propose also follows this second strategy, but as we will see it differs markedly from Reeve's.

1. Among those who claim that there is this inconsistency in Plato are: Adkins 1960, pp. 290-293; Annas 1981, pp. 260-271, esp. 269; Bloom 1968, pp. 407-408; Irwin 1977, pp. 163, 236-7, 242-3, 337-8 n. 61. Irwin holds that in both the *Phaedo* and the *Republic* Plato is sometimes attracted to a contemplative ideal, and that although this is not the predominant ideal of the latter dialogue, it misleads Plato into holding that the philosopher does not gladly undertake public service. For references to further literature, see Irwin 1977, pp. 337-8 n. 61; and Nicholas P. White 1979, pp. 195-196.

2. See White 1979, pp. 23, 189-196; a fuller treatment is contained in White 1986, pp. 22-46.

3. See Reeve 1988, pp. 201-203. Other attempts to show that returning to the cave has a self-interested justification can be found in: Beatty 1976, pp. 545-575; and Irwin 1977. I will not discuss the differences between their solutions and my own.

I

The first question we must ask is this: how convincing is the evidence drawn from our passage (*Republic* 519-521) that according to Plato philosophers are acting contrary to their best interests when they rule the ideal city? I believe that it is quite weak.

To begin with, there is an argument from silence: Socrates does not make any attempt to answer one of the questions Glaucon poses, and from this it might be inferred that he thinks no answer can be given. Glaucon asks whether the rulers have a worse life because they are required to rule, and Socrates replies that he is not aiming at the greatest possible happiness of the philosophers (519d-e). Nowhere in 519-521 or in the rest of the *Republic* does he return to Glaucon's challenge and spell out how the philosopher does profit from holding political office.[4] He argues that the requirement is just (520a-e), but not that it is defensible simply in terms of self-interest. And the absence of any such overt argument might be taken as a silent concession that the requirement cannot be defended in purely self-interested terms.

This by itself is not strong evidence, however, for there is a perfectly good explanation of why Plato does not, in this passage, attempt to show that ruling is in the best interests of the philosophers: he is still in the midst of constructing the ideal city, and is very far from completing his argument that justice pays.[5] He might think that to see why ruling is advantageous for the philosophers, we must have a fuller picture of what the philo-

4. There is a contrast here between the way Plato treats the question whether holding political office makes the philosophers worse off and the way he treats the earlier question, raised at the beginning of Book IV, whether the ban on private property among the guardians involves some loss of well being for them. He does return to the earlier question at 465e-466c and argues that the economic restriction on the guardians does not diminish their happiness. But there is no passage in which he makes a parallel claim about the requirement that philosophers rule.

5. I do not believe that at the end of the Book IV Plato has come to the conclusion of one argument for the thesis that justice pays, and that he then goes on to give new arguments in the remainder of the dialogue. Rather, I think that he only comes to the completion of his first defense of justice in Book IX at 580c, where he proclaims that the philosopher-ruler is happier than any of the individ-

sophical life involves and why it is so much better than any other kind of life. And although he does not, after completing his portrait of the philosophical life, return to its political component and show why it is advantageous for the philosopher to rule, he may think that it is the job of his readers to see for themselves how the general defense of justice in terms of self-interest can be applied to this particular case. Our failure to see how ruling benefits the philosophers may be just that—*our* failure— and so the fact that Plato does not spell this out for us does not by itself indicate that they do not benefit. Everything depends on how we construe his attempt to defend justice in self-interested terms, for if we misunderstand his general argument for this thesis we will also fail to see why justice is advantageous in this particular case.

II

It might seem, however, that our passage is not merely silent on the question whether and how ruling benefits the philosopher; some would go farther and say that it provides positive textual evidence that according to Plato ruling is *contrary* to the philosopher's good. I will now try to show that there is no such positive evidence, despite initial appearances.

To begin with, he says several times that the philosophers are *compelled* to rule and regard this as a necessity,[6] and this might be taken to mean that political activity is disadvantageous for them. Why should compulsion be applied, after all, if the philosophers can see that ruling is in their self-interest?

But a moment's thought is enough to see that this talk of compulsion cannot mean that the philosophers are actually being coerced to accept political office. Plato does not induce them to rule by threatening them with punishment; on the contrary, he

uals portrayed in Books VIII and IX. I present this interpretation more fully in Kraut (forthcoming). Plato says several times after Book IV that the nature of justice is still under examination (472b, 484a), and at 543d-544b he indicates that the best possible case for justice had not yet been given in Book IV. The idea that Books II-IV are not intended as a complete argument for justice is also backed by White 1986.

6. See 520a8, 520e2, 521b7, 540b4-5.

gives an argument that they should rule, and it is their acceptance of this argument that *persuades* them to hold political
office.[7] Furthermore, since they are quite capable of understanding the entire argument of the *Republic* for the thesis that justice
coincides with one's self-interest, they will come to see that in
fact they will not be sacrificing their good by holding political
office.

What then does Plato have in mind when he says that the
philosophers are compelled to rule, and that they will regard
ruling as a necessity? These statements do not mean or entail
that ruling is contrary to their good, for the claim that an act is a
necessity is entirely compatible with its being in one's best interests.[8] Surely what explains the talk of necessity and constraint
in this passage is the point that it is not up to the philosophers to
do whatever they think best in this situation. They are not free
to act in any way whatsoever because, in light of the great benefits they have received, they owe it to the city to make an equivalent return. This is precisely what Socrates emphasizes at
520a3-4: no one in the community is allowed to act in whatever
way she[9] thinks best; rather their activities are coordinated in a
way that promotes the good of the whole community. Now, it
would be a mistake to think that since the philosopher is not free
to accept or reject political office as she sees fit, she must be sacrificing her own good when she accepts this requirement.
Though the city is not giving the philosopher the option of
refusing political office, it might still be the case that were she to
refuse, she would be sacrificing her good because of the injustice
of her refusal. So Plato's talk of necessity should not be taken to

7. This point is well made by White 1979, pp. 24-5, n. 6. Note too that, as Plato
clearly indicates in our passage (519e4; cf. 421c1), it is possible to induce people
to act in certain ways by means of both persuasion and compulsion.

8. As an anonymous reader pointed out to me, Plato holds that reason is compelled to sort out the conflicting reports of the senses (524c7), but he of course
does not mean that doing so is contrary to its interests.

9. Here and throughout I use feminine pronouns as a reminder that Plato
expects some women to be in the ruling class. The basic idea is presented at
454b-457a and Plato himself issues a reminder at 540c, immediately after he restates the requirement that philosophers must rule.

suggest that the philosopher would do better for herself were she to act unjustly and refuse to rule.[10]

III

As we have now seen, we cannot infer a conflict between justice and self-interest from Socrates' silence about how ruling benefits the philosopher, nor from his statements that the philosopher will be constrained to hold political office whether she wants to or not. But there is one aspect of our passage that we have not discussed so far, and it might be thought to show decisively that according to Plato philosophers do sacrifice their own good in returning to the cave. For he says several times that the philosophical life is better than the political life, and that therefore the philosopher is rightly reluctant to give up a certain amount of philosophical activity in order to hold political office.[11] And it might be thought that these statements tell us explicitly and unmistakably that even though the philosopher acts justly when she accepts political office, she would be better off if she were able to violate this requirement and continue her purely philosophical activities.

But in reading the passage in this way, we would be running together two questions that must be kept distinct:

1. Is philosophical activity better than political activity?

2. Would the philosopher who has been trained by the ideal state be better off (a) to continue philosophizing, thereby violat-

10. Here my reading differs from that of White 1979. He says, "when he says that they are forced ... he means that they consent to rule in spite of their realization that they could be better off" (p. 192). I don't think there is any connection between doing what one thinks is less than best for oneself and being compelled to do something. To be compelled is to have one's freedom restricted, so that alternatives one might have chosen are not available. This is precisely the situation of the philosophers: they must hold office, whether they want to or not. But this leaves it entirely open that if they act with full understanding of why justice is always best for the agent, then they will take their fulfillment of a just requirement as best for themselves.

11. See 520e4-b10: the political life is worse than the philosophical life, and so the philosophers rightly look down upon holding office. For them, ruling is not a fine thing (540b4).

ing the just requirement that she rule, or (b) to spend some time ruling the city, thereby fulfilling the requirement that she hold political office?

The first question is the one that is clearly answered by the text, but it would be a great mistake to think that this by itself forces an answer to the very different question posed in (2).[12] For it may be that when philosophizing is undertaken in circumstances that make it unjust, then its injustice detracts from the value that it normally has, and makes it worse, all things considered, than justly ruling the city for a period of time. To put the point differently: We do not have to take (1) to make the extremely strong claim that engaging in philosophical activity is always the more advantageous option, regardless of the circumstances. It can mean that when all other things are equal, philosophy is better than politics. That would leave open the possibility that on occasions when philosophical activity would involve acting unjustly, and political activity is justly required, then the latter is the option that better promotes one's self-interest.

Of course, if this is what Plato thinks, then he should give some explanation of why just and unjust circumstances make so much difference. He must say why it is in one's interest to act justly even when doing so requires one to give up a certain amount of philosophical activity. But as I have already said, Plato's silence in this passage about why in this particular case justice is so advantageous, in spite of the fact that ruling is a worse activity than philosophical study, should not be taken to mean that he can give no argument for this.

I conclude that there is no positive textual support for the claim that philosophers would be better off to disobey the political requirement. The fact that philosophical activity is more worthwhile than political activity does not by itself show that

12. I think the inference from (1) to (2) is made by White 1979 when he says: "the task of a philosopher-ruler necessarily involves some sacrifice of the individual good of the person performing it. This is a point repeatedly emphasized by Plato" (p. 23). What is repeatedly emphasized by Plato is that philosophy is a better activity than ruling, not that when the philosopher justly obeys the political requirement she makes "some sacrifice" in her individual good.

49

unjust philosophical activity is more advantageous than acting *justly* by accepting the requirement that one hold office. If we believe that he promises in Book II to show that justice is always more advantageous than injustice, then nothing in our passage indicates that he wants to or needs to make an exception in this one case.

IV

We must now consider what resources Plato has for showing that the philosopher is better off to obey the political requirement than to disobey it. In this section, I will consider a recent suggestion of Reeve; in the next, I will propose my own solution.

Reeve thinks that philosophers are better off to obey the political requirement because their failure to do so would lead to civil war, and such strife would undermine their own happiness.[13] The good of the philosopher consists in "getting as much of the pleasure of knowing and learning the truth as possible throughout life,"[14] and ruling is a purely instrumental means to this goal. For if the philosopher refused to rule, the ideal city would be destroyed, and in the less than ideal city that would take its place the philosopher would have fewer opportunities to get "the pleasure of knowing and learning the truth."

This proposal is open to two objections. First, it commits Plato to a speculative and doubtful empirical calculation, one that he does not himself make in this text or any other. Reeve's idea is that the philosophers who have completed their education will enjoy more contemplative pleasure by remaining in the ideal city than they would if they were to flee to some other city and continue their theorizing there. But that empirical calculation would be true only if no other cities would allow them to continue their philosophizing. How can Plato's entire argument depend on the truth of this speculative claim?

Second, this interpretation makes no use of an indispensable premise Socrates relies on when he explains why the philosophers should rule: they have received a splendid education from

13. Reeve 1988, p. 202.
14. Reeve 1988, p. 248.

the city, and it is just that they should repay this debt by using that education for the benefit of the city. On Reeve's reading, this appeal to reciprocity does not by itself have persuasive force for the philosophers. Their real reason for ruling, as he sees it, is that the future benefits will outweigh the costs: the burden of ruling is offset by the increased philosophical pleasure one will have by remaining in the ideal city. But this reason is not only one that Plato fails to give; it makes irrelevant the one he does give. And surely when philosophers agree to rule, they must do so for the reasons stated in the text.

Another way of putting this point is that for Reeve the advantage of ruling has nothing to do with its justice; for what makes the political requirement just is the assumption that one should return good for good. If justice and maximal advantage happen to coincide in this situation, it would be, on Reeve's account, a fortunate coincidence. And surely Plato cannot afford to admit that justice and self-interest are so loosely connected. He wants to show that justice by its very nature must benefit us and that injustice is by its very nature harmful. So, if philosophers who have been trained by the ideal city are best off to rule for a while, this must depend on the fact that ruling is justly required. A successful interpretation of our passage must therefore not only show why the philosopher benefits from ruling; it must also derive the connection between ruling and advantage from the very considerations Plato presents in our text.

V

I turn now to my own solution. My assumption in what follows is that Plato's metaphysics plays a central role in his defense of justice. More specifically, I take him to be saying that the philosopher is the paradigm of a just person and that what makes the philosophical life better than any other is the fact that the objects that the philosopher knows, loves, and imitates—the Forms—are the most valuable objects one can possess.[15] What is

15. My first assumption—that the philosopher is the consummately just person—is not controversial; but I do not take it to be obvious why Plato thinks the philosophical life best. For further discussion of this issue, see Kraut (forthcoming). The interpretation I offer here depends heavily on the general framework provided by that paper. The crux of my view is that the Forms constitute the

crucial for our present purposes is Plato's notion that the Forms are arranged in a systematic order and that the philosopher's understanding of this order will inspire in her a desire to imitate them. This idea is put forward in a passage which precedes the one we have been discussing by some 20 pages, and which lays the groundwork for the claim that because of their understanding of the Forms philosophers will be in an excellent position to create a just political order (500b-501b). In this earlier passage, Socrates describes the Forms as constituting a *kosmos* in which no element is unjust to or unjustly treated by another (500c3-4); and he says that when the philosopher looks to this incorporeal system, she wants to become as similar to it as she possibly can (c5-d1). The thought here is that justice and injustice need not be relationships among human beings or parts of the soul; rather, justice among a certain group of elements consists in their having a relationship that is in some way harmonious and appropriate for that group of objects. The philosophers who grasp the Forms do not merely understand them one by one, each in isolation from the others, but view them as exhibiting a pattern; and their love of that pattern inspires in them a desire to imitate them.

How does this help with our problem of seeing why it is best for the philosopher to accept the just requirement that she hold political office? My suggestion is that Plato believes that certain relationships among people are fitting and harmonious; and that participation in these well-ordered relationships constitutes an imitation of the Forms. Accordingly, he also believes that if one violates fair requirements in human relationships, one is by that very fact *rejecting* the Forms as models of human behavior. The Forms constitute the highest harmonious order, and when human beings are related to each other in the pattern prescribed for the ideal city, their relationships with each other constitute a pattern which is the best political imitation of the Forms there can be. Conversely, if one recognizes that a certain political

---

supreme good because they exhibit the highest kind of order, and that human beings can possess this supreme good by entering into a certain kind of relationship with the Forms, a relationship that involves not merely understanding these abstract objects but loving and imitating them as well.

arrangement is just and that it is therefore appropriate for one to make a certain contribution to the well-being of the city, but one refuses to make this contribution, then one is consciously rejecting the Forms as a pattern to be imitated and one is thereby undermining one's own good. For the best sort of human life is one which is dedicated to the project of imitating the Forms and in which one never does anything to reject them as a model.

This suggestion is easily applied to the situation we have been discussing. When one has received a philosophical education and can use it to benefit those who have in some way contributed to that education, then one would be upsetting the proper order in human relationships if one were to refuse. One would be a creator of disorder by one's very failure to reciprocate, because harmony in human relationships involves each giving and receiving benefits that are peculiarly appropriate to the talents and needs of the individuals involved. So Plato's argument that philosophers should rule does not depend on the harmful consequences that might or might not follow an unjust refusal to govern. Rather, he is assuming that the injustice of the act of refusal is by itself a decisive objection to it, because that act of rejecting appropriate order in human relationships distances one from the Forms. Even if a single philosopher shirks her responsibilities, but other philosophers do not, and the city continues to function smoothly because of their additional efforts, that single philosopher would be violating the proper order among human relationships.

The idea I am attributing to Plato is that when we act justly, we should do so because we recognize a certain pattern of distribution to be fitting. The philosopher who returns to the cave is not doing so merely because she wants to benefit those who dwell there; rather, she does so because she remembers what others have done for her, and she recognizes that this way of repaying her debt is precisely what the situation calls for. The lover of justice is a lover of a certain kind of pattern in human affairs, and not merely a lover of other human beings. She does not just distribute benefits to others randomly, but distributes them in order to achieve a certain balance that is appropriate in human relationships. That is why Plato thinks there is a kinship between loving justice in social arrangements and loving the order among the Forms.[16]

If we understand Plato in the way I propose, then the *justice* of requiring philosophers to rule is intimately connected with the *advantage* of governing in this situation. One cannot profit from an act that dissociates one from the Forms, since imitation of the Forms is the goal at which one must always be striving, if one is to lead the best life.[17] The Forms are a just order, and we fail to imitate them if we refuse to do what is justly required of us in human relationships. Once the philosopher sees why ruling is just, she will agree that it would be contrary to her interest to continue her purely philosophical activities, even though such activity would in other circumstances be more advantageous than political activity.[18]

VI

16. My interpretation rejects the idea, endorsed by several scholars, that the philosophers' motivation for returning to the cave has nothing to do with the fact that in doing so they benefit others. See Cooper 1977, p. 157; and Annas 1981, p. 267. She says of the philosophers: "They are not seeking their own happiness. Nor are they seeking that of others. They are simply doing what is impersonally best." I am not sure how this can be reconciled with the fact, emphasized in our passage (519e1-520a3), that the philosophers must rule because well-being and benefits must be distributed to all components of the city, not just one. The philosopher's goal is to benefit-others-in-a-certain-pattern; the fact that she is not trying to benefit others, regardless of pattern, does not entail that the good of others is of no concern to her. Note that in saying this, I am also rejecting Cooper's suggestion that the philosopher's ultimate goal is to "maximize the total amount of rational order in the world as a whole" (Cooper 1977, p. 156). If that were her goal, then she would be required to engage in political activity even in a community that had not given her a philosophical education. At 520b Plato explicitly allows the philosopher to forego political activity in such a situation.

17. See 519c for the requirement that a good life have a single goal at which all actions aim. It would be no more plausible to take this single goal to be a mere aggregate than it would be to take the project of being a single human being to be a mere aggregate of projects. I take Plato to be assuming that personal unity cannot be achieved unless one aims at a unified ultimate end. This single best end is the imitation of the Forms.

18. This reading is supported by a well-known passage from the *Theaetetus*, in which we are told that we should pursue virtue in order to become as godlike as

Several objections to this interpretation must now be considered. First, it might be thought that I have lost sight of the philosopher's *reluctance* to rule. On my account, she should eagerly return to political office, because in doing so she imitates the Forms and thereby benefits herself. But as we have seen Plato emphasizes the point that the philosopher does not find ruling a particularly attractive activity: it is not a fine thing, but a necessity (540b4-5).

What this objection overlooks is that one can be eager to perform an act because of one of its features and reluctant to do it because of another. Clearly, the philosopher has no interest in the mundane and practical activities she must undertake in order to govern the community; that is, she has no desire to exercise power over others, to give them orders, to correct their errors, and so on. But this is entirely compatible with her loving a different feature of what she does when she returns to the cave: in these circumstances, exercising power over others is precisely what justice requires. And of course the philosopher must have a love of justice—a love, that is, not only of the moral Forms, but of people, institutions, and acts that participate in those Forms. So it would be a mistake to dwell exclusively on the philosopher's reluctance to rule and to overlook a different component of her complex attitude towards justly returning to the cave. She is no lover of political office, but she is a lover of justice. And surely this complex attitude will fully recommend her to those over whom she exercises rule: they should be assured that it is the love of justice and not the love of power and political honor that motivates her.

A second apparent difficulty for me is that I seem to have for-

---

possible: "My friend, there are two patterns set up in the world. One is divine and supremely happy; the other has nothing of God in it, and is the pattern of the deepest unhappiness. This truth the evil-doer does not see; blinded by folly and utter lack of understanding, he fails to perceive that the effect of his unjust practices is to make him grow more and more like the one, and less and less like the other. For this he pays the penalty of living the life that corresponds to the pattern he is coming to resemble" (176e3-177a3). I have used the translation of Levett in Burnyeat 1990. See Burnyeat's introductory essay, pp. 34-39, for discussion and references to further literature.

gotten that for Plato the justice of an individual human being does not consist in the external actions she undertakes but rather in the harmonious relationships among the parts of her soul. A just person must of course act in appropriate ways towards others, but it might be thought that what makes her treatment of others just (and advantageous) is simply the effect such treatment has on the harmonious relationship between her reason, spirit, and appetite. But my discussion of why it is good for the philosopher to rule the city apparently ignores this central feature of Plato's theory. For it might seem that on my account the philosopher benefits from ruling simply because she thereby returns good for good and in this way imitates the Forms.

To reply to this objection, I must clarify the interpretation I am proposing. I am not saying that according to Plato whenever someone acts in the way that is required by justice, she thereby imitates the Forms and benefits from her act. Rather, she benefits from her act only if it expresses a certain psychological state: she must be someone who loves justice for itself, and she must have a significant level of understanding of what this virtue involves. So, the philosopher will benefit from ruling because she recognizes and loves the order of the Forms, and tries to arrange her soul and her activities so that they imitate the Forms. It is no mere bit of behavior, considered apart from her psychological state, that benefits her. Rather, she benefits because the just act she performs expresses her love of the Forms, and her love of the Forms is a condition of the reasoning part of her soul.

But the objection against me might still be pressed in the following way: perhaps it will be said that according to Plato the only way to tell whether an act is just is to leave aside the question how one should treat others and to focus entirely on whether the act benefits one's soul by producing the right ordering of its elements. By contrast, on my reading, the argument for the justice of requiring the philosopher to rule depends crucially on the question how she should treat others. When the objection is expressed in this way, however, it can immediately

be seen as an unreasonable obstacle to any interpretation whatsoever. For it is an undeniable feature of the passage we have
been studying that Plato does appeal to some notion of proper
social relations when he defends the justice of the political
requirement. What this shows, I think, is that he does not intend
his identification of justice in the human individual with the
proper ordering of the soul as by itself a sufficient criterion for
deciding how to act on any occasion. As we are told at the end
of Book IV, justice involves the rule of reason, the help of spirit,
and the obedience of appetite; but surely that general formula
does not by itself have enough content to pick out the right
action in every case. Though reason must rule, it often has no
alternative but to consider the proper relationship among
human beings when it takes up the question of how to act; and
Plato's argument that the philosopher must rule shows his
acceptance of this point, for he does not justify the political
requirement by connecting it to the harmony of the soul.
Reason rules when it does what is best for the individual (441e),
but to determine what is best for us, we must take into account
the features of the world in which we live. Above all, we must
recognize the existence and harmonious arrangement of the Forms
and choose those acts that imitate them; and to do this we must
take into account what we owe those who have benefitted us.

A final objection—in this case, not to my interpretation but to
Plato's position as I understand it—arises from the fact that
according to Plato contemplating the Forms through purely
philosophical activity is itself an imitation of those abstract
objects.[19] So even if it is granted that the just acts that express
justice in the soul imitate the Forms, Plato is faced with a problem about why the philosopher should imitate them in one way
rather than another. If the philosopher ignores the political
requirement and continues to contemplate, she continues to imitate the Forms by virtue of her contemplation. If she rules, she
imitates them in a different way through just activity. How can

19. I take this to be the meaning of 500c-d, and assume that this is not controversial. By calling the Forms "abstract," I mean that they have no location in the
corporeal world.

Plato show that one way of imitating the Forms is better in these circumstances than the other?

I cannot think of a decisive argument on Plato's behalf, but I do not think his position is hopeless or even unreasonable. He must be relying on the idea that when one interrupts one's purely philosophical activity in order to do something else, one is not thereby rejecting the Forms as models to be imitated; for no human being can engage in this activity without interruption. Imitating the Forms is not a feasible ideal for us if it is taken to require some kind of uninterrupted activity. So taking time away from contemplation cannot by itself be regarded as a rejection of the ideal of imitating the Forms; otherwise we would be rejecting that ideal whenever we sleep. By contrast, by refusing to rule, even when one sees that in doing so one fails to participate in an organization of human beings that is just, one would not merely be interrupting an activity that imitates the Forms, but one would be rejecting the Forms as models. Or, to put the point differently, Plato thinks that it is more in one's interest to adhere to a principle of purity—never reject the Forms as models—than to make compromises so as to have the greatest possible amount of the best single activity. One can ask whether there are arguments to support this principle of purity, and I find no such arguments in the text. But this feature of my interpretation does not make it unacceptable. Nor does it make Plato's moral thought unattractive.

VII

If the interpretation I have presented is defensible, then it does not merely save Plato from the accusation that he has defeated his own purposes by providing a counter-example to the central thesis of the *Republic*. It also has important consequences for the way we understand some of the dialogue's major themes. For example, if I am correct, then Plato's conception of the human good is not intellectualist in the strongest possible sense: he does not believe that in all circumstances one best promotes one's own good by maximizing a purely intellectual activity, namely the contemplation of the Forms. If there is a single goal towards which we should always be striving, then it is the *imitation* of the Forms, not, more narrowly, their contemplation; and as we have seen, the project of imitating the Forms, though no mere aggregate, is diverse and does not consist solely in one kind of activity.[20]

Furthermore, the interpretation I have given allows us to see more clearly why Plato believes that the good of the individual citizen and that of the just political community must always coincide. He holds that each individual is justified in pursuing her greatest good, but at the same time he expects citizens of an ideal city always to do what is best for the community. Why is he so confident that these two dicta—(1) do what is best for yourself, (2) do what is best for the best community—will always coincide in the advice they give? The answer lies in his thesis that an individual does best to imitate the Forms, together with his conviction that the Forms themselves constitute a moral community of sorts. Taken together, these ideas support the conclusion that it can never be in my interest to subvert the system of distributive justice that is best for the community. For I would then disrupt my relationship with the Forms and deprive myself of the greatest good I can have.

Finally, I believe that the interpretation I have proposed indicates that in an important way Plato is not really an egoist after all. Admittedly, he does believe that one can never go wrong if one consults self-interest, properly understood, and does whatever is best for oneself. If that is egoism, then he is an egoist. But there is a stronger form of egoism that holds not merely that self-interest is *always one* proper guide to action, but that it is *necessarily* the proper guide, because there is no other. According to this stricter form of egoism, the good of the com-

---

20. My reading therefore gives us a way of showing, contrary to Annas and Irwin (see n. 1 above), that Plato is not ambivalent or confused, switching back and forth between a contemplative and a practical ideal. His view that contemplation is the single best activity allows him to say that the philosophers rule with reluctance, and this is compatible with his belief that ruling in these circumstances is after all in their best interests. If the contemplative ideal is to maximize one's contemplative activity, then it is not Plato's ideal in the *Republic*. If the ideal is to imitate the Forms, then it is Plato's.

munity, even an ideal community, by itself carries no weight as a reason for action; and so, should there be a conflict between the good of the community and one's own, the latter must of course take precedence.

Plato indicates twice that this is not his position, once in the passage we have been studying, and once in an equally well-known earlier passage, in which he insists on depriving the guardians of private property because of the good this would do for the community (419a-421c). In both cases, he holds that a social arrangement can be justified simply on the grounds that it creates an appropriate apportionment of happiness to the various groups that compose the community; the proper test of political institutions is not whether they make any one group of individuals as happy as they possibly can be. What this means is that the good of the group takes precedence over that of any portion of it; and this in turn entails that if my own greatest good should ever conflict with that of the community, the former should give way to the latter. Of course, as we have seen, Plato thinks that such a conflict cannot happen, because he upholds a conception of the individual's good that makes it coincide with that of the just community. But though he is assured that there can be no such conflict, he gives clear expression to his belief that the good of the whole community *would* justify limits on any one person's good, were such a conflict possible.[21]

If Plato is not an egoist in this strict sense, then why does he go to such great lengths to show that justice serves one's own good? Why does he not shrug his shoulders at the challenge of Thrasymachus, and reply that so long as justice serves the good of others, that is all the recommendation it needs? As I see it, the answer we should give to this question is not: "because he sees no other way to recommend something to an individual than to show that it promotes that individual's greatest good."

21. Here my interpretation differs from one I proposed earlier in Kraut 1973. There I tried to show that Plato does not attempt to prove that justice and self-interest (as normally construed) always coincide, but I now think that he does attempt such a proof. For further discussion of whether Plato is an egoist, see Irwin 1977, pp. 255-257; and Reeve 1988, pp. 269-270.

Rather, we should say that Plato recognized the desire for one's own good as one (not the only) powerful incentive, and believed that the stability of the community is undermined when its members think that the demands of justice and self-interest frequently come into conflict, coinciding only through good fortune. If we do not investigate where one's own good lies but simply accept prevailing and unreflective views about human happiness, we are likely to do great harm not only to ourselves but to others as well.[22] Both of these concerns—self-interest and the good of others—animate Plato's attempt to show that justice and one's own well-being necessarily coincide.[23]

University of Illinois

at Chicago

22. On this point, my reading is in accord with the one expressed by Waterlow 1972-73, p. 24: Plato thinks that the just man acts justly out of "a care and respect for the welfare and rights of others no less than his own."

23. I would like to thank the two anonymous referees for their comments on the penultimate draft of this paper.

KRAUT BIBLIOGRAPHY

Adkins, A.W.H., 1960: *Merit and Responsibility*. (Oxford).

Annas, J., 1981: *An Introduction to Plato's Republic*. (Oxford).

Beatty, J., 1976: "Plato's Happy Philosopher and Politics." *The Review of Politics* 38, pp. 545-575.

Bloom, A., 1968: *The Republic of Plato*, translated with notes and an interpretive essay. (New York).

Burnyeat, M., 1990: *The Theaetetus of Plato*. (Indianapolis).

Cooper, J.M., 1977: "The Psychology of Justice in Plato." *American Philosophical Quarterly* 14, pp. 151-157.

Irwin, T., 1977: *Plato's Moral Theory* . (Oxford).

Kraut, R., (1973): "Egoism, Love, and Political Office in Plato." *Philosophical Review* 82, pp. 330-44.

_____. Forthcoming: "The Defense of Justice in Plato's *Republic*." In R. Kraut (ed.), *The Cambridge Companion to Plato* .

Reeve, C.D.C., 1988: *Philosopher Kings*. (Princeton).

Waterlow, S. (1972-73): "The Good of Others in Plato's Republic," *Proceedings of the Aristotelian Society* 72, pp. 19-36.

White, N.P., 1979: *A Companion to Plato's Republic*. (Indianapolis).

_____. 1986: "The Ruler's Choice," *Archiv für Geschichte der Philosophie* 68, pp. 22-46.

Colloquium 3
Epicurean Poetics
Elizabeth Asmis

If one were to ask people to rank the contributions made by the Epicureans to philosophy, I would not be surprised if poetic theory were near the bottom of most people's lists, or altogether missing, whereas poetry itself might well be at the top. The ancient quarrel between philosophy and poetry seems to have played itself out in an extreme paradox in Epicureanism. Epicurus has the reputation of being the most hostile to poetry of any Greek philosopher. But some of his later followers were clearly devoted to poetry, and one of them, Lucretius, achieved a remarkable reconciliation between philosophy and poetry.

In this paper, I propose to investigate the road between Epicurus and Lucretius. What were Epicurus' views, and to what extent did his followers adopt, modify, or jettison his views? We know that in other areas Epicurus' followers went to great lengths to show that their views were consistent with those of their leader. The more innovative they were, it seems, the more they insisted on their orthodoxy. The problem of orthodoxy became especially acute at the time when Zeno of Sidon was head of the Epicurean school at Athens, about the end of the second century to the early 70's B.C.[1] The period of

Copyright © 1992 Elizabeth Asmis. From the paper read October 25, 1990, at Boston University as part of the 13th Annual Boston Area Colloquium in Ancient Philosophy.

1. The problem of orthodoxy is well attested in the areas of epistemology and ethics, as well as rhetoric and poetry. On epistemology, see Asmis 1984, esp. pp. 220-224. When Zeno of Sidon was head of the Epicurean school there was a very acrimonious debate among Epicureans on who observed Epicurus' teachings about whether rhetoric is a craft. This debate is discussed in detail by Sedley 1989; see also Asmis 1990, pp. 2400-2402. In his work Περὶ παρρησίας (fr. 45.8-11 Olivieri), Philodemus sums up the loyalty of Epicurus' followers in a statement which is virtually an oath of loyalty : καὶ τὸ συνέχον καὶ κυρι/ώτ[α]τον,

Elizabeth Asmis

Zeno and his immediate followers is also a time when the Epicureans showed an especially strong interest in poetry. Zeno and his student Philodemus of Gadara both offered comprehensive criticisms of poetic theories; and while Lucretius' great poem on the nature of the universe overshadows all contemporary poetry, Philodemus' epigrams are among the most elegant examples of this genre. There are just a few, well known bits of evidence about Epicurus' views on poetry. But these testimonies, in conjunction with the much larger and partially unfamiliar body of evidence concerning the later period, suggest that there is greater continuity between Epicurus and his followers than has been thought.

The allegorist Heraclitus (about the first century A.D.) pairs Epicurus with Plato as a detractor of Homer, while charging him with deriving his doctrines from the great poet. Heraclitus accuses Epicurus of condemning all of poetry, not just Homer; and he describes Epicurus as "purifying himself (ἀφοσιούμενος) from all of poetry at once as a destructive lure of fictitious stories."[2] He also charges that, although Epicurus condemned poetry, he was a "Phaeacian" philosopher who, by misinterpreting Odysseus' words to Alcinous, stole from Homer the notion that the supreme good is pleasure.[3] Another late author, Athenaeus, associates Epicurus with Plato as someone who expelled Homer from cities.[4]

But Epicurus' hostility to poetry is not as simple a matter as Heraclitus and Athenaeus make out. According to Heraclitus, the Homeric words that Epicurus misinterpreted were:
...ὅταν εὐφροσύνη μὲν ἔχῃ κατὰ δῆμον ἅπαντα,
δαιτυμόνες δ' ἀνὰ δώματ' ἀκουάζωνται ἀοιδοῦ
τοῦτό τί μοι κάλλιστον ἐνὶ φρεσὶν εἴδεται.

Ἐπικούρωι, καθ' ὃν ζῆν ἡ(ι)ρήμεθα, πει/θαρχήσομεν ("the basic and most important [principle] is that we will obey Epicurus, according to whom we have chosen to live").

2. *Homeric Problems* 79 and 4 (= U 229), including at 4: ἅπασαν ὁμοῦ ποιητικὴν ὥσπερ ὀλέθριον μύθων δέλεαρ ἀφοσιούμενος.

3. *Homeric Problems* 79 = partly at U 229.

4. *Deipnosophistae* 5, 187c = U 228.

When joy possesses all the people,
and banqueters throughout the house listen to the singer,
this seems to my mind most beautiful.[5]

Heraclitus has omitted three lines, coming just after mention of
the singer, in which Odysseus describes the abundance of food
and drink at the banquet. The whole passage is:

οὐ γὰρ ἐγώ γέ τί φημι τέλος χαριέστερον εἶναι
ἢ ὅτ' ἐυφροσύνη μὲν ἔχῃ κατὰ δῆμον ἅπαντα,
δαιτυμόνες δ' ἀνὰ δώματ' ἀκουάζωνται ἀοιδοῦ
ἥμενοι ἐξείης, παρὰ δὲ πλήθωσι τράπεζαι
σίτου καὶ κρειῶν, μέθυ δ' ἐκ κρητῆρος ἀφύσσων
οἰνοχόος φορέῃσι καὶ ἐγχείῃ δεπάεσσι·
τοῦτό τί μοι κάλλιστον ἐνὶ φρεσὶν εἴδεται εἶναι.

For I say that there is no more pleasant fulfilment than when
joy possesses all the people, and banqueters throughout the
house listen to the singer, sitting next to each other, and
alongside the tables are full of bread and meat, and the wine-
pourer draws drink from the mixing-bowl and brings it and
pours it into cups. This seems to my mind to be most beautiful.[6]

According to Heraclitus, Epicurus failed to notice that Odysseus
was driven by necessity to praise his host's way of life. What
Heraclitus fails to notice himself is that, in the very lines he has
cited, Odysseus is praising the joy of listening to the songs of a
poet.

Odysseus' words to Alcinous are among the most famous passages of poetry in antiquity.[7] Because they were thought to propose a view of the goal (τέλος) of life, they received much philosophical attention. Plato cited only Homer's description of food
and drink, omitting the lines dealing with the singer, to illustrate

5. *Homeric Problems* 79. These lines correspond to *Odyssey* 9.6-7 and 11.
6. *Odyssey* 9.5-11.
7. The history of these verses, dubbed Homer's "golden verses," is discussed
by Kaiser 1964, pp. 213-223.

the inadequacy of Homer's ethics.[8] Aristotle cited only the lines dealing with the singer as evidence that Homer believed that music is an appropriate leisure time activity.[9] Later authors associated the whole passage with Epicurean hedonism. Some, like Heraclitus, accused Epicurus explicitly of taking his hedonism from Homer.[10] More perceptively, Seneca derides the attempt to turn Homer into an Epicurean or any other philosopher. Seneca also describes the ostensible "Epicurean Homer" as one who praises peace, banquets, and songs.[11] Implicitly, the entire later tradition associates the full measure of Homeric conviviality, including poetic entertainment, with Epicureanism.

Although the charge of plagiarism is hardly plausible, it is not implausible, as Bignone has argued, that Epicurus cited Odysseus' words in his own writings.[12] Despite his reputation for being unlearned, Epicurus was not averse to citing verses for his own ends. Epicurus seems to have quoted a couple of verses from Sophocles' *Trachinians* to illustrate his claim that we natu-

8. *Republic* 3, 390a-b.

9. *Politics* 1338a27-30.

10. These references have been gathered by Bignone 1936; see also Kaiser 1964, pp. 220-221. Athenaeus (*Deipnosophistae* 12, 513a-c), quoting the entire passage at *Odyssey* 9.5-12, writes that "Odysseus seems to be the leader for Epicurus' notorious pleasure"; then he cites a defence of Odysseus similar to that of Heraclitus. Likewise, ps-Plutarch (*De vita et poesi Homeri* 2, 150) claims that Epicurus was misled by Odysseus' words to propose pleasure as the goal of happiness. A scholiast on *Odyssey* 9.28 and Eustathius (p. 1612, 10) also claim that Epicurus took the goal of pleasure from Homer. Exceptionally, the scholiast approves of Epicurus' notion of the goal, with the observation that he extended the Homeric goal to all circumstances of life.

11. Seneca (*Epistle* 88.5): nam modo Stoicum illum faciunt...modo Epicureum, laudantem statum quietae civitatis et inter convivia cantusque vitam exigentis ("they sometimes make him a Stoic..., sometimes an Epicurean who praises the condition of a government that is at peace and passes life among banquets and songs"). In a lighter vein, Lucian (*Parasite* 10-11), quoting "banqueters sitting next to each other" and "alongside the tables are full of bread and meat," suggests that Epicurus stole from Homer the goal of the parasite.

12. Bignone 1936, pp. 270-273, holds that Epicurus cited the verses polemically to show, against Aristotle, that the type of enjoyment praised by Odysseus is not the supreme good; instead, Bignone proposes, Epicurus wished to show that the supreme pleasure is the absence of pain and anxiety, that is, catastematic pleasure. In response to Bignone, Giancotti 1960, pp. 83-84, argues that Epicurus

rally avoid pain.[13] He might well have cited the famous Homeric verses to explain his complementary doctrine that we all naturally seek pleasure. By doing so, he would have staked a position within a philosophical tradition; nor need he have imputed any special insight to either Odysseus or Homer. If Epicurus did cite the passage, it is unlikely that he excluded poetic entertainment from the life of pleasure.

Plutarch is our main witness for Epicurus' attitude to poetry. He subordinates the charge that Epicurus shunned poetry to the general charge that he rejected all intellectual pleasures. In his treatise *It is impossible to live pleasantly according to Epicurus*, Plutarch alleges that both Epicurus and Metrodorus berated their intellectual forebears, including the poets, in the most abusive language. Two terms cited by Plutarch, apparently of the milder sort, are "poetic confusion" (ποιητικὴ τύρβη) and "the foolish statements (μωρολογήματα) of Homer."[14] Plutarch accuses the Epicureans of rejecting both historical investigation, including the study of poetry, and the mathematical studies of geometry, astronomy, and harmonics.[15] As an example of Epicurean philistinism, Plutarch cites a statement from Metrodorus' *On Poems* : "Don't worry," Metrodorus said, about admitting that you don't even know "on whose side Hector was, or the first lines of Homer's poetry, or the middle."[16] Plutarch also reports that the Epicureans urged their students to "hoist sail" in order to flee intellectual pleasures. In particular, he notes, Epicurus' entire entourage urged Pythocles not to "envy the so-called liberal education"; and they praised a certain Apelles for having kept himself entirely "pure" (καθαρόν) of learning.[17] These admonitions can be traced to Epicurus' own

---

cited the verses in partial agreement with Odysseus; for Epicurus approves of the kinetic pleasure of listening to songs and consuming food and drink, even though this is not the supreme good, catastematic pleasure. A passage in *PHerc.* 1012 (see below, n. 18) suggests that Epicurus cited Odysseus' words as expressing a commonplace opinion.

13. Diogenes Laertius 10.137 (= U 66).

14. 1087a = U 228.

15. 1092d-1094d.   16. 1094d-e.

17. 1094d, including: ὅπως οὐ ζηλώσει τὴν ἐλευθέριον καλουμένην παιδείαν.

Elizabeth Asmis

writings. Epicurus urged Pythocles in a letter: "Flee all education, hoisting sail."[18] According to Athenaeus, Epicurus' words to Apelles were: "I call you blessed, Apelles, because you set out for philosophy, pure of all education." Athenaeus adds that Epicurus was himself "uninitiated in the educational curriculum."[19]

The sail boat in Epicurus' *Letter* is an allusion to the boat in which Odysseus sailed past the Sirens.[20] In another treatise, *How a young person should listen to poets*, Plutarch explicitly associates the Epicurean hoisting of sails with the Homeric episode by asking: Should we protect the young against the deceptions of poetry by plugging their ears with wax (as happened to Odysseus' men), forcing them to flee poetry "by hoisting the sails of an Epicurean boat"; or should we protect them by binding them and straightening their judgment with reason (Odysseus' choice)?[21] The same Siren imagery is implicit in the description of poetry as a "destructive lure," which the allegorist Heraclitus attributes to Epicurus. Heraclitus' entire description of Epicurus as "purifying himself" (ἀφοσιούμενος) from this lure

18. 10.6 (= U 163): παιδείαν δὲ πᾶσαν, μακάριε, φεῦγε τἀκάτιον ἀράμενος. Quintilian (12.2.24) also quotes this advice. It is possible, as Bignone 1936, pp. 282-283 has suggested, that Epicurus included a polemic against Homer in the same letter to Pythocles. PHerc. 1012, whose author was conjectured by Crönert to be Demetrius the Laconian, contains an address to Pythocles, together with an attack on Homer, as follows (col. 48.8-13): "Ομη/ρος μὲν γὰρ οὐδὲν πλῆον / περὶ τῶν τοιούτων διέ/γνωκεν ἥπερ ο[ἱ] λοι[πο]ὶ ἄν/θ[ρω]ποι, ἡμεῖς δ[έ], ὦ Πυθό/κλ[εις... ("Homer recognized nothing more about such matters than the rest of mankind, but we, Pythocles....") The text is fr. 70 of Enzo Puglia's new edition of fragments 1980, p. 49. Bignone argued that Demetrius excerpted not only the address to Pythocles from Epicurus' letter (as is generally agreed), but probably also the preceding remarks on Homer. Puglia's new text strongly supports this suggestion. The issue under discussion is Homer's notion of enjoyment, as indicated by the word [ἀπό]/λαυσιν at lines 4-5. The claim that Homer knew no more than the rest of mankind also occurs in the arguments against grammar which are attributed by Sextus Empiricus "especially" to the Epicureans (Adv. math. 1.285 and 299, see below).

19. *Deipnosophistae* 13, 588a (= U 117), including: μακαρίζω σε, ὦ 'Απελλῆ, ὅτι καθαρὸς πάσης παιδείας ἐπὶ φιλοσοφίαν ὡρμήσας.

20. The Sirens' song was commonly taken to symbolize the attractiveness of learning in general and poetry in particular; see Kaiser 1964, pp. 109-136.

21. *De poetis audiendis* 15d.

seems to be based on the same well known core of testimonies cited by Plutarch and others. The purity demanded by Epicurus has a religious aspect; and Athenaeus responds to it by calling Epicurus "uninitiated."

Plutarch shows that Epicurus' opposition to poetry is part of a larger issue, education. Like Plato in the *Republic*, Epicurus believed that the whole traditional educational system, with its teaching of Homer and other poets, was a corrupting influence that prevented a person from achieving happiness. Epicurus also rejected the alternative curriculum proposed by Plato in the *Republic*, with its purged poetry and rigorous program of mathematics. Epicurus aimed to replace both types of education with Epicurean philosophy. Accordingly, he assured his students that it was an advantage not to be educated; and, unlike most philosophers, he welcomed the uneducated, both young and old, to his school.

But Plutarch's testimony, too, is ambivalent. Embedded within his attack is evidence that Epicurus was, in part, hospitable to poetry. On the one hand, Plutarch notes, Epicurus claims in his *Questions* (Διαπορίαι) that the wise person is a "lover of sights (φιλοθέωρον) and enjoys hearing and seeing Dionysiac performances (χαίροντα...ἀκροάμασι καὶ θεάμασι Διονυσιακοῖς) as much as anyone"; on the other hand, Epicurus does not permit musical or philological inquiry even over drink, but in his work *On Kingship* (Περὶ βασιλείας) "recommends even to music-loving (φιλομούσοις) kings that they should put up with military narratives and vulgar jesting at parties rather than with lectures on musical and poetic problems."[22] Plutarch thinks that these two positions are contradictory: how can the Epicureans care so

---

22. *Non posse suaviter vivi* 1095c (= U 5 and 20): φιλοθέωρον μὲν ἀποφαίνων τὸν σοφὸν ἐν ταῖς Διαπορίαις καὶ χαίροντα παρ' ὁντινοῦν ἕτερον ἀκροάμασι καὶ θεάμασι Διονυσιακοῖς, προβλήμασι δὲ μουσικοῖς καὶ κριτικῶν φιλολόγοις ζητήμασιν οὐδὲ παρὰ πότον διδοὺς χώραν, ἀλλὰ καὶ τοῖς φιλομούσοις τῶν βασιλέων παραινῶν στρατηγικὰ διηγήματα καὶ φορτικὰς βωμολοχίας ὑπομένειν μᾶλλον ἐν τοῖς συμποσίοις ἢ λόγους περὶ μουσικῶν καὶ ποιητικῶν προβλημάτων περαινομένους. ταυτὶ γὰρ ἐτόλμησεν γράφειν ἐν τῷ Περὶ βασιλείας... Diogenes Laertius (10.120) paraphrases the first claim as follows: μᾶλλόν τε εὐφρανθήσεσθαι τῶν ἄλλων ἐν ταῖς θεωρίαις ("[the wise person] delights more than others in spectacles").

Elizabeth Asmis

much about musical performances, if they shut their ears to discussions about musical and poetic matters, such as musical
modes, poetic styles, and so on?[23]

In a manner that is typical of him, Plutarch has juxtaposed two
excerpts that are not really in conflict with each other. In his
Questions, Epicurus challenges a distinction made by Plato in the
Republic.[24] Socrates argues that ordinary lovers of sights
(φιλοθεάμονες) and lovers of hearing (φιλήκοοι) differ from
philosophers (φιλόσοφοι) in that the former chase the sights and
sounds of sensible things, whereas philosophers seek the wisdom of knowing things in themselves. The lovers of sounds,
especially, are strangely unphilosophical, as Glaucon observes:
they are unwilling to participate in discussion and "run around
all the Dionysiac festivals" instead, "as though they had rented
out their ears to listen to all the choruses." True philosophers,
Socrates proposes, are lovers of sight in the special sense of
being lovers of the sight of truth.[25] Using φιλοθέωρος as a syn-
onym for φιλοθεάμων, Epicurus responds to Plato's distinction
by contending that the wise person loves the sights and sounds
of Dionysiac festivals as much as anyone.[26] The Epicurean wise
person does not forsake the objects of sense perception in the
pursuit of truth; for wisdom consists precisely in enjoying sensory experiences and having correct opinions about them.
Epicurus agrees that the wise person loves the sight of truth, but
insists that the love of truth encompasses the love of visual spectacles and auditory performances.

23. *Non posse suaviter vivi* 1095e-1096c.

24. *Republic* 5, 475d-476b. This attack on Plato is further evidence that
Epicurus studied Plato's dialogues.

25. 475d-e.

26. Boyancé 1947, pp. 91-92 suggests that Epicurus' attitude to Dionysiac festivals is a concession to established religious practice, rather than an endorsement
of poetic performances: the Epicurean, he proposes, will participate in religious
festivals, even though he does not share the ordinary person's beliefs; cf. Obbink
1984, pp. 607-619. Although the terms φιλοθέωρος, θεωρία, and θέαμα can apply
to religious spectacles, there is no reason to suppose that their scope is restricted
to religious worship here. As was customary, Epicurus regularly uses forms of
θεωρ- to refer to visual or mental viewing in general.

In this confrontation with Plato, Epicurus gives clear approval to the enjoyment of musical and poetic performances. In the second half of Plutarch's indictment, Epicurus rejects an entirely different use of leisure time, listening to lectures on musical and poetic problems. These are lectures given by musicologists and grammarians or literary "critics," experts who, according to Epicurus, make no contribution to happiness.[27] By contrast, Epicurus approves of philosophical inquiry about music and poetry. According to Diogenes Laertius, Epicurus held that the wise person "alone would discuss music and poetry correctly."[28] Epicurus himself wrote a book, not extant, *On Music*; and his friend Metrodorus, as we saw, wrote *On Poems*.[29] In advising kings to put up with military talk and buffoonery at parties rather than with musical and literary criticism, Epicurus does not advocate the former kind of entertainment, but suggests merely that it is more tolerable than the latter. Military talk, we may guess, might be useful for kings, even though a party is hardly the proper occasion for it, and buffoonery might be pleasant, whereas musicology and philology are neither. In his work *Symposium*, Epicurus showed that appropriate subjects of discussion at parties are indigestion, fever, wine, and sexual intercourse, —all topics that are useful for party-goers to know about.[30] But Epicurus does not imply here or elsewhere that one should fill one's leisure time with nothing but useful discussion. It is significant that he does not advise "music-loving" kings to give up music; he urges them only not to waste their time listening to learned discussions about it.

27. Plutarch pairs the "critics" with the musicologists (*Non posse suaviter vivi* 1095c, see n. 22 above). There is a fine line between "grammarians" and "critics." As Sextus Empiricus shows (*Adv. math.* 1.93), grammar included poetic criticism. Some who called themselves "critics" held that grammar is subordinate to "criticism"; among them, Crates held that, unlike the grammarian, the "critic" must be experienced in "all knowledge of speech (λογικῆς ἐπιστήμης)" (*Adv. math.* 1.79).

28. Diogenes Laertius 10.121.

29. Another friend of Epicurus, Colotes, discussed poetry in his work *Against Plato's Lysis*. It is difficult to extract any information from the few relevant fragments; see Crönert 1906, pp. 6-12; and Mancini 1976, pp. 61-67, esp. 61-63.

30. U 56-63.

Although Plutarch regards Epicurus' notion of entertainment as incredibly crude, his testimony indicates that Epicurus had a clear-cut position. Epicurus distinguished between two uses of poetry, education and entertainment, and condemned poetry wholesale as education, while welcoming it as entertainment. Plutarch charges Epicurus with just one type of inconsistency: excluding musical and literary learning from the appreciation of music and poetry. But Epicurus' dichotomy suggests a more serious inconsistency. How can the two uses of poetry, education and entertainment, be compartmentalized so neatly as Epicurus supposes? Is it possible for a person to derive enjoyment from poetic performances without being contaminated by morally bad subject matter? Plato did not think so. Epicurus seems to believe optimistically that one can. Presumably, Epicurus held that it is a sufficient protection to come to a poetic performance with a philosophically trained mind. Epicurus adopted an analogous position concerning religious ritual: the Epicurean participates in it freely, while discounting false religious beliefs. Both positions betoken a strong faith in human rationality.[31]

Unlike Plato, Epicurus did not propose to use a purified type of poetry as a propaedeutic to philosophy or happiness. Nor did he consider poetic form appropriate for teaching philosophical doctrines. In his list of things that the Epicurean wise person will and won't do, Diogenes Laertius reports that, although the wise person alone would speak correctly about music and poetry, he would not practice the composition of poems,[32] and that he would leave behind prose writings.[33] As the writings of Epicurus and his circle amply illustrate, the wise person uses prose, not poetry, to instruct others. What prevents Epicurus from making poetry a handmaid to philosophy is again, I suggest, his rationalism. Although there is no doubt that Epicurus and his followers practiced irrational indoctrination, it was

31. Ronconi 1963 argues that there is an irreconcilable conflict between Epicurus' theory, which makes him repudiate all of poetry, and his practice, whereby he cites poetry and recommends Dionysiac festivals.

32. Diogenes Laertius 10.121 (= U 568).

33. Diogenes Laertius 10.120 (= U 563): συγγράμματα καταλείψειν.

Epicurus' aim to persuade his students by an appeal to their intellectual powers, or, as he conceived it, by philosophical examination. He sought to mould their character by undisguised opinions, approved by a mental act of judgement on the part of each person. To this end, he required clarity as the only quality of good speech.[34] It is the function of clear speech to communicate clear opinions that are verifiable by each student on the basis of sensory experience. False tales, mimetic experience, public speeches are all rejected as educational tools because they do not engage a person in a clear vision of the truth.[35] What produces a happy life is "sober reasoning" in all circumstances;[36] and this depends on having a clear view of human nature, as imparted by the clear speech of philosophy.

Granted that the wise person will not use poetry to instruct others, why should he or she not compose poems for private enjoyment? There is some confusion about Epicurus' prohibition in the text of Diogenes (10. 121). All the manuscripts have: [τὸν σοφὸν . . .] ποιήματά τε ἐνεργεῖν οὐκ ἂν ποιῆσαι. Since the combination of the two infinitives is ungrammatical, all editors have accepted Usener's emendation of ἐνεργείᾳ for ἐνεργεῖν. According to Usener, Epicurus' meaning is that, whereas the wise person has poetic ability, he won't use this ability "in actuality."[37] This interpretation makes sense only if we understand the wise person's poetic ability in the very restricted sense of an ability to judge a poem philosophically: the wise person knows all that it is useful to know about poems, but he does not have the expertise that a practicing poet has. The wise person, therefore, does not compose poems "in actuality"—that is, not at all. Epicurus might have justified this absolute prohibition on the ground that the toil of learning the poetic craft outweighs the

34. Diogenes Laertius 10.13.

35. According to Diogenes Laertius (10.120), the wise person "will not make panegyric speeches" (οὐ πανηγυριεῖν). See further De Lacy 1939.

36. *Letter to Menoeceus* 132 (νήφων λογισμός).

37. Usener briefly explained: copia et facultas poeseos non minus in sapiente est, etsi carmina non facit. The contrast between the sage's ability, including his ability as a poet, and his actual practice is well attested in Stoicism (SVF 3.654-656).

enjoyment of practicing it; or he might have held that the wise man will have nothing to do with an inherently deceptive mode of expression.

But Diogenes' report admits of another interpretation. This is to take either ἐνεργείᾳ, as emended, or ἐνεργεῖν, understood as a gloss on ποιῆσαι, in the sense of "being busy at," or "making a practice of," or "practicing energetically"—meanings primarily associated with the corresponding adjective ἐνεργός and adverb ἐνεργῶς. In that case, Epicurus is not prohibiting the wise person from dabbling in the composition of poetry, but only from busying himself with it or practicing it in the manner of a professional poet. I shall return to this possibility.

In the centuries after Epicurus, his followers both defended and revised his position that poetry is to be rejected as education and welcomed as entertainment. Cicero signals a major shift in his book *On Ends*. He taunts his young friend Torquatus, a confirmed Epicurean, by pointing out that he, Torquatus, is devoted to history, poetry, and literature in general, whereas his master, Epicurus, shunned these studies and was altogether uneducated.[38] Torquatus comes to Epicurus' defence by asserting that, according to Epicurus, "there is no education except that which contributes to the learning of happiness" (*nullam eruditionem esse...nisi quae beatae vitae disciplinam iuvaret*). There is no reason why Epicurus should have spent his time reading the poets, "in whom there is no solid usefulness but only a childish delight" (*in quibus nulla solida utilitas omnisque puerilis est delectatio*) and whom, Torquatus admits, he reads at the urging of Cicero. Nor is there any reason, Torquatus continues, why Epicurus should have wasted his time on the Platonic curriculum of "music, geometry, arithmetic and astronomy." For unlike "the art of life," or practical philosophy, none of these arts contributes anything to happiness. Torquatus concludes that Epicurus is not uneducated (*ineruditus*), but those are who think they should

---

38. *De finibus* 1.25-26 and 71-72. Cicero appears to use *indoctus* (1.26 and 72) and *ineruditus* (1.72, cf. *parum...eruditus* at 1.71) as synonyms, corresponding to Greek ἀπαίδευτος.

study into old age what it is disgraceful for them not to have learned as children (*pueri*).[39]

Cicero's presentation is based on well known doxographical material. Similarly to Plutarch, he accuses Epicurus of rejecting all learning, as divided into literary studies and mathematics. But there is an important difference: the Roman Torquatus does not shun traditional studies as Epicurus is said to have done and to have advised others to do. As though aware of his failure to follow Epicurus' example and precept, Torquatus makes Cicero responsible for the deviation.[40] At the same time, Torquatus admits that literary and mathematical studies do not contribute to happiness, and that the study of poetry in particular is without "solid utility" and nothing but a "childish delight" (*puerilis delectatio*). The latter phrase recalls Plato's proposal in the tenth book of the *Republic* to set aside the "childish love" (παιδικόν...ἔρωτα) of poetry.[41] Torquatus does not set it aside; and he is uncomfortably aware that, whereas Epicurus spent his time in the serious pursuit of philosophy instead of literary and mathematical studies, he is devoting much of his time to a trivial pursuit.

This difference between Torquatus and Epicurus suits Cicero's polemical purpose. Throughout the discussion, Cicero aims to

39. *De finibus* 1.71-72: Qui quod tibi parum videtur eruditus, ea causa est quod nullam eruditionem esse duxit nisi quae beatae vitae disciplinam iuvaret. An ille tempus aut in poetis evolvendis, ut ego et Triarius te hortatore facimus, consumeret, in quibus nulla solida utilitas omnisque puerilis est delectatio, aut se, ut Plato, in musicis, geometria, numeris, astris contereret, quae et a falsis initiis profecta vera esse non possunt et si essent vera nihil afferrent quo iucundius, id est quo melius viveremus;—eas ergo artes persequeretur, vivendi artem tantam tamque operosam et perinde fructuosam relinqueret? Non ergo Epicurus ineruditus, sed ii indocti qui quae pueros non didicisse turpe est ea putant usque ad senectutem esse discenda.

40. Giancotti 1959, p. 24; and 1960, pp. 69-76 holds that there is total agreement between Epicurus and his followers, including Cicero's Torquatus. He suggests that Epicurus and his followers alike condemned only certain poems—those that present myths and appeal to the emotions—as having no utility, whereas they admitted other poems as having utility. This interpretation is in conflict, among other things, with Torquatus' blanket characterization of poetry as having no "solid utility" (as pointed out by Boyancé 1960, p. 442).

41. *Republic* 608a.

show that Torquatus' professed Epicureanism is incompatible with robust Roman values, as exemplified by Cicero himself. At the same time, Cicero's literary portrait of Torquatus stands for real Epicureans at Rome who were devotees of Epicurus and poetry at once; and we might expect some of them to resist the charge of deviating from their master. How would they defend their study of poetry, without the help of Cicero? Another look at Cicero's exposition suggests a possible defence.

Cicero's Torquatus presents a tightly constructed argument whose major premiss is a definition of "education" (*eruditio*) as "that which contributes to the learning of happiness." Torquatus attributes this definition to Epicurus himself. Accordingly, neither the traditional curriculum nor that of Plato counts as "education"; the only education in the proper sense is philosophy. The other studies, such as the "childish (*puerilis*) delight" of poetry, are properly the pursuits of childhood: it would be disgraceful for children (*pueri*) not to occupy themselves with them; but they do not make a person educated. To put the point in Greek, the curriculum of so-called liberal studies is παιδεία only in the etymological sense of being the occupation of children, παῖδες; it is not παιδεία in the proper sense in which education is a training for happiness.

The definition of education is not exemplified in the extant sayings of Epicurus, but might be said to capture his intent.[42] It is clearly a philosophical reinterpretation of the commonplace notion of education.[43] Using the new definition, Epicurus' followers could argue that when Epicurus urged Pythocles to "flee all education, hoisting sail" (παιδείαν δὲ πᾶσαν...φεῦγε τἀκάτιον ἀράμενος), he meant: don't be misled into thinking that what

---

42. Apart from the testimonies that have been cited, *Vatican Saying* 45 is the only extant text in which Epicurus uses the term παιδεία. Epicurus shows his contempt for those who flaunt their learning by observing that the study of nature, φυσιολογία, does not make people boast or show off "the education that is an object of rivalry among the many" (τὴν περιμάχητον παρὰ τοῖς πολλοῖς παιδείαν).

43. Cicero uses the ordinary definition at 1.26, when charging Epicurus with being uneducated: est enim [Epicurus]...non satis politus iis artibus quas qui tenent eruditi appellantur ("[Epicurus] is not sufficiently polished in those arts whose possession causes people to be called educated").

commonly passes for education is education; shun this spurious education and turn instead to real education. According to this interpretation, Epicurus was, in effect, using the term παιδείαν in quotation marks. Plutarch confirms this hypothetical exegesis by paraphrasing Epicurus' command to Pythocles as "do not envy the so-called liberal education."[44] What Epicurus did not mean, on the other hand, according to this exegesis is: avoid so-called liberal studies altogether. So long as a person shuns these studies as an education, he is free to enjoy them as a leisure-time activity or, to use the Aristotelian term, as διαγωγή. Epicurus' admonition to "hoist sail" does not mean, therefore, as Plutarch mistook it, that one should shut one's ears to poetry and all other learning. There is another option: it is possible to flee the Sirens, as Odysseus did, by experiencing the charm of their song while escaping its destructive influence. What one needs as a defence is the only true education, Epicurean philosophy.

It would not be surprising if Cicero was not convinced by this exegesis. The plain meaning of the testimonies is that Epicurus urged his followers to get away from traditional and Platonic education altogether. The hypothetical exegesis, however, proposes nothing that might not be held to agree with Epicurus' views. His approval of poetry as an enjoyment provides an opening for the acceptance of poetry as a leisure-time occupation, or διαγωγή, alongside the serious pursuit of philosophy. Epicureans like Torquatus could argue that they really do emulate Pythocles and Apelles, and even Epicurus, in the only way that matters: they keep themselves pure of so-called education by giving serious attention only to philosophy. Epicurus' followers are quite willing to admit a difference between Epicurus' practice and their own: he did not "waste" his time in poetry and other so-called liberal studies, whereas they spend time in such pursuits. But this difference, as Torquatus shows, does not amount to a difference in the estimation of these studies. Historically, the difference might be explained by the fact that Epicurus is the philosophical leader and they are the followers: as leader, he gave them the protection they need; and as followers, they may exploit it.

44. See above, notes 17 and 18.

Elizabeth Asmis

Sextus Empiricus provides a further glimpse of how Epicurus' followers related poetry to philosophy. In agreement with Cicero's Torquatus, Sextus reports that Epicurus held that learning (as ordinarily understood) makes no contribution to wisdom.[45] We have already seen that one type of learning rejected by Epicurus is the criticism of poetry as practiced by the grammarians. According to Sextus, the grammarians tried to show the usefulness of their discipline by arguing that, whereas poetry contains many "starting-points" (ἀφορμάς) for wisdom and happiness, these truths cannot be discerned adequately without the light shed by the grammarians. The ethical precepts of the philosophers, the grammarians maintained, are rooted in the ethical sayings of the poets; and this is true even of Epicurus, who stole his most important doctrines from the poets.[46] As the allegorist Heraclitus and others confirm, Epicurus had a reputation for stealing from the poets. With obvious reference to the Platonic expulsion of poets from cities, the grammarians also claimed that poetry is useful and even necessary for the welfare of cities.[47]

Against the grammarians, Sextus cites a series of objections which he says are due "especially" to the Epicureans.[48] In these arguments, poetry is analysed as harmful in three ways. First, although poetry contains some worthwhile statements, these are outweighed by many more statements that are harmful. Since poetry does not supply demonstrative proofs (ἀποδείξεις), which would allow listeners to distinguish between good and bad, listeners incline toward the worse course.[49] Second, whereas philosophers and other prose-writers teach what is useful by pursuing the truth, poets aim at all cost to move the soul (ψυχαγωγεῖν), and since falsehood moves the soul more than truth, poets pursue falsehood rather than the truth.[50] Third, poetry is

45. *Adv. math.* 1. 1; cf. *Adv. math.* 6. 27 (= U 229b).

46. 1.270-273.

47. 1.275-276.

48. 1.299: τὰ μὲν ὑπὸ τῶν ἄλλων λεγόμενα...καὶ μάλιστα τῶν Ἐπικουρείων. Sextus distinguishes these arguments from his own Pyrrhonist arguments.

49. 1.279-280.

50. 1.296-297.

a "stronghold of human passions," inflaming anger and the desire for sex and drink.[51] These arguments allow that poetry may occasionally be useful. But poetry can be useful only when the language is clear.[52] Moreover, even if it is occasionally useful for cities, it is not necessary to their welfare; nor, if it is useful for cities, does it follow that it is useful for individuals.[53]

Because they view poetry as predominantly false and harmful, we might expect Sextus' opponents of grammar to brand poets in general as corrupters of humankind and to join with Plato in banning all except morally useful poetry. Instead, they recognize a way of rendering poetry harmless: whereas grammar cannot bring any aid to poetry, philosophy can cancel out the harm and even extract some utility from it. For philosophy can distinguish the good from the bad in poems by supplying proofs. Whereas poetry unaided is harmful, it is harmless and can even be of some small moral benefit when joined by philosophy.

In this partnership, philosophy extends its help to poetry without being dependent on it in any way. "Genuine philosophers," Sextus' opponents of grammar claim, do not use the poets as witnesses; instead, their own argument is sufficient to persuade.[54] This is an attack not only on the grammarians, but also on the Stoic propensity to cite poets in support of their doctrines. The attack is reinforced by the claim that the assumptions of poets are far worse than those of ordinary individuals. Examples of how bad the beliefs of the poets are include the castration of Uranos by Cronos and the subjugation of Cronos by Zeus—stories defended by the Stoics by allegorical interpretation.[55] This implicit attack against the Stoics agrees with the Epicureans' rejection of allegorical explanation. Epicurus, it is argued, did not steal any doctrines from the poets: for his teaching is fundamentally different from that of the poets; or, if there

51. 1.298.
52. 1.278.
53. 1.293-295.
54. 1.280.
55. 1.288-291.

is a resemblance, what is admirable is not the mere assertion, but the philosophical proof; or the belief is shared by Epicurus with all of mankind, not just the poet.[56]

Although these arguments are clearly indebted to Plato and although Sextus may well have gathered his material from a variety of sources, the overall content and cohesiveness of the arguments show that the Epicurean school is indeed the main source of the arguments, as Sextus states.[57] The demand for clear speech, the distinction between civic and private life, the view that poetry does much harm, and, in general, the claim that learning is useless for happiness, are all fundamental tenets of Epicureanism. Sextus does not name any particular Epicurean; but we can go a little further in trying to pinpoint his source. The view that there is little or no utility in poems, and that poems inflame the emotions, is argued in detail in the writings of Philodemus of Gadara (ca. 110-40 B.C.).[58] In his book *On Music*, Philodemus is concerned primarily with the utility of music; but in the course of his discussion he has much to say about the utility of poems. With a systematic review of poems that are sung, he maintains that they have little or no utility, and that they do much harm by intensifying the emotions. Against an opponent, probably the Stoic Diogenes of Babylon, who agreed with Plato that music has the power to produce orderliness or disorder of the soul, he argues at length that if there is any moral utility in songs, it lies in the poems—or lyrics—, not in the musical accompaniment, and even then it is small. The harm done by poems, moreover, can be very great. Marriage songs, for example, are no more useful than cookery; if there is a moral benefit, it comes from the poems, not the music, and then it extends to only a few (if indeed marriage can be said to be a good).[59] Love songs do not help the passion of love either by

56. 1.283-286.

57. Apart from the general claim that the poets state many morally harmful beliefs, the most conspicuous debt to Plato is the charge that poetry is a stronghold of the passions (as designated by the Stoic term πάθη), with the bipartite division of passions into anger and the desire for food and drink.

58. Philodemus' views on poetry are discussed in more detail in Asmis 1991.

59. *On Music* 4, col. 5.25-37 Neubecker.

the music or by the poetry; in the case of most people, most poems inflame it.[60] In particular, Ibycos, Anacreon, and the like corrupted the young with the thoughts expressed in their love songs.[61] Also, poems that are sung as dirges generally do not heal grief, but most often intensify it.[62] Concerning poems in general, Philodemus brings his greatest indictment against poetry in his work *On Piety*, where he charges the poets, along with philosophers and others, of holding beliefs about the gods that are "impious and harmful to humans."[63]

In the fifth book of *On Poems*, Philodemus extends to all poems the claim that there is little utility in them, while showing that they have a goodness that is independent of the utility of their subject matter. Against Heraclides of Pontus, who followed Plato in demanding that poems be both useful and pleasing, he objects that

he eliminates (ἐκρ[απ]ίζει, literally "expels with the rod") from goodness the most beautiful poems of the most famous poets because they provide no benefit whatsoever; in the case of some poets [he eliminates] most poems, and in certain cases all poems.[64]

60. *On Music* 4, col. 6.5-8; I understand "poems" (from lines 4-5) with ὑπὸ τῶν πλείστων (line 7).

61. *On Music* 4, col. 14.7-13. Anacreon is cited likewise by Sextus Empiricus (*Adv. math.* 1.298) as a poet who "inflames" the "love-maddened."

62. *On Music* 4, col. 6.13-18.

63. *On Piety*, PHerc. 247, 7 = fr. 48, p. 20 Gomperz.

64. *On Poems* 5, col. 1.10-18 Jensen:
...τὰ κάλ-
λιστ[α] ποιήματα τῶν [δο-
κιμ[ω]τάτων ποητῶ[ν
διὰ τὸ μηδ' ἡντινοῦν
ὠφελίαν παρασκευ[ά-
ζειν, ἐνίων δὲ καὶ [τὰ
πλε[ῖ]στα, τινῶν δὲ πά[ν-
τα [τ]ῆς ἀρετῆς ἐκρ[απ]ί-
ζει.

Elizabeth Asmis

Echoing the Presocratic Heraclitus, who demanded that Homer and Archilochus be expelled (ἐκβάλλεσθαι) from the contests and flogged (ῥαπίζεσθαι),[65] Philodemus uses the compound verb ἐκραπίζει to show his disapproval of Heraclides' censoriousness. If utility is admitted as a criterion of a good poem, Philodemus argues, a large proportion of the most beautiful poems of the most famous poets will not qualify as good. Philodemus restates his objection later in book 5 in a survey of poetic theories that he owes to his teacher Zeno of Sidon.[66] Using the same verb ἐκραπίζειν, which occurs only in these two places, he now rejects the requirement for poetic utility in general on the ground that it

eliminates (ἐκραπ[ίζ]ει) many wholly beautiful poems, some containing what is useless, others containing..., and prefers many that are worse, as many as contain beneficial or more beneficial thoughts.[67]

Philodemus agrees with Zeno that utility is absent from many utterly beautiful poems and is not a requirement of good poetry. He obviously places a high value on poems that have no utility, and thereby shows why an Epicurean might wish to devote time to poetry, despite its moral deficiencies.

Like Sextus' opponents of grammar, Philodemus considers it the function of prose, not poetry, to be useful. Although the

65. DK 22 B 42.

66. Philodemus introduces his survey by saying that he will refute the opinions found in Zeno (*On Poems* 5, col. 26.19-23). Zeno classified these opinions for the purpose of criticism and may be assumed to be responsible for the analysis as a whole, including the objections.

67. *On Poems* 5, col. 29.9-17 Jensen:
...πολλὰ τῶν παν[κά-
λ[ων] ἐκραπ[ίζ]ει ποιημά-
των τὰ μὲ[ν ἀ]νωφελῆ,
τὰ [δὲ οὐδ' ἀνωφελ]ῆ περι-
έχοντ[α, καὶ π]ολλὰ πρ[ο-
κρίνει τ[ῶ]ν ἡττόνων,
ὅσα τὰς ὠφελίμους ἢ τὰς
ὠφελιμωτέρας περιείλη-
φε.

thrust of his argument in *On Music* is that any moral benefit associated with music comes from the words of songs, not the music, he does not consider poems suited for moral instruction. One reason, as Philodemus shows in an argument against the Stoic Cleanthes, is that poetic expression blunts any moral message that a poem might have. Against Cleanthes' claim that melody reinforces the moral impact of a poem and makes the thoughts more useful, Philodemus argues that melody not only fails to enhance but actually weakens the moral utility of the thoughts because the pleasure, as well as the special qualities of the sounds, distract the listener, because "the words are expressed continuously and not naturally," and so on.[68] The same argument applies to poems without music; in their case, too, the moral force of a poem is weakened by the attendant pleasure, the peculiarity of the sounds, and the unnatural diction. In general, Philodemus believes, poetic expression is not as clear as prose. He points out in *On Poems* that not every kind of clarity is permitted to poets nor does the permitted kind seem to fit all thoughts.[69] In agreement with Sextus' opponents of grammar, he draws a distinction between poems and "demonstrative discourses" (ἀποδεικτικοὶ λόγοι).[70] The kind of clarity that poems lack most conspicuously is the clarity of philosophical demonstration; and since this is an indispensable tool of moral instruction, the usefulness of poems is severely limited.

It follows that if ever poems are useful, prose would have been more useful. In *On Music*, Philodemus is not at all persuaded that the many examples of how poets stopped civil strife with their songs are historically accurate. But if Stesichorus and Pindar did indeed persuade their fellow citizens to put aside their differences, Philodemus writes, they did so by speech (λόγων) put in poetic form, not by the melodies; and "they would have succeeded better if they had tried to dissuade them

68. *On Music* 4, col. 28.16-35; cf. 26.9-14. At col. 15.5-7 Philodemus claims that music, like sexual pleasure and drink, distracts a person from paying attention to the misfortunes of love.

69. *On Poems* 5, col. 28.26-32.

70. *On Poems* 5, col. 29.33-36.

by prose."[71] Of prose, the best kind is philosophical prose, whose job it is to teach what is morally correct. Music, Philodemus points out, cannot console the distraught lover at all; only the words (λόγος) can do so.[72] Words, moreover, over-power sexual passion by "teaching what is futile, harmful, and insatiable."[73] The words of a song can do some teaching. But the teaching of moral truths is clearly the special prerogative of philosophical prose, using "demonstrative discourses" to show, among other things, that unless a limit is placed on desires, they are insatiable and cause great unhappiness. Philodemus there-fore suggests that instead of contributing music toward the acquisition of "erotic virtue," as Diogenes of Babylon seems to have claimed, the Muse Erato contributed "poetry or, better still, philosophy."[74] Since "everything has been attributed to the Muses", Philodemus reasons, we might as well make Erato responsible for contributing philosophy to the virtue identified as "erotic" by the Stoics. For music does not contribute one bit toward helping people who are in love. Poetry can help a little; but it can help only to the extent that it agrees with philosophy, which alone can show the full truth about love.

In his own quarrel with poetry, Philodemus agrees with Plato that poets have said "vulgar, bad, and contradictory" things about every virtue. If they were to have knowledge about virtue, Philodemus adds, "they would not have this knowledge as poets ([κ]αθ' ὃ ποιηταί), let alone as musicians."[75] Moral knowledge belongs to the philosopher; it belongs to poets—and here Philodemus parts with Plato—to create beautiful poems, whether morally beneficial or not. Drawing the same distinction between the proper function and an incidental attribute of a poem, Philodemus claims in his Zenonian survey of poetic theo-ries in *On Poems* that "even if [poems] benefit, they do not bene-

71. *On Music* 4, col. 20.7-17.

72. *On Music* 4, col. 15.1-5.

73. *On Music* 4, col. 13.16-24.

74. *On Music* 4, col. 15.15-23.

75. *On Music* 4, col. 26.1-7, including: οὐ / μὴν ἀλλ' οὐδὲ [κ]αθ' ὃ ποιη/ταὶ ταῦτ' εἰδεῖ[εν] ἄν, οὐχ ὅτι καθ' ὃ μουσικοί.

fit as poems (κα[θὸ πό]ημᾱτ᾽)."[76] Philodemus agrees with Sextus' opponents of grammar that it is not the aim of poetry to present the truth; hence, if poetry does impart moral truths, this is incidental to its function. Because it is not the job of the poet to discover or impart truths, the philosopher will not use the poet as a witness. In his work *On Rhetoric*, Philodemus picks out a favorite poet of many philosophers in order to make this point: "How would a philosopher pay attention to Euripides, especially since he has proof (πίστιν) whereas Euripides does not even bring in proof?"[77]

These similarities between Philodemus' position and Sextus' account suggest that Sextus may have drawn directly on Philodemus or one of his circle. Such a conjecture receives some support from the fact that in his book *Against the Musicians* Sextus cites a series of arguments that coincide even more closely with arguments found in Philodemus' *On Music*.[78] Philodemus, we know, was strongly indebted to his teacher Zeno, whom he greatly admired; and, as we have seen, in *On Poems* he used a summary of poetic theories prepared by Zeno.[79] Zeno wrote a work *On Grammar*, as well as a work *On the Use of Poems*, which are not extant.[80] A powerful and origi-

76. *On Poems* 5, col. 29.17-19: κᾶν ὠφελῇ, / κα[θὸ πο]ήματ᾽ οὐκ ὠφε/λεῖ.

77. *On Rhetoric* HV[1] v. 5, col. 27.10-14 (Sudhaus v. 1, p. 262): καὶ πῶς Εὐριπίδει φιλόσοφος / ἂν προσέχοι καὶ ταῦτα μη/δὲ πίστιν εἰσφέροντι / πίστιν αὐτὸς ἔχων; The type of proof used by a philosopher is demonstrative proof, ἀπόδειξις; πίστις is "proof" in a wider sense, which includes the proofs used by rhetoricians and, at times, poets. In Sextus' arguments, Euripides is called "the philosopher of the stage," and he is said to have held more reasonable views about the gods than Homer or Hesiod (*Adv. math.* 1.288-289).

78. *Adv. math.* 6.19-37. This section consists of the "more dogmatic," non-Pyrrhonist arguments against music (as announced at 6.4). Gigante 1981, pp. 215-221, showed that there is a close agreement between this section and Philodemus' *On Music*, and conjectured that Sextus is here indebted directly to Philodemus.

79. Many of Philodemus' writings contain summaries or transcriptions of Zeno's teachings; and some are derived entirely from him. Zeno had a strong interest in literature as well as in mathematics and logic. In addition to *On Poems*, Philodemus' other major work on literature, *On Rhetoric*, contains extensive excerpts from Zeno's writings.

80. PHerc. 1005, col. 10, contains a list of Zeno's works, including περὶ γραμ-

nal thinker, Zeno was remarkably adept at gathering material for his arguments from many sources and marshalling them in tight array against his opponents. It is plausible, therefore, that Zeno was the primary source of Sextus' arguments.[81]

Cicero, Sextus, and, above all, Philodemus show that at the end of the second century and in the first half of the first century B.C. the Epicureans reconsidered the relationship between poetry and philosophy. Although we have very little evidence about Epicurus, the testimonies suggest that whereas Epicurus emphasized the harmful educational influence of poetry and the need to replace poetic teaching by philosophy, his followers took the more hospitable view that it is not the function of poetry to teach and that philosophy may form an alliance with poetry, in which both pursuits achieve their own ends. In this partnership, the serious study of philosophy gives licence to Epicureans like Torquatus to spend their leisure time in the enjoyable, though fundamentally useless, study of poetry. As a sign of this more conciliatory view, Cicero's Torquatus describes poetry as having "no solid usefulness" (*nulla solida utilitas*). Torquatus recognizes that only philosophy can bring happiness; but since philosophy can render the enjoyment of poetry harmless, there is no reason why he should not indulge in this delight, which may even bring a little incidental moral benefit. Since Epicurus, too, admitted poetry as a form of enjoyment, there is no contradiction with Epicurus' doctrine; but a new place is given to poetry as a study subordinate to philosophy.

ματικῆς and περὶ ποιημάτων χρήσεως. *PHerc.* 1012, whose author is thought to be Demetrius the Laconian, contains two references to Zeno that may have been derived from Zeno's *On Grammar*; see Angeli and Colaizzo 1979, p. 76. There are no other testimonies about Zeno's *On Grammar*.

81. Crönert (1906, p. 119) previously suggested that Sextus' Epicureans are οἱ περὶ τὸν Ζήνωνα and that Sextus used Zeno's *On Grammar*. Crönert supposes, unnecessarily in my view, that Sextus derived his knowledge of Zeno's work from Aenesidemos. It is possible that Demetrius the Laconian, an associate of Zeno and Philodemus, also participated in the debate on the usefulness of poetry. *PHerc.* 1014 is entitled "Demetrius' *On Poems* 2", and has been attributed to the Laconian by the most recent editor, Costantina Romeo 1988. It is debatable, however, whether the author is the Laconian or the first century B.C. Peripatetic; see Romeo, pp. 21-25. The extant text shows a detailed acquaintance with Greek poetry and includes excerpts from Homer, Euripides, and others.

Philodemus is the outstanding example of a Greek Epicurean who conjoined the pursuit of poetry with philosophy. But he went considerably further than Cicero's Torquatus in the value he placed on poetry. As we have seen, Philodemus held that poetry can do much harm. In particular, he agreed with Epicurean tradition that Homer said many foolish and harmful things. His book *On Piety* (Περὶ εὐσεβείας) contains striking examples of how Homer propagated false and pernicious beliefs about the gods.[82] But Philodemus also believed that Homer provides beneficial moral guidance for rulers. In fact, Philodemus devoted an entire treatise to showing that Homer offers good advice on how to rule. The treatise is *On the Good King according to Homer*; and it has generally been regarded as an anomaly among Epicurean texts. In this work, which is dedicated to Piso, the father-in-law of Caesar and a leading politician himself, Philodemus proposes to extract from Homer "starting-points...for the correction of positions of power" (ἀφ[ορμῶν]...εἰς ἐπανόρθωσιν δυνα⟨σ⟩τε[ιῶν]).[83] With numerous examples from the whole range of human Homeric rulers—Odysseus, Nestor, Agamemnon, Achilles, Hector, Alcinous, Telemachus, the suitors, and others—and even some divine rulers, Philodemus gives a detailed analysis of how a ruler should behave both in peace and in war. It looks as though, contrary to Epicurus' alleged expulsion of Homer from the city, Philodemus has led him back.

Whereas Torquatus' devotion to poetry as something pleasurable but fundamentally useless can readily be regarded as an extension of Epicurus' position, the view that Homer is morally useful seems a reversal. Philodemus does bring Homer back into the city—the Roman city—as a politically useful poet; and this is a major turning point in the history of Epicurean poetics. Yet this apparent reversal can also be seen to fit a tradition of interpretation which claims to be faithful to Epicurus' thought. In particular, it fits the view that philosophy may ally itself with

82. For example, he denounces Homer's description of Ares, son of Zeus, as "mindless, lawless, murderous, a lover of strife and of battle" (*On Piety*, *PHerc.* 1088, 10 = fr. 95.22-28, p. 46 Gomperz). Other examples of Homeric impiety occur at fr. 37, p. 9 Gomperz; fr. 63, p. 34 Gomperz; and fr. 145, p. 59 Gomperz.

83. Col. 43.16-19 Dorandi.

poetry in such a way as to illuminate the truths that are found incidentally in poems. Philodemus recognizes that Homeric poetry contains a great deal that is harmful, not just in its theology, but also in its depictions of the misuse of power, notably by Achilles, and most of all, by the suitors. But, according to Philodemus, Homer also shows, through Nestor, Odysseus and others, how the misuse of power is to be corrected. These "starting-points for the correction" of power need to be illuminated by the philosopher—not anyone else; and this is the job that Philodemus undertakes for Piso, a Roman ruler who is in a position to practice what he is taught.[84] As philosophical interpreter of Homer, Philodemus guides Piso through a reading of Homer by drawing attention to statements that are morally beneficial. The treatise is unique as an example of Epicurean literary criticism, according to which the only legitimate critic is the philosopher, distinguishing what is morally valuable from what is morally harmful. Although Philodemus' procedure resembles that of other philosophers, the theoretical underpinning is wholly different. He does not use the poet as a witness for moral truths, but identifies truths on the basis of his own philosophical understanding.

Philodemus, therefore, extends Epicurus' acceptance of poetry by admitting it not only as a pleasant, but also as a morally useful, pastime. He also made another extension, which concerns the enjoyment of poetry. For the most part, Philodemus seems to follow Epicurus closely on how poetry is to be enjoyed. Indeed, much of what he says about the pleasure of listening to poetry looks like an amplification of Epicurus' remarks. In his book *On Music*, Philodemus mentions that the Homeric poems "have indicated, as they ought to, that music is appropriate at parties."[85] One obvious piece of evidence is Odysseus' speech to Alcinous. I suggested earlier that Epicurus may have quoted the words; Philodemus surely has them in mind, and may be following Epicurus. Homer, of course, attests that not just music, but the recitation of poems is appropriate at

84. At col. 25.20 Dorandi, Philodemus refers to himself as a "philosopher."
85. *On Music* 4, col. 16.17-21.

parties; and Philodemus agrees with him. Philodemus approves of Diogenes of Babylon for admitting Homer, Hesiod, and other poets to the entertainment at parties, even though he does not approve of Diogenes' reasons.[86] Philodemus proposes, in effect, to recreate the good cheer of Homeric parties by bringing in Homer himself, together with other early poets and their successors, as singers of tales; and this position is not essentially different from that of Epicurus.

Just as Epicurus recommends the enjoyment of Dionysiac festivals, so Philodemus points out that there is an abundance of public entertainments for one's listening pleasure; indeed, he observes, there is such great scope for participating in them that one can easily get tired of them.[87] Like Epicurus, Philodemus restricts participation to being a member of the audience, in the belief that the acquisition of technical musical skill adds nothing to happiness. The availability of public shows, Philodemus points out, makes it futile to toil at learning musical skills oneself; only the small-minded, who have nothing worthwhile to do, think they need to toil at learning music in order to get enjoyment for themselves.[88] Musical learning and practice, Philodemus argues, are toilsome and "shut us out from the things that are most decisive for prospering."[89] What is most decisive for happiness is, of course, the study of philosophy; but Philodemus presumably also has in mind the companionship of friends. The "continuous inactivity of the person who sings in boy-like fashion or is busy at playing the lyre (κιθαρίζο[ντ]ος ἐ[ν]εργῶς)," Philodemus implies, excludes the activity of friendly social intercourse.[90] Expertise in musical theory is no less an obstacle to happiness than skill in performance, since it requires practice for its perfection.[91] Philodemus supports Epicurus' ban on musical and literary lectures by commenting that "to have

86. *On Music* 4, col. 17.2-13.

87. *On Music* 4, col. 37.16-29.

88. *On Music* 4, col. 37.8-15.

89. *On Music* 4, col. 37.31-34: τῶν κυριωτά/των πρὸς εὐετηρίαν ἐκκ[λ]εί/ουσαν.

90. *On Music* 4, col. 37.36-39.

91. *On Music* 4, col. 38.22-26; Philodemus claims that the required practice "removes [us] from the things that tend toward happiness."

Elizabeth Asmis

something to say [about music] at parties and other gatherings"
is "not demanded of all...and may even be laughed at if a
philosopher should do it."[92] In general, "it is vastly better to
have good cheer (εὐθυμίαν) than uselessness (ἀχρηστίαν) by giving a display or working out some other detailed interpretation."[93]

These warnings against musical expertise would seem to apply
just as much to poetry. But there is a problem. Philodemus not
only studied poetry and wrote about it as a philosopher; he also
composed poetry. In one of his epigrams, he calls himself
μουσοφιλής, "beloved of the Muses"; and although he might
well have extended the meaning of this term to include service
to the Muse of philosophy, he draws attention specifically to his
poetic creativity. For he promises his addressee Piso, to whom
he dedicated *On the Good King according to Homer*, that Piso will
hear "things far sweeter than [in] the land of the Phaeacians" at
the party to which Philodemus invites him.[94] Piso, we may
guess, loved Homer; and Philodemus, it appears, places himself
ever so ironically among the successors of Homer himself.
Philodemus composed only light epigrams; but he displays considerable poetic skill. How could he justify this activity if
Epicurus did indeed prohibit the wise person from composing
poems?

At this point I would like to return to the alternative interpretation of Epicurus' prohibition. It is possible that Philodemus and
others interpreted Epicurus to mean that the wise person does
not make a practice of composing poetry: unlike the lyre-player
who plays ἐνεργῶς, keeping himself busy with this activity, the
wise person does not busy himself with composing poetry. If he
composes poetry, he does so as an amateur, not a professional.

92. *On Music* 4, col. 38.12-19.

93. *On Music* 4, col. 38.25-30: καὶ μυρί[ωι κ]ρεῖτ/τ[ον ἔχ]ειν τὴν εὐ[θυ]μίαν / ἢ τὴν
ἀχρηστίαν ἐ[πι]δει/κ[ν]υμένου[ς ἢ τ]ῶν ἄλλων / τι τῶν ἐκ τῆς διεξόδου
π[ε]/ραίνοντας. The verb περαίνειν is also used by Plutarch in his report of
Epicurus' prohibition of musical and poetic lectures (*Non posse suaviter vivi*
1095c, see note 22). Although the verb is commonplace, it is possible that
Philodemus and Plutarch are drawing on the same text by Epicurus.

94. *Palatine Anthology* 11.44. David Sider drew my attention to the reference to
the Phaeacians; please see his commentary.

Accordingly, he does not spend a great deal of effort at acquiring the skill, so that the pleasure of exercising the skill is not outweighed by the toil; nor does he deprive himself of any opportunities for happiness, or of any "good cheer" at parties. This interpretation could have been placed on either an original prohibition phrased simply as ποιήματά τε οὐκ ἂν ποιῆσαι or on a prohibition augmented by ἐνεργείᾳ.[95] Whatever the original wording, it is unlikely that Epicurus meant to leave a loophole for poetic composition. But his followers might reasonably have argued that he did not intend his prohibition to apply to the amateur efforts of someone who practices poetic composition only incidentally, not "as a poet."

If Philodemus justified the composition of poems as an amateur pleasure, this is a further extension of the acceptance of poetry as a leisure-time occupation, or διαγωγή. The amateur composer does not use poetry for the serious purpose of instructing others. To educate others, he uses prose, just as Epicurus demanded. Philodemus' own writings exemplify this demarcation between prose and poetry. His epigrams might have some incidental moral utility, but they are not intended to teach.

Philodemus, then, represents a new kind of Epicurean, who studies poetry with enjoyment and even profit, and who may even compose poems as a pastime. This Epicurean is cast in a new mould, but one which is carefully calculated to fit the standard established by Epicurus. But there is also a wholly different new Epicurean. Lucretius exploited the seductive beauty of poetry to educate others and spared no labor to make poetry a suitable vehicle for philosophical instruction. By combining the two uses of poetry, education and enjoyment, that Epicurus had kept strictly apart, Lucretius seems to preclude any way of reconciling his approach to poetry with that of Epicurus.

Lucretius does not, however, use poetry without offering a defence of his method; and this defence may be regarded as his

95. See pp. 73-74 above. If Epicurus wrote the simple prohibition, a later interpreter may have added ἐνεργεῖν as a marginal explanation which subsequently crept into the text.

Elizabeth Asmis

own novel exegesis of Epicurus' views on poetry. In a famous image, Lucretius compares himself to a doctor who smears honey around the cup of bitter medicine in order to trick the child into drinking the healing potion. The reason for this trickery, Lucretius explains, is that the doctrine of Epicurus generally seems "too cheerless" (*tristior*) to people who are not acquainted with it.[96] Lucretius proposes to use poetry as a lure to attract the ordinary person to Epicurean philosophy. But this is not all. Lucretius does not regard poetry simply as a necessary device, dictated by the antipathy of his audience. Instead, what makes him so enthusiastic about his work is that poetry makes a positive contribution to the presentation of philosophy. Not only does its sweetness differ from the bitterness of the doctrine, but also its clarity differs from the obscurity of Epicurus' discoveries. Lucretius takes great pleasure in his poetic toil "because I fashion such lucid songs about an obscure subject matter" (*quod obscura de re tam lucida pango/carmina*).[97] As he assures Memmius, he will not spare any labor "in seeking by what words and what song I may be able to spread clear light over your mind."[98] Lucretius aims to dispel the darkness of his listeners' ignorance by illuminating the discoveries of Epicurus with the language of poetry.

In claiming clarity for his verses, Lucretius asserts, paradoxically, a continuity of his method of teaching with that of Epicurus. Whereas Epicurus assigned clarity to prose alone, Lucretius now claims this quality for poetry. If poetry has clarity, it is an entirely appropriate vehicle for imparting philosophical truths. Lucretius is so intent on proving the suitability of poetry as a philosophical medium that he does not shun any technical difficulties; indeed, he goes out of his way to give a full presentation of philosophically difficult material. His poem is a "demonstrative discourse" (ἀποδεικτικὸς λόγος), aiming to move

96. *De rerum natura* 1.936-950, including (943-945): quoniam haec ratio plerumque videtur / tristior esse quibus non est tractata, retroque / volgus abhorret ab hac.

97. 1.933-934.

98. 1.143-144: quaerentem dictis quibus et quo carmine demum / clara tuae possim praepandere lumina menti.

the soul (ψυχαγωγεῖν) in such a way as to lead it to the truth. In combining what other Epicureans kept apart, Lucretius reaffirms the traditional link between divine inspiration and poetic expression. Lucretius symbolizes his source of inspiration by Venus, a deity who represents both his love for Epicurus and the expression of this love in his poetry. If called to account by Epicurus for using poetry to instruct others, he might reply: "You have inspired me to attempt a feat that no one has tried before: to illuminate your teachings in poetry. I do not deviate from your path; but you have shown me a path by which I may lead others to a clear vision of your divine truth."

We do not know whether Lucretius associated with Philodemus and his friends. There is no sign in Philodemus' writings that he ever conceived that a poem such as Lucretius' might be compatible with Epicurus' teachings. Yet I suspect that if he ever came to know Lucretius' poetry, he would have been so impressed by its exceptional beauty and clarity that he would have welcomed Lucretius as an associate in his own efforts to spread Epicureanism to the Romans.[99]

The University of Chicago

99. I am very grateful to Dirk Obbink for many helpful comments on an earlier draft of part of this paper.

Commentary on Asmis

David Sider

Professor Asmis has done us all a service by her investigation of what the term Epicurean poetics means. The view that has become standard handbook fare is that Epicurus was himself impervious to the charms of poetry and that his charge to his disciples was to avoid it absolutely, both the listening and the composing. Not everyone of course held to this extreme statement of his position, but it was easy enough to believe that anyone who wrote prose on so stylistically plain a level as Epicurus would, almost *a fortiori*, be insensitive to the charms of poetry. Secondly, that the most famous piece of Epicurean literature was itself a poem could be regarded as all the more interesting if Epicurus himself abjured the writing of poetry.

Nor did this view derive *e nihilo*. There seemed to be sufficient ancient testimony to support it. Cicero, for example, says of Philodemos: *non philosophia solum sed etiam cereris studiis quae fere ceteros Epicureos neglegere dicunt perpolitus*, "he is expert not only in philosophy but also in other skills which almost all other Epicureans are said to neglect" (*In Pisonem* 70). As Cicero's very next sentence makes clear, these other skills include, or are coextensive with, the writing of poems, and indeed, Cicero admits, quite elegant ones at that. Thus, for Philodemos as well as his contemporary Lucretius, although one wrote in the slightest of genres, the epigram, while the other wrote in the weightiest of genres, the didactic epic, the very idea of Epicurean poetry would seem to remain something of an challenge, which would have to be confronted before verse composition could begin.

David Sider

Moreover, whereas Cicero speaks of contemporary Epicureans, Diogenes Laertius, not only our most complete ancient source for the teaching of Epicurus, but also one of the most sympathetic, seems to have been an unambiguous witness to the hostility of Epicurus himself to poetry. Asmis, however, has just shown us that his prohibition was probably not intended to be absolute. She suggests that the unconstruable infinitive ἐνεργεῖν in Diogenes should either be emended as Usener did to ἐνεργείᾳ, but with the sense "energetically"; or understood as a gloss with this same sense on the infinitive ποιεῖν. Reading the dative is preferable, as it (or some synonymous expression) would have been written presumably by Epicurus himself and thus have formed an essential part of his original statement. The infinitive as gloss would have to have come from an interpreter later than Diogenes Laertius who, like Elizabeth Asmis, would have reasoned that Epicurus allowed for the writing of poetry by Epicureans. Ἐνεργείᾳ could well have appeared in his *Choices and Avoidances* (Περὶ Αἱρέσεων καὶ φυγῶν), where Epicurus classifies εὐφροσύνη, the very word used by Homer in the Phaeacian passage, and χαρά, "joy," as kinematic pleasures. If, however, as seems likely, ἐνεργεῖν is to be emended, then ἐνεργῶς, which is equally possible paleographically, provides the desired sense unambiguously.[1] Epicurus's statement would thus be noticeably similar to Philodemos' in *De Musica* which Asmis cites later where he objects to someone's κιθαρίζοντος ἐνεργῶς, "be busy [i.e., overbusy] at playing the kithara" (Book 4, col. 37.38f).

Also in favor of Asmis' interpretation of this Diogenes passage is its general context. Between his transcription of Epicurus's letters to Pythokles and to Menoikios, Diogenes inserts a number of do's and dont's for this wise man, who in this parlance is none other than the Epicurean.[2] It is noteworthy that, although drawn from several Epicurean sources, these ethical guidelines often take the following form: The wise man will in general

1. Cf. D.L. 10.136 = Epic. 2 U = 7 Arr. ἡ δὲ χαρὰ καὶ ⟨ἡ⟩ ἀπονία κατὰ κίνησιν ἐνεργείᾳ βλέπονται.

2. Strictly speaking, these maxims are attributed to Epicurus or his followers, but nobody I think would argue that a prohibition against poetry was added by a later Epicurean without the master's own authority.

avoid activity X but will engage in it under certain circumstances. He shouldn't marry, for example, but may yet find some reason for doing so. He shouldn't get drunk, but if he does so then let him not babble. He will avoid the usual business of the state but will occasionally sue somebody. And so on. The notion that the Epicurean will not write poetry but if he does he will not do so actively fits perfectly into this Diogenean context. This would seem to provide futher confirmation of Asmis' thesis. It should be pointed out, however, that Diogenes seems, in his usual cut-and-paste style of composition, to have suppressed a clause or two. Although commentators and translators usually connect the two clauses under discussion with an "although" or a "but," they are in fact linked by two τε's: Literally, "Only the wise man would converse correctly concerning music and poetry; *and* [to adopt Asmis' sense of the passage] he would not write poems enthusiastically." Ignored are the fact that the infinitive of each clause is accompanied by an ἄν, which makes it unlikely that one clause was subordinated to the other. There would seem to be suppressed protases of future less vivid conditions here, which in turn follow upon suppressed prohibitions: In full, then, we may flesh out Epicurus's original statements as follows: (1) "Nobody should spend time discussing music and poetry, but if it should be done only the wise man would do so correctly." And (2) "The wise man should not write poetry but if he should do so he would not do so too seriously."

This analysis, as I have said, not only fits Diogenes' context, it separates what are too often linked in discussions of Epicurus's views of poetry, the analyzing of poetry and the writing of poems, and leaves open the possibility of an Epicurean doing one, like Lucretius, or both, like Philodemos. And it may be worth noting that Diogenes attributes no prohibition to Epicurus concerning the mere listening to poetry. This too supports Asmis' general thesis.

One should also add to her discussion of Lucretius and Philodemos that there were several, some might say many, other poets who considered themselves Epicureans. The earliest of these may be Epicurus's friend Metrodoros of Lampsakos, who had been credited with the philosophical poem credited merely to "Metrodoros" in *Anth. Pal.* 9.360, and who has been put forth as the possible author of a recently published hexameter fragment on the birth of Aphrodite.[3] None of this, however, is very secure. We are on surer ground with Titus Albucius in the Second Century B.C., who is called a *perfectus Epicureus* by Cicero (*Brutus* 131) and an *aridus [poeta]* by Fronto (*De Eloquentia* p. 13 van den Hart]. Krebs may be right in thinking that Albucius left behind some sort of *Lehrgedicht*, i.e., a didactic poem with an Epicurean message, although he is more certain than the evidence actually warrants.[4]

In the first century B.C. there are the poets Plotius Tucca and Lucius Varius Rufus, who edited the *Aeneid* after Vergil's death, and who are addressed more than once by Philodemos in his prose treatises, which suggests very strongly that they were regular members of the Epicurean circle which met in and around Naples. Donatus in his life of Vergil furthermore specifically attests to the Epicureanism of Varius.[5] This makes it quite likely, if not certain, that Varius' hexameter poem *De Morte*, dealt with this central Epicurean subject, again along Epicurean lines. Our understanding of Lucretius' diatribe against the fear of death would probably be much enhanced were Varius' poem extant.[6] There is also the obscure Pollius Felix, whom Statius credits in

3. Gerhard 1909, p. 104; Maresch 1987, pp. 26-51, esp. 27, 30f., 35 (text), 46-8 (comm.). For these references and for much useful discussion on the nature of Epicurean poetry I am grateful to Dirk Obbink.

4. "Albucius (2)," RE 1 (1892) 1330f.

5. Donatus vita Verg. 68 [*Vergilius*] *audiuit a Sirone praecepta Epicuri, cuius doctrinae socium habuit Varium.* Cf. Jerome *Chron.* ad ol. 140.4 *Varius et Tucca Vergilii contubernales poetae habentur illustres*, although not everyone agrees that Tucca was in fact a poet; cf. Naumann 1938.

6. It does not tell against this interpretation that at least some of the extant fragments of this poem (p. 100 Morel) seem to concern Marc Antony: consolation literature often uses the death of a friend or relative (or in this case a Roman leader) as an obvious point of departure for a disquisition on the nature of death and how it should be borne by those left behind. Ungar 1870, p. 78 argues for its being a Lehrgedicht; cf. further Rostagni 1961; *RE* 8A1 1955, col. 412, s.v. L. Varius (21) Rufus; Gigante 1990, 56ff.

his *Silvae* with writing a Hesiodic, i.e. didactic, poem which is
worthy of Epicurus (2.2. 112ff.):

huc ubi Pierias exercet Pollius artes
seu voluit monitus, quos dat Gargettius auctor[7]
seu nostram quatit ille chelyn seu dissona nectit
carmina sive minax ultorem stringit iambon.

Less obscure a poet than Pollius Felix is Vergil, who spent time
with the two most famous Epicureans in Naples, Siron and
Philodemos, and who, I am convinced, wrote at least some of
the Epicurean poems in the *Catalepton*, most notably 5, which
not only refers to Siro (as does 8) but whose point clearly recalls
that of Philodemos' *Epigram* 17 (*A.P.* 11.41).[8] Horace is a different case when it comes to philosophical affiliation, but he too
consciously drew upon Epicurean doctrine in some of his poems
(as well as many other schools of thought).[9] Nor should we forget that Diogenes Laertius, who seems to have considered himself an Epicurean (10.138), wrote many epigrams.[10] Thus,
although this brief census may well be incomplete, there are

7. I.e., Epicurus called after his Attic deme; cf. D.L. 10.1, Suidae vita.

8. Cf. AJP 108 (1987) 315 f. The presence of Vergil and Plotius in the
Herculaneum papyri, long conjectured, has been recently confirmed; cf. Gigante
and Capasso 1989, with frontpiece plate. For ancient literary testimony, cf.
Crönert 1906, 125 f.

Vergil's patron Maecenas also wrote poetry with an Epicurean flavor; cf.
Ferguson 1990, 2263f. Ferguson 2268 also suggests Vergil's friend Octavius
Musa, who was in the Naple circle, but we do not know if his poetry was in any
way Epicurean.

9. Horace's use of philosophical themes is far too complex to deal with here; in
brief, though, we can say that like Philodemos he uses what in a philosophical
treatise would be doctrine as poetical topoi. Thus although in one poem he calls
himself *Epicuri de grege porcum* (*Ep.* 1.4.16), in another epistle he more truthfully
says that he is *nullius addictus iurare verba magistri* (1.1.14). Cf. De Witt 1939, pp.
127-34; Fraenkel 1957, pp. 254-7. Note in partucular *Odes* 1.31, which ends with
distinctly Epicurean and Philodemean echoes in praise of the simple needs of
the good life (cf. Nisbet-Hubbard's comm., pp. 348, 355f.), including the composing of poetry (*nec cithara carentem*).

10. That 10.138 indicates Diogenes was an Epicurean, or at any rate more
Epicurean than anything else, is argued by (i.a.) Gigon 1986, p. 137. For an
assessment of Diogenes' epigrams, cf. Mejer 1978, pp. 46-50; Gigante 1986. At
1.63, Diogenes mentions that his *Pammetros* contained poems on famous men "in
all meters and rhythms, in epigrams and in lyrics"; cf. Mejer 1978, p. 48 n. 102 for

enough names to show us that however broad the term
Epicurean poetics is, allowing as it does for the poetry of
Lucretius, Philodemos, and Horace, it is not so oxymoronic as is
often thought.[11]

Asmis strengthens her case when she analyzes Epicurus's attitude toward poetry as though it were a form of reader-response
criticism. That is, Epicurus's criterion for the acceptability of a
particular piece of poetry lies not in its particular content but in
how it is received by a particular audience. The ancient testimony brought to the fore by Asmis connecting Epicurus with the
Phaeacians and Odysseus is especially pertinent. Whereas earlier scholars looked at the elements of the *telos* listed by Odysseus
in isolation, it now seems better to view them as complementary
parts of the larger whole that is the proper banquet scene which
can serve as a model for those held in an Epicurean Garden.
Poetry now takes its rightful place, at least in Epicurus's eyes, as
but one contributory element of pleasure. But straining too hard
for pleasures, we know, can only bring pain; in the case of poetry this would entail too much attention paid to what, after all,
cannot, whatever its claims to do so, contribute to our happiness. Poetry is thus reduced by Epicurus to *Tafelmusik*, which
should no more be paid attention to let alone analyzed than the
music that comes over the phone when we are put on hold.

In more Epicurean terms, poetry is classifiable as a natural but
unnecessary pleasure, which adds variety to already existing
pleasures without, like necessary pleasure, ameliorating pains.

---

a list of the meters in the extant poems. Gigante 1986 pp. 39f. argues that the
many epigrams on the death of philosophers earn Diogenes "un posto nella let-
teratura antica περὶ θανάτου."

11. After Horace the Epicurean views found in the poets tend to become more
literary motifs and borrowings (often from Philodemos), and hence less meaningful from our point of view. There is little of value in Disch 1921, who discusses Vergil, Horace, Tibullus, Propertius, and Ovid. Cf. the remarks of Courtney
1991, pp. 11-14, on several seemingly Epicurean poems: "Petronius is in no
sense propagating Epicurean doctrine, but is quite willing to allow his characters
to justify their acts by recourse to a superficial Epicureanism."

In a banquet setting it is equivalent to fancy food.[12] If listening to poetry is thus barely tolerated, Epicurus's view of composing it must have been similar to that of Athena who thought that however beautiful the sound of the aulos, the playing of the instrument was infra dignitatem.

In classifying poetry as a natural but unnecessary pleasure, Epicurus is thus, like Plato, stripping it of any claims made on its behalf to offer valuable ethical precepts that could lead to happiness. Poetry, that is, makes claims that gourmet food does not, so that it is not surprising that Epicurus would have followed Plato in cautiously treating poetry as a rival whose admittance into philosophical society can be allowed only under circumscribed conditions. That he himself knew his Greek poetry well and could make poetical allusions with ease has been recently brought out by Diskin Clay,[13] but the overall impression Epicurus produced in ancient readers is that he depended on no predecessors in his arguments, that "there is no external authority in them; the voice is the voice of Epicurus."[14] The allusions pointed out by Clay and Asmis, therefore, were probably made in passing; it seems unlikely that Epicurus would have based an argument on a poetic passage. As Asmis properly reminds us, poetry formed an essential part of Greek culture and as such demands emotional and critical detachment, however difficult it must have been to maintain *ataraxia* while listening to Homer.

We should not, however, miss the irony of Epicurus's using a literary allusion to Odysseus and the Sirens when he warns Pythokles to set sail and flee all culture. For in couching his admonition to Pythokles in this form, Epicurus demonstrates precisely how literature should be treated: Listen to it, he seems

12. Cf. KD 29 with scholion·

φυσικὰς καὶ ἀναγκαίας
ἡγεῖται ὁ Ἐπίκουρος τὰς ἀλγηγόνος ἀπολούσας,
ὡς ποτὸν ἐπὶ δίψους· φυσικὰς δὲ οὐκ ἀναγκαίας
δὲ τὰς ποικιλλούσας μόνον τὴν ἡδονήν, μὴ
ὑπεξαιρουμένας δὲ τὸ ἄλγημα, ὡς πολυτελῆ σιτία.

13. 1983, p. 16 with n. 12, p. 78 n. 58.
14. D.L. 10.26; cf. Sedley 1976.

to be saying, and use it, i.e., make allusions to it; but do not suc-
cumb to its charms. Epicurus's specific warning to Pythokles
had a notable echo in Stokely Carmichael's famous dictum of
the 1960's: "When I hear the word "culture" I reach for my
gun." In Carmichael's phrase the *word* "culture" makes the
same point attributed to Epicurus by Plutarch, that one should
not envy τὴν ἐλευθέραν καλουμένην παιδείαν, "the *so-called* liberal education" (Plut. 1094d = 164 U), which is all too often used
to convince people of their social inferiority. Rather than being
the philistine Plutarch says he is, Epicurus seems instead to have
been working to break down the social barriers maintained in
large part by the ability to parade's one cultural credentials. The
line of Metrodoros quoted by Asmis which says in effect 'Don't
worry if you can't quote Homer at the drop of a hat', reinforces
this very point. (All the more so if we believe Epicurus's charge
that Metrodoros lacked originality, for he would probably have
taken the phrase from Epicurus.)

If thanks to Asmis we now have a good idea of what Epicurean
poetics meant to Epicurus himself, we are also better prepared
to examine what it meant to his later followers. We can certainly
agree with her that the continuity between Epicurus's and
Philodemos' poetical theory is unbroken. If nothing else, we
should note with Asmis the various Epicurean writings on the
subject, from Epicurus's own Περὶ Μουσικῆς and Συμπόσιον,
and Metrodoros' Περὶ Ποιημάτων, Demetrios Lacon's Περὶ
Ποιημάτων, through the many titles on these subjects over
Philodemos' name.[15] Many of the statements she quotes from
Philodemos' *De Musica* could have been said by Epicurus himself. Others, including the famous statement quoted by Asmis
that a poem insofar as it is a poem does not benefit, are sophisticated extensions and elaborations of Epicurus's basic beliefs.

Against this theoretical background, then, of Epicurean *poetics*,
what could be the nature of Epicurean *poetry*? Lucretius' is
clearly one way to go: proselytizing poetry in the service of
Epicureanism. If in Philodemos' phrase it is not the poetry as
such that benefits, the poetry will nonetheless have justified

15. See now Dorandi 1990.

itself if it turns the reader to a better way of life thanks to its honey-sweet charms. Epicurus himself would not have needed such a poem, so it is probably Philodemos' style of poetry that would have appealed to him more than Lucretius', especially as Lucretius seems to have composed more for the reader whereas Philodemos' epigrams, almost certainly recited *viva voce* before audiences in Herculaneum, would have fitted in better with the dinner parties that Epicurus considered an important part of the good life as lived in the Garden. We can probably get a good idea of Epicurus's ideal banquet from his Συμπόσιον, which Athenaios tells us described a banquet whose company, unlike those in Plato and Xenophon, comprised only Epicurean philosophers, whom Athenaios calls "prophets of atomism" (56 U).[16] It is just such an audience as this that Philodemos had on the bay of Naples, in his and Siron's modest houses and in the more grand villas of their Roman acquaintances who were their students and patrons, sometimes both at the same time. As I have argued at greater length elsewhere,[17] before this sophisticated audience Philodemos could compose and recite poems which were appreciated primarily for their Hellenistic grace. That is, as with much Hellenistic poetry, especially in epigrams, the wit often lies in the striking combination of old and new. This could take several forms, one of which is the ringing new changes on familiar topoi. Philodemos could depend upon his particular philosophically inclined audience to catch allusions not only to Epicurus but also to Sokrates, Plato, Aristotle, and perhaps even more obscure thinkers. If this if true, then there is no need to look for philosophical consistency let alone Epicurean orthodoxy in the 35 or so poems we can credit to Philodemos.

As an example, we could look at the poem alluded to by Asmis in which he calls himself μουσοφιλής, a friend of the muses. We should not lose sight of the fact that this occurs in a poem in which Philodemos invites a wealthy Roman to take part in a dinner party in honor of Epicurus, and thereafter to become Philodemos' patron. In such a context the—φιλης part of the

16. Athen. 5.187b = 56 U ὁ δὲ Ἐ. ἅπαντας εἰσήγαγε προφήτας ἀτόμων..
17. Sider (forthcoming).

word along with two other examples of the stem φιλ—in this poem remind us of some other meanings; first the friendship that was to prevail in an Epicurean setting, and second the Latin *amicitia* that, perhaps euphemistically, defined the mutual relationship between patron and poet.[18] Asmis has also alerted me to the likely significance of Philodemos' telling Piso that if he comes tomorrow he will hear things sweeter than the Phaeacians. If Epicurus himself cited the Phaeacian feast in the *Odyssey* as a model of his school's own dinner parties and as a result he was referred to as the Phaeacian philosopher, then Philodemos is almost certainly alluding to this particular Epicurean passage, which in turn alludes to Homer. A perfect example of Hellenistic poetic wit that could also serve as a perfect example of one person's—Philodemos' if not Lucretius'—idea of Epicurean poetic theory in action.

Fordham University

---

18. Cf. White 1978; Saller 1989.

ASMIS/SIDER BIBLIOGRAPHY

Angeli, A., and Colaizzo, M., 1979: "I Frammenti di Zenone Sidonio", *Cronache Ercolanesi* 9, pp. 47-133.

Asmis, E., 1984: *Epicurus' Scientific Method* (Ithaca, N.Y.).

_____. 1990: "Philodemus' Epicureanism." in *Aufstieg und Niedergang der römischen Welt*, ed. by W. Haase, part 2, vol. 36.4 (Berlin), pp. 2369-2406.

_____. 1991: "Philodemus' Poetic Theory and *On the Good King* according to Homer." *Classical Antiquity* 10, pp. 1-45.

Bignone, E., 1936: *L'Aristotele perduto e la formazione filosofica di Epicuro*, vol. 1 (Florence).

Boyancé, P., 1947: "Lucrèce et la poésie." *Revue des Etudes Anciennes* 49, pp. 88-102.

_____. 1960: Review of Giancotti 1959, in *Revue des Etudes Anciennes* 62, pp. 441-45.

Clay, D., 1983: *Lucretius and Epicurus.* (Ithaca).

Courtney, E., 1991: *The Poems of Petronius.* (Atlanta).

Crönert, W. 1906: *Kolotes und Menedemos* (Munich).

De Lacy, P., 1939: "The Epicurean Analysis of Language." *American Journal of Philology* 60, pp. 86-90.

De Witt, N.W., 1939: "Epicurean doctrine in Horace." *Classical Philology* 34, pp. 127-34.

Disch, H., 1921: *De poetis Aevi Augusti Epicureis.* (Bonn).

Dorandi, T., 1990: "Filodemo: gli orientamenti della ricerca attuale." *Aufstieg und Niedergang der Römischen Welt* 2.36.4, pp. 2328-2368.

Ferguson, J., 1990: "Epicureanism under the Roman Empire." *Aufstieg und Niedergang der Römischen Welt* 2.364, pp. 2257-2327.

Fraenkel, E., 1957: *Horace.* (Oxford).

Gerhard, G.A., 1909: *Phoinix von Kolophon.* (Leipzig and Berlin).

Giancotti, F., 1959: *Il Preludio di Lucrezio* (Florence).

_____. 1960: "La poetica epicurea in Lucrezio, Cicerone ed altri." *Ciceroniana* 2, pp. 67-95.

Gigante M. and Capasso M., 1989: "Il ritorno di Virgilio a Ercolano." *Studi Italieni di Filologia Classica* 7, pp. 3-6.

Gigante, M., 1981: *Scetticismo e Epicureismo* (Naples).

_____, 1986: "Biografia e dossografia in Diogene Laerzio." *Elenchos* 7, pp. 34-44.

_____. 1990: *Filodemo in Italia* (Florence).

Bibliography

Gigon, O., 1986: "Das dritte Buch des Diogenes Laertios." *Elenchos* 7, pp. 133-82.

Griffin, M., and Barnes, J., edd., 1989: *Philosophia Togata. Essays on Philosophy and Roman Society* (Oxford).

Kaiser, E., 1964: "Odyssee-Szenen als Topoi." *Museum Helveticum* 21, pp. 109-136 and 197-224.

Mancini, A., 1976: "Sulle opere polemiche di Colote." *Cronache Ercolanesi* 6, pp. 61-67.

Maresch, K., 1987: *Koelner Papyri (P. Koeln)* 6 = *Papyrologica Coloniensia* 7, pp. 26-51.

Mejer, J., 1978: *Diogenes Laertius and his Hellenistic Background.* (Wiesbaden).

Naumann, H., 1938: "Suetons Vergil-vita." *Rheinisches Museum* 87, pp. 364-9.

Nisbet, R.G.M. and M. Hubbard, 1970: *A Commentary on Horace's Odes Book 1.* (Oxford).

Obbink, D., 1984: "*POXY.* 213 and Epicurean religious ΘΕΩΡΙΑ." *Atti del XVII Congresso Internazionale di Papirologia* (Naples), pp. 607-619.

Puglia, E., 1980: "Nuove Letture nei PHerc. 1012 e 1786 (Demetrii Laconis opera incerta)." *Cron. Erc.* 10, pp. 25-53.

Romeo, C., 1988: *Demetrio Lacone, La Poesia* [PHerc. 188 e 1014] (Naples).

Ronconi, A., 1963: "Appunti di estetica epicurea." in *Miscellanea di Studi Alessandrini in memoria di Augusto Rostagni* (Turin), pp. 7-25. Reprinted 1972 as "Poetica e critica epicurea." in *Interpretazioni letterarie nei classici* (Florence), pp. 64-90.

Rostagni, A., 1961: "Il *De Morte* di Vario." *Virgilio Minore*, pp. 391-404.

Saller, R., 1989: "Patronage and friendship in early imperial Rome." In *Patronage in Ancient Society*, Wallace-Hadrill, A., ed., pp. 49-62. (London).

Sedley, D., 1989: "Philosophical Allegiance in the Greco-Roman World." in Griffin and Barnes 1989, pp. 97-119.

_____. 1976: "Epicurus and his professional rivals." In *Études sur l'Epicurisme antique*, Bollack , J., and Laks, A., edd. , pp. 119-59. (Lille).

Sider, D. (forthcoming). "The Epicurean Philosopher as Hellenistic Poet." In *Philodemus and Poetry*, Obbink, D., ed.

Ungar, R., 1870: *Varii de morte eclogae reliquiae.* (Halle).

White, P., 1978: "Amicitia and the profession of poetry in early imperial Rome." *Journal of Roman Studies* 68, pp. 74-92.

Colloquium 4

The Idea of the Will in Chrysippus, Posidonius, and Galen

Jaap Mansfeld

Das Primäre und Ursprüngliche ist allein der W i l l e, das θέλημα, nicht βούλησις: die Verwechslung dieser beiden, für welche nur Ein deutsches Wort vorhanden, ist Quelle des Missverstehns meiner Lehre. θέλημα ist der eigentliche Wille, der Wille überhaupt, wie er in Thier und Mensch erkannt wird: βουλή aber ist der überlegte Wille, *consilium*, der Wille nach erfolgter Wahlbestimmung: den Thieren legt man keine βουλή, wohl aber θέλημα bei: weil in den neuern Sprachen nur Ein Wort für beide ist, so sind die Philosophen uneins, ob sie den Thieren Willen beilegen sollen, oder nicht; die es zugestehn, denken θέλημα, die es leugnen, βουλή.*

I

One often reads, or hears, that the Ancients had no theory, or concept, or idea of the will in our sense of the word. Perhaps the best known recent promotor of this view is A. Dihle, who devoted an entire and very learned monograph to this issue.[1]

I shall not, of course, address this huge subject as a whole, but only look at part of it. My not entirely original point of departure is a rather obvious question, namely: do we moderns, or post-moderns if you wish, really have a clear-cut concept of the

* Schopenhauer's philology is not good enough, but his point is worth taking. For the quotation, part of a note on Anaxagoras jotted down in 1825, see Frauenstädt 1864, p. 338, or Hübscher 1970, p. 213 f.

1. Dihle 1982. Trimmed-down German transl. by the author: Dihle 1985 (I shall refer to the English original). Cf. also Dirlmeier ³1964, pp. 327 f. n. 3. who however is aware that "Vieles was wir als Wille (= Energie) bezeichnen, wäre griechisch θυμός."

will which the ancients did not have? There is no separate article on *Will* in the *Encyclopedia of Philosophy*,[2] a useful and familiar work of reference, although it has an article on *Choosing, Deciding,* and *Acting,* and others on *Determinism,* on *General Will, The,* and on *Volition,* and although its index *sub voce* "will" provides a list of names starting with the medieval Arab philosopher al-Farabi and going all the way down the alphabet to the nineteenth-century German psychologist Wilhelm Wundt. The indexes of a number of books concerned with ethics in the ancient world do not have an entry for "will" either, although some of them have one for Williams; but this is by the way.

Dihle, in the book I have just cited, does not begin by telling us what is his theory, or definition, of the will.[3] He seems to suppose that we, having heard of Schopenhauer and Nietzsche and of course having been told as children by our parents that where there's a will there's a way, already know what we mean when using the word, and apparently wants us to find out what he has in mind by studying his book and discovering in the process what it is that according to him is lacking in the conceptual world of Greek and even Roman antiquity until Augustine and the full-blown Christian concept of the will made their appearance.[4]

What I have noticed is that Dihle wants a will that is a separate faculty to be distinguished from reason on the one hand and from desire and the emotions, or passions, on the other. He finds such a will in the world of the Old Testament. In the first place, he argues, God's often inscrutable and even whimsical will has as its counterpart a human will that is willing to accept whatever God ordains. You, a human being, do not want something to occur and try to make it happen, but conversely: what-

2. Edwards 1967.

3. The helpful definition to be found s.v. '[4]will' in Hornby, Gatenby and Wakefield [16]1972 runs: "mental power by which a person can direct his thoughts and actions, and influence those of others."

4. Cf. the account and apposite criticism of Dihle's approach by Kahn 1988. It does not seem that Dihle has seen Schopenhauer's *Die Welt als Wille und Vorstellung.* For Augustine's doctrine of the will see esp. the *De trinit.* bks. IX-XI, on the 'trinities' memoria-intelligentia-voluntas and res–sensus–voluntas.

ever occurs is what you want,[5] and neither reason nor the emotions are at issue. But I believe that there is a major difference between the active and influential will of the God of early Judaism and this kind of human will. I suggest that we call the latter passive, and it is fairly easy to point out a counterpart in Greek thought. The accomplished Stoic too accepts whatever it is that God has ordained, and the difference with the Jewish attitude as depicted by Dihle in my view is not a question of the idea of the will as such, but of the theology that is involved, for the wholly rational Stoic God is entirely free of whimsy. This brings me to the second aspect of the idea of the will in the world of the Old Testament as distinguished from that in Greco-Roman thought which is underscored by Dihle and other scholars. The God of early Judaism is able to do whatever he wants; he creates the world through acts of his will without having to take into account any factors that would constrain his freedom of action, and once our world has been created he is in no way hampered by mathematical or physical laws, even working what we may call miracles whenever this suits his convenience. In this respect, the God of Christianity is his worthy successor, and quite a number of Christian holy men are said to have been able to work miracles as well, which seems to imply that they may be credited with a kind of will analogous to the entirely autonomous creative will of God. But according to the conceptions of the Divinity, or of the gods, held by philosophers and other members of the Greek and Greco-Roman intelligentsia, God's will, or his freedom to act, is limited by the laws of mathematics and physics,[6] and the creator of the world—in those philosophical systems where such a creator occurs—has to work with a kind, or several kinds, of what we may call raw material, something which is already there right from the start and which

5. This is to ignore the passages in the Old Testament where people do not accept God's will.

6. A good instance of this view is at ps.Plutarch (Aëtius), *Plac.* 880F ~ Aët. I 7.3: ἀναιρείσθω ... ὁ ποιητικὸς λῆρος σὺν Καλλιμάχῳ τῷ λέγοντι [Fr. 586 Pfeiffer]· 〈〈εἰ θεὸν οἶσθα, / ἴσθι ὅτι καὶ ῥέξαι δαίμονι πᾶν δυνατόν.〉〉 οὐδὲ γὰρ ὁ θεὸς δύναται πᾶν ποιεῖν· ἐπεί τοί γε εἰ θεός ἐστι, ποιείτω τὴν χιόνα μέλαιναν τὸ δὲ πῦρ ψυχρὸν κτλ. The Stoic God, in a sense, *is* the laws of mathematics and physics, or these laws are an aspect of what he is.

Jaap Mansfeld

imposes its own constraints on whatever he makes, or does.[7] (Even the omnipotent God of Stoicism, who in principle is capable of doing whatever suits his convenience without effort by merely exercising his will, is bound by the laws and inexorable concatenation of causes he has created himself; in Seneca's words: "he always obeys, he has commanded once"[8]). If *per analogiam* we translate this state of affairs into human terms, there would accordingly be room for the idea of a human will which, given the circumstances in which it has to operate and

7. This important distinction between the God of Moses and the Demiurge of (especially Platonist) Greek thought was already stressed by Gal., *De usu part.* XI 14, II pp. 158.2-159.19 Helmreich, a passage quoted and discussed by Walzer 1949, pp. 11 ff., 23 ff., and made much of as a *Leitmotiv* by Dihle 1982, p. 1. The Skeptic critics of Stoicism already argued that the Stoic God is capable of anything by a mere act of his will, see Cic., *De nat. deor.* III 92 (*SVF* II 1107, a text partly quoted by Walzer 1949, p. 28, and cavalierly treated by Dihle 1982, pp. 133-4 and notes): "vos enim ipsi dicere soletis *nihil esse quod deus efficere non possit*, et quidem sine labore ullo; ut enim *hominum membra* nulla contentione mente ipsa et voluntate moveantur, sic numine deorum omnia fingi, *moveri*, mutarique posse. Neque id dicitis superstitiose atque aniliter sed physica constantique ratione; materiam enim rerum, ex qua et in qua omnia sint, totam esse flexibilem et commutabilem, ut nihil sit quod non ex ea quamvis subito fingi convertique possit, eius autem universae fictricem et moderatricem divinam esse providentiam; haec igitur *quocumque se moveat, efficere possit quidquid velit*." In this passage (as in the next to be quoted) we should notice the correlation between the omnipotent divine will and human volition pertaining to bodily motion. For a parallel of (Posidonian rather than Chrysippean?) Stoic provenance see Cic., *De divin.* I 120 (*SVF* II 1213): "... efficit in avibus divina mens ut tum huc tum illuc volent alites ... . Nam si animal omne *ut vult* ita utitur *motu sui corporis*, prono, obliquo, supino, *membraque quocumque vult flectit*, contorquet, porrigit, contrahit, eaque ante efficit paene quam cogitat, quanto id deo est facilius, cuius numini parent omnia!" (my italics in both passages). Pierluigi Donini points out (*per litt.*) that the disappearance of the entrails at the moment of sacrifice adduced by the Stoics (*De div.* I 118 ff.) "è veramente molto simile al miracolo giudaico e cristiano (e come una violazione delle leggi di natura è trattata e contestata da Cic. nel libro II, 37)." Pease, note to *De nat. deor.* III 92 "nihil esse quod deus efficere non possit" excellently quotes Philo, *Opif. mu.* 46, πάντα γὰρ θεῷ δυνατά, and Matth 19:26 παρὰ δὲ θεῷ πάντα δυνατά. It is interesting to compare the utterance of the pneumatic divine principle of the Naassenes ap. Hipp., *Ref.* V 7.25, γίνομαι ὃ θέλω καὶ εἰμὶ ὃ εἰμί.

I shall say more about the volitional paradigm (moving a limb etc.) later in this paper; for the idea in a passage of Aristotle see *infra*, n. 56.

8. *De provid.* V 8, "semper paret, semel iussit."

110

given the constraints from which human action cannot free itself, may be able to accomplish what it sets out to do. However, what I have to admit —and where, accordingly, Dihle and others seem to be right—is that there is no evidence that those Greeks who thought, or at any rate wrote, about such matters, ever thought of the will as an autonomous function, or part, of the psyche, which does not depend on reason and which can be firmly distinguished from desire and the emotions. To put it differently, one may say that in Greek psychology, or philosophy of mind, there is no room for the idea of the will as an autonomous theme.

II

I now wish to proceed to my topic, that is to say to the contention that in the philosophy of mind of at least some Greek philosophers—and/or—scientists the idea of the will does play an important part. In my view, the question has up till now often been approached from the wrong side; I mean the side of what the Germans call *Wortphilologie*, a term I propose to translate "dictionary philology." Classical philologists and historians of ancient thought have taken our word "will" (or its equivalent in their own language) as their starting-point, they have looked for Greek equivalents of this term and of its relatives, as a rule have found quite a handful of such equivalents (nouns, adjectives, verbs),[9] and concluded that in Greek thought nothing corresponds to what they somewhat cavalierly call our idea of the will.

I do not wish to suggest that such equivalents from the world of the dictionaries are entirely irrelevant, and shall be using them from time to time. But I prefer to choose a different spring-board. There may be any number of complicated theories concerned with the will, but there is at any rate one association to be connected with the term which will be immediately obvious. It is used even by Augustine when he wants to illustrate his concept of the will. He tells us that, in the Garden of

9. ὄρεξις, ὁρμή, προαίρεσις, (ἐ)θέλω, βούλομαι, ἑκών, etc. In his useful book (Bourke 1964), pp. 5 ff., V. J. Bourke advocates this approach as well, although in practice he dodges the limitations imposed by it.

Eden, "sexual desire was controlled by the will, very much like the *movements of the hands and feet*" (my italics).[10] In that period of bliss, erections apparently were at one's beck and call.

That we are able to move our limbs and most of our muscles if we want to, that is to say that for example I do move or bend my finger if such is my will, is the intuitively obvious instance of an act of will and its instantaneous consequence. It is even hard to distinguish between cause and effect. To do something in a larger sense, such as to perform an action (evil or good) I want to perform or to make an object (ugly or beautiful) I want to make, or to persevere in pursuing a line of conduct I have committed myself to, is merely the result of an act, or rather a plurality, of acts of will in a sense which sometimes is very close to metaphor, the word "will" in such cases indeed being a mere word, a kind of dummy used to represent what may be a very complicated configuration of actions, intentions, motives, traits of character, outside influences and whatnot.

What I propose to do is to study the type of will involved in moving one's finger— a case of the exercising of will, needless to say, most of the time one fortunately is entirely unaware of. Reflecting on what this sort of will involves, one remembers that some people cannot move some of their limbs even if they want to, because something dreadful has happened to them. The will is there, or the intention is there, but there is no follow-up. They do not have the capacity, power, or strength, that is required to move a finger, or a leg. As a matter of fact, we habitually associate the notion of "power," or "strength," with that of "will," and (metaphorically) speak of will-power, of a strong will, of a strong-willed person, or even of a strong person *tout court*; others we call weak, because their conduct is characterized by what sometimes is called weakness of will. Will without capacity does not make much sense, and it is therefore not a coincidence

10. Dihle's paraphrase (1982, p. 128) and cf. *ibid.* n. 26 to p. 128; my italics. At *De civ. Dei* XIV xvi.28, Augustine speaks of "membra ... nutu voluntatis acta, non aestu libidinis incitata." Further material is to be found in Bourke's chapter "Will as Dynamic Power," (1964) p. 103 ff., who believes that this idea of the will begins with Augustine.

that Augustine—to return to him for a moment— speaks of "the will and *power* [voluntas et potentia] of God."[11] The God of Christianity is in a position to do whatever he wants because he is all-powerful.

Using the notion of "strength" as our lodestar, we may hope to find out something about certain aspects of the theory of the will in classical antiquity.

III

It is often said that man as depicted in the Homeric poems does not have a clear-cut *personal* identity; what we may call the psychic aspect of his *persona* is believed to be a set of autonomous entities. In Homer, however, one must distinguish between words denoting organs, or places, in the body and the same words as denoting aspects of psychic phenomena, and the fragmentation of the Homeric *persona* has been exaggerated.[12] The author of the Hippocratic treatise *Sacred Disease* (whom I would like to identify as Hippocrates) is in favour of the unity of

11. E.g. *Conf.* VII iv, where he is addressing God: "Nec cogeris invitus ad aliquid, quia voluntas tua non maior est quam potentia tua. Esset autem maior, si te ipso tu ipse maior esses: voluntas enim et potentia dei deus ipse est." On the divine will and power and the formula "omnis potentia naturalis est voluntas" in Victorinus see Benz 1932, pp. 79 ff. For Cicero in the *De fat.* on "potestas" and "voluntas" (which he connects with one another but still distinguishes) see infra, n. 20, n. 24. For a similar combination see Lucr. II 251-286 (but note that at 256-7 the required terminology has been introduced by emendation); cf. further *infra*, n. 25. In these passages both Cicero and Lucretius are concerned with the large problem of free will v. determinism; what they say is certainly relevant to the more microscopic topic of the present paper, but cannot be dealt with now.

12. See e.g. the classic view of Snell [3]1955, esp. p. 33, on ψυχή, θυμός, and νόος as "getrennte Organe" and on the fact that Homeric poetry "das Ganze der Seele ... eben nicht kennt." Cf. also Buffière 1956, pp. 256 ff., on Homeric views of psychic functions and on the attempts to find Plato's psychology in Homer. Jahn (1987) has demonstrated that in Homer the variations between θυμός, φρένες, ἦτορ, κῆρ and κραδίη as denotations of psychic phenomena (not organs) is dependent on metrical reasons and to be explained in the same way as the use in oral poetry of the *epitheta ornantia* pertaining to persons. We should further observe that in the epics the brain does not possess any function connected with thinking or the emotions, whereas the heart, the θυμός etc. do have such functions. Greek philosophers beginning with Plato tried to read back their own psychology into the epics.

Jaap Mansfeld

the person. He firmly argues that the brain is the source of our
pleasures, sorrows and fears, that we think and make judgements with it, and that it is the organ affected with certain dis-
eases of the mind (ch. xvii). He adds (ch. xx) that it provides
understanding (σύνεσις), and that those who argue that the
heart is the organ with which we think and feel pain and anxiety
are wrong; he actually calls it the cause (αἴτιος) of distress and
its physiological symptoms, such as shivering, of joy and of
thought (φρόνησις).[13] He therefore is acquainted with a view
which is in favour of a unified psychic *persona* with the heart as
its centre which he rejects, and to which he opposes his own
view of the unified psychic *persona* with the brain as its centre.
It would seem that he makes a distinction (though not in technical language) between reasoning on the one hand and the emotions on the other.

The philosophers Plato and Aristotle—about whom I shall say
as little as possible—distinguished different parts, or at least
functions, of the one human psyche. The main division argued
by them is that between reason on the one hand and what is
irrational, or not rational, or emotional, on the other: desire,
rage, the affections in general. To mention only some of his
major works Plato, in the *Republic* (which is mainly concerned
with ethics) and in the *Timaeus* (which is mainly concerned with
physics) contends that we have to distinguish three parts of the
soul, each of which has its own location in the body: reason in
the head or brain, anger (or the spirited part) in the heart, and
desire and the rest somewhere below our waist-line. This
Platonic fragmentation of the one psyche is to some extent coun-
tered by Aristotle, who even says that it does not matter
whether one speaks of parts or of functions (*De iuventute*
467b17) and who firmly puts everything in one place, that is to
say in the heart (and not, as the author of *Sacred Disease* had

13. See e.g. Penfield 1958, p. 3: "This [scil., the role attributed to the brain] was
a great step forward in the fifth century before Christ, and one that was forgotten or ignored by the philosophers and physicians who followed him [scil., the
author of *Sacred Disease*]." I have argued that the author is Hippocrates in
Mansfeld 1980. For Galen's attitude towards this treatise see below, text to n. 34,
n. 35, n. 36.

114

argued, in the brain), but still distinguishes between at least two major groups of psychic functions.

Such a dualist view of the psyche, or the psychic functions, was rejected by the majority of the Stoics.[14] They still made a distinction between reason and the four main kinds of primary emotions, or affections, or passions (the *pathe*: distress, fear, pleasure, and desire), all five of which may determine our attitudes and/or actions, but they argued that there exists only a single psychic part or faculty embracing, in a way, both reason and the passions, the so-called dominating part (ἡγεμονικόν), that is to say reason, or the mind, and that the various affections are merely cases of reason gone wrong in various ways; in Seneca's words, reason and the affections have no "separatas sedes ..., sed affectus et ratio in melius peiusque mutatio animi est" (*De ira* I 8.3).

From the physical point of view, the soul is said by Chrysippus and his followers to consist of a kind of warm vapour, called *pneuma*.[15] This *pneuma* always possesses what they call *tonos*, that is to say tension: a sort of strength.[16] But psychic tension may be present in a variety of ways. The pneumatic soul of the person who is not dominated by one of the affections is characterized by what is called "good tension" (εὐτονία), which pre-

---

14. On the Stoic notion of the will see Bonhoeffer 1890, pp. 232 ff., who in a chapter devoted to "Der Wille" discusses ὄρεξις, ὁρμή, ἐπιβολή, πρόθεσις, παρασκευή, προαίρεσις. See further Voelke 1973, esp. pp. 30 ff., 56 ff., with whom to some extent I find myself in agreement. See also Inwood 1985, pp. 53, 96-7. For the Stoic theory of the passions see e.g. Bonhoeffer 1890, pp. 261 ff.; Long and Sedley 1987, Vol. I, pp. 410 ff., Vol. II, pp. 404 ff., where a number of relevant texts have been collected, translated, and explained; and Vegetti 1989, pp. 225 ff.

15. This is also the view of Posidonius according to Diog. Laërt. VII 157 = Pos. F 139 E.-K. (cf. also *infra*, n. 78). Bourke 1964, p. 104, writes: "The Stoics thought of the *pneuma* (vital spirit) as the efficient cause of organic functions and movements; this is especially so in the case of Chrysippus. However, there is no effort to identify the *pneuma* with will." It will become clear that I believe the view expressed in the second sentence to be mistaken.

16. See e.g. Hahm 1977, pp. 171 ff., who quotes numerous passages; Long and Sedley 1987, Vol. I, pp. 282 f., 288; and *infra*, n. 18 and n. 19. For the double, i.e. inwards and outwards, "tensile movement" constitutive of each thing see e.g. Nemes., *De nat. hom.* 2, p. 18.5 ff. Morani (*SVF* II 451, L.-S. 47J), but I know of no evidence proving that the term τονικὴ κίνησις goes back to Chrysippus.

sumably implies that it has the right sort of quality (produced by outward tension) and unity (produced by inward tension). But the soul of someone in a passionate state, e.g. distress, has the wrong sort of tension. In a somewhat neglected passage in Diogenes Laërtius' faithful account of Stoic philosophy,[17] we read that the affections are caused by physical transformations (τροπαί) in the pneuma. The technical term for this kind of change, *trope* or "turning," is familiar from Zeno's and Chrysippus' accounts of elemental change:[18] fire turns into air, air into water, water into earth, and conversely. The affections are often explained as a kind of contracting (as in fear) or dilating (as in desire), and these changes are easily understood as tensile. Elemental change too may be described in terms of contraction and dilation. Consequently, what happens on the macrocosmic scale also occurs—though to a less drastic extent, because the *pneuma* remains *pneuma*—in the microcosm of the psyche. The *hegemonikon*, when making a weak or wrong judgement, i.e. when perverting itself, weakens its good tension and so turns into a condition characterized by a different degree of tension, for instance a condition of distress. What we should

17. Diog. Laërt. VII 158, αἰτίας δὲ τῶν παθῶν ἀπολείπουσι τὰς περὶ τὸ πνεῦμα [scil., τοῦ ἡγεμονικοῦ] τροπάς. Von Arnim failed to include this crucial sentence in the chapter "De affectibus" in SVF III (we have to make do with the not wholly clear snippet from Clement printed at SVF III 433), and only printed it as part of SVF II 766. Sen., *De ir.* I 8.3, speaks of "mutatio." Marc. Aur. XI 19, p. 228.9-10 Farquharson says τέσσαρας μάλιστα τροπὰς τοῦ ἡγεμονικοῦ παραφυλακτέον διηνεκῶς. Why precisely four? Exactly. Cf. also ps.Plut., *De libid.* (Fr. Tyrwh. 1), ch. 1, the soul changing shape (ψυχὴν ... μετασχηματιζομένην) under the influence of the passions which make it expand or contract. At Diog. Laërt. VII 158, we should either read αἰτίας (adjective) or, preferably, emend to αἴτια, i.e. physical causes. As to τροπὴ in this context see also Plut., *De virt. mor.* 446 F (SVF III 459, p. 111.27-29; L.-S. 65G; cf. also Pohlenz 1965, pp. 12 f.): ἔνιοι δέ φασιν οὐχ ἕτερον εἶναι τοῦ λόγου τὸ πάθος οὐδὲ δυοῖν διαφορὰν καὶ στάσιν, ἀλλὰ ἑνὸς λόγου τροπὴν ἐπ᾽ ἀμφότερα, λανθάνουσαν ἡμᾶς ὀξύτητι καὶ τάχει μεταβολῆς. For τροπή Long and Sedley 1987 *ad loc.* refer to another passage in the same work. It is clear that Plutarch simplifies matters; the two parties he talks about are reason on the one hand and the set of the four affections on the other.

18. See e.g. the reports *ap.* Ar. Did. Fr. 38 Diels (= Heracl. Fr. 53 (c1) Marcovich) at SVF I 102, p. 28.17 and *ap.* Ar. Did. Fr. 21 (= Heracl. Fr. 53 (c2) M.) at SVF II 413, p. 137.4. One must assume the term was taken over from Heraclitus, see *Vorsokr.* 22 B 31 = Fr. 53a M., πυρὸς τροπαί· πρῶτον θάλασσα κτλ.

The Idea of the Will in Chrysippus, Posidonius, and Galen

note is that the condition of good, that is to say rational, tension of the soul, or of its ruling part, is said to be one of *strength*, and the condition characterized by one of the four main affections one of *weakness*.[19] Strength seems to be correct, or right, reason considered from a particular angle, that is to say in relation to choosing-deciding-acting. In a passage from book IV of his treatise *On the Affections*,[20] Chrysippus explicitly draws a parallel between physical strength, that is to say the *power* we have to

19. See e.g. the verbatim fragment from Chrysippus *On the Affections* (hereafter *Aff.*) bk. IV, the so-called *Therapeutikon*, ap. Gal., *De placitis Hippocratis et Platonis* (hereafter *PHP*) V 2.26-27, p. 300.2-12 De Lacy (cf. *SVF* III 471): καθάπερ γὰρ ἐπὶ τοῦ σώματος θεωρεῖται ἰσχύς τε καὶ ἀσθένεια, εὐτονία καὶ ἀτονία ..., κατὰ τὸν αὑτὸν ... τρόπον ἀνάλογόν τινα πᾶσι τούτοις καὶ ἐν ψυχῇ λογικῇ συνίσταταί τε καὶ ὀνομάζεται, [...] ὡς οἴομαι, ἀπὸ τῆς τοιαύτης ἀναλογίας τε καὶ ὁμοιότητος καὶ τῆς ἐν αὐτοῖς συνωνυμίας γεγενημένης· καὶ γὰρ καὶ κατὰ ψυχήν τινας λέγομεν ἰσχύειν καὶ ἀσθενεῖν καὶ εὐτόνους καὶ ἀτόνους εἶναι .... , οὕτω πως καὶ τοῦ πάθους ... λεγομένου κτλ. Cf. also Ar. Did. *ap.* Stob. II, *Ecl. eth.* pp. 62.24-63.1 Wachsmuth (cf. *SVF* III 278), a passage which seems to echo Chrys. *Aff.* IV, ... ὥσπερ ἰσχὺς τοῦ σώματος τόνος ἐστὶν ἱκανὸς ἐν νεύροις [the "sinews" one needs in order to move a limb], οὕτω καὶ ἡ τῆς ψυχῆς ἰσχὺς τόνος ἐστὶν ἱκανὸς ἐν τῷ κρίνειν καὶ πράττειν ἢ μή (my italics). In the same section Arius Didymus tells us that the ἰσχὺς of the soul is a δύναμις which comes about through the exercise of virtue (p. 62.17 ff.).

20. Verbatim *ap.* Gal., *PHP* IV 6.5-6 (*SVF* III 473; my italics): ἔτι δὲ καὶ κατὰ τοῦτ' ἴσως (ὡς) οἱ ἐπὶ τοῦ σώματος λέγονται τόνοι ἄτονοι καὶ εὔτονοι εἶναι κατὰ τὸ νευρῶδες τῷ δύνασθαι ἡμᾶς ἢ ἀδυνατεῖν ἐν τοῖς διὰ τούτων ἐπιτελουμένοις ἔργοις, καὶ ὁ ἐν τῇ ψυχῇ λέγεται τόνος ὡς εὐτονία καὶ ἀτονία. [...] ὥσπερ γὰρ ἐν δρόμῳ καὶ ἀνθέξει τινὸς καὶ τοῖς παραπλησίοις ἤδη, ἃ διὰ τῶν νεύρων ["sinews"] ἐνεργεῖται, ἔστι τις ἐπιτελεστικὴ κατάστασις καὶ ἐνδοτική, τῶν νεύρων προεκλελυμένων καὶ ἀνειμένων, ἀναλόγως καὶ ἐπὶ ψυχῆς ἐστι τοιοῦτον νευρῶδες, καθὸ καὶ κατὰ μεταφορὰν ἀνεύρους τινὰς λέγομεν καὶ νεῦρα ἔχειν. On this passage see Manuli 1988, pp. 211 f. For the idea of force or strength as connected with the regent part see also the verbatim fragment from bk. I of Chrysippus' *On the Soul* (hereafter *De an.*) quoted by Gal., *PHP* III 5.28, p. 206.15-18 (= *SVF* II 896), τούτοις πᾶσι συμφώνως καὶ τοὔνομα τοῦτ' ἔσχηκεν ἡ καρδία κατά τινα κράτησιν καὶ κυρείαν ἀπὸ τοῦ ἐν αὐτῇ εἶναι τὸ κυριεῦον καὶ κρατοῦν τῆς ψυχῆς μέρος, ὡς ἂν κρατία λεγομένη. Cf. also *infra*, n. 24. Prof Kidd (*per litt.*) reminds me that Plat., *Rep.* III 411b, speaks of the θυμὸς cut out ὥσπερ νεῦρα ἐκ τῆς ψυχῆς (this passage is adduced by Plut., *De virt. mor.* 449E and alluded to at *De coh. ir.* 457B-C), and refers to Philod., *De ir.* cols. xxxi.24 ff. and xxxiii.25 ff. In the first of these passages, Philodemus' opponents are identified as Peripatetics, while Plut., *De coh. ir., loc. cit.*, does not identify those who held this view; see Pohlenz 1896, pp. 331 f., and cf. Indelli 1988, p. 210. Vegetti 1990, pp. 11 ff., who also discusses the passages in Plato (adding *Laws* I 664e) and Philodemus, argues in a most interesting way that the metaphorical use of *neuron* in Chrysippus and Plato derives from the meaning "bow-string" (a meaning, by the way, which "nervus" has in Latin), that the

move, or to hold fast to something because our sinews are strong and not limp or slack, and strength of soul: in the soul, too, there must be something that is tendon-like, or "sinewy" (νευρῶδες). A really strong *hegemonikon*, viz. one never making a weak, i.e. wrong, judgement is affection-proof.[21] This sinewy something in the soul, with reference to which Chrysippus says we call strong *personalities* "sinewy," is rather close to what we would call a strong will. We may observe that Chrysippus makes no bones about the fact that he avails himself of a metaphor.

When looking at these conditions and events from the psychological side we should point out that, according to the Stoic theory, action, or a change of temper, is preceded and instigated by a movement, or change (κίνησις), of the soul, viz. impulse, or "conation." "Conation" is De Lacy's convenient translation of *horme*; the latter is also described by the Stoics as *logos parataktikos*, i.e. reason which gives the command to act. This follows upon a presentation (φαντασία) in the soul, and an action or change of temper occurs in accordance with a conation. Actions performed when reason has gone wrong and "anger"—my conventional translation of *thymos*—or one of the other affections

---

metaphorical use of *tonos* in Chrysippus derives from the meaning "spring," and that what matters is their combination: " ... è nella costruzione delle catapulte che si erano prodotte la saldatura fra *neura* (corde elastiche formate da tendini) e *tonoi* (molle a torsione costruite da matasse di tali cordi" (*ibid.*, 13). Another metaphor is at issue as well, viz. that of the puppet moved by its strings; cf. Plat., *Nom.* I 644e2, ταῦτα τὰ πάθη ἐν ἡμῖν οἷον νεῦρα ἢ σμήρινθοί τινες σπῶσίν ... ἡμᾶς κτλ., Arist., *De mot. animal.* 7.701b2 ff., Marc. Aurel. X 38, In fact, the metaphorical use of *neura* is older even than Plato (cf. Aristoph., *Ran.* 862, τάπη, τὰ μέλη, τὰ νεῦρα τῆς τραγῳδίας, cited Liddell and Scott s.v. νεῦρον, 2), and Chrysippus *expressis verbis* refers to popular parlance. Also compare the little speech of Wealth in the abstract from Crantor at Sext., *M.* XI 53, ἐν δὲ πολέμοις νεῦρα τῶν πράξεων γίνομαι. For *tonos* see also supra, n. 16. The Academic critic (Carneades) *ap.* Cic., *De fat.* 9 and 23-5 (texts in which the terms "voluntas," "potestas" and "motus voluntarius" are linked together, cf. *supra*, n. 11) seems to ignore Chrysippus finer physiological and psychological points.

21. Cf. Posidonius' point against Chrysippus according to Galen's paraphrase at *PHP* V 2.5, p. 296.3-4 (= Pos. F 163.15-16 E.-K.; cf. L.-S. 65R): ἀπαθῆ μὲν γὰρ γίγνεσθαι ψυχὴν τὴν τοῦ σοφοῦ δηλονότι. Obviously, Posidonius uses a Chrysippean tenet against his opponent.

holds sway are said to be caused by an excess of (a particular) *horme*. Clearly, such a horme is called excessive because the condition of the psyche of which it is a movement is excessive in the sense that reason has converted itself into a different state and so no longer holds sway *qua* reason but exists in the form of a passionate soul (see the illuminating account of Seneca, *De ira* I 7.1-8.3), with rudiments of right reason in a minority position.

Chrysippus illustrates this state of affairs by means of his famous simile[22] of the walking as compared to the running man, that is to say by using volition pertaining to physical motion as a *tertium comparationis*. The man who walks represents the person whose psyche is in a state of good tension, that is to say someone whose actions are controlled by reason, someone whose soul produces a series of *hormai* that are according to reason. The running man represents the person carried away by anger or any other of the affections. When someone walks in accordance with a *horme*, the motion of his legs is not excessive, "so that he can stop whenever he wants (to stop)."[23] The verb used by Chrysippus for "he wants," ἐθέλει, belongs to the family of words from the dictionary connected with the idea of the will (we shall see that he also uses βούλομαι). It is clear that the *horme* which leads to walking is what we would call an act of will, and that the counter-order or counter-*horme* to stop walking likewise is an obvious instance of volition. The running man, however, is not able to stop whenever he wishes, even if he wants to do so. The movement of his legs "is excessive (and) opposed to the *horme*,"[24] that is to say is stronger than the wish,

22. Verbatim quotation from *Aff.* bk. I at Gal., *PHP* IV 2.14-18; printed at *SVF* III 462 (cf. L.-S. 65J); for its continuation see *infra*, n. 24. The first quotations in n. 23 and 24 are from this fragment.

23. ὥστε καὶ στῆναι, ὅταν ἐθέλῃ. Cf. the expressions used by Galen in his attempted refutation: e.g. p. 244.13-14, εἰ στῆναι βούλοιντο, 244.28-9, στῆναι βουληθέντες, 244.38 οὐκέθ᾽ ἡ βούλησις ἱκανή, and especially 244.32, where he points out that someone running while drawing the weight of his body backward "has full control over stopping" (αὐτοκράτωρ ἐστὶ τοῦ στῆναι; the rather strong term αὐτοκράτωρ only occurs here in the *PHP*). At p. 246.7-8 Galen says that if a conation is caused by reason alone "it can be stopped and aroused again by a mere act of will" (διὰ μόνου τοῦ βουληθῆναι; De Lacy's transl.). Cf. also *infra*, n. 26, n. 31, for Chrysippus' use of βούλομαι.

119

or will, to stop at once (the *horme* to run of course no longer is at issue the moment one wants to stop). In the same way, Chrysippus says, the irrational *horme* itself, for instance the *horme* to be depressed or to act in anger, is opposed to reason (λόγος); an angry person, or a person deeply in love, is not obedient to reason, just as the legs of a running man do not instantaneously obey the command to stop running. We may conclude that the *horme*, or the will to act, is a permanent feature of the pneumatic ruling part of the soul as a whole,[25] which is

24. πλεονάζει παρὰ τὴν ὁρμήν (cf. Sen., *De ir.* I 7.4, "quarundam rerum initia in nostra potestate sunt, ulteriora nos vi sua rapiunt nec regressum relinquunt"). See also the verbatim quotation from *Aff.* bk. I–the sequel to the passage about the walking and the running man—at *PHP* IV 4.24-25 + 30 (*SVF* III 476; for the idea of strength involved here cf. *SVF* II 896, quoted supra, n. 20), where he says that "such conditions are out of control (ἀκρατεῖς), as if the men had no power over themselves (οὐ κρατούντων ἑαυτῶν), just as those who use their tension for running are carried along because they have no control (οὐ κρατοῦντες) over a movement of this kind. But those who are moving according to reason (κατὰ τὸν λόγον) ..., control (κρατοῦσιν) their motions and the conations pertaining to them ..." (transl. De Lacy, modified; I believe that p. 256.11 κρατοῦσιν is continued at 256.29 ff.). One may assume that the moral agent to be compared to a man walking possesses the virtue ἐγκράτεια, a sub-species of the primary virtue σωφροσύνη according to e.g. Ar. Did. *ap.* Stob. II, *Ecl. eth.* p. 60.21 (*SVF* III 264, p. 64.22-23); defined *ibid.*, p. 61.11-12 (*SVF* III, p. 64.34-35): ἐγκράτειαν δὲ ἐπιστήμην ἀνυπέρβατον τῶν κατὰ τὸν ὀρθὸν λόγον φανέντων. According to a verbatim fragment of Chrysippus quoted by Plut., *De Stoic. rep.* 1041A-B (*SVF* III 297), he said that what is done in accordance with ἐγκράτεια is a κατόρθωμα. For Cleanthes' definition of ἐγκράτεια, involving the τόνος, ἰσχὺς and κράτος of the soul see Plut., *op. cit.* 1034D (*SVF* I 563).

The Epicurean account of the relation between "innata potestas" and "voluntas" resulting in voluntary motion (Lucr. II 251-86, cf. *supra*, n. 11), though at first glance similar to Chrysippus', is far less satisfactory from a physiological and psychological point of view. Carneades *ap.* Cic., *De fat.* 23, moreover points out that the argument would have been better if it had been confined to "quendam animi motum voluntarium" and had made no appeal to the swerve. The account of volition at Lucr. III 136 ff. (L.-S. 14B) likewise is less satisfactory than Chrysippus', but this passage at least says something about the force (*vis*, 159) of the corporeal *animus* which communicates itself to the contiguous and equally corporeal *anima* which, being diffused throughout the body, is capable of setting this in motion (for the mechanics involved see Lucr. IV 877 ff., = L.-S. 14E).

25. Cf. Long and Sedley 1987, Vol. II, p. 420: "volition is a natural and necessary function of reason"; Inwood 1985, p. 53: "An impulse [*horme*] is little more than an "intention," "act of will," "decision" or *Entschluss*, because of its role as the cause of an action."

operational not only when the soul is wholly rational but also when it has turned its coat and, having made the wrong sort of judgement, has given in to its own passion, passion itself indeed *being* this wrong judgement. The mechanism relative to action or feeling remains the same, but the physical condition of the soul has changed; from being calm, rational, and well-tuned it has for instance turned to being afraid, which in physical terms means that the *pneuma* has contracted and cooled (has become chilled with fear, so to speak).

Another interesting example of an affection provided by Chrysippus—a sub-species of the primary affection distress this time—which outruns the command of reason is to be found in his comment, in *Aff.* book II, about people who "weep against their will,"[26] that is to say who cannot stop weeping even if they want to; he adds that it is hard, perhaps even precluded, in cases such as these to indicate precisely why stopping is impossible. I assume that one of his motives is that existing causes may remain hidden to human knowledge (cf. *SVF* II 973).

<h3 style="text-align:center">IV</h3>

According to our evidence as preserved by Galen, to whose for many reasons invaluable treatise *On the Doctrines of Hippocrates and Plato* we also owe the Chrysippean passages I have cited so far, it is precisely here that Posidonius' critique of Chrysippus' psychology and *Psychopathologie des Alltagslebens* finds something important to get hold of.[27] Posidonius, to some extent a heterodox Stoic and presumably a less interesting philosopher than Chrysippus, had a reputation for always wanting to know "why?" This time, he very much wants to establish a causal explanation for all forms of irrational human behaviour, and he contends that Chrysippus' monistic psychology fails to provide

26. Verbatim *ap.* Gal., *PHP* IV 7.16, p. 284.12 (*SVF* III 466; cf. L.-S. 650), μὴ βουλόμενοι κλαίειν κλαίουσι (my italics). I quote De Lacy's transl.; a literal translation would be "although they do not want to whine, they whine." It should be noted that κλαῦσις is a sub-species of the primary affection λύπη according to ps.Andron., Περὶ παθῶν p. 227.59 Glibert-Thirry = *SVF* III 414, p. 100.41 (κλαῦσις δὲ δάκρυσις λυπουμένου νεύοντος ἐπὶ τὸ χεῖρον).

27. I know that Galen also quotes other Posidonian arguments against Chrysippus. See further below.

this.[28] Posidonius argues that we must distinguish between different psychic functions (not parts) that exist independently of one another, but which are all in one and the same place, that is to say in the heart.[29] In other words, what in his view we have to accept is that the affections are not, *pace* Chrysippus, modified, or perverted, forms of reason, or transformations of the one psychic *pneuma*, but manifestations of psychic functions that are different from reason. In a way, this amounts to a return to the psychology of Plato, as Galen—who is able to adduce explicit statements of Posidonius in praise of Plato's tripartite psychology—never tires of pointing out. Anger and desire according to Posidonius are kinds of animals, or children, within ourselves that have to be soothed or even let loose for a while because, being irrational, they are impervious to argument. In this context, the idea of the will plays an important part. Criticizing Chrysippus' failure to provide a causal explanation for the fact that some people weep against their will, Posidonius[30] asks for the reason why "most people often weep although they *do not want to* (μὴ βουλόμενοι) because they *lack the force* (μὴ δυνάμενοι) to check their tears, whereas in others, who want (βουλόμενοι) to go on crying, the tears stop all of a sudden. Obviously (Posidonius continues), this occurs because the pressure of the affective motions is so hard that they cannot be controlled by *their will* (ὡς μὴ κρατεῖσθαι πρὸ⟨ς⟩ τῆς βουλήσεως), or because

28. For what follows compare Walzer 1962b, pp. 148 ff., who emphasizes Posidonius' influence on the *De morib.*, and Kidd 1971, pp. 200 ff.

29. E.g. F 146 E.-K. *ap.* Gal., *PHP* VI 2.5. The question whether one may speak of parts or functions continued to be much debated; see e.g. the interesting discussion in ps.Plut., *Utrum pars an facultas animi affectibus subiecta sit* (Fr. Tyrhw. 2), and Porphyry, *De animae facultatibus, ap.* Stob., *Eclog. phys.* I 49.25a, pp. 350.8 ff. Wachsmuth. On Posidonius' reception of Plato's psychology Jaeger 1914, pp. 62 ff., is still worth reading; see also Vander Waerdt 1985 and De Lacy 1988, pp. 51 ff. For the spirited part as an animal that has to be soothed cf. also Galen's own view (clearly dependent on Posidonius') at *De affect. dignot.* 5, p. 20.12-4 Marquardt 1884-1893, vol I, but note that *ibid.* 4, p. 15.15-16 he says χρὴ παιδαγωγῆσαι τὸ ἐν ἡμῖν θυμοειδὲς τῷ λόγῳ κτλ. (as a matter of fact, Galen's argument in this treatise is the traditional one that one may become a morally good person by overcoming the passions in a rational way, viz. by heeding the advice of one's betters).

30. Part verbatim, part paraphrase *ap.* Gal., *PHP* IV 7.36-39 (cf. *SVF* III 467) = Pos. F 165.151-172 E.-K. I have modified De Lacy's transl.; italics are mine.

they have petered out to such an extent that they can no longer be aroused by *their will.*" Posidonius then argues that this proves the existence of a *conflict* between reason and the affections and so the existence of opposed functions of the soul[31]—in fact, of the three functions Plato had called parts, that is to say of (1) reason, (2) anger, and (3) desire. And we may note that

31. For this notion of conflict (already at Plat., *Rep.* IV 439e ff., where however the battle of anger, or perhaps rather indignation, against desire is at issue; the passage is quoted and discussed piecemeal by Gal., *PHP* V 7.44 ff.) cf. e.g. the standard Middle Platonist account at Alcin., *Didasc.* ch. 24 (the chapter devoted to the tripartite soul), pp. 176.37-177.14 Hermann, on the struggle between reason and each of the other parts (cf. Dillon 1977, pp. 290 f., who however in my view should have avoided saying that the poetic quotations in Alcinous which were already used by Chrysippus "flatly contradict his [scil., Chrysippus'] theory of the soul"). For the evidence in Plut., *De virt. mor.*, see Babut 1969, pp. 60 f. For the evidence in Philo see Runia 1986, pp. 301 ff. Pierluigi Donini points out (*per litt.*) that the conflict of psychic functions is also found in Alexander of Aphrodisias, e.g. *De an.* p. 27.6, and *De an. mant.* pp. 118.5 ff.

Although Alcinous posits that each of the parts must κατὰ λόγον be in a different place, his psychology is very close to Posidonius'; indeed, because he does stick to the three locations of the Platonic parts it is virtually indistinguishable from Galen's (for the two different views of the νεῦρα found in *Didasc.* ch. 17 see however *infra*, n. 78). Galen's relation to Middle Platonism is still largely unexplored (a paper dealing with this topic by P. L. Donini is forthcoming in *ANRW*), one of the obstacles being the fact that he studied Plato for himself and quotes him extensively; for the latter aspect of Galen's relation to Plato see De Lacy 1972 and De Lacy 1988, pp. 43 ff. For the trilocation in Alcinous and Galen see Whittaker 1990, p.127 n. 378.

From the passage quoted in the text it would appear that *boulesis* even according to Posidonius is a function of the rational part of the soul, because it is after all an irrational part that in his example is vainly told to stop or may be ordered to keep going. Desire, one of the primary affections, is defined by Chrysippus *ap.* Gal., *PHP* IV 1.3 (cf. *SVF* III 463, p. 115.35; context: quotations of definitions from the beginning of bk. I of *Aff.*) as ἄλογος ὄρεξις. We need not doubt that the definition of *boulesis*, one of the three primary *eupatheiai*, as εὔλογος ὄρεξις (Diog. Laërt. VII 116 ~ *SVF* III 431, p. 105.20, cf. Long and Sedley 1987, 65F; ps.Andron., *op. cit.* p. 235.21 ~ *SVF* III 432, p. 105.27) derives from Chrysippus too. According to the stricter form of the theory, only the Wise Man has it, cf. Cic., *Tusc.* IV 12 (*SVF* III 438, p. 107.1-4; for the relation of *Tusc.* IV 11-32 to Chrysippus Περὶ παθῶν see Fillion-Lahille 1984, pp. 82 ff.): "... cum constanter prudenterque fit, eiusmodi appetitionem [scil., *horme*] Stoici βούλησιν appellant, nos appellemus voluntatem. Eam illi putant *in solo esse sapiente*, quam sic definiunt: voluntas est, quae quid cum ratione desiderat" (my italics). But we have noticed that Chrysippus, just as Posidonius, uses the verb βούλομαι in relation to ordinary people too (*supra*, n. 26). For *boulesis* as will in an anti-Stoic argument of

123

Jaap Mansfeld

Posidonius (just as Chrysippus) links the concept of will with that of power, or strength.

To argue in favour of a tripartite psychology the way Plato did is a quite complicated affair; to defend a revised form of this tripartite psychology against a quite successful, utterly sophisticated and very influential monistic theory about the soul, as Posidonius did, is an even more difficult undertaking. Galen, who about three centuries later in the *PHP* defends the Platonic position (which he also attributes to Hippocrates), gratefully uses Posidonius against Chrysippus, but does so in a rather devious way. What apparently matters to him most is that two major Stoics disagree among themselves and not what Posidonius really may have been up to, for such a disagreement (διαφωνία) proves that even from a Stoic point of view the issue is in a way still undecided. Galen is for instance rather coy about the fact that Posidonius did not assign different locations in the body to the different functions of the soul,[32] and he only quotes him extensively where what he says fits his own Platonizing argument in that it helps to undermine the

Plutarch concerned with moving one's limbs and the will and power of the supreme divinity see Plut., *De comm. not.* ch. 33, 1076D-F (partly printed at *SVF* II 937, 3rd text). It is not certain whether Chrysippus spoke of τὴν τοῦ Διὸς βούλησιν because Plutarch does not quote verbatim. I note in passing that the term for "voluntary movements" used by Chrysippus' pupil Diogenes of Babylon, in a fragment quoted verbatim *ap.* Gal., *PHP* II 8.44, p. 166.1 (*SVF* III Diog. Bab. 30, p. 216.21), is κατὰ προαίρεσιν κινήσεις, although according to the stricter formulation of the theory (see Adler *s. vv.* αἵρεσις and προαίρεσις rather than Inwood 1985, pp. 240 ff.) *prohairesis* belongs with *boulesis*; much later, Epictetus calls the δύναμις which opens and closes the eyes etc. προαιρετικὴ (*Diatr.* II 23.8 ff.). Though it is sometimes doubted that Chrysippus introduced the *eupatheiai*, the doctrine is attested for *Aff.* by Gal., *PHP* IV 4.8, p. 252.12-15 (*SVF* III 440; von Arnim oddly fails to print this in the appropriate place): Chrysippus stipulated that a sharp distinction be made between αἰσχύνεσθαι and αἰδεῖσθαι and between ἥδεσθαι and χαίρειν. (For Galen's not unparalleled impatience with such fine distinctions [cf. Plut., *De virt. mor.* 449A-B; *De vit. pud.* 529D, ἡμῖν χρῆσθαι τοῖς ὀνόμασιν ἀσυκοφαντήτως δότωσαν (scil., οἱ Στωικοί)] see *infra*, text to n. 56, and n. 61. Now αἰσχύνη is a sub-species of the primary affection φόβος (cf. e.g. ps. Andron., *op. cit.*, p. 229.61 = *SVF* III 409, p. 99.1), as αἰδὼς is a sub-species of the primary *eupatheia* εὐλάβεια (cf. e.g. ps.Andron., *op. cit.*, p. 237.38 = *SVF* III 432, p. 105.29), whereas ἡδονὴ is of course a primary passion, just as χαρὰ is a primary *eupatheia*.

32. Cf. *supra*, n. 28 and text thereto.

Chrysippean position, and to the extent that it agrees with what according to him is Plato's main point: three irreducibly different parts of the soul in three different places. What is most remarkable indeed is that Galen, to whom we owe substantial quotations of Chrysippus' treatise *On the Soul*, never refers to Posidonius' *On the Soul*, a treatise which must have contained at least three books.[33]

This attitude finds a noteworthy counterpart in Galen's treatment of *Sacred Disease*. In the introduction of Erotian's little dictionary of Hippocratic terms published in the first century CE, the treatise is listed among the genuine works.[34] In the enormous mass of surviving writings by Galen, there are only three references to it, all without an author's name; according to a scholium at the beginning of the text of *Sacred Disease* in an important manuscript, Galen said that though important it was not genuine on account of its different style and lack of Hippocratic acumen.[35] Other references collected by Grensemann show that the physician Herodotus (a somewhat later contemporary of Erotian) and Caelius Aurelianus, that is to say Soranus (ca. 100 CE), believed the treatise to be genuine.[36] Galen's view therefore seems to be a dissident one, and one surmizes that his reason for rejecting it and generally being rather reticent about it is the fact that its author, as we have noticed above, argues that the brain is the organ of both reason and the emotions and that his doctrine is in fact very much at odds with Galen's Platonizing tripartition and trilocation of the soul.

33. Pos. F 28a E.-K.; see further *infra*, n. 75. I note in passing that some among Galen's arguments against Chrysippus' psychological monism very much resemble those of Plut., *De virt. mor.*

34. Nachmanson 1918, p. 9.10.

35. *CMG* V 9, 2, p. 206.13 ff. Heeg, *CMG* V 10, 2 ,2, p. 348.19 ff. Wenkebach-Pfaff, and Gal. XVIIIA p. 356.6 ff. Kühn, conveniently accessible (together with the scholium from Marcianus Venetus 269 fol. 84 v) in Grensemann 1968, p. 48. Most remarkably, there is not a single reference in the *PHP*. One may assume that among other things Galen believed its anatomy to be unworthy of Hippocrates.

36. Grensemann 1968, pp. 48 f., 49 f.

Jaap Mansfeld

V

We had therefore better leave Posidonius for the moment and concentrate on what Galen himself has to say. For in Galen's own account we do not merely find arguments in favour of one view which is opposed to another *equally* arguable view, but something else as well, namely what he calls scientific proof for the theory that is correct. To put it somewhat crudely: according to Galen the venerable ancients, that is to say the greatest of all philosophers, Plato, and the greatest of all physicians, Hippocrates, had the right sort of insight about the human soul, so Posidonius has to be applauded because he took their side against the new-fangled psychological monism of his own school. But it is a different matter altogether to *prove* that Plato (and Hippocrates) were right, and so still are, and this is what Galen sets out to do.

Galen was not only famous as both a practising and an experimental physician, but he was also a person familiar with the history of medicine; he was not only quite good as a philosopher, but also someone familiar with the history of philosophy, and he was an accomplished dialectician to boot—as rare a combination then as it is now. He proves to his own satisfaction that Plato is right by firmly putting the question of the parts of the soul in a physiological and anatomical context and by performing a number of rather gruesome vivisections which he never tires of describing. He claims that this experimental method is an apodeictic method which should settle all disputes: "the evidence of dissection alone compels even those who hold the contrary view to acknowledge the truth against their will" (*PHP* VI 5.21). Furthermore, assuming the role of the dialectician, he skilfully grants his major opponent, Chrysippus, that those among the Stoic's arguments which prove anger, or the spirited part of the soul, to be in the chest or the heart are entirely right, for such arguments merely confirm what Plato said. The main thrust of Galen's inquiry is therefore concerned with the location of the ruling part of the soul, that is to say of reason, for if one can actually prove this to be in the head Chrysippus has been beaten, and one can no longer afford to speak, *more Chrysippeo*, of one and the same soul as at one time operating as a reasonable and at another as an angry entity. Here Galen the logician enters upon the stage, who constructs the first premise of a hypothetical syllogism which according to him is granted by all the parties in the dispute, philosophers as well as physicians, viz., the ruling part is located where the *nerves* have their beginning.[37] The contents of the second premise, viz. that concerned with the *place where* the nerves actually do have their beginning can only be determined by means of anatomical experiment, including vivisection. It is in this context that we come across Galen's views concerned with the will. What we shall see is that, notwithstanding the important differences that exist, he shares one assumption with Chrysippus, viz. that the will is very much a matter of strength.

The discovery of the nerves, and more specifically of the sensory and motor functions of the nerves, as is well-known, is the immortal accomplishment of the great Hellenistic physicians-and-anatomists Herophilus and Erasistratus in the third century BCE.[38] They both discovered that the nerves have their beginning near or in the brain (although they disagreed as to

---

37. E.g. *PHP* p. 66.19-20, ὅπου τῶν νεύρων ἡ ἀρχή, ἐνταῦθα καὶ τὸ τῆς ψυχῆς ἡγεμονικόν; cf. also *infra*, n. 75. A brief introduction to Galen is found in Donini 1982, pp. 124 ff. For brief accounts of the *pneuma*tology see Verbeke 1945, pp. 206 ff., and Temkin 1950; a short substantial overview of the psychology is in Moraux 1981, pp. 92 ff., and an account of the neurology in Souques 1936, pp. 191 ff.; Daremberg 1841, pp. 43 ff., is still useful. For the methodology von Müller 1897 is still indispensable; see also Frede 1987. On Galen's exegetical methods see the preliminary remarks of Manuli 1983. On the scope of the *PHP* compare Vegetti 1986. See also Manuli 1977. On Galen's public anatomical performances see Vegetti 1981, pp. 54-5. On the affections and the role of *thymos* as "dinamica psicologica" in the *PHP* and other Galenic works see Manuli 1988, pp. 185 ff. See now also Lloyd (1991), esp. pp. 409 ff. on Galen's interpretation of the psychology of Hippocrates and Plato in the *PHP* and elsewhere.

38. Solmsen 1968, pp. 569 ff., is still worth reading. The fragments of Erasistratus have been edited by Garofalo (1988) (difficult to consult but good to have); those of Herophilus in the splendid edition with commentary and essays by von Staden 1989 (on the nerves see von Staden 1989, pp. 159 f., 250 ff.); see also Vegetti 1990, from which moreover much may be learned about the connection between the nervous system, the soul, and the idea of strength.

127

which part of the brain is at issue), and according to the tradition they therefore put the regent part of the soul in the head.[39] Galen uses this discovery and further refines the theory and the experimental investigations that go along with it.

Aristotle had argued that in humans the heart is the centre of sense-perception and thought as well as the organ which commands bodily movements.[40] In order to prove that the heart has the indispensable physical leverage and force (ἰσχύς), he had argued that it has a large number of *neura* (νεῦρα)—a word which in Aristotle's time meant "tendons," "sinews," "strong fibres," and did not yet have the meaning "nerves" which it slowly acquired after Erasistratus and Herophilus. (Chrysippus and Posidonius still used it in the ancient sense). Galen quotes a passage attesting this view from the *On the Parts of Animals* which he says is unworthy of its author, and refutes him by a number of arguments, one of which turns on the distinction between nerves and sinews.[41] The fibres Aristotle calls *neura* are not nerves. And even if they were nerves, and even if there were a good many of these in the heart (*quod non*), Aristotle's point according to Galen still is beside the point, for what matters is the origin (ἀρχή) of the nerves. As a matter of fact, in the lost first part of book one of the *PHP* Galen had given a summary account of the anatomy of the nerves and demonstrated that some nerves issue from the brain, others from the spinal medul-

39. I am not now concerned with the details; see Mansfeld 1990, pp. 3092 ff.

40. For the heart as the source of the blood-vessels and as the centre of sense-perception and bodily movements see the chapters on the heart and its functions at *De part. an.* III 4 and *De iuv.* 3-4 and 14; cf. also *De sens.* 2.438b25 ff., and *De mot. an.* 8-9. The view that the brain is the centre of sense-perception is rejected at *De part. an.* II 10.656a17 ff.

41. *PA* III 4.666b14-16 at *PHP* I 8.3, p. 92.1-5, the only Aristotelian passage quoted verbatim in the *PHP*; for the various meanings of νεῦρα ("sinews," "nerves") see also *infra*, n. 78. It may seem odd that Galen does not quote from the *De mot. an.*, which deals rather extensively with the dominating role of the heart and with the connate *pneuma* as the physical counterpart of *orexis* providing strength (*ischus*) to the animal; see Nussbaum ²1985, pp. 143 ff., and the remarks of Vegetti 1990, p. 27 n. 13, on the *pneuma* in ch. 10. But in this work Aristotle does not mention the *neura* of the heart (although at 7.701b1-10 he compares the movements of puppets by means of ropes to that of animals by means of "*neura* and bones"). Cf. also *infra*, n. 56.

la, and that the spinal medulla itself grows from the brain.[42] In one of his more neglected works, the *On the Motion of the Muscles*,[43] Galen explains voluntary motion by telling us at length that the commands issued by the regent part of the soul in the brain are transmitted by the motor nerves which (in a physiologically rather complicated way) use the muscles as levers to move the limbs, and this is also his view in the *PHP*.[44] There is no perceptible interval in time between the will e.g. to bend one's finger or one's leg and the act itself.[45] We should add that Galen praises Aristotle for using two correct premises, "the first, that some *considerable strength* is needed for voluntary action, and the second, that the brain does not possess any such strength" (my italics).[46]

We should say something about the experiments and experiences Galen adduces in proof of the thesis that there is a chain of command and of strength stretching from the brain to the muscles. If one of the ventricles of the brain of an animal is wounded, or if pressure is applied to it, the animal "will immediately

42. See the collection of references at *PHP* p. 68 De Lacy. The monobiblos *De nervorum dissectione* has been preserved (II 831-856 K.; no modern edition). Cf. *infra*, n. 78.

43. *De motu musculorum* libri duo (IV 367-464 K.; no modern edition).

44. See e.g. I 10.11-17, where he refers inter alia to the treatise cited *supra*, n. 43. Vegetti 1990, p. 15, points out that Gal., *PHP* VII 4.1-3 argues that although the experiments concerned with the *pneuma* in the brain [for which see below] prove this to be instrumental in regard to sensation and bodily movement, it is not certain whether there is "some *pneuma* in each nerve." According to Galen, there are three possibilities: (1) there is a connate *pneuma* in the nerves that is struck by the *pneuma* which comes like a messenger from the centre of command; (2) there is no such *pneuma* in the nerves, but *pneuma* flows into them "from the brain at the moment that we wish to move a part of the body"; and (3)— a rather obscure suggestion—there is a "flow of power without material substance" by means of a "transmission of qualities to continuous bodies." *Ibid.*, VII 4.21, he states that he does not believe that there are passages (scil., for the *pneuma*) in all the nerves.

45. *PHP* II 5.36, p. 134.26-29, οὐδείς ἐστι χρόνος αἰσθητὸς ἐν τῷ μεταξὺ ... τοῦ βουληθῆναι κάμψαι τὸν ἄνθρωπον δάκτυλον ἢ τὸν πόδα καὶ αὐτῆς τῆς ἐνεργείας. For the idea of the instantaneous in a similar passage in Aristotle see *infra*, n. 56.

46. *PHP* I 9.7, p. 96.29 ff., ἓν μὲν ὡς ἰσχύος δεῖ τινος οὐκ ἀγεννοῦς εἰς τὰς κατὰ προαίρεσιν ἐνεργείας κτλ.

Jaap Mansfeld

lose motion and sense-perception, breath and voice";[47] Galen
tells us that he has often given public demonstrations of this
fact. He adds that if, during cranial surgery, you merely press
the brain too hard with the instrument you have inserted underneath the bones to protect the membranes of the brain from
damage, "the patient is rendered incapable of sense-perception
and of all voluntary movement."[48] Nothing of the sort occurs
when one manipulates the heart: "I once allowed someone,"
Galen continues, "to hold a heart with a smith's tongue, since it
jumped out of his fingers because of the violent palpitation; but
even then the animal suffered no impairment of sense-perception or voluntary movement. It uttered a loud scream, breathed
without hindrance, and kept all its limbs in violent motion."[49]
Two other experiments are perhaps even more interesting.[50]
Galen tells us that in his (lost) treatise *On the Causes of
Respiration* he described "all the muscles and the organs moved
by them and the motor nerves that transmit the "psychic
power" (δύναμιν τὴν ψυχικὴν)," and that in another treatise (also
lost), *On Voice*, he did the same for the organs of speech, the
muscles that move these organs, and the nerves that come down
to these muscles from the brain.[51] The proper organ of the voice
is the larynx, which contains a number of specialized muscles; if
you sever an animal's trachea below its larynx, it loses the
capacity to use its voice. If you happen to have a patient who
has been wounded in this way, you may request him to say
something, but he will not be able to do so, however much he
may *want to*[52] and however much he exerts the muscles of his
epigastrium, chest, and larynx. This of course is a perfect
instance of an act of will which remains without results. The

47. *PHP* I 6.5, p. 78.32-33, ἀκίνητόν τε καὶ ἀναίσθητον, ἄπνουν τε καὶ ἄφωνον
εὐθὺς ἔσται τὸ ζῷον. This point is often rehearsed in the *PHP*.

48. *PHP* I 6.6, p. 80.2-3, ἀναίσθητός τε καὶ ἀκίνητος ἁπασῶν τῶν καθ᾽ ὁρμὴν
κινήσεων ὁ ἄνθρωπος ἀποτελεῖται.

49. *PHP* I 6.7.

50. For what follows see *PHP* II 4.17-42.

51. *PHP* II 4.38-39.

52. p. 120.19, προθυμηθήσεται, 120.23-24, ὅταν προθυμῆται φθέγγεσθαι τὸ ζῷον,
120.32-33, ἐπειδὰν θελήσῃ φωνῆσαι τὸ ζῷον.

130

same effect, Galen continues, is produced when you sever, or block with ligatures, the nerves leading from the brain of an animal to the muscles which are necessary for the production of voice. As a matter of fact, the blocking or cutting of any motor nerve paralyzes the muscle it enters, and the will becomes impotent. This is also proved by the last experiment I wish to cite. Galen wants to establish that the spinal medulla derives its powers (δυνάμεις) from the brain, and does so by telling us that "when it is cut at any point whatever, all that is above the cut is preserved unharmed, but the sense-perception and motion of what lies below (the cut) is immediately destroyed, and all the muscles that receive nerves from it become insensate and motionless."[53]

Cruelty towards animals was indispensable to Galen's demonstrations; we may feel uneasy about this lack of feeling for moral or sentimental reasons, but from a purely scientific point of view his method is impeccable.

Galen's terminology for voluntary motion is not monotonous; the expressions "motion καθ᾽ ὁρμὴν" and "motion κατὰ προαίρεσιν" which occur a number of times in the PHP mean exactly the same thing, although in the first case Galen uses a word that is originally a Stoic technical term and the second time one that is originally Aristotelian. His formula for the motor nerves is κινητικὰ νεῦρα[54] as well as προαιρετικὰ νεῦρα, the word προαιρετικὰ suggesting that it is the involvement of the will which distinguishes motion from sense-perception.[55]

53. PHP VII 8.11.

54. PHP p. 456.19-20.

55. PHP p. 96.9.13; see also von Staden 1989, pp. 250 f., who argues that Herophilus may have introduced the term προαιρετικὰ νεῦρα and that Erasistratus may have spoken of κινητικὰ νεῦρα. For κίνησις προαιρετικὴ see e.g. Gal., De nerv. diss. 1, II p. 831.2 Kühn. It is not a coincidence that according to Augustine—De Trin. XI ii.5, vi.10, vi.12—seeing too depends on the "voluntas animi," see Dihle 1982, pp. 125 and 232 f., n. 15. But Augustine, ibid. XI viii.15, argues in a rather sweeping way that this holds for all the senses: we may look in another direction or close our eyes if we do not want to see something, and we may also close our ears and nose; when distracted or thinking about something else, we do not listen to what is being said, or may fail to notice what we

Jaap Mansfeld

Often enough, Galen tells us that words are a matter of secondary importance as long as we know and make clear what we are talking about, and there is a passage near the end of chapter one of book one of his *On the Motion of the Muscles* which nicely illustrates this point:[56]

... the (motions) of the muscles are psychic and by aid of conation (*horme*). It makes no difference at all whether you say that the motions of the muscles occur by aid of choice (*prohairesis*), or voluntarily (*hekousios*), or by aid of the will (*boulesis*). Whatever expression one uses, the only aim that must be

are reading. We may close our mouth, i.e. refuse to take something, or spit out something we do not want to taste. We may avoid touching something, or push or throw it away if we are already touching it.

56. IV 372.14-373.4 K.: ... αἱ δὲ τῶν μυῶν [scil., κινήσεις] ψυχικαί τε καὶ μεθ' ὁρμῆς. εἴτε δὲ μετὰ προαιρέσεως λέγοις τὰς τῶν μυῶν γίνεσθαι κινήσεις, ἢ ἑκουσίως, ἢ μετὰ βουλήσεως, οὐδὲν διοίσει. ἑνὸς γὰρ ἐν ἅπασι τούτοις ἐστοχάσθαι δεῖ, τοῦ διορίσασθαι τὴν κίνησιν αὐτῶν ἀπὸ τῆς τῶν ἀρτηριῶν τε καὶ φλεβῶν κινήσεως· ὥστ', εἰ καὶ μὴ ἱκανὸς εἴης ἐν ὀνόμασιν ἐνδείξασθαι τὴν διαφοράν, αὐτάρκως ὃ βούλῃ δηλώσεις. As Pierluigi Donini points out (*per litt.*), in Galen the fine Aristotelian distinctions (see *Eth. Nic.* III 1-4) between *hekousion* and *prohairesis* have been flattened out. He adds that, according to Aristotle, moving a limb presumably would be a case of *hekousion*. Cf. also *supra*, n. 41. See further Donini 1989, pp. 76 ff., and his reference, *ibid.*, p. 77 n. 24, to *Eth. Nic.* III 4.1111b8 ff., where it is said that children and animals possess *hekousion* not *prohairesis*, and where instantaneous actions are also said to be *hekousia*. One may add *Eth. Nic.* III 1.1110a14 ff., where those actions which depend on one's moving one's limbs are said to be, in a way, *hekousia* (ἡ ἀρχὴ τοῦ κινεῖν τὰ ὀργανικὰ μέρη ἐν ταῖς τοιαύταις πράξεσιν ἐν αὐτῷ ἐστίν. Moerbeke translates "etenim principium movendi organicas partes in talibus operationibus in ipso est"). Dirlmeier [3]1964 fails to comment on these passages, and so do Gauthier and Jolif 1959. Thomas Aquinas' comments are not entirely adequate. Commenting on the passage in ch. 1, he says "Aliter tamen esset si ipse non moveret membra, sed ab aliquo potentiore moverentur. Ea autem quae fiunt ex principio intrinseco sunt in potestate hominis, ut ea operetur vel non operetur, quod pertinent ad rationem voluntarii. Unde manifestum est quod tales operationes prope et vere sunt voluntariae. Sed tamen simpliciter, idest in universali considerando eas, sunt involuntariae, quia nullus quantum est in se eligeret operari aliquid talium nisi propter timorem ... " (Spiazzi 1949, Lib. iii, l. i, pp. 112 f.). Commenting on the passage in ch. 4, he says "Pueri et alia animalia communicant ipso voluntario, inquantum scilicet proprio motu aliquid sponte operantur ... . Non autem communicant electione, quia non operantur ex deliberatione, quod requiritur ad electionem: ergo voluntarium est in plus quam electio" (Spiazzi 1949, Lib. iii, l. v, pp. 124 f.). I cannot deal here with Plotinus' intellectualistically oriented discussion (which takes its starting-point from Arist., *Eth. Nic.* III 1 ff.) of what is in

kept in sight is that of making a sharp distinction between the motion of the muscles and that of the veins and arteries so that, even if you were not entirely successful in indicating this difference by means of the terms (used), you will make clear what you want (to say) without being dependent (on such terminology).

So much for *Wortphilologie*, at least inasfar as Galen is concerned.[57]

VI

With the support of this scientific account of the relation between will and strength in voluntary motion and of the role here played by the ruling part in the brain, Galen now is in a position to apply this finding in the context of the Platonic (and, as he affirms, Hippocratic) tripartite psychology, and to transform a physiological doctrine into one concerned with moral questions. His ally against Chrysippus is, again, Posidonius. For Posidonius, who himself follows Plato, argues that human behaviour is determined by the part, or rather function, of the soul that is *strongest*. What is more, Galen the dialectician even is capable of accommodating Chrysippus' view concerned with *strong* and *weak* souls;[58] he merely gives it a different twist by sharing out strengths and weaknesses among the three different parts of the Platonic psyche. What we may call the will which determines those of our actions or forms of behaviour which can

one's power, and/or in the power of the first principle, in *Enn.* VI 8 [39], Περὶ τοῦ ἑκουσίου, καὶ θελήματος τοῦ ἑνός, but wish to point out that in the important introductory paragraphs concerned with what may be true for humans he does not speak of the question concerned with the moving of one's limbs.

57. One may compare the passage applauding Plato for not being a stickler for words as long as it is clear what is meant (in this case, desire or its opposite), *PHP* V 7.32: τῷ τε γὰρ ὀρέγεσθαι καὶ τῷ ἐπιθυμεῖν καὶ τῷ ἐφίεσθαι καὶ τῷ ἐπινεύειν ἐπορέγεσθαί τε καὶ θέλειν καὶ βούλεσθαι καὶ προσάγεσθαι καὶ μέντοι καὶ τοῖς ἐναντίοις αὐτῶν ἐπὶ τοῦ ἑνὸς πράγματος φαίνεται χρώμενος, τῷ ἀβουλεῖν καὶ μὴ ἐθέλειν (on this passage see also De Lacy 1988, p. 46). On the other hand, one may indulge in a bit of *Wortphilologie* with regard to Galen himself. See for instance the interesting formula βουλήσει τε καὶ δυνάμει at Marquardt 1884-1893, vol. II, p. 3.7 (cf. p. 3.15-16). The context is about the acquisition of knowledge and what one needs to acquire it.

58. E.g. *PHP* IV 6.8.

be considered from a moral point of view is nothing but the dominating strength, or force, of a particular function, or part, of the soul. In a sense, each of the three parts therefore has a will of its own. I shall illustrate this development by providing a few examples.

Anticipating to some extent an important argument of Posidonius quoted in a later book of the *PHP*,[59] Galen writes as follows in the third book:[60]

... as a horseman is to a horse or a hunter to a hound, so reason is to anger. For with greater justice the naturally superior rules and prevails in all things, the horseman over the horse, the hunter over the hound, reason over anger. ... (but) sometimes a disobedient horse, running in wild disorder, has car-

59. *PHP* V 6.31 = F 166.6-14 E.-K.; see further below. Cf. Kidd 1988 *ad locc.*, (ii) Fragments 150-293 and Kidd 1983, pp. 111 f.

60. *PHP* III 2.5-6; De Lacy's transl., slightly modified, italics mine. In what follows (up to the end of ch. 3), Galen elaborates this point at length; cf. also Gal., *De affect. dignot.* 5-6, pp. 20.11-21.10, and *De morib.* (Περὶ ἠθῶν) pp. xxvii-xxviii and xxxix Kraus (the *De morib.* has been translated by Mattock 1972, pp. 235 ff.; see further *infra*, n. 75, n. 82, and nn. 83-87 and text thereto). Note, however, that in F 166 Posidonius only mentions the horse, not the hound. For horse and hound in relation to courage and spirit see Plat., *Rep.* II 375a11 ff.; the guardians (who corrrespond to the spirited part) are compared to dogs e.g. at *Rep.* II 375a ff. and III 416a (cf. De Lacy 1984, p. 661). Foals as well as puppies are found at Xenoph., *Mem.* IV 1.3 (Socrates' views on education) and *Oec.* 13.7-8, and horse and hound at Hor., *Ep.* I 2.63-67 (on how to curb anger). The parallels in Plato and Xenophon have eluded Gigante 1987, pp. 45 f., who (commenting on Hor., *loc. cit.*) refers to Philod., *De lib. dic.* Frs. 87 and 52 Olivieri, passages without animals; note that Philodemus refers to Xen., *Oec.* 13.7-8 at *De oecon.* col. vii, p 23.6-7 Jensen, see the apparatus *ad loc.* The passages in Plato and Xenophon have also eluded Walzer 1962c, pp. 171 f. n. 2, and Stern 1956, p. 92, who both provide various further parallels. Posidonius (F 176 E.-K.) is of course thinking of the myth of Plat., *Phaedr.* 246a ff. (no dogs there). The horse-and/or-hound comparison seems to be a *topos*. which allows itself to be mixed with the image of the *Phaedr.*

At *PHP* IX 2.25 (followed by Platonic proof-texts in IX 3) and *De anim. mor.* 4 (including Platonic proof-texts), Galen tells us that the faculties of reason are strengthened by training (ὑπὸ ... τῶν γυμνασίων αὐξάνεσθαί τε καὶ ῥώννυσθαι, *Script. min.* II, p. 25.23-24) and weakened by sloth; cf. also *De affect. dignot.* 4-5. In a similar way, he argues that the lower parts of the soul grow if we give in to our passions (e.g. *De affect. dignot.* 3 ff., *De morib.* ch. I). But he fails to provide a description in physiological terms for their growing strength.

ried along his rider, defeated through *weakness* (ἀρρωστίᾳ δυνάμεως) or ignorance of horsemanship; and a *strong* anger (θυμὸς ... ἰσχυρός), moving violently toward an untimely act of revenge, has sometimes dragged with it a reason that is weak (ἄρρωστον) or ignorant. If they have *strength* (ῥώμην) and knowledge, reason will always rule over anger, and the charioteer over the horse; but if they lack either or both of these, then there is a risk that the worse will *overpower* (ἐπικρατῆσαι) what is naturally superior.

So reason, even if it possesses knowledge, according to Galen will be unable to hold anger in check as long as it lacks the required strength.

In his critical comments on Chrysippus' simile of the walking and the running man,[61] Galen makes the same point in a different way. He argues that each part of the soul is capable of setting a conation (ὁρμή) in motion.[62] If such a conation, or act of will, is caused by one of the three parts of the soul alone while the others are inactive, it is determined by this part alone. But if more than one such part is involved, then—assuming there is a conflict between reason and anger, or reason and desire—the stronger part (τὸ ἰσχυρότερον) will prevail, that is to say either reason, or anger, or desire. And if reason is galloping along with the irrational power, the latter's conation will never come to a stop. Galen here again follows Posidonius, who had said that "the conation is *sometimes* generated ... as a result of the judgement of the reasoning part, but *often* as a result of the movement of the affective part" (my italics).[63] We may add that according to Galen, who as is his habit illustrates the point by one of his invaluable verbatim quotations, Posidonius in book one of his

61. See *supra*, text to n. 22.

62. *PHP* IV 2.37-38. Cf. Gal., *De affect. dignot.* 3, p. 5.14 ff., where the πάθη are said to be caused διὰ τὴν ἄλογον ὁρμήν, and the affections listed (θύμος καὶ ὀργή, καὶ φόβος, καὶ λύπη καὶ φθόνος, καὶ ἐπιθυμία σφοδρά) pertain to the spirited as well as to to the desiderative part of the soul.

63. Pos. F 169.82-84 E.-K. *ap.* Gal., *PHP* V 5.21, p. 320.27-28: γεννᾶσθαι γὰρ τῷ ζῴῳ τὴν ὁρμὴν ἐνίοτε μὲν ἐπὶ τῇ τοῦ λογιστικοῦ κρίσει, πολλάκις δ᾽ ἐπὶ τῇ κινήσει τοῦ παθητικοῦ. Cf. also the expression διὰ τῆς παθητικῆς ὁλκῆς ("pull'; note the physical metaphor), F 169.80 E.-K.

Jaap Mansfeld

On the Affections gave a sort of summary of Plato's remarks on education (presumably of the arguments of the *Republic* and *Laws*),[64] and stated that the affective part of the soul should be prepared in such a way as to be most amenable to the rule of the rational part. At first the rational part is small and weak (ἀσθενές), but it becomes big and strong (ἰσχυρὸν) about the fourteenth[65] year, "which is the proper time for it to take control and to rule, as a kind of charioteer, the team of horses conjoined with it, namely desire and anger, as long as these are neither excessively *strong* nor *weak*" (my italics). It should, however, be noticed that according to Posidonius (who, as usual, is arguing against Chrysippus) weakness of soul, although being a necessary condition, is not always a sufficient condition for being moved affectively. "When two persons have the same weakness (τὴν αὐτὴν ἀσθένειαν) and receive a like impression of good or evil, one is moved affectively, the other not; and one is moved more, the other less."[66] The reason for this difference according to him is that one person may be used to this sort of thing, and the other not.[67]

A further noticeable passage, involving both Posidonius and Galen, is found in book five of the *PHP*.[68] Galen here seems to paraphrase an argument of Posidonius against Chrysippus;[69] he argues that there are three "identifications" (τριῶν ... οἰκειώσεων), corresponding to the form (εἶδος) of each of the soul's parts[70], viz. with pleasure through the desiderative, with victory through the spirited, and with the morally good through

64. *PHP* V 5.32-35 (Pos. F 148 E.-K.).

65. Orthodox Stoic doctrine, see e.g. Diog. Laërt. VII 55 (*SVF* III Diog. Bab. 17), Aët. IV 11. 4 (*SVF* II 83).

66. *PHP* IV 5.33-34 (Pos. F 164.42-50 E.-K.).

67. For this reason, Posidonius advises us to prepare ourselves beforehand for whatever may befall (προενδημεῖν ... τοῖς πράγμασι), see *ap.* Gal., *PHP* IV 7.6-11 (F 165.17-53 E.-K.). Note however that we do not need a tripartite soul for this form of spiritual training.

68. *PHP* V 5.8-9 (= Pos. F 160 E.-K., *SVF* III 229a). For the pursuit of pleasure and that of dominance and victory by the two lower powers of the soul according to Posidonius see F 158 E.-K. *ap.* Gal., *PHP* IV 7.33-35.

69. Kidd's argument (1988) (ii), pp. 617 ff., seems convincing.

70. Posidonius would have said "powers."

the rational part. The "ancient philosophers," he continues, were the only ones to acknowledge this triple relationship. We are in a position to fill in the names of these unidentified ancients: Pythagoras and Plato.[71] As a matter of fact, Plato in the ninth book of the *Republic*,[72] where he resumes the exposition of the three parts of the soul begun in the fourth, argues that each of these parts has its own specific pleasure and desire, and its own specific reign:[73] the desiderative part wants food, drink, sex, or money, the spirited part wants[74] to be dominant, to win, and to gain prestige, and the rational part is always directed towards knowing the truth. Plato here attributes a specific motivation to each of the soul's parts, and I believe that we may assume that Posidonius had this passage in mind when he argued that the ancients accepted that each of the parts of the soul has its own *oikeiosis*; in its turn, this argument supports his view that each part has a *horme*, or rather a series of *hormai*, of its own.

That we should think of Posidonius rather than of Galen with regard to the remark about the ancients (though of course Galen fully agreed with Posidonius) finds some support in the second chapter of the fourth book of the *PHP*. Galen here provides a

71. Pos. T 101 E.-K. *ap.* Gal., *PHP* IV 7.18-20 (where he argues that the Platonic tripartition of the soul should also be attributed to Pythagoras), and T 95 E.-K. *ap.* Gal., *PHP* IV 7.39. Cf. also the reference to "the ancient philosophers" at *De morib.* p. xxvi Kraus and Walzer's comments (1951), p. 149. See further Burkert 1972, p. 74 n. 22, Vander Waerdt 1985, pp. 387 ff., and Whittaker 1990, p. 75 n. 11, 87 n. 73.

72. *Rep.* IX 580d ff.; in Pos. F 160 E.-K., various echoes can be detected. I am grateful to T. Tieleman for having reminded me of these passages. A further important parallel for the highest sort of *epithymia* is in the account of the etymology of Hades at Plat., *Crat.* 403a-404b.

73. 580d7-8, τριῶν ὄντων τριτταὶ καὶ ἡδοναί μοι φαίνονται, ἑνὸς ἑκάστου μία ἰδία· ἐπιθυμίαι ὡσαύτως καὶ ἀρχαί. The "reigns" pertain to the fact that different parts may, and do, dominate in different individuals. For the specific desires of each of the parts cf. also De Lacy 1988, p. 44, and Vegetti 1989, pp. 131 f. Pierluigi Donini points out (*per litt.*) that an echo of this idea is found at Arist. *De an.*, III 9.432b5 ff. (tripartition of *orexis*); cf. also Donini 1988, pp. 92 f.

74. 581a10, ὁρμῆσθαι, seems significant in view of the role attributed to *horme* in Stoic theory.

cento of quotations from the *Timaeus* and the *Republic* which prove that Plato spoke of three parts of the soul in three different locations. He includes a single snippet from the passage in *Rep.* IX referred to above, and it is not the most significant one, or at the very least not one that can be understood apart from its Platonic context.[75]

VII

In order to conclude my argument, I would like to point out one major inconsistency of Galen's. To be sure, he had diligently studied, quoted, and even digested Chrysippus, and Posidonius, and Plato, and Hippocrates and the great anatomists (one of his teachers, Pelops, in fact being an important anatomist himself), and he had carried out sophisticated scientific experiments of major importance. But Plato had not spoken about the motor nerves at all,[76] and Chrysippus, although admitting ignorance in anatomical matters,[77] was at least consistent in arguing (just as Aristotle had done) that the origins of physical motion must be sought in the heart, i.e. in the place in the body where he located the main psychic functions. According to Posidonius' Platonizing revision of Chrysippus' psychology, the three differ-

75. *Rep.* IX 581e6-582a2 at *PHP* VI 2.12, p. 370.19-23: "When therefore, I said, the pleasures of each form [i.e., part of soul] and the very way of life are in dispute, not only in regard to the nobler or more shameful, or worse or better, kind of life, but even in regard to what is more pleasant and less distressing, how shall we know who among them comes closest to the truth?" The three different kinds of desire of the three parts of the soul are treated at required length at Gal., *De sequel.* 2, *Script. min.* II pp. 35.16-36.8, and at *De morib.* pp. xxxviii-xxxix Kraus (where Galen speaks of "the three souls"). A compendium of the whole *Rep.* was included in the lost parts of Galen's Πλατωνικῶν διαλόγων σύνοψις, cf. Kraus and Walzer 1951, p. 2 f.

76. For Plato, there is no problem in that the self-activating soul simply is ἀρχὴ κινήσεως (e.g. *Phaedr.* 245c-e).

77. *SVF* II 897, third text, *ap.* Gal., *PHP* I 6.13. In the polemical passages at *PHP* II 5.69-71 (= *SVF* II 898) and 94, Galen attributes the view that the nerves issue from the head to Chrysippus, but this reading of what Chrysippus means (βούλεται λέγειν), *pace* Manuli 1977, p. 181, is not borne out by the fragment from Chrys. *De an.* bk. II quoted by Galen as the proof-text (see also *infra*, n. 80). At *De foet. form.* 4, IV p. 674 Kühn (= *SVF* II 761, first text), on the other hand, Galen states that Chrysippus and many other Stoics as well as Peripatetics affirm that the heart is the first part of the embryo to be formed and that it is φλεβῶν καὶ νεύρων ... ἀρχήν.

138

ent functions (or powers, *dynameis*) of the soul are in one and the same place, whereas according to Galen in the *PHP* (following Plato) there are three different parts in three different places.

I can see no major difficulty in Posidonius' attribution of conation (ὁρμή) to each individual psychic power, for they are functions of one and the same soul and are all in one place, so that communication should not be too difficult and a chain of command can therefore be imagined.[78] One may even make an

78. The surviving evidence suggests that Posidonius did not deal with the nerves; the fact that Galen is silent on this point also tells us something, for he would surely have played off Posidonius' view against that of Chrysippus if it had been significantly different and more like his own. According to F 28a + b E.-K., Posidonius in the third book of his *On the Soul* said that the psychic *pneuma* is diffused in the bones; according to Diog. Laërt. VII 138 = F 21.5-6 E.-K., he said in his *On the Gods* that the soul (as a ἕξις) "is diffused through the bones and the *neura*" (κεχώρηκεν διὰ τῶν ὀστῶν καὶ τῶν νευρῶν). Kidd 1988 (i), p. 140, must be right in translating "bones and sinews" (cf. also Sext., *M.* VII 19 = Pos. F 88 E.-K). It therefore appears that according to Posidonius it is the all-pervading soul as warm *pneuma* (cf. *supra*, n. 15), not the *pneuma* in the nerves which moves the muscles, and this of course also was Chrysippus' view (cf. e.g. the perambulating regent part *ap.* Sen., *Ep.* 113.23 = *SVF* I 525 ~ II 836, second text, and the text from Calcidius quoted *infra*, n. 80).

That disagreement as to the function of the νεῦρα (and so about the reference of the word) existed is attested by Cic., *Luc.* (= *Ac. pr.* II) 124: "sed redeo ad animum et corpus. satisne tandem ea nota sunt nobis, quae nervorum natura sit, quae venarum? (but the *nervi* in the Stoic anatomical doctrine at *De nat. deor.* II 139 *nervos a quibus artus continentur* are "sinews," though Pease, who has a rather confused note *ad loc.*, says "probably including both nerves and sinews")." We should observe that *ibid.*, 122 (= Deichgräber 1930, Fr. 66), Cicero refers to the well-worn epistemic argument of the Empiricist physicians against the anatomists, viz. that the opening up of the living body may interfere with the functions of its parts. His remark about the "nervi" is followed by a short discussion which is concerned with the contrasting views of the experts about the nature and even the existence of the "animus"; he also briefly mentions the traditional question "trisne partes habeat ut Platoni placuit, rationis irae cupiditatis, an simplex unusque sit" (cf. also *Tusc.* I 20). The main bone of contention in the *PHP* did not begin with Galen (cf. also *supra*, n. 31), but is already found in the collections of *Placita* (see further Mansfeld 1990, pp. 3085 ff., 3128 f., and passim); for the collection used by Chrysippus see Mansfeld 1989. We should note that in Alcin., *Didasc.* ch. 17, p. 172.27-31, νεῦρα means "sinews" (περιέθηκαν ... τοῖς ... ὀστοῖς πρὸς σύνδεσιν αὐτῶν νεῦρα· καὶ διὰ νεύρων μὲν κάμψεις ἐγένοντο καὶ ἄρθρων συνδέσεις), but that in the same chapter, p. 173.5-7, *pace* Whittaker 1990, p. 122 n. 330, it clearly means "nerves." I find the same phenomenon in another syncretistic document, the *Pythagorika Hypomemnata* cited by Diogenes Laërtius from the *Successions* of Alexander Polyhistor (*Vorsokr.* 58 B.1a, FGrH 273F93; for

effort to understand the reason why Chrysippus and Posidonius did not feel compelled to accept the theories of the nervous system which had been developed by the great anatomists. It is not certain whether according to Herophilus the motor nerves are filled with *pneuma*; possibly, he conceived of them as a sort of strings used for pulling or slackening the muscles. According to Erasistratus, however, the nerves are a sort of channels, or tubes, containing *pneuma*, and it is this *pneuma* which has the sensory and motor functions.[79] But if you are convinced that the soul itself is a material *pneuma*, and that it has, as its further parts, a sort of *pneuma*-streams linking the regent part with the senses, the trachea, and the reproductive organs—in fact with the body as a whole, and assume that it causes locomotion,[80] you may

---

the date, apart from Festugière 1945, see Burkert 1972, pp. 53 ff., 74 ff.). At Diog. Laërt. VIII 29 = *Vorsokr.* I p. 450.4 νεῦρα in the list σάρκας τε καὶ νεῦρα καὶ ὀστᾶ καὶ τριχὰς means "sinews," but at VIII 31 = *Vorsokr.* I p. 450.22 it means "nerves" (δεσμά τ' εἶναι τῆς ψυχῆς τὰς φλέβας καὶ τὰς ἀρτηρίας καὶ τὰ νεῦρα—this triplet is modelled after Erasistratus' τριπλοκία τῶν ἀγγείων, see Festugière 1945, p. 427, and Erasistratus Frs. 36 and 200 Gar.). Alcinous' sentence on the nerves is parallel to Galen's statements about the origin of the spinal medulla and of the nerves (cf. *supra*, n. 37 and text thereto; n. 42 and text thereto): τὸ ἡγεμονικὸν ... περὶ τὴν κεφαλὴν καθίδρυσαν, ἔνθα μυελοῦ τε ἀρχαὶ καὶ νεύρων κτλ. It appears that Galen's only contributions to the traditional debate are the much advertised experiments with which he supported the anatomy of the Hellenistic anatomists and his incorporation of their theory of the nervous system in a Platonist psychology. In Calc, *In Tim.*, this anatomy is not adduced in the chapters on the seat of the regent part and only at issue in the those dealing with vision (chs. 236 ff., commentary on *Tim.* 45b2-d3), see my paper (Mansfeld 1975), pp. 27 ff. We may add that Galen in his abstract of the *Timaeus*, Kraus and Walzer 1951, p. 55.18-22, refers to *PHP* VII, "ubi etiam plura (invenies)," and to bk. XIII of his lost treatise *On Proof.*

79. For Herophilus see von Staden's well-argued criticism of Solmsen (von Staden 1989, pp. 255 ff.) (but I do not share his view of Galen as a generally reliable interpreter of the views of others [von Staden makes much of *De trem.* 5 = Her. T 141 von St.], and the dubious text of Rufus, Her. T 80 von St., is obscure). For Galen's *non liquet* see *supra*, n. 44. There can be no doubt, however, about Erasistratus' position, see Solmsen 1968, pp. 573 ff. (cf. e.g. the explanation of paralysis at *Anon. Fuchsii* p. 550 = Erasistr. Fr. 241 Gar.; for the *pneuma* moving the muscles see Erasistr. Fr. 39 Gar.). See also Souques 1934, pp. 357 ff.

80. See the verbatim fragment from bk. I of Chrysippus' *De an.* (*SVF* II 885) *ap.* Gal., *PHP* III 1.10 ff.: ἡ ψυχὴ πνεῦμά ἐστι σύμφυτον ἡμῖν συνεχὲς πάντι τῷ σώματι διῆκον κτλ. See further Chrysippus *ap.* Calc., *In Tim.* 220 (*SVF* II 879) on the regent part as a spider in its web (Calc. p. 233.19 ff. Waszink = *SVF* II p. 236.12 ff.); the further parts of the soul "per universum corpus porriguntur omniaque

well believe that the strings and/or tubes are irrelevant, and especially so if the experts disagree among themselves about the physiology of the nervous system. You would have to bother even less with those who submit that the soul is a cause of motion in an immaterial way.

But Galen, unlike Posidonius, is not really in a position to attribute a *horme* to the irrational parts which is capable of gettings things done, because this gets him into difficulties with his own theory of the chain of command stretching from the ruling part, that is to say from the reason somewhere in the brain, through the motor nerves (either by means of the *pneuma* or perhaps rather by means of an immaterial force) to the muscles that have the parts of the body execute the movements they have been ordered to perform. His to the modern mind so immensely gratifying experimental method, which is his outstandingly important original contribution to the traditional debate concerned with the parts, or powers, of the soul and their location in the body, proves to be utterly damaging to the main point he wants to make in the *PHP*. Because there are no motor nerves issuing from either the heart (the seat of anger, according to Galen) or the liver (the seat of desire, according to Galen), the two non-rational parts of the soul are in fact precluded from moving any muscle; there is, in the literal sense of the word, no way in which they can determine our actions, because it is reason, and reason alone, which makes the muscles move by means of the connecting nerves. As Galen says himself, *De mot. musc.* 1, IV p. 373.6-7 Kühn, "motion of animals according to conation cannot happen without muscles" (κίνησις μὲν οὐκ ἂν γένοιτο τοῖς ζῴοις οὐδεμία καθ' ὁρμὴν ἄνευ τῶν μυῶν). So what he should have argued[81] is that, when desire or anger proves to be stronger than reason, reason actually goes along with either anger or desire and so has the muscles go through the appropriate

---

membra usque quaque vitali spiritu complent reguntque et moderantur innumerabilibus diversisque virtutibus nutriendo adolendo *movendo motibus localibus*" etc. (my italics; Calc. pp. 232.22-233.2 W. = *SVF* II p. 235.31-34). Another illuminating simile for the soul is that of the octopus and its arms (Aët. IV 4.4 = *SVF* II 827; Aët. IV 21 = *SVF* II 836); see further Rolke 1975, pp. 404 ff.

81. And to some extent does argue, see e.g. *supra*, text to n. 60; but in such passages the role of the muscles is not taken into account.

motions, e.g. those involved in stabbing someone, or in over-eating. But in what physiologically acceptable way, one may well ask, can the irrational parts of Galen's Platonic psyche prove themselves to be stronger than reason and impel it to issue commands to the muscles that for instance have to move the knife? They simply cannot gather the clout they need. The idea of force or strength, transferred by Galen to the irrational parts of the soul, proves to be an empty metaphor[82], or at the very least a conception which is incompatible which his account of the brain and the motor nerves and all the cruel experiments he performed to prove this account true.

82. At *PHP* IV 6.35-36, Galen argues (against Chrysippus) that there is βίαν τινὰ τὴν κινοῦσαν ... πᾶσι τοῖς ἐμπαθέσιν ὁρμάς, ... ἐν τοῖς ἀνθρώποις. At *PHP* VII 3.2, summarizing his previous investigations, he states that he has proved (1), that the part of the soul which is in the head is among other things the cause of voluntary motion; (2), that the part which is in the heart is among other things the cause of the "tension" of the soul (τόνος; Manuli 1977, p. 157, translates "la sua attività per sé consiste nel dare vigore all'anima"; cf. *PHP* VI 8.44, and also Plut., *De virt. mor.* 442A, τὸ ... τῷ λογισμῷ παρέχον ἰσχὺν καὶ δύναμιν, θυμοειδές), of firmness in executing the commands of reason and, "in passion," of the "boiling of the innate heat" (cf. also *PHP* III 1.30); and (3), that the liver is the seat of desire. In physiological terms, this "tension" of the soul produced by the heart is presumably to be explained by the fact that the heart according to Galen produces part of the *pneuma* that is transformed into psychic *pneuma* in the *reta mirabilis* (see e.g. Vegetti 1990, pp. 12, 16 f., 19). Obviously, it is again precluded that the parts of the soul in the heart and the liver are the cause of voluntary action, and it is in no way clear in what way they could manage to overrule reason.

In the *De morib.*, p. xxxii Kraus, Galen argues that the spirited soul must be "strong and firm." He continues: "The essence of this strength, which enables man to be patient and steadfast in what he does, is, as far as I can see, Natural Heat, for the more powerful the *movement* of the Natural Heat, the more a man *moves*" (tr. Mattock 1972; my italics). For the natural, or innate, heat (ἔμφυτος or σύμφυτος θερμασία or θερμότης, or σύμφυτον θερμὸν) see *PHP* VIII 7, with prooftexts from Hippocrates and Plato. For the heart as τῆς ἐμφύτου θερμασίας ἀρχὴν see *PHP* VI 8.75, p. 424.3. Cf. also Manuli 1988, pp. 196 ff., on the Galenic vital *pneuma*. But one fails to see in what way the natural heat would be able to cause movement without reaching the muscles; according to Galen the heart is the source of the involuntary movements of the veins and the arteries (cf. e.g. De Lacy 1988, p. 55). Furthermore, the function of this strong spirited part, *more Platonico*, is to hold desire in check, not to act in anger on its own. It seems that in this passage Galen has the innate heat perform the tasks of the Stoic *pneuma*. For statements about the strength and weakness of each of the "three souls" see also *De morib.* pp. xxxiii, xxxix Kraus.

What may have helped him to loose his footing is the fact that Posidonius called the parts of the soul *dynameis*, that is "powers," and powers after all seem to be able to get something going.

Galen himself may have been fully aware of the problem involved in reconciling his account of human physiology with his moral philosophy. In the surviving Arabic abstract of the *De moribus*[83] (the Greek original is lost), p. xxvi Kraus, he writes as follows:

I have explained this[84] in the book that I wrote on *The Views of Hippocrates and Plato*, and I have shown there that man possesses something that is responsible for thought, something else that is responsible for anger and a third thing that is responsible for desire. *It makes no difference how I refer to these things in this book* [viz., in the *De moribus*], whether as *separate souls*, as *parts of* the *one* human soul or as *three different faculties* of the *same essence*.[85]

He goes on by telling us that he will designate these separate souls, or parts, or faculties, as the rational or cogitative soul, the passionate or animal soul, and the appetitive or vegetative soul. So now we have three souls.

In the same page, Galen explains what he means by the type of movement he calls by the name of "action":

when someone moves something from one place to another the movement of his *hand* is an action produced by the person and his hand.[86] This illustrates spatial movement ...

Although the volitional paradigm is maintained the nervous sytem has no place in the *De moribus*, and in this important essay in moral philosophy Galen silently drops one of the main points proudly established in the *PHP*, viz. that we have to

83. I quote from Mattlock's translation (1972).

84. The relation between the soul and (characteristic) behaviour, etc.

85. Italics in this sentence are mine. For the (Platonic) desires of the three souls in this treatise see supra, n. 75.

86. My italics.

Jaap Mansfeld

assume three different parts of the soul which are located in three different places in the body. At *De moribus* p. xlv Kraus, he explicitly explains action as the consequence of a desire that follows upon a decision without entering into the physiological details:

> ... thought and scrutiny are followed by a decision upon one of the things investigated and examined by thought from among those which occur in the imagination. Then, if that which is decided upon is something that can be done, and not something that can only be known, the decision to do it is followed by the desire that it should be done. This *deliberate movement* that it makes subsequently *sets in motion the hands, feet, tongue, larynx, chest, eyes, mouth or other similar members.* [...] What I mean by imagination is every movement that is produced by the soul because of the movements that happens to it when a change occurs in the body.[87]

In this passage, the three souls have indeed, *more Posidonio*, become "different faculties of the same essence," and although the nervous system is conspicuously absent a chain of command can perhaps be imagined.[88] We may therefore say that, rather than confirming Plato's insight concerned with the three places for the three parts of the soul, Galen makes the difficulties which inevitably are entailed by the strongly argued physiological tripartition and trilocation of the soul as confirmed by scientific proof (the position of the *PHP*) stand out in glaring conspiciousness.

Although it is of course easy to argue from the vantage-point of hindsight, nothing forces us to be be silent about the fact that,

87. My italics. Posidonius had said that the emotional movements of the psyche are always consequent upon the condition of the body (F 169.85-93 E.-K. *ap.* Gal., *PHP* V 5.22-23, but Galen goes a bit further); Kidd 1988 (ii), 623, appositely refers to *De sequel.* ch. 11. An account which is not dissimilar to Galen's in the *De morib.* is found at Plut., *De virt. mor.* 442CE: when a conation (ὁρμή) occurs and reason (λογισμός) so to speak shakes the reins, breath and sinews and bones grow taut and are obediently drawn together; the feet of someone who has in mind to run are εὔτονοι, etc. Cf. also Plut., *De gen. Socr.* 588E-589A (see Babut 1969, pp. 56 f., 142 f.), and Sen., *De ir.* I 7.3-4.

88. We may notice that the innate heat (cf. *supra*, n. 82) plays no role here.

after all, neither the heart nor the liver in our view are parts of the psyche in the sense wanted by Galen and that, although Chrysippus chose the wrong location in the body for the conscious mind, his unitarian psychology and psychopathology[89] in a plurality of ways are more interesting than the fragmentation of the psyche argued by Galen and his chosen predecessors. The modified position in the *De moribus* is not only opportunist but also inevitable; it reveals that Galen's physiology on the one hand and his moral philosophy and philosophy of mind on the other are not co-ordinate.

It has hopefully become clear that the idea of the will plays an important part in Galen's psychology. However, it would in my view be true to say that most of the time it remains a mere idea, and that Chrysippus' account of volition (as linked both with his physical explanation of the mind-and-soul and with his moral philosophy) is rather more satisfactory and consistent than Galen's.*

Utrecht University

89. We have noticed *supra* (text to n. 13) that the author of *Sacred Disease* too argues in favour of a unitarian view, but his psychology and physics (if these terms are allowed here) are of course far less sophisticated than Chrysippus', and in his doctrine the will does not seem to play a part.

* Thanks are due to Pierluigi Donini, Ian Kidd, David Sedley, Teun Tieleman, Mario Vegetti and the BACAP referee for comments on versions of this paper. Dr Sedley's Commentary is published in this volume. I am grateful to Prof Vegetti for a preview of his paper "Lo statuto epistemologico della medicina in Galeno," and to Henri van de Laar who checked the references and compiled the index.

Colloquium 4
Commentary on Mansfeld

David Sedley

Jaap Mansfeld's elegant and instructive paper seems to me largely persuasive in its relative evaluations of the positions of Chrysippus, Posidonius and Galen. In it he makes it clear that he is concerned neither with will in its trivial sense as the wish to act—no one could deny that the Greeks had *that* concept —nor with will as in "free will." His aim is rather to try and locate, within the chosen ancient psychological theories, that mental power which has the causal efficacy to translate thought or intention into action.

Even that may seem to leave at least two separate questions: (a) what enables us to do this *at all*? (b) what power is it that is present more abundantly in strong-willed than in weak-willed people?

Galen's anatomical exploitation of the nervous system, in the wake of the less informed speculations of Aristotle about the heart and the pioneering researches of Herophilus and Erasistratus, seems directed at the first question. But moral psychology tends to be concerned principally with second. Certainly the two questions can in principle be brought under a single theory, such as the Stoic theory of pneumatic tension. Galen's physicalist approach to mind, especially in works like *QAM*, likewise gestures towards a unitary solution. But it remains important to recognize that the two problems had very different histories, and I am not sure that both can constitute one and the same problem of the will. I shall say no more about the

Sedley

specifically physiological issues, except to congratulate Mansfeld on his neat critique of Galen's stance at the end of the paper.

The second question has a strongly Socratic history, and we can never afford to forget the Socratic origins of Stoic moral psychology. Socrates himself implicitly denied the distinction in question (b) between strong- and weak-willed people: everyone is fully motivated towards what they believe to be good. Reason itself is desiderative of good, and, since there is no conflicting mental force over which reason has to exert itself, there is no place or need for an *autonomous* will.

Plato, in introducing the tripartite soul, rescues the empirical distinction between strong and weak will. Mansfeld suggests the Greeks had no concept of the will as an *autonomous* function or part of the psyche, distinct from reason on the one hand and desire or the emotions on the other. But isn't the Platonic *thumoeides* a strong candidate for this role? In *Rep.* 4 the *thumoeides* is our internal police force, analogous to the policing role of the auxiliaries in the state. Cf. *Tim.* 70a, "That part of the soul which partakes of courage and spirit, since it is a lover of victory, they planted nearer to the head, between the midriff and the neck, in order that it might be obedient to the reason and, in partnership with it, forcibly control the tribe of desires when they completely refused to yield voluntary obedience to the rational orders from the citadel." In *Rep.* 4 the *thumoeides* functions as the natural ally of reason, unless corrupted by bad upbringing, and even then, we are told, it could never take the side of appetite against reason. Just as the rulers in the state are too few numerically to enforce their dictates without the help of the auxiliaries, so too the reasoning element in the soul is too small (cf. 442c5) to control the appetites without the spirited element's support. Reason is itself motivat*ed* towards good, but it lacks the motivat*ing* force to drive the whole soul.

This sounds awfully like willpower. Even the story of Leontius, who knew he shouldn't gawp at corpses but gave in, to the dismay of his *thumoeides*, is a story of failure of

147

will—Plato's first acknowledgement that you can act against knowledge. It's true that Leontius' *thumoeides* also expressed indignation, and anger is undoubtedly a prominent feature of the *thumoeides* that goes beyond will, as does its goal of honor or victory. So it is right to say that Plato isn't precisely distinguishing *will* as an independent function. But in so far as he is acknowledging a role for will here, he does make it *independent* of reason and desire. People's strength of will can vary independently of the strength of their reasoning powers. Indeed, the auxiliaries in the ideal state have much stronger will than reasoning power.

But Posidonius, despite his debt to Platonic psychology, does not take up the policing role of the *thumoeides*. He regards the battle for psychic domination as one between reason on the one side and two irrational forces on the other—appetite and anger—without conceding any positive intermediary role to the *thumoeides*. This is not surprising for a Stoic, who would inevitably regard both elements alike as having morally indifferent goals (roughly, wealth and honor), and reason alone as correctly motivated. Thus Mansfeld is absolutely right to read Posidonius' psychology as he does: there is a direct competition between three motivating forces, and, by and large, the strongest wins.

What I want to do is develop Mansfeld's point by taking up some hints in his paper and asking what this "strength" actually amounts to. It strikes me that it will make an enormous difference whether the motive power exercised by reason is an independently variable property, or is merely a function of the state of reason. Plato regards it as independently variable, and so in his own way does Galen, when he makes knowledge and psychic strength distinct desiderata in the moral agent (*PHP* 3.2.5-6). But the Stoics surely do not.

Posidonius repeatedly correlates an agent's intellectual strength with his set of beliefs (*PHP* 4.5.33, 35, 37, 41; 5.5.21): e.g. "the weaker (of two persons), who supposes that what has befallen him is greater . . ." (4.5.33), and "the causes of all false

suppositions arise in the contemplative mind through ignorance, and in the practical mind through the pull of the affections, but false opinions precede this pull, because the reasoning
part has become weak in judgement" (5.5.21). It appears that in
the case of the reasoning faculty its strength *is identical with its
degree of understanding*. Given a Stoic physical analysis of the
hegemonikon as pneuma, there is no puzzle in principle as to why
the very strength that is its perfected rationality should be identical with the degree of tension that gives it the causal efficacy
needed to dominate the two irrational forces. Indeed, it is a
familiar Stoic doctrine that this same strength is also the cohe-
sive physical property that enables a sage's soul to continue to
exist after his death (*SVF* 2.810). No dividing line should be
expected between the soul's intellectual strength and its tensional strength. It is precisely because pneuma is the locus and
cause of intelligence that all intellectual states *are* pneumatic
states.

Posidonius presumably therefore holds, as surely any Stoic
should be expected to, that a reasoning element that had complete understanding would *eo ipso* be strong enough to control
the other two elements. Posidonius gives reason its own intrinsic strength, so that it has no need to call on the support of the
thumoeides to police the appetites, as in the Platonic soul, or to be
accompanied by an independent property of psychic strength,
as in Galen's account.

Can we now work back from Posidonius to Chrysippus?
Chrysippus did, like Posidonius, correlate the soul's "strength"
with its degree of understanding, and there seems to me good
reason to think that he saw the two as identical. Galen alleges
that what Chrysippus calls "strength" must be an irrational
force, distinct from judgement, but it is instructive to see that,
despite extensive verbatim quotation from Chrysippus, he can
find no clear textual support for the claim. And no wonder. The
official Stoic definition of the soul's "strength" is "sufficient *tension* in *judging* and in acting and refraining from acting" (*SVF*
2.278). This, typically of Stoicism, simply refuses to detach ten-

sional from intellectual properties as if they belonged to two different levels of analysis.

But even if it is true that for Posidonius psychic strength does the work of will in translating thought into action, can we say the same for Chrysippus, as Mansfeld is perhaps suggesting we should? What worries me is that with a monistic psychology, such as Chrysippus has, the *hegemonikon*'s degree of understanding should be irrelevant to its efficacy in producing action. All agents, wise and foolish alike, surely act by and large as their *hegemonikon* directs. Indeed, if anything the *hegemonikon* of the foolish agent has *more* efficacy, since its passionate impulses are excessively zealous ones which push it too hard, like a runner out of control. Could Chrysippus doubt that the money-lover is at least as highly motivated to seek money as the sage is to act rightly?

Chrysippus does nevertheless say things which strongly suggest the view Mansfeld advocates. Galen reports him as saying that "sometimes we abandon correct judgements because the soul's tension yields and does not persist to the end or fully carry out the commands of reason" (4.6.3), and that "since all inferior men act in this way, abandoning their course and yielding for many causes, it might be said that they act in every case weakly and badly" (4.6.11). This sounds very much like failure of will: a soul which is weak because its *pneuma* lacks the appropriate tension can flag, and fail to stick to its resolves.

But when we bear in mind that the soul's pneumatic weakness is identical with its lack of understanding, the picture changes. For the Stoics, opinion is "weak supposition," ἀσθενὴς ὑπόληψις, and this weakness consists at least partly in its lack of an adequate cognitive foundation. Hence the opiner is easily led to change his mind (cf. SVF 3.177, the bad assent to false impressions ὑπ' ἀσθενείας): only knowledge is not subject to dissuasion, opinion is inherently changeable. If so, the soul's weakness of resolve will be identical to its inability to stick to its judgements. It weakly believes that what it has decided on is right, but it lacks the understanding to guarantee its retaining that belief when confronted with dangers and temptations. You may believe, rightly, that you should have your tooth extracted, but your false belief that pain is an evil can easily oust that belief when the time comes. Thus your soul's lack of tension, its pneumatic weakness, is to be equated with its imperfect state of understanding of the relative values involved, and its consequent inability to stick to its judgements.

If this is on the right lines, does Chrysippean psychic strength amount to the same thing as strength of will? Chrysippus does, as Mansfeld emphasizes, go out of his way to describe it in terms which suggest that idea: the soul can be, as it were, sinewy or without sinew, well or badly tensioned, just like the body, and its successes in enforcing its decisions depend on those qualities. But it is important to notice that in saying this he is repeatedly appealing to popular linguistic usage: "the tension in the soul *is called* good and bad tension" (4.6.5), "*we metaphorically call* some people without sinew or sinewy" (4.5.6), "For *we do in fact say* that some persons are strong or weak also in soul, and firm or soft, diseased or healthy; and *we speak in this way* of affection, infirmity, and the like in the soul" (5.2.27). I take it that Chrysippus was trying to bridge the gulf between ordinary ways of talking about passions and his own intellectualist theory. Just as elsewhere he tried to accommodate rather than ignore the popular view of passion as irrational, explaining that "irrational" meant in effect "unreasonable," so too here I suspect his aim was to accommodate the popular view that some people are endowed with more moral fibre than others, while nevertheless identifying that fibre with a state of reason.

I am therefore led to suggest one small modification to the picture expertly sketched by Mansfeld. The will, as a form of motive power, *was already acknowledged in popular usage.* Chrysippus' aim was to reinterpret that popular view in the light of his Socratic intellectualism. The reinterpretation involves identifying our will not only with our pneumatic state but also, and inseparably, with our intellectual state of understanding. Agents with the necessary understanding pursue their objectives single-mindedly, agents who lack it waver and are easily persuaded to modify or abandon their objectives, even where those objectives were correctly chosen in the first place. Whether this is an acknowledgement of the power of will, or an attempt to eliminate it in favor of the power of understanding, seems to me quite a difficult matter to determine.

Christ's College, Cambridge

Babut, D., 1969: *Plutarque, De la vertu éthique* (Paris).
Benz, E., 1932: *Marius Victorinus und die Entwicklung der abendländischen Willensmetaphysik* (Stuttgart).
Bonhöffer, A., 1890: *Epictet und die Stoa* (Stuttgart; repr. Stuttgart 1968).
Bourke, V.J., 1964: *Will in Western Thought* (New York).
Burkert, W., 1972: *Lore and Science in Ancient Pythagoreanism* (Cambridge, Massachusetts).
Buffière, F., 1956: *Les mythes d'Homère et la pensée grecque* (Paris).
Cambiano, G., ed., 1986: *Storiografia e dossografia nella filosofia antica* (Torino).
Daremberg, Ch.-V., 1841: *Exposition des connaissances de Galien sur l'anatomie, la physiologie et la pathologie du système nerveux* (Paris).
De Lacy, Ph., 1972: "Galen's Platonism," *American Journal of Philology* 93, pp. 27 ff.
_____1978-1984: *Galen, On the Doctrines of Plato and Hippocrates*, CMG V 4, 1, 2; 3 vols. (Berlin, vol. I ³1984, vol. II 21984, vol. III 1984).
_____1988: "The Third Part of the Soul" in Manuli and Vegetti 1988, pp. 43 ff.
Deichgräber, K., 1930: *Die griechische Empirikerschule* (Berlin, repr. Berlin/Zürich 1965).
Dihle, A., 1982: *The Theory of Will in Classical Antiquity* (Berkeley etc.).
_____1985: *Die Vorstellung vom Willen in der Antike* (Göttingen).
Dillon, J.M., 1977. *The Middle Platonists: a Study of Platonism* (London).
_____ and Long, A.A., edd., 1988: *The Question of "Eclecticism": Studies in Later Greek Philosophy* (Berkeley etc.).
Dirlmeier, F., 31964: *Aristoteles, Nikomachische Ethik*, Aristoteles Werke Bd. 6 (Berlin).
Donini, P.L., 1982: *Le scuole l'anima l'impero: La filosofia antica da Antioco a Plotino* (Torino).
_____1988: "Tipologia degli errori e loro correzione secondo Galeno" in Manuli and Vegetti 1988, pp. 65 ff.
_____1989: *Ethos: Aristotele e il determinismo* (Allessandria).
Edwards, P., ed., 1967, repr. 1972: *The Encyclopedia of Philosophy* (New York/London).
Ferrari, G.A., 1984: "Meccanica 'allargata'" in Giannantoni and Vegetti 1984, pp. 225 ff.
Festugière, A.-J., 1945: "Les <<Mémoires Pythagoriques>> cités par

Bibliography

Alexandre Polyhistor." *Revue des Études Grecques* 58, pp. 1 ff. (repr. in *Études de philosophie grecque* (Paris 1971), pp. 371 ff.).

Fillion-Lahille, J., 1984: *Le De ira de Sénèque et La philosophie stoïcienne des passions* (Paris).

Fortenbaugh, W.W., ed., 1983: *On Stoic and Peripatetic Ethics: The Work of Arius Didymus* (New Brunswick/London).

Frauenstädt, J., ed., 1864: *Aus Arthur Schopenhauers handschriftlichem Nachlaß* (Leipzig).

Frede, M., 1987: "On Galen's Epistemology" in Frede, M., *Essays in Ancient Philosophy* (Oxford), pp. 279 ff.

Garofalo, I., 1988: *Erasistrati Fragmenta* (Pisa).

Gauthier, R.A., and Jolif, J.Y., 1959: *Aristote, L'Éthique à Nicomaque, T. II*, Commentaire, prem. partie. Livres I-V (Louvain/Paris).

Giannantoni, G. and Vegetti, M., edd., 1984: *La scienza ellenistica* (Napoli).

Gigante, M., 1987: *La bibliothèque de Philodème et l'Épicurisme romain* (Paris).

Grensemann, H., 1968: *Die hippokratische Schrift >>Über die heilige Krankheit<<* (Berlin).

Haase, W. and Temporini, H., edd., 1990: *Aufstieg und Niedergang der Römischen Welt II* Vol. 36.4 (Berlin etc.).

Hahm, D.E., 1977: *The Origins of Stoic Cosmology* (Columbus, Ohio).

Hornby, A.S., Gatenby, E.V. and Wakefield, H., [16]1972: *The Advanced Learner's Dictionary of Current English* (London).

Hübscher, A., ed., 1970: *Arthur Schopenhauer, Der handschriftliche Nachlaß*, vol. 3, Berliner Manuskripte (1818-1830) (Frankfurt a. M.; repr. München 1985).

Indelli, G., 1988: *Filodemo, L'ira* (Napoli).

Inwood, B., 1985: *Ethics and Human Action in Early Stoicism* (Oxford).

Jaeger, W.W., 1914: *Nemesios von Emesa: Quellenforschungen zum Neuplatonismus und seinen Anfängen bei Poseidonios* (Berlin).

Jahn, TH., 1987: *Zum Wortfeld 'Seele-Geist' in der Sprache Homers* (Munchen).

Kahn, Ch.H., 1988: "Discovering the Will: From Aristotle to Augustine" in Dillon and Long 1988, pp. 234 ff.

Kidd, I.G., 1971: "Posidonius on Emotions" in Long 1971, pp. 200 ff.

_____1983: "*Euemptosia*—Proneness to Disease" in Fortenbaugh 1983, pp. 107 ff.

_____1988: *Posidonius*, Vol. II: The Commentary (Cambridge etc.).

Kraus, P. and Walzer, R., edd., 1951: *Galeni compendium Timaei Platonis*, Corpus Platonicum Medii Aevi, Plato Arabus Vol. I (London).

Lasserre, F. and Mudry, Ph., edd., 1983: *Formes de pensée dans la Collection Hippocratique* (Genève).

Lloyd, G.E.R., 1991: 'Galen on Hellenistics and Hippocrateans: contemporary battles and past authorities', in Lloyd, G.E.R., *Methods and Problems in Greek Science* (Cambridge etc.), pp. 398 ff.

Long, A.A., ed., 1971: *Problems in Stoicism* (London).

_____ and Sedley, D.N., 1987: *The Hellenistic Philosophers*, 2 vols. (Cambridge etc.).

Mansfeld, J., 1975: "Alcmaeon: 'Physikos' or Physician? With some remarks on Calcidius' 'On Vision' compared to Galen, *Plac. Hipp. Plat.* VII" in Mansfeld and de Rijk 1975, pp. 26 ff.

_____ and de Rijk, L.M., edd., 1975: *Kephalaion*, Festschr. de Vogel (Assen).

_____ 1980: "Plato and the Method of Hippocrates," *Greek Roman & Byzantine Studies* 21, pp. 341 ff.

_____ 1989: "Chrysippus and the Placita," *Phronesis* 34, pp. 311 ff.

_____ 1990: "Doxography and Dialectic: The *Sitz im Leben* of the 'Placita'" in Haase 1990, pp. 3057 ff.

Manuli, P., 1977: "Galeno e l'antropologia platonica" in Manuli and Vegetti 1977, pp. 157 ff.

_____ 1983: "Lo stile del commento: Galeno e la tradizione ippocratica" in Lasserre and Mudry 1983, pp. 471 ff. and in Giannantoni and Vegetti 1984, pp. 375 ff.

_____ 1988: "La passione nel *De placitis Hippocratis et Platonis*" in Manuli and Vegetti 1988, pp. 185 ff.

_____ and Vegetti, M., 1977: *Cuore, sangue e cervello: biologia e antropologia nel pensiero antico* (Milano).

_____ and Vegetti, M., edd., 1988: *Le opere psicologiche di Galeno* (Napoli).

Marquardt, J, Müller, I. von and Helmreich, G., edd., 1884-1893: *Claudii Galeni Pergameni Scripta minora*, 3 vols. (Leipzig)(repr. Amsterdam 1967).

Mattock, J.N., 1972: "A Translation of the Arabic Epitome of Galen's Book Περὶ ἠθῶν" in Stern, Hourani and Brown, 1972, pp. 235 ff.

Moraux, P., 1981: "Galien comme philosophe: la philosophie de la nature" in Nutton 1981, pp. 87 ff.

Müller, I. von, 1897: "Ueber Galens Werk vom wissenschaftlichen Beweis," *Abh. philos.-philol. Cl. d. Kön. Bay. Ak.* Bd. 20

(München), pp. 403 ff.

Nachmanson, E., ed., 1918: *Erotianus, Vocum hippocraticarum collectio cum fragmentis* (Uppsala).

Nussbaum, M., 1978, ²1985: *Aristotle's De Motu Animalium* (Princeton).

Nutton, V., ed., 1981: *Galen: Problems and Prospects* (London).

Penfield, W., 1958: "Hippocratic preamble: The brain and intelligence" in *The Brain and its Functions* (Oxford 1958), pp. 3 ff.

Pohlenz, M., 1896: "Ueber Plutarchs Schrift Περὶ ἀοργησίας," *Hermes* 31, pp. 321 ff.

_____1965: "Zenon und Chrysipp" in *Kleine Schriften* I, ed. Dörrie, H. (Hildesheim).

Rolke, K.-H., 1975: *Die Bildhaften Vergleiche in den Fragmenten der Stoiker von Zenon bis Panaitios* (Hildesheim/New York).

Runia, D.T., 1986: *Philo of Alexandria and the Timaeus of Plato* (Leiden).

Snell, B, ³1955: "Die Auffassung des Menschen bei Homer" in Snell, B., *Die Entdeckung des Geistes* (Hamburg), pp. 17 ff.

Solmsen, F., 1968: "Greek Philosophy and the Discovery of the Nerves" in Solmsen, F., *Kleine Schriften* Vol. I (Hildesheim), pp. 536 ff.

Souques, A., 1934: "Que doivent à Hérophile et à Erasistrate l'anatomie et la physiologie du système nerveux?," *Bulletin de la société française d'histoire de la médecine* 28, pp. 357 ff.

_____1936: *Étapes de la neurologie dans l'antiquité grecque* (Paris).

Spiazzi O.P., R.M., ed., 1949: *Thomae Aquinatis In decem libros Ethicorum Aristotelis ad Nicomachum expositio* (Torino/Roma).

Staden, H. von, 1989: *Herophilus: The Art of Medicine in Early Alexandria* (Cambridge etc.).

Stern, S.M., 1956: "Some Fragments of Galen's On Dispositions (Περὶ ἠθῶν) in Arabic," *Classical Quarterly* 6, pp. 91 ff. (repr. as Study III in S. M. Stern, *Medieval Arabic and Hebrew Thought*, London 1983).

_____, Hourani, A. and Brown, V., edd., 1972: *Islamic Philosophy and The Classical Tradition*, Festschrift R. Walzer (Oxford).

Temkin, O., 1950: "On Galen's Pneumatology," *Gesnerus* 8, pp. 180 ff.

Vander Waerdt, P.A., 1985: "Peripatetic Soul-Division, Posidonius, and Middle Platonic Moral Psychology," *Greek Roman and Byzantine Studies* 26, pp. 373 ff.

Vegetti, M., 1981: "Modelli di medicina in Galeno" in Nutton 1981, pp. 47 ff.

_____1986: "Tradizione e verità: Forme della storiografia filosofico-scientifica nel *De placitis* di Galeno" in Cambiano 1986, pp. 227 ff.

_____1989: *L'etica degli antichi* (Roma/Bari).

_____1990: "I nervi dell' anima" in *Il vivente e l'anima*, <<BioLogica>> n. 4, pp. 11 ff.

Verbeke, G., 1945: *L'évolution de la doctrine du pneuma du Stoïcisme à S. Augustin* (Paris/Louvain).

Voelke, A.-J., 1973: *L'idée de volonté dans le Stoïcisme* (Paris).

Walzer, R., 1949: *Galen on Jews and Christians* (London).

_____ and Stern, S.M., edd., 1962a: *Greek into Arabic:* Essays on *Islamic Philosophy* (Oxford).

_____1962b: "New Light on Galen's Moral Philosophy (From a recently discovered Arabic source)" in Walzer 1962a, pp. 148 ff.

_____1962c: "A Diatribe of Galen" in Walzer 1962a, pp. 171 ff.

Whittaker, J., 1990: Alcinoos: *Enseignement des doctrines de Platon* (Paris).

Colloquium 5

Philosophy and Literature: The Arguments of Plato's *Phaedo*[1]

Christopher Rowe

My aim in this paper will be to contribute to the understanding of the *Phaedo* as an entity in itself, by examining some of the connections between its parts. That the *Phaedo* is a highly articulated whole is, I think, beyond dispute;[2] but there is no clear agreement either about the relationships between its parts or about what sort of whole it is.[3] Even if no such agreement is possible, there is, I think, still plenty of room for discussion of the issues.[4]

1. This paper, in its present form, is for the most part an annotated version of the one originally delivered at Brown University in January 1991; the notes include an indication of my responses to points raised on that occasion (particularly by my respondent, Professor Thomas Tuozzo), by audiences later in the year at the Universities of Amsterdam and Perugia, and by an anonymous commentator for the *Proceedings*.

2. That, for example, all the arguments somehow contribute to a single, complex conclusion (however we may define the "arguments": see below), or that the arguments and the dramatic action are connected, cannot reasonably be denied; even if this leaves out two significant elements, i.e. Socrates' "autobiography", and the "myth", the *Phaedo* already thereby possesses a rather higher degree of overt structural organisation than many or most other Platonic dialogues.

3. My own primary concern will be to examine the relationships between the arguments, and between the characters who propose and respond to them, from which there will emerge a specific explanation of the combination in the dialogue of argument and action. About Socrates' autobiography, and the "myth", I shall have little or nothing to say, for reasons which will become clear; in any case, they deserve full treatment in their own right, for which I have no space in this paper, and whatever view is taken of them is unlikely to affect my conclusions.

4. As this already suggests, I shall be offering a highly determinate reading of the dialogue. In a preliminary seminar paper at Brown, I presented an argument against those who, for whatever reason, are inclined to deny the existence of any

Christopher Rowe

Most of the items in any modern bibliography on the *Phaedo* are naturally concerned with parts or aspects of the dialogue in isolation, for example the individual arguments for immortality (if I may so describe them, in the traditional way[5]), or those stretches which look like promising quarries for Plato's metaphysical ideas; and commentaries are themselves usually so preoccupied with particular problems that issues about the overall structure tend be neglected (though Gallop's philosophical commentary[6] is more helpful than most). There are, however, three relatively recent books whose titles, at least, suggest a concern with the dialogue as a whole: those of Bostock,[7] Burger[8] and Dorter.[9] Of these, Bostock's turns out to be restricted wholly to what he calls "the philosophical interest of the dialogue;" it "has nothing to say of its considerable literary merits and dramatic power," because, he says "it stems from a course of lectures designed for undergraduates . . . who were studying the *Phaedo* as their first introduction to philosophy."[10] Burger and Dorter,

enforceable limits on the interpretation of (Platonic) texts. I do not of course claim that my own interpretation of the *Phaedo* exhausts its meaning, or that it is invulnerable either to general arguments of a skeptical nature or to specific objections which I have failed to foresee or answer. I do claim that if the relevant parts of the dialogue are read in the way I shall suggest, they represent an internally coherent and consistent ordering of elements; and that if it is at all legitimate to prefer one interpretation, of any work, over any other, the discovery of such an ordering is one plausible basis for making the choice. While any work, whether by Plato or by anyone else, may turn out to be internally incoherent, inconsistent, or ambiguous, the interpreter has no reason to begin by assuming it to be so; and there is strong evidence, as I hope to show, that the *Phaedo* is not like this.

5. Of the four arguments, according to the usual division, the first (the "cyclical" argument, or the argument from opposites) requires combination with the second (from recollection), if it is to fulfil Cebes' original requirements (70b2-4), and the second with the first (77c1-d5); only the last two (that from the alleged "affinity" of soul to the unchanging, and the final argument) appear as selfstanding "arguments for immortality"— though if Cebes is prepared to attribute the same description separately to the first and the second too (as he implicitly does at 73a2-3), it will do no harm to go on doing the same.

6. Gallop 1975.

7. Bostock 1986.

8. Burger 1984.

9. Dorter 1982.

10. Op. cit. p. v.

however, both resist this kind of approach: thus Burger tells us that ". . . no argument can be immediately isolated from its context; its significance, particularly if it is or appears to be unsound, can be grasped only by taking into account its function in the whole,"[11] while Dorter's view is that

". . . no prior decision should be made as to the importance or unimportance of the dramatic form for the dialogue. Since Plato wrote in a literary way, whoever tries to understood him as he understood himself must consider the literary elements as well as the arguments. One may finally conclude that the literary elements serve no purpose beyond ornamentation, but this should be a conclusion reached after serious consideration, not a prior assumption."[12]

The basic principles being expressed here seem reasonable enough (though one might jib at some of the terms used by Dorter), and they will in fact be the ones that I shall employ in this paper.[13] It may serve certain pedagogic purposes to separate out the arguments of the dialogue and treat them in isolation; but from a wider point of view, it seems a disappointingly limited way of reading Plato, and one which does him scant justice not only as a writer (however loud the protestations of his literary qualities), but as a philosopher. A verdict on an argument rapidly turns, at least by implication, into a judgement on the mind that constructed it; but such a judgement cannot properly be reached until we have investigated the *purpose* of the argument, as measured by the way in which it is introduced, presented and received. Since verdicts on the arguments of the *Phaedo* are usually somewhat negative, Plato tends to come off rather badly (on occasion, or indeed rather more often, he is made to seem—as Burger puts it—like "a rather primitive or careless thinker").

11. Op. cit. p. 3.

12. Op. cit. pp. 3-4.

13. What is it to write in a non-literary way? How do we draw the line between "literary elements" and "arguments?" However, a fair working example of the kind of division Dorter had in mind is probably provided by Bostock.

Christopher Rowe

Such an approach also implies that, as a philosopher, he either shared or ought to have shared the same narrow interest in the arguments as such; that is, that on each occasion he was, or ought to have been, attempting simply to construct the best argument of the type that would appeal to one sort of modern academic philosopher. Whether he ought to have been doing that is a matter of opinion, but there is, as I shall suggest, clear evidence that he was not in fact doing it,[14] and that—for better or for worse—he views philosophy in a somewhat different way from those who claim to be his modern counterparts.[15] This general point too I share with Burger and with Dorter (and with others[16]), but not its application. I shall not comment directly on the ambitious readings of the dialogue which they use it to support; instead, I shall simply outline my own argument, which

14. It is of course consistent with this to hold both that his ultimate concern would have been with finding persuasive arguments, whether about immortality or anything else, and that this is the concern of the characters in the dialogue. (As Tuozzo rightly said, my later argument directly implies this latter point.) The question I raise is simply whether each and every piece of argumentation must be assumed to be presented as persuasive (as we shall be likely to imply, if we satisfy ourselves with establishing its strengths and weaknesses), or whether we should ask of any if it might not have some further purpose in its context within the conversation. Perhaps, from a dramatic point of view, any character who proposes an argument must be usually be supposed to be serious about it; but the author is not bound by the same limitations as his characters.

15. The difference I allege is not over the *aims* of philosophy, if these might broadly, and no doubt naively, be characterised as the discovery or demonstration of the truth by argument (see preceding note), but rather over the conditions under which someone may properly be said to be doing it. For Plato, or at least for the Socrates of the *Phaedo*, the requirements seems to be (i) that whoever is talking is talking to one or more other people, (ii) that they are talking about the right sort of subject (i.e. that it is one of those that Socrates thinks important), and (iii) that both sides are willing and able to treat what is said critically. (The justification for this list of requirements will, I hope, be provided cumulatively in what follows.) If so, any utterances or argument *by itself* would not count as "philosophical", while a set of utterances which we might want to treat as "rhetorical" (i.e. merely persuasive, lacking adequate support of the appropriate kind) would count as such, provided requirements (i)-(iii) were fulfilled. Thus e.g. — as I shall argue — there would from Socrates' point of view be no difference in kind between his "defence," on the one hand, and the arguments for immortality, to which they give rise, on the other; nor between the two parts of the argument from affinity. See esp. p.163-4 below.

16. See e.g. Stokes 1986.

can then be judged against theirs on the basis of the evidence.

*****

I begin with the third of Socrates' arguments for immortality, the argument from "affinity," which is by common consent one of the weakest. I claim that he is shown to be fully aware of its limitations, although he suppresses these in his final statement of the conclusion; and that in the light of Simmias' and Cebes' objections, he goes on actually to abandon it. If this claim of mine can be made good, then we shall have a clear practical example of the need (as urged by Burger and Dorter) to consider each argument in its context, since this section of the dialogue will have presented us with the acknowledged *failure* of an argument. In this case, the analysis of the particular way or ways in which Socrates fails will be only the first, and easiest, task, for the interpreter; the next task will be to ask how the argument fits into the strategy of the whole work, and indeed what that strategy is, since it will already have been demonstrated that it does not consist simply in piling up a series of arguments for the chosen thesis. I take the affinity argument as my starting-point because it seems to me to establish this elementary but fundamental lesson with special clarity, and also because, taken together with Simmias' and Cebes' objections, and Socrates' reactions to them, it represents the most important part of the development of what I shall call the philosophical action of the dialogue.

I shall here summarize a much longer analysis of the affinity argument which I have given elsewhere.[17] In brief, when at 80b9-10 Socrates claims that ". . . it belongs to soul . . . to be absolutely indissoluble, or something close to this," what he means to claim is that he has shown that we have reason to believe *either* that the soul is in principle incapable of being dissolved, because incomposite, *or* that, though composite, it will in fact remain permanently undissolved into its parts (which would fairly be described as "something close to" absolute indivisibility). This is a reasonably accurate statement of what the

17. Rowe 1992.

argument justifies. On the one hand, Socrates has only said that it is "most likely"[18] that unchanging things like the forms—to which the soul is alleged to have "affinity"—are incomposite (that they are unchanging only strictly entails that they are not in fact divided or dissolved); on the other, by his use of the verb προσήκειν, he carefully avoids suggesting that he has proved anything. If property F is said to προσήκειν item x, no more need be meant than that we should expect x to be F, as the sequel shows: what is said (in 80b8-9) προσήκειν the body, i.e. to be quickly dissolved, is admitted in 80c-d hardly to be true of it at all. Even if the soul were like the forms in some respects, we might say that Socrates should not even have tried to base anything on that; but he does at least show a healthy awareness that it does not justify the conclusion that therefore the soul is, must be, like them in some further respect.

Yet when we reach 84b, we find Socrates giving the final conclusion of the argument without any qualifications of this sort at all: "there is *no danger*," he says there, "that (the soul which has lived the right kind of life) will fear . . . that it will be torn apart in its separation from the body . . . " It is this unqualified statement of the conclusion which immediately gives rise to Simmias' and Cebes' objections, although even before these are made, Socrates has himself said that "there are many ways in which [the preceding argument] leaves room for misgiving and counterattack."[19] The objections themselves are followed by Socrates' warning against "misology," which concludes[20] with a comparison of himself with those uneducated people who care only about winning a debate, and not about the truth of the subject about which they are speaking—presumably the eristics, the class represented by Euthydemus and Dionysodorus in the *Euthydemus*. The only difference, he says, is that whereas their aim is to make what they say seen true to their audience, his is, or rather will be, to convince himself, not his audience, "except

18. μάλιστα εἰκός 78c7.
19. 84c6-7.
20. 91a-c.

incidentally."[21] That of course is a rather considerable difference, since he has been marked out from the beginning as the complete philosopher; his λόγοι, if he is convinced by them, will therefore have to have passed the most stringent test available. Yet the comparison of himself with the eristics probably cannot be treated as merely ironical, for the sudden switch to the future tense in 91a6-7—"it seems to me that I *shall* differ from them only to this extent"—leaves open the possibility that he had earlier been behaving exactly like them, and putting the production of conviction in his audience before the truth. The reference here must be primarily to the argument from affinity, which was after all what gave rise to the present crisis in the discussion. Socrates' point is not necessarily that it was in itself a bad argument, merely that he claimed too much for it: the latter part, from 80c to 84b, did nothing to justify the move from "may reasonably be expected to be ἀδιάλυτον" to "*will* not be dissolved." But he must in that case now regard it as inadequate (as he was already showing signs of doing at 84c). That does not of course yet amount to a justification of my claim that he *abandons* it, since he will reply to Simmias' and Cebes' objections, and could simply try reverting to this original and more circumspect version of the conclusion. Later, however, as we shall see, he does appear to turn his back on the argument altogether.

Looked at in the way I have suggested, the inadequacies of the argument from affinity form an essential part of the movement of the dialogue. Through the objections from Simmias and Cebes, which they trigger, we pass on to a new and more ambitious set of λόγοι from Socrates—his excursus on explanation, and the final argument, on whose strength he is content, at least provisionally, to rest:[22] for the moment, he has succeeded in convincing himself—and Simmias and Cebes—of the truth of the proposition that the soul is deathless, and imperishable. That Plato was aware of the weakness of the affinity argument, especially since Simmias and Cebes point it out, is surely not in doubt; what matters, for anyone who is interested in the dia-

21. 91a8-9.
22. 107b4-9.

logue as such, is why he should have bothered to have Socrates put it forward. The clear answer is that it both contributes to the development of the plot,[23] and simultaneously teaches us something about philosophical argument in general: that it depends upon a commitment to finding truth, and not merely on an ability to convince those who happen to be listening.[24]

But it is equally clear that the philosopher cannot be satisfied with talking to himself. He has to argue his case in open forum, and submit it to examination by others. The idea of philosophy as mutual interchange is fundamental to the *Phaedo* as a whole. The question will always be: "are there counter-arguments to what I am now saying, which I cannot see myself?" This is what Socrates seemed temporarily to forget at the end of the affinity argument, only to be brought up short by Simmias and Cebes (though if they had not intervened, he would apparently have backtracked himself). The others, we discover, were thoroughly convinced by the argument;[25] Simmias and Cebes, however, are made of different stuff. If the mere ability to persuade is not enough for Socrates, it is certainly of importance to him to persuade *them*. Philosophy, if that means actually moving forward in the search for the true, is evidently not a matter of talking with just anyone; one must be talking to someone who, like the two Thebans, is capable of seeking out weaknesses, and proposing alternative avenues of inquiry. This will not in itself be a guarantee against error, but it is the only test available.

Simmias and Cebes have of course been crucial to the development of the conversation from the beginning: it is they who start it off, and who keep it going throughout. In this role they appear, if not as Socrates' equals, at least as close to that.[26] They

23. So forming a kind of false climax: compare Agathon's speech in the *Symposium*, and Socrates' second speech on love in the *Phaedrus*, both of which similarly tease us, momentarily, with a sense of closure.

24. Philosophy, then, is a dangerous game; we can never be quite sure of having played according to the rules (cf. Simmias' reference to "human weakness" at 107b1).

25. 88c-d.

26. Tuozzo objected to this that "neither of them ever in fact directs a dialectical investigation by assuming the questioner's role," and that when they are

are imbued with the Socratic conception of philosophy,[27] and are veterans of numerous previous discussion with the man himself.[28] The same may be supposed to be true of the others present,[29] but in the action of the dialogue they are mostly reduced to the status of mere onlookers, of an intellectual calibre inferior to that of these two—well-meaning, but too easily persuaded.[30] It has often been held that Simmias and Cebes are Pythagorean opponents of Socrates: even if they were Pythagoreans, for which it seems to me the evidence is extremely slight, the fact is scarcely given much prominence in the *Phaedo* itself. They may have heard Philolaus, but the dialogue gives much more emphasis to their familiarity with Socrates' methods and ideas.[31] (They are, for instance, as thoroughly committed to the hypothesis of the existence of forms as he is,

unhappy with a conclusion, they respond with speeches, which though insightful, "express that insight by means of an image." I doubt whether their objections to the affinity argument can be written off so easily; and if they do not direct any "dialectical investigation" of the type familiar from the "Socratic" dialogues, they certainly ask questions. The real issue, however, is once more about what constitutes "philosophy" (see n. 15 above), or dialectic. The philosopher/dialectician in Plato is not always the one who gets to ask the questions; in the *Phaedrus*, in fact, the position is reversed— it is his λόγοι which get to be questioned (*Phaedrus* 276a, 276e-277a, 278c-e). What matters is that Socrates, Simmias and Cebes are all involved in a particular type of conversation (i.e. in which each is properly critical of the others) and on a particular type of subject (whether or not the soul is immortal is, of course, a matter of crucial importance to Socrates). Socrates certainly still plays the leading part in that conversation; but Simmias and Cebes are not afraid to tackle him, and match argument with argument —which surely justifies my description of them.

27. See esp. Simmias' speech at 85b10-d10, which prepares the way for his and Cebes' objections.

28. 75c-d, 78d.

29. 59a, d.

30. 88c; cf. also the intervention of the confused, anonymous objector at 103c5-6.

31. I believe it true to say that the only evidence for regarding Simmias and Cebes as Pythagoreans comes from the *Phaedo* itself: a) they have associated with (συγγίγνεσθαι) and heard Philolaus, who is undoubtedly a Pythagorean; b) Simmias sponsors the theory of soul as a kind of ἁρμονία which Echecrates, also certainly (?) a Pythagorean, is firmly attached to. But neither συγγίγνεσθαι nor hearing someone necessarily implies adherence to his school; and if it does imply it, Simmias and Cebes are quite certainly (also) Socratics. Nor does the fact that someone who belongs to a particular school accepts an idea necessarily

which is hardly something we should expect them to have got from Philolaus. Perhaps they can only fictionally have got it from Socrates, but that is a different matter.)[32] Their actual role is as partners in the discussion, of sufficient intelligence and articulateness, and openness of mind, to help drive it forward. So it is, perhaps, that the Socrates of the *Phaedrus* singles out "Simmias the Theban" as the one person who might have brought more λόγοι into existence than Phaedrus—except that the λόγοι which captivate *Phaedrus* are of a rather different kind.[33] The theory of soul as an attunement—whatever the origin of the theory—is put forward by Simmias only as an extension of his original objection to the affinity argument, and he abandons it as soon as he is faced with a choice between it and the hypothesis of forms. What Phaedo reports is a conversation between like-thinking but critical minds, collaborating in the construction and demolition of arguments; a process which can be called philosophical just to the extent that the collaboration is successful.

---

imply that the idea belongs to the school; even if it did imply it, someone else's accepting it does not necessarily imply that the someone else belongs to that school, unless perhaps the idea is central to its doctrines. But the attunement theory is actually at odds with other central ideas associated with Pythagoreanism (immortality, transmigration), and Aristotle, for one, does not describe it as Pythagorean, even though he has plenty of opportunity to do so, having just referred to the Pythagorean doctrine of transmigration (*De anima* I. 3-4). At least since Burnet, it has been usual to treat the whole dialogue as being set in a Pythagorean *ambience*, because *Phaedo* relates the conversation in Echecrates' home town of Phlius, where others are reputed to have shared his Pythagorean leanings. But the setting in Phlius is already sufficiently explained by the fact that Philus is on the way from Athens to Elis, *Phaedo's* native city, that Echecrates and Phlius are a long way from Athens, and news of Socrates' last day in prison have not yet reached them, and that Echecrates, being philosophically minded, is naturally interested in such news (see McQueen and Rowe 1989). Finally, if it is sufficient for being a Pythagorean that one accepts at least one Pythagorean doctrine, then the Socrates of the *Phaedo* is Pythagorean because he accepts transmigration; but he rejects the harmony-theory, the acceptance of which by Simmias is allegedly one of the grounds for treating him as a Pythagorean. (See further below, on 61d-e.)

32. See p. 167-8 below.

33. *Phaedrus* 242a-b; cf. below on 62e-63a.

Cebes begins the serious questioning, at 61d, by asking Socrates how he can accept the universal prohibition on suicide, and yet propose that "the philosopher will be willing to follow the dying." Socrates' response is to ask whether he and Simmias haven't heard Philolaus talking about such things, when he was in Thebes—presumably because he counts Philolaus, as opposed to Evenus, who has just been ironically dismissed, as a true philosopher.[34] Simultaneously, the association of Cebes and Simmias with Philolaus suggests the same of them. Socrates goes on to remark delightedly, at 62e-63a, on Cebes' diligence in questioning (Cebes has just pointed out an apparent inconsistency in his position): "he's always sniffing out some argument or other, and he's not at all willing to believe at once what anyone may say." Simmias, not to be outdone, immediately adds his weight to Cebes' objection, after which Socrates launches into a defence of himself, "as if in a court of law."

We should then expect a set speech; instead, Socrates presents his defence by means of his usual procedure of question and answer—a point which is underlined by the interruption of the jailer, who says that he ought to "converse" (διαλέγεθσαι) as little as possible, and Socrates' reaction to this: tell him to go away, and if talking interferes with the working of the poison, let him prepare to give me as many doses as necessary.[35] The philosopher, then, will defend himself in the mode which belongs to his activity. We might be tempted, despite this, to classify what Socrates has to say as rhetorical rather than philosophical, insofar as it contains more persuasive, and frequently

34. Cebes' responses at 61d7 and e6 suggest that Philolaus endorses the first of the two propositions paradoxically paired by Socrates (the prohibition against suicide), but not the second (that philosophers will want to die as soon as possible)— as, according to Socrates, any philosopher should (c6). There is no necessity to assume that the mention of Philolaus is in any way connected with his status as a Pythagorean; it may be enough simply that he is a prominent philosopher who had visited Thebes when Simmias and Cebes were there. There is equally nothing to suggest that the ἄλλοι τινές whom Cebes says he also heard speaking against suicide were Pythagoreans (so incidentally downplaying Philolaus as an influence on him), although they might have been (61e7-8); since Socrates too is against it, the doctrine was not exclusively Pythagorean.

35. 63d-e.

hyperbolic, description than argument. But there is no indication that Socrates, or Simmias or Cebes, see it in this way; rather the contrary, since the *"defence"* merges seamlessly into, and provides the starting-point for, the arguments for immortality that follow.[36] Cebes accepts nearly everything else Socrates says about philosophy and philosophers: we may suppose he has heard most of it before,[37] and if he accepts the idea of separate forms, as he evidently does, his acceptance of the main line of Socrates' defence is probably guaranteed in any case. Nonetheless, he has a question: how will Socrates deal with the fact that people in general are afraid that the soul perishes when a man dies?[38] What he thinks himself, he doesn't say; later, Socrates is required to persuade him and Simmias *as if* they were afraid of such a thing.[39] This reception by Cebes of Socrates' defence is part of what makes it a piece of philosophy in Socrates' terms. In general, for Socrates, what distinguishes a philosophical λόγος from a rhetorical one, as from an eristic λόγος,[40] is ideally a combination of intention and reception: that what is said is said with the expectation of its being received critically, and that it is so received, puts it firmly within the context of φιλοσοφία, *qua* the search for wisdom.[41] Both philosopher and orator seek to persuade, but from different motives.[42]

The terms of Cebes' interjection at 69e show his true worth as a collaborator in the discussion. He points out in effect that the definition of death which Socrates has proposed begs the crucial

36. Cf. n. 15 above.

37. If, that is, he has been a regular member of Socrates' circle: see p. 160-1 above.

38. 69e-70b.

39. "ὡς δεδιότων;" or rather, not ὡς ἡμῶν δεδιότων, but there is perhaps a child even in us who fears such things"– i.e., as Socrates has jokingly suggested, that the soul may literally be blown apart on its separation from the body, especially if death occurs in a high wind (77d-e).

40. See 90e-91c, with p. 158-9 above.

41. Such a view emerges especially clearly from a combination of 90e-91c, 85c-d (Simmias' excursus on methodology), and 99-101 (Socrates on his "second sailing," where he implicitly endorses Simmias' position).

42. For which see *Gorgias passim,* and those parts of the *Phaedrus* which criticise contemporary rhetoric.

question, whether the soul which is separated from the body at death really is something which has "power" and "directing intelligence" (as Socrates had gone on to assume), or whether it is rather something so insubstantial, as most people suppose, that it might immediately be dispersed. (What "most people" think is evidently related to Homeric ideas: that a soul can go beneath the earth "like smoke," and that the souls of the dead are witless.[43]) Anyone—unless he is a supporter of the attunement theory to be introduced later by Simmias—can accept that death is the separation of soul from body, but Socrates needs more than that (as he himself hinted at 66e5-6[44]). There may also be signs of at least some resistance to other parts of his defence: we may notice, for example, Simmias' "it seems so" at 65a3, in response to Socrates' description of what is "clear" about the philosopher's attitude to physical pleasures; contrast his unstinting acceptance of Socrates' next point ("what you say is absolutely true").

Similarly with Cebes in the course of the following argument (the "cyclical" argument): while he has accepted the premises proposed by Socrates, he shows some reluctance about agreeing to what it is to be got from them.[45] "You say, don't you, that being dead is opposite to living? "I do." "And that they come to be from each other?" "Yes." "So what is it that comes to be from that which is living?" "What is dead." "And what comes to be from what is dead?" "I have to agree that it is what is living." "Then it is from what is dead, Cebes, that living things and living people come to be?" "It seems so." "Then our souls do exist in Hades." "Apparently." Then again, when Socrates proposes that there must be some opposite process to dying, Cebes answers with an ambiguous "Absolutely, I suppose."[46] Admittedly, he makes no direct criticisms of the argument, nor does he object when at 77c Socrates represents him and Simmias as having accepted it (fairly enough, given that he took on board

43. *Iliad* 23. 100-104.
44. δυοῖν θάτερον, ἢ οὐδαμοῦ ἔστιν κρήσαθαι τὸ εἰδέναι ἢ τελευτήσασιν ...
45. 71d6ff.
46. 71e11 πάντως που.

all of its steps, however reluctantly); moreover, his contribution at 72d4-5, at the end of the argument itself, could be taken as implying that it has his full endorsement. But that remark in fact strictly only applies to Socrates' last move;[47] and if Cebes had any enthusiasm for the argument as a whole, it has certainly evaporated by 77c—while he may not explicitly object to Socrates' saying that he had accepted it, he has to be reminded about it, and takes no notice of Socrates' claim that it amounts to a "proof," preferring instead his offer of something new. Simmias, for his part, has just contradicted it, by asking innocently "what's to prevent [a man's soul] from coming to be . . . from some other source (i.e. than the dead)?"[48] In these circumstances, it is hard to suppose that when Cebes and Simmias later say, at 91e4, that they accept some of the previous λόγοι but not others, the "cyclical" argument is meant to be one of the "some." If they did not voice any objections, they have only themselves to blame if Socrates himself treats it as a good argument. On the other hand, if he has not succeeded in persuading them, no real advance has been made. We may think of his exhortation at 91c2-4: "if I seem to you to be saying something true, give me your agreement; but if not, resist with all the resources of argument, taking care that in my zeal I do not deceive both myself and you, and go off like a bee leaving its sting behind."

If Cebes was unhappy about the consequences of accepting the premises of the cyclical argument, he should presumably have "resisted" by withdrawing his agreement to them. He could have pointed out, among other things, that the "opposites from opposites" principle will work only in the case of comparatives, and of contradictories, not of contraries; and that there are not in fact always complementary pairs of processes between opposites, as Socrates proposes. Quite what Plato would have identified as the flaws in the λόγος as a whole, we can only guess; but that he knew that there was *something* wrong with it is, I think, reasonably well established. It is there, perhaps, as a deliberately

47. οὐδὲ μία μοι δοκεῖ (sc. μηχανὴ μὴ οὐχὶ πάντα καταναλωθῆναι εἰς τὸ τεθνάναι . . . , ἀλλά μοι δοκεῖς . . .

48. 77b5-7.

unsatisfactory first attempt, which will call for replacement. The absence of any critical assessment of it may be explained partly by the fact that that would take our eye away from the second and more important part of Cebes' original challenge, to show that what survives death "possesses power and intelligence,"[49] which is answered by the argument from recollection.[50] Cebes conveniently obliges by remembering the basis of this new argument himself;[51] it is thus his desire to contribute which is responsible for cutting off any discussion of the cyclical argument, not Socrates himself. By the time the recollection argument is finished, it is too late, and Socrates is able to say "but the two of you did accept the previous one," while simultaneously recognising that it has not satisfied them. But the situation does also neatly illustrate Socrates' later lesson, about the need to resist if he appears not to be speaking the truth. (Other methodological points are similarly anticipated in the dialogue: so, for example, aspects of the hypothetical method which Socrates will favour have been in play long before he formally describes it at 99-101.[52])

Still, Cebes' helpfulness in preparing the way for the next argument more than makes up for his lapse, if that is what it is (the dialectical model of philosophy presupposes cooperation as well as criticism). The way in which he reports the theory of learning as recollection, and proposes it as another consideration in favour of the soul's immortality, strongly suggests a covert reference to the *Meno*.[53] If so, then the *Phaedo* is correcting the *Meno*, since as Simmias will point out,[54] the theory—if true—will only indicate the soul's pre-existence, not its capacity to survive death. In the fictional context of the dialogue, however, Cebes has learnt about it from Socrates (it is "that *logos* which you are always in the habit of putting forward"[55]), and Simmias is cor-

49. 70b2-4.

50. See 76c12-13.

51. 72e.

52. Cf. n. 40 above, and pp. 169-70 below.

53. See esp. *Meno* 86a-b.

54. 77a-b.

55. 72e4-5.

recting Cebes: Socrates' own conclusion from the theory is carefully restricted to pre-existence. Here all three are working together, as they have before; just as Cebes refers to what he has *often* heard about from Socrates, so the latter refers, in talking to Simmias, to what "we" do in "our" question-and-answer sessions.[56] Simmias' role in the argument itself is also far from being a passive one. They end with a joint conclusion: that the argument stands or falls with the existence of forms—the beautiful, the good, the equal, and the rest. Simmias declares that their existence is perfectly plain to him, and consequently gives his complete endorsement to the argument (as Cebes does later on his own account[57]). Socrates himself treats the existence of the forms as hypothetical ("*if* the things we are always harping on exist . . . "[58]); Simmias' considered position is that it is a "hypothesis worthy of acceptance."[59]

From the point of view of the overall strategy of the dialogue, this acceptance of the form-hypothesis, and the stress on its strength and importance, matter as much as the argument from recollection itself. The latter, even if it does not help towards establishing immortality, still has the crucial function of showing that the disembodied soul is something substantial and capable of thought (it will also be useful as a first line of defence against Simmias' attunement-theory). But the form-hypothesis will be the basis of the final and allegedly most powerful argument,[60] and cannot appear as a *deus ex machina*, a sudden and arbitrary proposal. The process of its introduction of course began way back, during Socrates' "defence"; now we have been given a practical demonstration of its importance, and it is placed more firmly centre-stage, where it will be kept by the affinity argument. From the dramatic, or fictional, perspective, the conversation has made its first real gains, provisional though they may be: if forms exist, then the three main characters are agreed that

56. 75d1-3; similarly (to Cebes) at 78d1-2.
57. 92a2-3.
58. 76d7-8; cf. 100b4-7.
59. 92d6-9.
60. 100b3-9, 102a10-b2.

the soul must at any rate pre-exist its attachment to the body, as a conscious, thinking entity.

How good, or bad, the recollection argument is, is not relevant to my present purposes;[61] what concerns me here is simply how it is received by the characters within the dialogue, and its general contribution to the structure of the whole. It wholly persuades Simmias and Cebes, and is the only one of Socrates' arguments which does so, with the exception of the last: the rider which Simmias attaches, with Socrates' approval, to his acceptance of that[62] would apply equally to his acceptance of the recollection argument. But their endorsement is immediately followed by a complaint about just how little has been achieved. "It appears," Cebes says, echoing Simmias, "that half, as it were, of what is needed has been demonstrated:"[63] "half, as it were," because it is not the important half. The soul might pre-exist, but that is perfectly consistent with its coming to the end of its existence on its separation from the body. The position that Cebes began by attributing to people in general, and from which he probed Socrates' defence, remains thereby untouched—if we ignore the cyclical argument, as he and Simmias do. It is against a restatement of this position, after a further short homily on the supreme value of philosophical inquiry,[64] that Socrates launches the abortive argument from affinity.

Following that, Simmias shifts up a gear. He makes a statement of his own methods:[65] a man (if he is really a man) must exhaustively test what is said about subjects like the present one; he must either learn how things are from others, or discover it for himself—or, failing that, take the best and least refutable λόγος available, and cling to that. Having made an effective assault on the affinity argument as such,[66] he then seems to go

61. For a detailed analysis of this and other arguments, see my forthcoming commentary on the *Phaedo*.

62. 107a8-b3.

63. 77c1-2.

64. 77e-78a.

65. 85c-d.

66. 85e3-86b5.

Christopher Rowe

on to apply the procedure he has described, abandoning the populist position he has represented so far, and taking up the more specialized theory of soul as attunement. This, for the moment, is "the best λόγος available" to him. Socrates later describes it as a "hypothesis;"[67] and it is reasonable to suppose that when Simmias talks in 85c about "taking the best and most irrefutable λόγος" (or rather "most difficult to refute"), he is referring to the same sort of general procedure envisaged by Socrates at 100a as part of his δεύτερος πλοῦς—that is, that "taking the best and δυσεξελεγκτότατος λόγος" is in principle the same as Socrates' "hypothesising the strongest λόγος on each occasion."[68] Simmias treats the attunement theory genuinely as a hypothesis, being prepared to abandon it in favour of another when that seems better;[69] he may also be said to apply it in the same way that Socrates says that he applies each of his hypothetical λόγοι "positing as true whatever seems in accord with it . . . , and whatever does not as not true,"[70] insofar as it leads him to assert the perishability of soul, and deny its capacity to survive death. He may be his own man, but the kind of man he is bears a striking resemblance in method, as well as attitude, to Socrates himself.

Simmias, then, grasps the initiative, and Cebes follows suit; together, they seem to the others, dismayingly, to undermine not only the affinity argument as such, but everything Socrates has previously said. "All of us who heard them were disagreeably affected by what they said . . . , because we had been fully persuaded by the previous argument, yet now they seemed to throw us into confusion again, and make us doubt, not only the arguments put forward before but also things yet to be said, for fear that we were worthless judges, or even that the things themselves might be inherently doubtful."[71] Echecrates echoes these feelings that Phaedo reports: ". . . it occurs to me to say to

67. 94b1-2.
68. 100a3-4.
69. 92c11-e3.
70. 100a4-7.
71. 88c1-7.

176

myself something like this: 'What argument shall we ever trust in now? How thoroughly persuasive was the argument that Socrates gave us, and yet now it has fallen into discredit.'"[72] He adds the immediate reason for his reaction; Simmias has reminded him that he is himself an adherent of the view that "our soul is a kind a attunement."[73] The result is that "I very much need once again, as if from the beginning, some other argument which will persuade me that the soul of the dead person does not die with him."[74] The reversal is complete: we seem to be right back where we started.

Socrates, undeterred himself, rallies the company with a warning against misology, and the skepticism of the antilogicians; then comes the passage at 90-91, which I took as an admission of error in the way he had finally presented the affinity argument, as conclusive rather than merely plausible. A page or so later, Simmias is found talking about λόγοι which base their (alleged) proofs on τὰ εἰκότα ("what is plausible," or "likely," or "probable"), and describing them as ἀλαῃόνες,[75] "impostors": both descriptions fit Socrates' argument well, the second at least in virtue of what he appeared to claim for it. Once again, Simmias appears as being at one with Socrates; he has no need of his lessons himself, as the others, and Echecrates, have (and perhaps, too, the intended readers of the dialogue).

The battle lines are set, and Socrates advances against what he calls Simmias' and Cebes' λόγος.[76] On being asked to choose between the attunement theory and the theory of learning as recollection, Simmias chooses the latter, on the grounds that it was firmly based (on the hypothesis of the existence of the forms, which thus acquires still further prominence), as the former was not. With the reinstatement of the recollection argument (though Cebes had himself explicitly proposed to retain it),[77]

72. c9-d3.
73. d3-6.
74. d6-8.
75. 89c3-4.
76. 87a, 88a.
77. 88b5-6.

the discussion is back where it was at 77a-b: we again have
"half, as it were" of what is required, i.e. that soul pre-exists
body (in intelligent form), but not the other and more important
"half," that it survives death (or rather, as Cebes has insisted,
that it is *altogether* immortal, and imperishable). After two more,
disappointingly *ad hominem* arguments against the attunement
theory,[78] Socrates turns his attention to Cebes' challenge. He
appears to accept his criticism of the affinity argument: as he
puts it in his recapitulation of Cebes' objection, a demonstration
that the soul is something strong and godlike, even when combined with its pre-existence, is insufficient to indicate its immortality.[79] There is no suggestion here that its strength and godlike
nature was actually demonstrated, or at least there ought not to
be, if Socrates is merely restating what Cebes said, as he claims
to be. Cebes accepted that the soul was stronger and longer-last-
ing than the body, but his analogy with the weaver suggested
that it was still consistent with that that it should perish before
the body—or rather, before the last body which it "weaves."
This in itself implies a rejection of the affinity argument as such,
since on this account the resemblance to the forms, on which
Socrates relied, is minimal, at least so far as concerns their
unchangeability. Cebes then went on to say that if one were
hypothetically to concede even more to Socrates' position, and
grant both that the soul pre-existed the body, and that it was
capable of surviving numerous cycles of conjunction and separation from it, that still would not be sufficient to prove our fears
about death to be irrational, because the soul might be worn out
by the process, and perish in one of the separations; indeed, in
that case it would be irrational not to fear death. Socrates no
doubt still holds that the soul does resemble the forms in the relevant respects, but that is a different matter. The affinity argument as such is, I conclude, well and truly buried; a different
tack if needed.

78. "Disappointingly *ad hominem*," because they are valid only against
Simmias' version of the theory, not against other and more interesting versions
of it.

79. 95c4-d4. Actually, he says only that *"you say* that it is insufficient:" but the
fact that he responds to Cebes' challenge by constructing a new argument
strongly suggests that he accepts the point.

The long section which follows, leading up to and including the final argument, is either monologue, or involves a minimal contribution from anyone except Socrates: a lone objection, involving an elementary confusion, comes from an anonymous member of the audience;[80] Cebes says that what this person has said does not trouble him, though he is troubled by many other things (he does not, however, expand on what these are);[81] and that, until the very end, is all. The passage is also largely independent of anything that has gone before. Since my main concern is with interactions in the dialogue between characters and arguments, I shall therefore content myself with the sketchiest of remarks about it. The major part revolves around the form-hypothesis: Socrates first sets up some puzzles about coming-into-being and perishing, which he claims that the methods of the scientists—relations, perhaps, of the proponents of the attunement theory—are unable to resolve; then, having described the kind of theory of explanation which he would have liked then to offer, he introduces his own "homely" kind, based on the form-hypothesis, and recommends it on the grounds that it provides an apparently unobjectionable way out of the puzzles in question. Since the hypothesis has proved its usefulness, he now feels entitled to employ it to construct his promised argument, which results in a conclusion of the type demanded by Cebes. The only point relevant to my immediate purposes is the simple fact of the centrality to the argument of the forms. They were in the foreground long before; now they are put to (more or less) triumphant use. That they exist, and that particulars can, or may, be explained in terms of their participation in them, is the key concept in the dialogue. But to be of any use in forwarding the discussion, it has to have the agreement of Socrates' partners. Even when they are playing a more passive role, as here, the presence of Simmias and Cebes *as philosophers in the Socratic mould* is essential.

80. 103a4-10.

81. 103c5-6. This brief contribution from Cebes further lifts him above the level of the majority of those present (see p. 160-1 above): if the anonymous objector needs Socrates' clarification in 103a11-c4 (as Plato evidently thought we might), he does not; at the same time it is hinted that he has other, perhaps more serious, problems with Socrates' argument.

Cebes does, however, contribute a vital step to the last argument, by conceding that what is deathless must be everlasting.[82] (Whether he should have made this concession is disputable, or at any rate disputed; but Socrates seems to think he should—and as a matter of fact I agree with Socrates.) And it is Simmias, not Socrates, who enters a qualification to the argument:

"... neither do I have any further grounds for doubting [that the soul is *athanatos* and imperishable]; however, in view of the size of the subjects of the arguments, and having a low regard for human weakness, I am compelled still to entertain some doubt in my own mind about what has been said."[83]

Socrates accepts this: "Right: not only that . . . , but—both that is well said, and what's more, our initial hypotheses [those of 102ab], even if they carry conviction with the two of you, still, they must be examined more clearly." But he ends on an upbeat note:

"and if you analyse them adequately, I think, you will follow out the argument [i.e. the one that will establish the soul's immortality], to the limits of human capacity; and if this very thing becomes clear [the reference, perhaps, is to the results of further analysis of the hypotheses, together with their consequences for the argument], you will look for nothing further."[84]

The implication, I think, is both that the hypotheses ("that each of the forms exists, and that the other things have the names of these very things by coming to share in them"[85]) are fundamentally correct, and that an argument based on them, of the sort just presented, will be sufficient—within the limits Simmias has suggested—to give us the required result: the soul is indeed immortal. If victory has not quite been achieved, and further

82. 106d2-4.
83. 107a8-b3.
84. b4-9.
85. 102b1-2.

discussion is needed ("*if indeed* the soul is immortal," Socrates goes on[86]), yet it seems close. After all its vicissitudes, the conversation has, more or less, justified his optimism in the face of death (or so he thinks).

*****

My aim has been to propose, or perhaps to reassert, a view of the *Phaedo* as a dramatic representation of the activity of philosophy, in which the three actors perform a complex and carefully articulated dance of λόγοι. The dialogue is, of course, also dramatic in a more obvious sense—in terms of its real action; but it simultaneously diverts our attention away from that, and mostly downplays its importance in favour of what the protagonist, Socrates, regards as more significant, the business of serious conversation. Its overt subject is death, but its real focus is on the question about how life itself is to be conducted. There can hardly be any doubt that Plato is serious about the idea of the soul surviving death, since it is one that he proposes repeatedly in other dialogues. It never appears, however, except in connection with the question about the nature of the best human life. Since this is a question that is raised elsewhere in different contexts (in the *Symposium*, for example, or in the *Philebus*), the choice of the theme of immortality might even in a sense be regarded as incidental. That would from most points of view be a perverse judgement; much of the effect of the work derives from the tension between the dispassionateness (mostly, though not always) of the arguments at its core and the apparently traumatic events that frame them and provide their immediate motive. Yet the chief spectacle is of philosophers going about their business, and discussing immortality as the conversation happens to turn to that, just as they have discussed other topics before. The main singularity of the *Phaedo*, apart from its setting, lies in its sustained demonstration of what co-operative dialogue can be, when individuals come together in a common understanding of and commitment to the ideals of philosophy. No other Platonic work is in this respect quite like it.

University of Bristol

86. c2.

Commentary on Rowe
Thomas M. Tuozzo

Professor Rowe distinguishes two opposing approaches to Plato. One seeks to isolate discrete arguments embedded in a Platonic dialogue and to evaluate the validity of their reasoning and the plausibility of their premises. This method necessarily focusses on particular passages where it appears that something like a formal argument can be reconstructed from the questions and answers of the interlocutors, and treats the dramatic context of these exchanges as philosophically unimportant. The other approach holds that the philosophical content of a dialogue can be determined only by seeing the dialogue as a whole, and, in particular, that dramatic context and the character of the inter-locutors are crucial for the understanding and evaluation of a dialogue's arguments. Rowe takes this second approach to the arguments of the *Phaedo*, and I find myself in complete agreement with him on the value and indeed necessity of doing so. Unfortunately, this approach produces extremely divergent interpretations (as the books of Burger[1] and Dorter[2] cited by Rowe make plain), and offers less hope of a definitive assessment of a Platonic dialogue than the approach that focusses narrowly on argumentative passages (theoretically) does. Nevertheless, like Rowe, I think the attempt at this more ambitious sort of interpretation is eminently worth making—to quote from the myth in the *Phaedo*, καλὸς γὰρ ὁ κίνδυνος—and although I disagree with Rowe on a number of important points,

1. Burger 1984.
2. Dorter 1982.

these disagreements should be seen within the context of my broader agreement with him on this crucial methodological issue.

Rowe maintains that to evaluate the philosophical contribution of a Platonic dialogue on the basis of an evaluation of its arguments is to assume that "on each occasion [Plato] was attempting simply to construct the best argument of the type that would appeal to one sort of modern academic philosopher" (p. 156). If one does make such an assumption, then Plato is charged with the errors of any fallacious arguments his characters give. Now Rowe believes that several arguments in the *Phaedo* —notably the cyclical and affinity arguments—are fallacious. But since Plato "views philosophy in a somewhat different way from those who claim to be his modern counterparts" (p. 156), we cannot move from an evaluation of an argument to a judgment on its author "until we have investigated the purpose of the argument, as measured by the way it is introduced, presented and received" (p. 155). That is to say, we must consider its dramatic context.

Now I agree with Rowe that Plato is not interested solely in producing the best argument on each occasion. But I think that Rowe's own view of what Plato is up to in the *Phaedo* is perilously close to his caricature of one sort of modern philosopher. In what follows I shall show how this is so, and suggest ways in which Plato may be even further away from a single-minded concern with deductive argument.

Rowe acknowledges the importance of dramatic context for understanding the arguments in the *Phaedo*, and certainly the personalities of the characters that give and listen to these arguments are a crucial part of the dramatic context. But Rowe insists that between the personalities of Socrates, Simmias and Cebes there is no difference—at least none that affects the arguments or their presentation in the dialogue. Simmias and Cebes are "philosophers in the Socratic mould" (p. 174); they "appear, if not as Socrates' equals, at least as close to that" (p. 160). And what do Socratic philosophers do? They "collaborat[e] in the construction and demolition of arguments," which activity "can be called philosophical in part just to the extent that the collaboration is successful" (p. 162). Aside from the requirement for success (which I do not understand), this activity seems remarkably like that of modern, argument-oriented philosophers. Of course, Socrates and company are not to be confused with Plato, and depicting philosophers engaged in constructing arguments is not precisely the same thing as constructing arguments yourself. Indeed, Rowe exploits this distinction in order to avoid having to saddle Plato with arguments Rowe considers straightforwardly fallacious. For Plato wishes to *depict* philosophical activity, i.e., collaboration in the construction and demolition of arguments, as well as to engage in it himself. To depict the demolition of arguments, you have to produce arguments susceptible to demolition (after all, we want to illustrate progress towards the truth, not degeneration into error or the triumph of sophistry); therefore, you must show your philosophers making mistakes in order to illustrate their coming to each other's rescue. In so doing Plato is able to illustrate common errors to avoid—claiming your argument proves more than it does, aiming for mere persuasion rather than the truth—as well as the general need for collaboration.

On Rowe's view, then, the arguments in the *Phaedo* fall into two groups: the fallacious ones Plato introduces merely to illustrate philosophical activity, and those of which Plato himself approves. The latter group turns out to comprise the recollection argument and the final, ontological argument for the soul's immortality—just the arguments that have been found most nearly successful, or most interestingly fallacious, by commentators concerned solely with the validity of the arguments in the *Phaedo*.

This near-convergence of Rowe's view with that of those who take an "arguments-only" approach to the *Phaedo* suggests that perhaps Rowe has not done full justice to the relation of the dramatic context to the arguments. In the first place, Rowe must treat the cyclical, recollection, affinity and ontological arguments as isolated, logically independent arguments, which can be neatly sorted into the fallacious and rejected on the one hand, and the sound (in Plato's eyes) on the other. There are difficulties in so treating them, however, some of which Rowe sees and attempts to overcome. Thus Rowe thinks that, though the affinity argument is carefully worked out and fails only because Socrates "appear[s] to claim" (p. 159)[3] that it proves more than it does, it is nonetheless thoroughly—and rightly—rejected by the three philosophers. (It is "well and truly buried" [p. 159].) So too Rowe holds that the cyclical argument is rejected by Socrates, Simmias, and Cebes, although none of them voices a criticism of it. That the fallacies in the argument are ignored may seem to contradict Rowe's thesis that fallacious arguments are included just so the collaborative activity of detecting their fallaciousness can be illustrated; Rowe is undecided between two opposing ways of dealing with this problem. (Either Plato is here illustrating a way of dealing with an egregious argument by tactfully ignoring it and replacing it with a better one [p. 166], or he is illustrating the trouble you get into if you do so ignore it [p. 167].) The only sign that Rowe finds in the dialogue that the cyclical argument is rejected is Simmias' question at 77b, which Rowe thinks is in contradiction with the cyclical argument. Simmias asks: "What prevents it [the soul] from coming to be *and coming together* (συνίστασθαι) from some place else and existing before it arrives in a human body?"[4] The word συνίστασθαι here suggests how this query can be consistent with the cyclical argument. That argument had only purported to show that soul, as the principle of life, must persist after death. It did not show that a soul remains whole and does not decompose into smaller elements, which might recombine in other ways (and with elements from other souls) to animate another body. The recollection argument has supported some sort of intelligent continuity between the soul before and after birth; but the

3. The affinity argument is often thought to have only a probable conclusion, and to be accepted by Simmias and Cebes; they are just not content with a probable conclusion. In one of his seminars Rowe argued that the argument is in fact meant to exhibit an error that Simmias and Cebes detect.

4. The reader should note that my translations sometimes imply an understanding of the text different from Rowe's.

specter of dissolution after death and radical recombination before rebirth still remains. Simmias raises this specter, and Socrates immediately addresses it in the affinity argument, which accordingly supplements, not replaces, the cyclical argument.[5] Furthermore, Plato incorporates a reference to the cyclical argument in the final, ontological argument (103ab). Although only an aside brought in to help make a metaphysical distinction, nonetheless this mention is significant. The metaphysical distinction could have been made without reference to the cyclical argument; Plato may well refer to it here to indicate that his most sophisticated argument is meant to supplement, not replace, the earlier, simpler one. At any rate it cannot be said that the cyclical argument is contemptuously ignored after 77d.

Rowe's insistence that the arguments can be divided into the good and the bad, with the latter included only to provide illustrations of philosophical self-correction, prevents him from seeing how the arguments might build on one another. This treatment of the arguments in isolation sits oddly with Rowe's intention of seeing the dialogue as a whole. Indeed, the sort of unity he sees in the series of arguments comes down, as it must, to what may justly be called a "merely" literary one—marked by such devices as "false climax" (p. 160), the wish to avoid a "deus ex machina" (p. 168), etc. This further suggests that Rowe's attempt to find a deeper unity between argument and dramatic context has miscarried.

I turn from Rowe's treatment of the arguments themselves to his treatment of the characters of Simmias and Cebes. In order to make them out to be Socratic philosophers, Rowe must minimize their Pythagorean affiliation. I find this move unconvincing. While it is true that later reports of their being Pythagoreans may be ultimately based on the *Phaedo*, Philolaus, with whom they are twice said to have associated (61de), is amply attested as an important Pythagorean.[6] (The suggestion that Philolaus merely serves as the type of the true [Socratic?]

5. For this interpretation of 77b, see Dorter, pp. 70-71.
6. See the chapter on Philolaus in Burkert 1972, pp. 218-298.

186

philosopher [p. 161] seems to me too easy.) Furthermore, Rowe makes nothing of the fact that *Phaedo* is narrating the conversation to Echecrates, whom we know from Aristoxenus to have been a Pythagorean.[7]

More important for our purposes than any prior philosophical orientation on the part of Simmias and Cebes, however, is their skill at Socratic philosophizing. Even after Rowe's paper, I am afraid that I cannot see that either of them ever pinpoints the fallacy Rowe thinks the affinity argument—or Socrates' claims for it—commit. Indeed, they do not develop the objections they raise at the end of this argument dialectically, but rather express them by means of well-chosen images.[8] Now if Socratic examination of a proposal or argument consists quite generally in "seeking out weaknesses and proposing alternative avenues of inquiry" (p. 160), as Rowe maintains, then perhaps these image-dependent responses count as philosophy at a high level. But if adherence to the systematic procedure of the method of hypothesis is necessary, then the performances of Simmias and Cebes must be put down as those of gifted, but undisciplined trainees.[9]

7. Wehrli fr. 19, cf. fr. 18, p.13,30-34. Aristoxenus tells us in fr. 19 that he was personally acquainted with Echecrates.

8. Simmias argues that the affinity argument could be used to show that an attunement would survive a lyre's destruction; since this is absurd, the affinity argument will not help us if the soul is something like an attunement of the body. Cebes, on the other hand, argues that the affinity argument could be used to show that a weaver must survive the coat he died in; since this is absurd, the affinity argument will not help us if the soul is something like a weaver and the body its coat. Their mode of arguments is very much like that of Thrasymachus in *Republic* I: when Socrates argues that the skilful ruler, like all possessors of a skill, is concerned with the good of that which he rules over, Thrasymachus objects that such an argument would prove that the skilful shepherd is concerned with the good of his sheep. Since this is absurd (as Frank Perdue and his chicken factories show), Socrates' argument will not work if the skilful ruler is like a shepherd and the city the flock he exploits. Although Simmias and Cebes certainly share more in common with Socrates than Thrasymachus does, and Simmias, especially, seems to have given some thought to methodological issues, I do not really see that in point of dialectical ability they stand very much higher than Thrasymachus.

9. Simmias' gropings towards something like the method of hypothesis (85c-d) should not obscure the fact that in accepting the attunement theory as proof that the soul is not immortal without confronting that theory with the hypothesis

There is another non-philosophic side to Simmias and Cebes, one that is extremely important for understanding the arguments Socrates addresses to them. At the end of the recollection argument, Simmias and Cebes ask for more argument for the soul's immortality. Rowe suggests that they have understandable reservations about the cyclical argument. But Cebes gives a rather different reason. Responding to Socrates' remark that Simmias and Cebes seem to have a child's fear of what will happen to their souls after death, Cebes says:

> Attempt to persuade us out of this, Socrates, as though we were frightened. Or rather, not as though we were frightened, but perhaps there is a child in us who fears such things. Try to persuade him over not to fear death like the bogeyman. (77e)

The idea here that the arguments to follow will be directed at the frightened child in Simmias and Cebes suggests that the arguments have an important emotional component, and so cannot be adequately treated as pure exercise in the construction and demolition of arguments. Socrates' reply strengthens this impression:

> You must sing incantations (ἐπᾴδειν) to him (sc. the frightened child) every day until you have charmed him away (ἐξεπᾴσητε). (77e)

Cebes immediately laments the imminent passing of that "good enchanter" (ἀγαθὸν ἐπῳδόν), Socrates, which suggests that Socrates' contributions to the dialogue function, in part, as the needed incantations. This certainly includes the affinity argument, which immediately follows the call for incantations, and presumably the ontological argument as well. But it also includes the great myth of the true earth and the soul's afterlife, which Socrates explicitly says is the sort of thing one should "as it were chant to oneself" (ὥσπερ ἐπᾴδειν ἑαυτῷ, 114d). Why does Plato liken his arguments to incantations, and how are they related to the other sort of incantation Socrates produces in the

---

from which the soul's immortality was proved (the theory of Forms) Simmias has made a methodological error—as he himself readily admits (92d-e).

dialogue, the myth? Although this question is obviously too large to go into in detail here, it is I think crucial for understanding the relation between the dramatic context and the arguments in the *Phaedo*; accordingly I shall conclude with some brief and sketchy remarks on this topic.[10]

It is, I think, essential to the "incantation" theme in the *Phaedo* that Simmias and Cebes are *not* Socrates' philosophical equals. I have already suggested that their ability to philosophize is not yet on a par with Socrates'; the fear they have for the soul's fate after death also contrasts with Socrates' own equanimity. That their fear is characterized as that of a "child within them" suggests that it is to some extent irrational, and so must be in part dealt with through non-rational means. Socrates' incantations work on both a rational and an emotional level; that is, they contain, in addition to reasoning, certain considerations, often in the form of pictures or images, which appeal to the emotional predispositions of the listeners. Although the non-rational appeal is more prominent in the myth and reasoning more prominent in the arguments, both elements are to be found in both types of incantation. If this is indeed what Socratic incantations are like in the *Phaedo*, then they must be fashioned in part to meet the psychic needs of Socrates' interlocutors.[11] Far from being his own attempts to produce the best arguments he can, Socrates' incantatory arguments are to some extent the product of the philosophic rhetoric described at *Phaedrus* 271b: carefully pegged to the souls of his audience.

Socrates' arguments are not, of course, merely rhetorical; but their rhetorical dimension provides an alternative explanation for the fallacies in them. Socrates' arguments in the *Phaedo* have a dual purpose: the rhetorical one of producing the conviction in his hearers that the soul is immortal, and the dialectical one of provoking their active reflection on and eventual understanding of this immortality. It is clear that Socrates thinks it very impor-

10. My remarks are inspired by Dorter, pp. 1-10.

11. Thus I disagree with those commentators who hold that the mythic and non-rational element is ineliminable from even the highest philosophical understanding. See, for example, White 1989.

tant that his interlocutors—and Plato his readers—believe in the immortality of the soul. But not everyone is capable of a philosophical understanding of the reasons for and the nature of that immortality. Hence Plato has Socrates present arguments that seem to prove a certain sort of immortality, and may suffice for some people, while all the time containing elements of fallacy and ambiguity that leave more philosophically gifted listeners vaguely uneasy and prick them on to further inquiry.[12] Such inquiry may result in a deeper understanding of the soul's immortality. The arguments in the *Phaedo* may on this view be seen to constitute a series of such breakthroughs to deeper understanding, such that each prior stage, accepted as true by those who can proceed no farther, is seen to be an approximation or image[13] of the truth by those who move on to the next stage. So understood, the arguments form a closely-linked progression, and not a collection of independent attempts to establish the soul's immortality. Furthermore, on this view we may hold, as I am inclined to do, that the final, ontological argument also contains a fallacy,[14] which Socrates expects Simmias at least (and Plato the most gifted reader) eventually to detect. Such a reader, armed with the τέχνη λόγων, the method of hypothesis, will not at that point fall into misology, but rather, heeding Socrates' advice to scrutinize the hypotheses more clearly and follow out their consequences, will go on to win ever greater understanding of the soul and its immortality.

University of Kansas

12. In the live version of these comments I argued, following Dorter, that the manuscript text of the conclusion of the cyclical argument (72d) manifests the two levels on which Socrates' arguments work and should be spared the excisor's knife. I refer the reader to Dorter, p. 43.

13. Socrates' production of such images is to be distinguished from Cebes' and Simmias' dependence on images for expressing their thought, since Socrates is guided by a deeper understanding that is not dependent on the images he creates for the less philosophically advanced. For Socrates' view in the *Phaedo* that images are inadequate for the highest sort of understanding (a view admittedly more prominent in the *Republic*), see 100a.

14. I agree with a line of criticism going back to Strato of Lampsacus; see Wehrli frr. 123 (m) and 124 (k), translated in Hackforth 1955, pp. 196-197.

ROWE/TUOZZO BIBLIOGRAPHY

Bostock, D., 1986: *Plato's Phaedo* (oxford).

Burger, D., 1984: *The Phaedo: A Platonic Labyrinth* (Yale).

Burkert,W., 1972: *Lore and Science in Ancient Pythagoreanism* (Cambridge, Massachusetts).

Dorter, K., 1982: *Plato's Phaedo: An Interpretation* (Toronto).

Gallop, D., 1975: *Plato, Phaedo*(Oxford).

Hackforth, R., 1955: *Plato's Phaedo* (Cambridge).

McQueen, E.I., and Rowe, C.J., 1989: "Phaedo, Socrates, and the Chronology of the Spartan War with Elis." *Methexis* 2 (1989), pp. 1-18.

Rowe, C.J., 1992: "The 'Affinity' Argument in the *Phaedo*." Forthcoming in a special issue of *Revue Philosophique* on Plato, ed., by M. Canto-Sperber.

Stokes, M.C., 1986: *Plato's Socratic Conversations: Drama and Dialectic in Three Dialogues* (London).

Wehrli, F., 1950: *Die Schule des Aristoteles*, Heft V: *Straton von Lampsakos* (Basel)

_____. 1967: *Die Schule des Aristoteles,* Heft II: *Aristoxenos*, 2nd ed. (Basel and Stuttgart).

White, D., 1989: *Myth and Metaphysics in Plato's Phaedo* (Selinsgrove, London and Toronto).

The Ascent in Plato's *Symposium*
Richard Patterson

My principal question is slightly odd in that the person to whom it is addressed—the Diotima of Plato's *Symposium*—appears to have answered it quite explicitly. The question is, "how do we ascend the ladder of love, even to the vision of Beauty itself?" Her answer is, to rephrase Lewis Carroll's King of Hearts: "start at the bottom; proceed in proper order to the top; then stop, and enjoy." She does also suggest that we are somehow carried upward by the force of *eros* as it attaches to a sequence of ever higher kinds of beauty; that this progression of attachments and reattachments is (at least) accompanied by rational discourse; that, at each stage, beauty is a stimulus to creative activity; and that a guide plays some role in all of this. But let us begin with Diotima's own words—or rather with a certain fourth-hand report of the words put into the mouth of this fictional priestess by her creator, the character of Socrates in Plato's *Symposium*:

> It is essential, she said, for anyone who would approach this matter correctly, to begin at an early age by drawing near to beautiful bodies, and first, if properly led by his guide, to experience *eros* for a single body, and thereby to beget fair discourse (210a4-8); then he must realize that the beauty of any one body is a brother to that of any other body, and that if he is to pursue beauty of form (τὸ ἐπ' εἴδει καλόν), it would be most foolish not to consider the beauty of every body to be one and the same (210a8-b3).

Having realized this, he must become the lover of every beautiful body, and slacken his *eros* for any single body, look down on it, and consider it a small matter (210b4-6).

Next he must deem beauty in souls more admirable (τιμιώτερον) than that in bodies, so that if someone possessed little beauty, but a fitting soul, that would be sufficient to love him and care for him, to seek out and beget *logoi* of a sort that would improve the young (210b6-c3),

so that he will then be made to see the beauty in practices and laws (ἐπιτηδεύματα, νόμοι, 210c3-4),

and to see that this is all akin (συγγενές) to itself (210c4-5), so that he considers bodily beauty a thing of little consequence (210c5-6).

After practices he must proceed to branches of understanding (μαθήματα, ἐπιστήμαι), so that he may see the beauty of these (210c6-7),

and, looking upon much beauty, no longer slavishly love any one beauty, any fair boy or man or any one practice, a servile fool and simpleton, but rather, looking out upon and contemplating the great sea of beauty, give birth to many, and beautiful, and magnificent *logoi* and thoughts in philosophy that is free of envy and jealousy (210c7-d6)

until, thus strengthened and magnified, he should catch sight of a single sort of learning, whose object is beauty of this sort (210d6-e1). . . .

Here we must for a moment leave Socrates and his instructress in *ta erotica* for a closer, more prosaic look at the ground she has covered. First, there are a few landmarks that even blind cupid could not miss. For one thing, among the forward steps, some involve generalization—seeing the kinship of instances of beauty within a given level—while others involve ascent from one level to another. Thus the lover proceeds on the horizontal plane from *eros* of a single beautiful body to that of bodily beauty in general (or beauty of [bodily] form, *eidos*), from *eros* of vari-

194

ous practices and laws to perception of the kinship of all such beauty. Meanwhile on the vertical plane the *erastes* ascends from bodily to spiritual beauty, then to *eros* of practices and laws, next to the various branches of understanding, and finally to that one kind of learning whose object is Beauty itself.[1] Most important for present purposes, Diotima conveys the power of *eros* as a potentially uplifting force, as in the Charioteer Myth of the *Phaedrus*, even as she repeatedly makes us aware of the presence of reason or *logos*—in the *logoi* apparently generated at each level and in the person of the guide or teacher whose presence is clearly indicated if not belabored.[2]

Let us return now to the question of how those vertical steps are to be accomplished. On close inspection, Diotima's remarks

1. The generalization process is one of many issues that will be set aside or only briefly discussed here. Others include the question of precisely how many levels there are (here I assume a distinction between that of souls and that of laws and practices, even though this has been contested); the relation of the earlier speeches to the levels of Diotima's ascent; the concept of immortality invoked at the top level and its relation to Diotima's earlier remarks on the subject; the mystery religion symbolism that frames the entire process; the question of why Diotima is a woman; the nature of the begetting of true virtue following upon the vision of Beauty itself; the *logoi* of the *Republic* as illustrating the kind of noble *logoi* Diotima has in mind concerning the beauty of bodies, souls, practices, and varieties of understanding; the larger connection of the ascent to Plato's metaphysics of image and reality; the details of the role of the "guide" mentioned by Diotima and of the relationship between the lover and the initial beloved–both bearing on the themes of *eros* and pedagogy in Plato; the individual as object of love in Plato; links between the ascent and the "theory of recollection"; comparisons with the πρῶτον φίλον of the *Lysias* and with the charioteer myth of the *Phaedrus*. The present paper, which concentrates on how one is to achieve the vertical steps, is part of a longer work in progress that will respond to many important discussions (by Vlastos, Santas, Sinaiko, Rosen, Robin, Dover, Halperin, *et al.*) not taken up explicitly here.

2. Neither *eros* alone nor autonomous reason could achieve the ascent. (For a recent, emphatic, statement of the need for both, see J.M.E. Moravcsic 1971, pp. 285-302.) Elsewhere I have tried to draw reason and *eros* into very close connection on grounds that the "reasoning part" of the soul is not a cold, detached, or disinterested calculator, but on the contrary has its own natural, necessary, and characteristic erotic attachments (as well as its own brand of spiritedness; Patterson 1987, pp. 325-350). It is also worth emphasizing that the function of *logoi* is not, on my account, to "articulate the ethical norms that hold desire in check" (in Prof. Lawrence's words). Their function in the ascent is rather the positive one of revealing to *eros* its genuine and highest object, hence of making possible its full and most intense expression.

are not quite so satisfying as they might have at first appeared: "next he must deem the beauty of souls more admirable...," "he will be made to see the beauty in practices...," "next he must proceed to branches of understanding...." What we would like to know is *how* these upward steps are supposed to come about, and this she does not pause to explain. What we lack and should keenly desire is, to begin with, an account of how reason gets involved in this process in the first place; then a specification of what reason takes as its subject matter—a question that must be posed at every level of the ascent; then an account of what exactly it says about its subject in those "noble" or "improving" or "philosophical" *logoi*; next an explanation of how its saying whatever it says manages to reveal a new object of *eros*; and finally, an explanation of how *logos* shows that this new object is superior to the old and, more precisely, superior in a way that brings about the reorientation of *eros* toward that new object.

The general form of my answer to these tightly intertwined questions will be this: at each level of the ascent the lover is stimulated by the object of *eros* to bring forth *logos*—*logos* which attempts to say, of its object, what is so wonderful about it, what makes it so beautiful. (This encomiastic impulse comes naturally to human beings, as several of Plato's dialogues testify.) Once that has been identified in *logos*, it becomes apparent that what the lover really found so attractive was not quite what he took it to be, for *logos* reveals that the original object was only beautiful insofar as it embodied, expressed, or, to adopt a more Platonic terminology, imaged or reflected, the new beauty brought to light by *logos*. This new beauty is now preferred not just because it is the source of the old, but because of the particular way in which it is that source: the beauty for which one experienced *eros* really *was*, all along, this newly revealed beauty. The lover then realizes that he had previously desired this new beauty all along, but desired it only as embodied or reflected in that earlier object, and without recognizing the nature of the true beloved.

Once the lover's eyes have been opened to all of this, no further explanation is needed for the fact that *eros* now attaches to the "new" beauty. This process repeats until the vision of Beauty itself has been attained. There alone dwells a beauty beautiful in and of itself and not merely as the reflection or embodiment of any further beauty; thus there alone can the process find its natural and final end.

There remains the large project of substantiating this account in detail. To this end let us begin again at the beginning with a single beautiful body. It is important that, as Diotima remarks, one approach even this "rightly" (ὀρθῶς), or that even here one be led rightly.[3] We are not dealing, even at this entry level, with the pure animal lust described by Pausanias in terms of the "earthly" Aphrodite (181bff.).[4] At the same time it would be pathetically anticlimatic (and unjustified) to entirely desexualize

3. For the guide, who is not to be identified with the lover or with the beloved (or, *pace* Nehamas and Woodruff 1989, p.57, n.90.), see 210a6-7 ("if he who is led is led correctly"), 210e2-3 ("whoever is instructed [παιδαγωγηθῇ] in matters of *eros* up to this point, observing beautiful things in order and correctly") and 211b7-c1 ("this is the correct way to go or be led by another [ὑπ' ἄλλου ἄγεσθαι] to *ta erotica*"). Since a lover's *logoi* are not necessarily edifying or improving or philosophical (as the *Lysis* reminds us), I believe this guidance must involve some shaping and directing of the lover's *logos* (and possibly some matching of the lover with appropriate erotic objects). Moreover we know very well that for Plato "fair discourse" (καλός λογος) will not include the sort of thing produced by Agathon or Hippothales, but will certainly include *logoi* concerned with goodness, virtue, and the like, and that make people better. (Recall Diotima's description at 209b-c of the lover teeming with *logoi* about virtue and about what the good man must be and do—*logoi* by which he tries to educate the beloved.) These will at the same time be philosophical *logoi*, delivered without envy or jealousy. So Diotima's various descriptions of the lover's *logoi* ("fair *logoi*," 210a; "*logoi* that make the young better," 210c; "fair *logoi*...in philosophy without envy or jealousy," 210d) should not be taken in some uninformatively vague way, or as introducing different (and unspecified) sorts of *logoi*. Toward the end of the paper I will try to bring out the strong kinship between correct praise of a beloved beauty and philosophical discourse about the nature of beauty.

4. There is no textual warrant for supposing that one must begin "as basely as possible," or in a "crudely" physical way, or from the "utter depths." Moreover from Plato's point of view it would be a great mistake to imagine that *eros* as such derives from corporeal sexuality (and, perhaps, attaches to higher objects only by somehow rechanneling [sublimating] an essentially corporeal desire).

Richard Patterson

the passage on this basis alone. What Diotima has in mind is an attitude towards physical beauty that is passionate, but that also gives rise not (simply) to sexual response, but to fair discourse (γεννᾶν λόγους καλούς, 210a7-8) as well. I believe we find some indication of what this involves in that memorable scene from Plato's *Charmides* in which Socrates catches a brief glimpse behind the cloak of the stunningly beautiful Charmides, and "takes the flame," feeling "as if he were out of his wits" (155d-e). This is not precisely the state of mind in which one begets "noble discourse," and it is only with considerable effort that Socrates is able to compose himself for his customary dialectical duties. But if one had to say what it was about Charmides that made him so beautiful at the bodily level—or better, why a glimpse of his body could so arouse Socrates—one might begin with an earlier detail of that same scene. Between the announcement of Charmides' imminent arrival and the moment when Socrates first catches sight of him, Plato, as author of the scene, takes the trouble to have Crito inform Socrates that the young man is not only the great beauty of the day, but possesses also a soul "most beautiful and good" (154e4); that he is even a "philosopher," and "quite a poet, as he seems to others and not just to himself" (154e8-155a1). It is the connection between psychic and bodily beauty, to be developed at several points in this and many other dialogues, that I wish to bring into the discussion of the initial phase of the ascent passage. Here we have at

As I understand Plato, the inborn desire for Beauty itself is (contrary to Freud) the origin of all the lower levels of *eros* on Diotima's ladder. It would be equally mistaken to identify Platonic *eros* for truth and beauty with any milk-toast conception of "Platonic love." One can be sure at the very least that Plato has in mind an intensity of feeling describable (as at *Republic* 490a-b) in overtly sexual terms.

One must start "while still young" with love of a beautiful body because we simply do find ourselves initially "tangled up in the world of bodies" (in Prof. Lawrence's apt phrase). It is no objection to this (*pace* Prof. Lawrence) that Diotima's imagined remarks are addressed to Socrates, for the "Socrates" to whom she speaks is not the Socrates who addresses the assembled party at Agathon's house and who professes to have some understanding of *eros*, but a younger figure who expressely lacks initiation into even the lower mysteries of love. In any case it is not true that the older, wiser Socrates of most of Plato's dialogues is unable to feel the allure of physical beauty, as a celebrated passage of the Charmides (quoted and discussed just below) is meant to indicate.

first only a juxtaposition of the two (as in, "This lad Charmides has everything, Socrates"), and one whose basis must still be confirmed by Socrates' examination of Charmides' soul (154e). But shortly thereafter Socrates reveals, in criticising the physicians of Greece, his conviction that psychic and bodily beauty are not merely juxtaposed. Our Greek physicians, says Socrates, neglect the fundamental insight of the Thracian Zalmoxis that

> all good or evil, whether in the body or in the whole person, originates...in the soul, and overflows from thence...and the cure of the soul must be achieved by the use of certain charms, and these charms are fair words, and by them temperance is implanted in the soul, and where temperance comes and stays, there health is speedily imparted, not only to the head, but to the whole body. (156e-157a)

These remarks prefigure Charmides' own first attempt to say what temperance is: "doing everything in an orderly and quiet way, whether walking in the street, conversing, or doing anything else" (159a). Although this first attempt is handily refuted, Socrates never questions its suggestion that physical bearing and carriage, the general way one "handles oneself," in every situation, expresses an inward temperance (or the opposite). Nor will he call into question his own earlier opinion that all true goods of the body flow from a proper condition of the soul. On the contrary, these suggestions are taken up and developed in other works.

The *Republic*, for example, provides many passages to the same effect—in its censure of certain kinds of bodily imitation (387e-388b, 390c, 396e), and in its praise of the "accents and bearing" of the just person in every sort of situation (400d-e), and elsewhere. Let the following passage represent this strand of the work:

> Good speech, then, harmony, grace, and good rhythm follow upon a good character (εὐηθείᾳ): not that simplemindedness we euphemistically call goodness of heart, but that truly good and fair cast of mind (τὴν ὡς ἀληθῶς εὖτε καὶ καλῶς τὸ ἦθος κατέσκευασμένην δάνοιαν, 400d-e).

Richard Patterson

Ultimately the point about bodily beauty extends very far indeed: grace in painting, architecture, household furniture, and even in the natural bodies of plants and animals are the brethren and images (μιμήματα) of sound mind and good disposition (σώφρονός τε καὶ ἀγαθοῦ ἤθους, 401a).[5]

Returning now to the *Symposium* itself, a familiar passage from Alcibiades' speech about Socrates will conclude the main point I wish to make about bodily beauty:

You should also have seen him at our horrible retreat from Delium. I was there with the cavalry, while Socrates was a foot soldier. The army had already dispersed in all directions, and Socrates was retreating together with Laches. I happened to see them just by chance, and the moment I did I started shouting encouragements to them, telling them I was never going to leave their side, and so on. That day I had a better opportunity to watch Socrates than I ever had at Potidaea, for, being on horseback, I wasn't in very great danger. Well, it was easy to see that he was remarkably more collected than Laches. But when I looked again I couldn't get

5. These passages and others to follow show that we should guard against the understandable temptation to think of bodily beauty narrowly as "good looks"—just as we should avoid thinking of "fair *logos*" as limited (in Plato's view) to pretty speeches in the style of Agathon. As Plato might put it, bodily beauty includes the beauty of bodies in motion as well as at rest, so that it can readily encompass not only a "pretty face," well-formed limbs, and the like, but also posture, carriage, gait, and so on up through more complex bodily motions and qualities, including what we might call "observable behavior."

But it is equally important to avoid taking even "good looks" in a superficial sense. Such things as well-formed faces and bodies might not seem *to us* to stem from a sound mind, and they may not (especially in the very young, and in animals and plants!) stem from any qualities of mind of their possessor. But this cannot excuse us from taking seriously what Plato has Socrates say, apparently in earnest, on this point. In fact there is a natural Platonic reading of those remarks quoted from the *Republic*: the "natural" beauty of plants, animals, and as yet untutored humans is just an especially successful expression of an intelligible Form whose instantiation is part of the rational cosmic plan carried out by the Demiurge. This extends, in the *Timaeus*, even down to the Demiurge's devising of the "fairest possible" primary bodies (53b; cf. *Sophist* 265c on the "divine craftsmanship" responsible for the bodies of plants and animals). Thus even this aspect of bodily beauty can be traced upwards to an unexpected (psychic) source at the highest levels of cosmic government.

your words, Aristophanes, out of my mind: in the midst of battle he was making his way exactly as he does around town,...with "swagg'ring gait and roving eye." He was observing everything quite calmly, looking out for friendly troops and keeping an eye on the enemy. Even from a great distance it was obvious that this was a very brave man, who would put up a terrific fight if anyone approached him. This is what saved both of them. For, as a rule, you try to put as much distance as you can between yourself and such men in battle; you go after the others, those who run away helter-skelter. (220e-221c; trans. Nehamas and Woodruff)

Plato seems to have written with a special relish about this incident in the retreat at Delium, not only for the sake of what it said about Socrates, but also for the contrast it afforded with the celebrated general Laches. In the dialogue of that name Socrates has another famous general, Nicias, declare in the presence of Laches that one important advantage of learning the art of fighting in armor is that it will "lend one a more impressive appearance at the right time, that is to say, at the time when his appearance will strike terror into his enemies." (182c) Shortly thereafter Plato has Laches himself try to say what courage is: he replies with complete confidence, "Socrates, I see no difficulty in answering. He is a man of courage who does not run away, but remains at his post and fights against the enemy. There can be no mistake about that." (190e) Plato's final comment on the general is Alcibiades' unflattering description of his discombobulated retreat, and his appearance in retreat, at Delium.

To this matter of cool, calm, and collected outward appearance as a reflection of inner courage or self-possession, one could add a long series of passages from the *Symposium* highlighting Socrates' abnormal and, in the popular estimation, sometimes comical behavior, all with the clear implication that his visible activities nonetheless expresses inner virtue. One thinks, for example, of Socrates' physical reaction—or rather, lack of reaction—to the sexual advances of the beautiful Alcibiades; of his uncomplaining endurance under the harsh conditions of winter

201

military campaigning; or of his oblivious perseverance while wrestling with a philosophical problem—lost in thought on a neighbor's porch, or standing abstracted from sunrise to night-fall (and, to the astonishment of the Ionian troops at Potidea) all night as well. The final detail of this last incident is especially revealing: at sunrise of the second day Socrates "said his prayers to the sun and went away." The outward practice is conspicuously pious—as if to give the lie to some things the historical Aristophanes, and certain accusers mentioned in the *Apology*, had said about Socrates. But beyond this, it recalls the concluding paragraph of the *Symposium* in which Socrates, having emerged as the sole survivor of a long night of drink and discussion, tucks in Aristophanes and Agathon, stops by the Lyceum for a bath, spends the rest of the day as usual and, toward evening, makes his way home to rest. In both passages Socrates' deportment illustrates in extreme form a certain power of mind over body—or rather, of visible bodily behavior as an expression of inner strength far exceeding the normal capacities of the soul.

These facts about bodily beauty as a reflection of inner beauty are, I suggest, precisely the facts that "noble *logos*" *about* the nature of bodily beauty must reveal. If so, I think we can fairly say that our initial lover of bodily beauty now realizes that what seemed so attractive in a broad array of admirable qualities of body, and of visible practices described and enacted in the *Charmides, Laches, Republic, Symposium* and elsewhere, was not anything intrinsic to them or even, strictly speaking, anything bodily or visible at all. Rather, these presumed bodily qualities were so attractive and so stirred our admiration because they showed courage in the face of great danger, self-possession in the face of powerful temptation, and so on. Or, perhaps, they were simply well-formed and healthy embodiments of the fair bodily form intended by their natural begettor. In a word, these outward, bodily things were attractive because they embodied or reflected inner courage, self-possession, wisdom, grace, dignity, piety, or, more broadly, fair disposition of the soul.

In terms of Plato's metaphysics of image and reality, one could say that bodily beauty as such no longer appears to the lover to be genuine beauty; all it really is (so it now seems) is an image of a true beauty which one now takes to be essentially psychic in nature. Of course further revelations await the lover of psychic beauty. But in the meantime it will seem obvious that what had been found so admirable and captivating was not these visible bodily behaviors and qualities themselves, but rather the unseen psychic excellence they embodied and enacted. Thus insofar as the lover was stirred by perception of these outward things, he or she was already implicitly a lover of the excellence they exemplified rather than of these visible bodily motions and conditions as such. With recognition of that truth, the *erastes' eros* for the supposed graces and beauties of the body will now begin to attach to those unseen inner virtues whose beauty was only "bodied forth" by things seen. This amounts not so much to a *transfer* of *eros* to a new object, but to an awakening to the fact that those beauties of soul or mind are what one was actually attracted to all along.[6]

The key to the next upward step is similar in design. Again *eros* gives rise, with the right sort of guidance, to appropriate *logos*, *logos* focusing now on the origin and nature of beauty (goodness, excellence) in the soul. This *logos* in turn brings about the realization that spiritual virtue not only arises from, or is inculcated by, fair laws, practices, and institutions, it actually *is* a kind of law or stable complex of institutions and practices established in the soul. The view we find in dialogues closely related to the *Symposium* (above all the *Republic* but also, I would argue, the *Phaedo* and *Phaedrus* as well), is that fully developed virtues do not exist entirely independently of one another, as if one could be truly courageous but unjust, truly wise but intemperate. Rather in their true form they all exist together as aspects of a single psychic harmony in which all "parts" or "aspects" of the soul, under the guidance of wisdom, find and carry out their own proper functions. This Socrates actually refers to in the *Republic* as a "constitution" (*politeia*) founded in the soul (590e3). Thus the truly just citizens of the just city share

6. This is not to say that bodily beauty, even including bodily behavior, is an infallible indicator of psychic beauty. (Recall Adeimantus' unjust man, who draws about him a deceptive image of justice; *Republic* 365c).

with that city a constitution—a complex of laws and practices—whose embodiment *is* their virtue. From this abstract point of view the institutions, relations and patterns of activity of the city do not appear as something *peculiar* to cities, or as anything *essentially* civic. Rather, institutions and practices—above all that complex of the two that we may call a *politeia*—are something more general, something instantiated alike by just souls and cities. Justice may be written larger in the city, but it is the same as justice in the soul.[7]

Given all of this it follows, as with the first step upwards, that one ascends by virtue of a realization, achieved through *logos* about the origin and nature of the beauty of the beloved, that what one found so beautiful was all along a higher beauty. In this second instance, *eros* for the virtuous soul is found to be *eros* for the *virtue* exemplified in a soul, where such virtue is in turn found to be a constitution, a supremely propitious *politeia* of virtue—constituting laws and practices informing the soul. Again there follows not so much a transfer of *eros* from fair souls

7. Dramatically speaking, Diotima can hardly insert here the moral psychology of the *Republic*. (Nor does my claim about psychic excellence as an inner constitution depend either on taking the *Republic*'s political theorizing at face value as a blueprint for Utopia, or on presupposing that Diotima's (or Socrates') auditors will have overheard such views being discussed in the Piraeus!) Still I do not think Diotima's audience will find it difficult to make sense of her remarks, even if only in their own terms rather than what I take to be Plato's. Indeed, piety, justice, courage, and so on might well be even *more* plausibly equated at that level with good practices. (Recall Charmides' first definition of self-control and Laches' characterization of courage.) It has frequently been observed that the religious *nomima* of the city (which Socrates was accused of neglecting) are probably not something like opinions or a credo, but customary observances, or what we would call religious practices. So, too, for the "common" tests of justice cited at the end of *Republic* IV (442d-443b), which appear to be what we would call fair practices. Thus Diotima's remarks can be readily understood independently of any distinctly Platonic theory of virtue. This situation is reminiscent of an important feature of *all* the earlier speeches as well, in that they are clearly intelligible to all the symposiasts even though their leading claims about *eros* all have, from a Platonic point of view, a deeper reading unsuspected by their proponents. This establishes, for the platonistic reader of the *Symposium*, an ironic distancing of these characters—much as there is of Oedipus for any reader of the *Oedipus Tyrannus* familiar with his family history. We are aware, as they are not, of the sense in which their words actually are true and important. Here we begin to come in view of Plato the comic and tragic poet.

to the beauty of laws and practices as the discovery that the true object of *eros* was in fact the beauty of right laws and practices. Even beautiful souls are beautiful only insofar as they exemplify a beauty that is not, in and of itself, psychic in nature; thus one loves beautiful souls only insofar as they reflect the beauty of good practices and institutions. But this perspective, too, we shall find subject to revision.[8]

Such revision will take place if *eros* for this new beloved should give birth once again to noble *logos* of the appropriate kind. On the present hypothesis this will be *logos* concerned in a specific way with the beauty of the new favorite: what makes these fair practices, laws, institutions (or constitutions) so beautiful?

The citizen of a fair city or nation might be brought by a variety of means to revere that polity's constitution. In our own nation we hear often of the Constitution as expressing "the wisdom of the founding fathers." On the assumption that the founding fathers were truly wise, it is still presumably true that they established the Constitution because it was a wise form of government (and not vice-versa, as the Socrates of the *Euthyphro* might put it). If so, it follows that our form of government is (rightly) beloved because it is the embodiment of wisdom—that it is beloved not just for being ours, but for its wisdom. The same holds for the fair practices, laws, and institutions referred to by Diotima. For if they are beautiful only

8. Notice that ascent is not motivated, here or at any other stage, by dissatisfaction with the current beloved (*pace* T. Irwin 1977, pp. 170). Becoming dissatisfied with—or better, placing in proper perspective—the old beloved *follows* apprehension of a higher object. (Here I agree with Price's criticism of Irwin in Price 1989, pp. 170.) I also agree with Price that achieving this new perspective does not entail abandonment of the previous beloved; he (or she or it) is still an exemplification of beauty rather than of ugliness. (On Diotima's use of "καταφρονήσαντα," "disdaining" (210b5), see Price, p.44.)

As for Price's own suggestion about the ascent, I would agree that "each stage justifies *itself* once the guide has prompted its achievement: to perceive the new beauty is to appreciate it...Love may be the best helper...not because it provides reasons, but because, in a promising soul well prompted, it is receptive of, and responsive to, the opening of new vistas" (p.42). Still, this leaves unanswered the main question I am trying to address here, namely, *how* is the soul prompted, *how* are new vistas opened to view?

insofar as they manifest or embody genuine wisdom or understanding (μάθησις, ἐπιστήμη), then our *eros* for their beauty is in fact *eros* for their wisdom, whether we first realize this or not. Plato has Socrates speak in the dialogues of many ἐπιστήμαι and *pseudo-ἐπιστήμαι*: statecraft, sophistry, medicine, cookery, legal justice, rhetoric, gymnastics, cosmetics, etc. The leading characteristics of the true ἐπιστήμαι are (1) they aim at the welfare or benefit of their objects rather than at the mere production of pleasure, and (2) they rest upon rational principles that may be explained and learned and taught, rather than on shrewdness or cunning, or on some idiosyncratic knack or on mere experience. (See esp. *Gorgias* 462a-465c.) One could say a great deal more about the further marks of Platonic ἐπιστήμη in general, and about the nuances of Plato's views on the more important individual ἐπιστήμαι. But the main point would remain the same: what we find so valuable, beautiful, and desirable about beautiful practices and laws—beyond the fact that they themselves constitute, or reliably achieve, the possession of some genuine good—is that they achieve these goods not by luck or by intuitive cunning, but by objective and secure understanding of the nature of their subject matter. This holds for the making of good shoes, the cure of disease, skill in navigation, and so on for all the genuine arts (τεχναί).

In a nutshell it follows, as the night the day, that what we value about practices, laws, and virtuous constitutions of the soul is the wisdom they embody, where wisdom is understood as another Platonic name for full and true comprehension of some truly good end, and the objectively right way of achieving it. Thus the beauty of wisdom or understanding is not just a necessary condition of the beauty of virtues, practices, and laws. Rather its beauty is what we value in them, what accounts for their hold on us, in the first place. They appear beautiful to us insofar as they exemplify a beauty that properly belongs to wisdom. But again, the lover may eventually rise above even this elevated point of view.

Having now awakened to the fact that what we really value and desire in ἐπιτήδευματα and laws is not these practices or laws in and of themselves, but the beauty of the wisdom or understanding they exemplify, we find ourselves on the fourth level of the ascent, that of lovers of understanding or wisdom of all kinds—of μαθήματα in general. It is at this point that we survey the "wide sea" of all beauty apprehended so far, and "give birth to many, and beautiful, and magnificent *logoi*...in philosophy" (210d). In point of fact we have already glimpsed the way to level five, that of the single ἐπιστήμη or *mathema* of beauty itself; for when we try to say what so powerfully attracts us about kinds of understanding in general, we find it lies in the fact that understanding constitutes or produces genuine good(s). Of course questions will arise if one sort of good, or the goodness of one sort of ἐπιστήμη, should find itself in competition with the claims of another. Or, if certain goods are not in direct competition so as to make them mutually exclusive, it may still be a major question whether one is subordinate to the other. To answer such questions would require a kind of learning or understanding that adopted a wide perspective indeed. Plato himself held an extreme view on the matter: at this level we reach a kind of study or understanding whose object is a single subject matter called what-is-beauty or Beauty itself. If, as I think Diotima (and Plato) thought, beauty is in fact goodness, only termed "beauty" when considered as object of desire, then we have in the *Symposium,* as in the *Republic,* the fundamental conviction that there is a single, objective nature of goodness itself. And that is why the ultimate end of all learning or education (μαθήσις or παιδεία) will be, as the *Republic* indicates, understanding of the good, but also, as the *Republic* and *Symposium* agree, love of Beauty itself (see *Republic* 403c).

What do these rather grand pronouncements mean for our ascent? Above all, they mean that if anything is to be really, objectively, beneficial or good, there must be a norm of goodness beyond that found directly in any individual ἐπιστήμη or μαθήμα. Otherwise we would find ourselves in the position of declaring that some carpenter, say, has built a fine house, and of awarding a nice prize—one cave dweller to another—but with as yet no answer to the question of whether the building of this home, or perhaps this entire housing development, is itself a good thing. The Platonic view would be that for any allegedly good product of any particular art or science—short of understanding of beauty or goodness itself—one can always ask whether the result, or the very exercise of that understanding, is genuinely beneficial, or only something that tickles our fancy so that we are pleased to call it "beautiful" or "good."

The point emerges in a strongly worded passage of the *Republic*:

> You have often heard that the greatest thing to learn is the idea of good by reference to which just things and all the rest become useful and beneficial. And now I am almost sure you know that this is what I am going to speak of and to say further that we have no adequate knowledge of it. And if we do not know it, then, even if without the knowledge of this we should know all other things perfectly well, you are aware that it would avail us nothing, just as no possession either is of any avail without the possession of the good. Or do you think there is any profit in possessing everything except that which is good, or in understanding all things else apart from the good while understanding and knowing nothing that is fair and good? (505a-b).

The parallel between possession of the good and knowledge of the good suggests a conclusion about the latter which Socrates leaves unspoken. It is not merely that goodness itself is a great deal better than other goods: rather, it is only insofar as there *is* such a thing, objectively speaking, as goodness, that anything else *could be* objectively good at all. As Socrates puts it, it is only by virtue of the good itself that just things and other advantageous things become beneficial. Just things and other truly advantageous things are nothing more (or less) than manifestations of goodness: true justice is one sort of genuine good, courage another, carpentry (properly exercised) a third, and so on for all genuine ἐπιστῆμαι and their objects. Put the other way round, if goodness were ultimately a matter of individual or group opinion none of these things, or anything else, *could possi-*

bly be truly or "really" good, but only good according to some-one.

The parallel on the side of knowledge would be that there could not be any genuine understanding or knowledge of any sort—where knowledge has a normative, Platonic sense on which it essentially involves understanding of the relation, direct or indirect, of its object to goodness—unless there were, objectively speaking, such a thing as knowledge of goodness itself. Hence no one ever could achieve full comprehension of the goodness of any good thing without apprehending the nature of goodness itself.

The concluding lines of the paragraph quoted just above from *Republic* VI draw out one important consequence:

> This [the good] every soul pursues, and all its actions are done for its sake. It divines that it is something but is per-plexed and cannot adequately grasp what it is, *nor does it have about this the firm opinion which it has about other things, and because of this it misses the benefit, if any, even of those other things.* Should we say that those ...to whom we entrust every-thing must remain in such darkness about so great and so important a subject? (505d-e)

To bring all of this back to the *Symposium*: we ascend from *eros* for μαθήματα or ἐπιστήμαι in general to *eros* for ἐπιστήμη of Beauty itself by coming to see not just that the latter is a neces-sary condition of the beauty of the former, but that the beauty we so valued in those other kinds of understanding is in fact, as we now see, the beauty or goodness in knowing what is objec-tively good or beautiful. That is, we now realize that we desired μαθήματα or ἐπιστήμαι only insofar as we took them to consti-tute different manners of grasping some genuine good. What we desired was apprehension of genuine goodness, wherever it should occur.

Still, if Beauty itself is to stand alone at the top (even above *understanding* of Beauty), as Diotima's exposition indicates, then we still have one step to go. This step is not so hard to describe, even if it may be very difficult to achieve, given what has gone

209

Richard Patterson

before. What do we value in the understanding of beauty or goodness? Why do we so desire it? The answer can be stated simply: because it is supremely beneficial (χρήσιμα καὶ ὠφέλιμα), in the words of *Republic* 505a4, commenting on how things other than the Good itself ("just things and the rest") become good. Here again we encounter a very strong claim. It is not just that knowledge of what is objectively good or beautiful is a necessary condition for achievement of genuine goods in life, or even simply that it is a necessary and sufficient condition. The crucial point is rather that all the goods encountered so far—of the body and of the soul, of practices and laws, of all particular ἐπιστήμαι—essentially *are* good only insofar as they exemplify wisdom or understanding *of* what is good and beautiful. This may seem rather surprising taken just by itself, but it is little more than a summation of the various relationships we have examined step-by-step between each level of beauty and its successor.[9]

With this last step upwards, as with all previous steps, our efforts to say, in beautiful or noble *logos*, what is beautiful about that beauty for which we experience *eros* (the μάθημα concerned with beauty), brings us to the realization that what we really found so valuable and desirable was not after all the beauty of that object in and of itself, but was in fact a higher beauty. And the beauty or goodness exemplified in that highest μάθημα is, and can be, none other than Beauty or Goodness itself. [10]

9. Moravcsik (*op. cit.*) and Plotinus are right in saying that each higher level is the *aitia* of its successor. But since there are numerous ways in which one thing can be an *aitia* of another, I have thought it best to simply describe the relation involved without at first invoking the concept of an *aitia* at all. Plotinus' discussion is exceptionally full and interesting. (See esp. I.6. and V.9.2. My thanks here to native Plotinian guide Steve Strange.) Still, it is not clear to me that what Plotinus means by this aitiological relation is the same at each step, or that each level's being an *aitia*—in the way he takes it to be an *aitia*—can successfully explain its being more beautiful than the level of which it is an *aitia*. I hope to treat his views in the detail they deserve on another occasion. For the present let it suffice to say that I have tried to describe a type of aitiological relation which can explain the upward movement of *eros*, and to show how that same relation can be plausibly viewed as linking all the rungs of Diotima's ladder.

10. This is not to say anything positive and definite ("capture in a concept") the nature of Beauty itself. Indeed, we shall see in a moment that Diotima's own

210

For once, the newly discovered beauty leads us no higher. As Diotima says, Beauty is not the beauty *of* anything else—not of "hands or face or body, of soul or wise law" or even of wisdom itself, but rather the Beauty reflected or embodied in each of the lower forms of erotic attachment. This has two important consequences. First, we now for the first time apprehend a beauty that cannot be unmasked as an image of some higher, genuine beauty. From this vantage point *all* previous beauties appear as participants in Beauty itself. This does not collapse the hierarchy, or the necessary order of the steps of the ascent, for it remains true that bodies must participate in Beauty by reflecting psychic excellence, souls by exemplifying a good *politeia*, and so on. Thus to understand the nature of these beauties it will be necessary to see the relation of each to its successor, hence, as Diotima says, to be led to the apprehension of beautiful things in proper sequence (210e). Second, our efforts to describe Beauty itself will be essentially negative ("it is not *of* anything else"; "it neither waxes nor wanes," "it is not beautiful here but ugly there," "it is not beautiful at one time, ugly at another," etc., 211a-b). These *logoi* reveal no further positive object for which *eros* might then strive. Accordingly there is also no further question possible as to *why* we desire beauty: on the one hand, if we desire anything rightly, even beautiful bodies, we desire Beauty itself, whether we realize it or not. At the same time if beauty is goodness, then possession of true beauty is happiness, and there is—as Diotima observes—no further question about why one desires happiness.

***

To this account of how the ascent actually works, I would like to add a few much more programmatic remarks about the general conditions under which ascent may take place—in particular, about the motivation for procreation of *logos* at each step. I

description of Beauty is almost entirely negative. But this should not be allowed to obscure the fact that *preparation* for the final initiation involves lengthy, arduous training and strengthening of the mind's capacity to grasp ever higher manifestations of beauty. Beauty itself will not appear "of a sudden" or in any other way to anyone who is not ready to gaze upon it; nor is "self-surrender" to Beauty possible for anyone incapable or unworthy of being possessed.

alluded earlier to the natural impulse of the *erastes* to "sing the praises" or extol the beauty of the beloved. This establishes a connection between the begetting of *logos* and the main "program" for the evening's entertainment at Agathon's symposium: each speaker is to praise *eros*, and as it happens they all (including even Socrates, prior to his encounter with Diotima) mistakenly conceive of and praise *eros* as something beautiful and desireable rather than as a desire for the beauty it lacks. Socrates will forcefully correct this view in his interrogation of Agathon before proceeding to his own praise of *eros*. From a more panoramic point of view the entire work is in effect Platonic praise of Socrates and thereby the life of philosophy—and ultimately, as it turns out, Beauty itself. Here as elsewhere Plato would appropriate a traditional function of the poets, only with a very different conception of the end to be served and the means to that end. [11]

By the same token it seems to me plausible that the begetting of *logos* does after all result in part from a kind of dissatisfaction; dissatisfaction not with the current beloved, however, but with one's state of ignorance about the nature of the beauty of the beloved. I believe this is an important factor with the lover who approaches beauty or is led to it "correctly." This would connect the ascent with Plato's perpetual theme, enunciated earlier in Diotima's speech, of awareness of one's own ignorance as not only a necessary condition for pursuit of understanding, but also as a powerful goad to philosophic activity. It also brings out a strong internal connection between the ascent passage proper and the preceding Socratic refutation of Agathon who had, after all, made a very pretty speech (so Eryximachus sin-

11. He thus in effect criticizes encomiastic *logoi* as traditionally and popularly conceived and also demonstrates what encomiae should be. (For a recent discussion of Plato's misgivings about traditional praise poetry, and for some sobering observations on Alcibiades' praise of Socrates in the *Symposium*, see Andrea Nightingale 1991.) I have argued elsewhere that Plato does something similar with regard to comedy and tragedy (Patterson 1982, pp. 76-93). That is, he does not simply criticize such genres from a philosophical point of view, but typically tries to best their practitioners at their own game, demonstrating at the same time how the thing (e.g. composition of true tragedy or comedy) really should be done "in the service of art and truth" (as Helen Bacon has put it; Bacon 1989).

cerely, and Socrates ironically, declare; 198a,b). As Agathon finally admits under Socratic cross-examination, he had not in fact known what he was talking about (201b). This clears the way for Socrates' presentation of Diotima's teaching as it enacts dramatically the necessary propaedeutic to that ascent. This confirms from a different direction the earlier supposition that we can make some educated guess about the *content* of the noble *logos* mentioned at various stages of the ascent: it is in each case *logos* about the nature of the beautiful ἐρώμενος. But is also suggests something rather definite about the nature of the "guidance" received by the lover. As observed earlier, although the lover can be expected to praise the beauty of the beloved, he does not automatically produce *logoi* that are "noble" or that "improve the young," or, at a higher stage, that constitute "philosophy free of envy and jealousy." What sort of *logoi* might these be? My suggestion (defended only very briefly above) has been that they are the sorts of *logoi* recommended and practiced in the dialogues generally: first (where necessary) an explicit and sincere recognition of one's own ignorance; second, an attempt to remedy that ignorance by appropriate investigation of a given subject.

I find further confirmation of this suggestion in the fact that these two motivations—to praise and to understand the object of *eros*—are not necessarily distinct. They *may* diverge, of course: in lovers attracted simply by the pleasurable bodily aspects of the beloved, or needing but lacking proper guidance, the desire for understanding may be entirely absent or lie forever dormant. But in the sort of lover capable of initiation into the higher mysteries and "correctly led" to matters of love the two will converge. For such lovers as these, the act of praise is not just the attribution to the beloved of whatever good qualities come to mind. This was the approach practiced by the other symposiasts but rejected by Socrates (198e). A true encomium, he says, is based on truth (even if not the whole truth) about the object of praise (198d-199b). As love is the one thing Socrates will claim to know something about, so will he now praise *eros* by speaking truly about its origin and nature (199b). The true act of *praise* thereby becomes a *logos* saying truly why the beloved is so beautiful: one praises "correctly" or "speaks well" about the beloved by declaring truly what makes the beloved genuinely beautiful. This requires the sort of understanding possessed not by the traditional composers of praise poetry, or by any of Socrates' fellow symposiasts, but by the philosopher alone.

Emory University

I would like to thank Joseph Lawrence, Andrea Nightingale, Michael Pakaluk, Cindy Patterson, Steve Strange and an anonymous reader for valuable comments on earlier drafts of this paper.

Colloquium 6
Commentary on Patterson

Joseph P. Lawrence

Let me try already from the outset to get to the heart of what separates my understanding of Plato from Patterson's. Patterson regards Plato as a "Platonist," primarily involved in the elaboration of a "theory of ideas." I do not. Patterson understands Plato's conception of Eros as being essentially identical with what has entered common discourse under the rubric of "Platonic Love." Again, I do not. Linked with Patterson's understanding of Plato as a Platonist is his apparent conviction that Plato articulated a single, internally coherent doctrine. He bears this out insofar as he looks to the "ascent passage" in the *Symposium* for a way of illuminating the structure of the *Republic* and vice versa. In contrast, I understand the two dialogues as decisively opposed, as embodying the internal tension which, without attaining a final resolution, works itself out in the extraordinary fullness of Plato's dialogues: the tension between Eros and Logos. Patterson resolves, without ever really facing, this tension, by maintaining that Plato accommodates only the erotic passion for form. According to his interpretation, Plato affirms the love of bodies only to the degree that they are conduits of the virtuous life which in turn derives from devotion to the forms and to the Good above all. While this may in fact be true for the dialogue character, Socrates, who after all had to be trained in erotics by Diotima, it is not true for Plato himself. As preliminary evidence let me quote the epitaph that Plato wrote after the death of Dion, the prince of Syracuse: "Oh Dion, you are the one who inflamed my heart with raving love."[1]

1. Diogenus Laertius, III, 30, quoted by Ute Schmidt-Berger 1985, pp. 135.

Joseph P. Lawrence

The *Symposium* leaves unresolved the question of whether Socrates might have expressed similar emotion towards Alcibiades. What does, however, seem clear is that, as Stanley Rosen has pointed out, Diotima places Socrates' erotic capacity into doubt.[2] She finds it inappropriate that he is so astonished at the frenzied irrationality (ἀλογία - 208c) with which the entire animal realm (207b) seeks to sustain itself through sexual intercourse and reproduction. And, more important in the present context, she questions Socrates' ability to properly comprehend the erotic ascent to a vision of the beautiful (210a). Socrates' astonishment at propagation is related to his prior reluctance to acknowledge a middle between the beautiful and the ugly (201e-202b): it is precisely his fixation on the realm of forms and its corresponding principle of logic, the principle of the excluded middle, which obstructs his understanding of Eros, itself a principle of *mediation* only to the degree that it is rooted in nature, so deeply rooted, in fact, that it draws from the darkness and indeterminacy of nature's most primal ground. Socrates' very commitment to the logical renders difficult his comprehension that beings are generated out of not-being (205b).

It is in this regard that we must understand Diotima's implicit assertion that the way into the ascent necessitates as its precondition a *descent*.[3] A guide is necessary to point the initiate towards an erotic encounter with a beautiful *body*. As if to emphasize that we are beginning as deeply, or if you will, as *basely* as possible, Diotima later tells us that the body must be that of a young boy (211b). Homoeroticism reflects, by its very sterility, an unadulterated sexuality which requires strict moderation by virtue before it can give rise to the propagation of spiritual goods. That the goal is indeed spiritual should not detract

2. Rosen 1987, pp. 221-263.

3. The theme of prior descent is implicit in the more general Platonic procedure of creating aporia as the precondition of authentic inquiry. The first step of virtually any of the dialogues is decisively negative: Socrates elicits opinions in order to refute them and thereby create the acknowledgment of ignorance that must precede the search for truth. This is accomplished in the *Symposium* simply by letting the speeches of the sophists and poets precede the speech of Socrates-Diotima.

attention from the fact that its point of departure is physical, even crudely so. To a certain extent we are, to use Pausanius's distinction (180e), referred here not to heavenly but to earthly Eros — *for what is decisive, in opposition to Pausanius's own "heavenly" standpoint, is passion, not calculative detachment.*

While Patterson's point is well taken that the element of grace which renders such a body beautiful is a function of a higher, spiritual kind of virtue, he fails to see that *beauty* is given when the spiritual shines forth in and through the *physical.* If his account were correct, we would not be directed towards a body, but directly towards the virtuous soul. There would be no need for a prior descent. Diotima would in fact have begun with an explicit *warning* that we avoid physical eroticism.[4] Rather than emphatically insisting that we begin by affirming our passion for a *beautiful* body, she would have stressed the appropriateness of loving someone like Socrates, that is, someone who is physically ugly, but spiritually beautiful. Even when we find ourselves advanced to a higher stage where the beauty of the soul is at issue (210c), we still find that such a soul must be attached to a body that has at least *some* beauty. Although Patterson might be able to get around this criticism by asserting that beauty of the soul will *always* create at least some semblance of beauty in the body (though why Socrates himself was shortchanged will be hard to understand), he still provides us with no understanding of why we shouldn't simply begin at level two. It will not do to say that this is necessary because most of us are too tangled up in the world of bodies: Diotima is, after all, speaking to *Socrates.* Any concern that *he* might not be able to follow her will have to do not with his inability to orient himself around purely intelligible ideas, but instead with his relative inability to feel the allure of the physical.

If one wonders why we must begin at such a low level, the answer is given in Diotima's final summation of her enthusiastic speech (211d). We are assured that the vision of the truly beautiful will elevate us beyond our infatuation for pretty boys. But at the same time it will retain the passionate character of such

4. *Krüger, G. 1973, p. 179.*

infatuations by so entrancing us that we are willing to forsake meat and drink in order to gaze steadily upon it. In other words, not cognitive appropriation, but enthusiastic self-surrender must finally determine our relationship to the beautiful itself. By arguing his way around the stage of physical eroticism, Patterson pays an enormous price: he loses the sense of *passion* which must finally permeate our relationship even to the most absolute sphere.

That this is the case is further reflected in Patterson's tendency to read the *Symposium* through the optic of the *Republic*. The goal of erotic striving, the beautiful, he identifies with the good, and that he equates with the beneficial or advantageous. This is, of course, not totally wrongheaded, despite the way it conflicts with certain elements of our Christian and above all our Kantian heritage. Moreover, there is the passage in the *Symposium* itself in which Diotima gets Socrates to identify the pursuit of the beautiful first with the pursuit of the good and then with the pursuit of happiness. I would, however, like to appeal to Socrates' reluctance to follow these quick identifications as an indication that they are in fact too narrowly reductive.

I will return to this in a moment. For now, I will settle for the observation that on Patterson's reading the project of ascent becomes that of enlightening our self-interest or, to use his phrase, clarifying our desires. Related to this step is his apparent assumption that this enlightenment can be autonomously executed by the systematic application of *reason*. Erotic ascent becomes the project of a kind of *erotechnique*, the mechanism of which he has set out before us. The general idea is clear and true to the text. The encounter with beauty so fills our souls that we give birth to words of praise. These *logoi* in turn help reveal to us the next higher stage of beauty, which is in fact the *truth* of the stage we are at. I agree with Patterson on this point, but would emphasize that it is not primarily a logical movement. For the speeches thus generated are characterized primarily by their *beauty* and beauty bespeaks a fullness that cannot be given determinate form. In other words, they must be understood as essentially *poetic* utterances, inspired precisely to the degree that they are not products of the understanding.

Perhaps I should explain my point here more fully. On Patterson's account, the logoi of bodily beauties disclose the origin of those beauties in virtues which have nothing bodily about them. Logoi, as crystallizations of desire's *intent*, are stripped of desire itself, until they can serve to articulate the ethical norms that hold desire in check. This is true insofar as it clarifies the path of ascent, but it is false to the degree that a poetic logos, by virtue of its rhythmic resonance, retains within itself a bodily moment. Diotima speaks of *beautiful*, not of logical speech; she speaks, that is, of that which not only reveals and itself constitutes the goal of desire, but is itself still fraught with desire. Beauty is truth, but truth in the mode of its *appearance*, its sudden and unpredictable emergence out of the ground of its ambiguous expressions. The vision of beauty is not attained by logical insight, but must, as Diotima says, "burst upon us" (210e). We are reminded here of the language of the *7th Letter* (341c/d) — and of the Divided Line. There is no discursive path that can guarantee final insight.

What would, I think, have helped here is a realization that the ascent passage at the end of the Socrates-Diotima speech is anticipated in the more general ascent which unfolds through all of the speeches of the *Symposium*. The project of enlightening our self-interest through the application of rational technique is indeed the project that hovers, with more or less clarity, before the three sophists who speak in the beginning: Phaedrus, Pausanius, and Eryximachus. This assertion on my part may come somewhat as a surprise, at least with regard to Phaedrus, who clearly equates Eros with physical love and, by designating him the "oldest of the gods" (178a), seems to identify him with primal nature. In other words, the general ascent seems to afford too direct a parallel with the ascent passage we have considered to be very helpful. This would be the case, except that Phaedrus depicted Eros only in order at the end of his speech to turn to something more praiseworthy. The gods, he said, honor the beloved, like Achilles, who acts for the sake of his lover far more than they honor the lover, for the lover's actions are not his own, precisely because he is "filled by the god," whereas the beloved acts on his own (180b). The highest praise is to be given to those whose accomplishments are autonomously executed, not to those who are inspired instruments of erotic passion.

This position is reinforced by Pausanius who in good sophistic form suggests an explicit contractual arrangement, which can be summed up as the exchange of sex for education in virtue (184c). Like Lysias in the *Phaedrus*, Pausanius clearly prefers the one who, in the spirit of cold calculation, pretends to love over the one who has given himself over to the power of Eros. Eryximachus follows through with a proposal for using Eros to attain the "advantageous" by subordinating it to technological manipulation (186b). While Patterson might distinguish his own position from that of the sophistic physician by stressing the goal of mental over physical health, he would presumably be committed to the notion that a sufficiently rational discussion would be all that is necessary to produce perfect accord between them.

What I would caution, however, is that a discussion which unfolds in this manner could never achieve anything more than the best state of affairs in *Hades*, for that is where Plato has clearly located Socrates in the dialogue. I refer not only to the general atmosphere of drink and homoerotic sensuality, to Aristophanes' grotesque depiction of dismembered and bleeding bodies groping for a reunification they can only momentarily enjoy (191a-192e), or to the way the effeminate and decadent Agathon presides over the entire affair, but more specifically to Socrates' opening remarks in his own speech about his fear that, armed with the Gorgon's head of Gorgias's eloquence, Agathon might strike him as dumb as stone (198c). The image is an image from hell.

I want, then, to criticize Patterson for leaving out of his account any reference to the utter depths that constitute the erotic point of departure. In doing so, however, I run into the danger of

making the opposite mistake. For I have thus far only enunciated the poetic moment within philosophy, whereas the task faced
by the Socrates of the *Symposium* was to distinguish philosophy
not only from sophism, but from poetry as well. Poetic exuberance by itself numbs the listener, while philosophical discourse
sparks a desire to participate in further dialogue.[5] The beauty to
which Diotima refers awakens "fruitful discourse" and provides
for "a golden harvest of philosophy" (210e) — and this does in
fact express itself in the *mathemata* and *epistemai* to which
Patterson refers.

Eros, as described by Diotima, is the son not only of poverty or
Penia, that is of blind desire, but also of the master of cunning,
Poros, who is the very spirit of calculation (203b-d). He is
described, moreover, as both a philosopher and a sophist. It is
his inheritance that facilitates those distinctions (for instance the
distinction between beautiful bodies and physical beauty as
such) that Patterson correctly depicts as leading the initiate from
stage to stage. Were Eros *only* blind desire, he would lose himself in the devotion to corporeal beauty. An additional, rational
ability is essential, for it helps solve the problem posed by most
enthusiastic speeches which, like Agathon's, are simply beautiful words with no meaning. When, lacking essential insight, we
surrender ourselves to enthusiastic exuberance we are always in
danger of mistaking the appearance of the good for the good
itself.

This is, however, a danger not only for the poet but for the
sophist as well, which is why we have to come back to the distinction that must be made *within* the common inheritance of
Poros, that is, the distinction between sophistry and philosophy.
Sophism claims to know when it doesn't, whereas philosophy
modifies its cognitive claims in relation to its own highest
knowledge, the knowledge that it does not know that ultimate
which is needed to truly secure any knowledge whatsoever. The

5. Compare the applause and speechlessness that followed Agathon's poetic
flourishes with Aristophanes' willingness to follow immediately upon Socrates'
speech with a question and defense of his own position. Socrates' speech generated further discourse in a way in which Agathon's speech did not.

sophist elevates relative claims to the status of true knowledge. The philosopher does not claim true knowledge in any positive and determinate way, but appeals to its possibility to disclose the relative and therefore inadequate nature of the "truths" that humans command. It is thus in an essentially negative form that philosophy attains its highest knowledge, a knowledge which should not therefore be disparaged, but recognized as the only form of wisdom accessible to human beings. It has, moreover, a positive correlate, the apprehension of the beautiful as an apprehension of the unknowable *formlessness* of that eternal One that reflects itself in all that is.

What this means, however, is that while the distinction between philosophy and sophism is an easy one to make — philosophy modifies its claims in a way that sophism does not —, the distinction between philosophy and poetry is one that cannot be finally and decisively completed, insofar as such completion would only be given where philosophy became science, which is impossible.

What must be clearly grasped is that this impossibility does not constitute a *defect* in philosophy, but instead a sign of the sublimity of its call and function. The *epistemai* to which Diotima refers at the penultimate stage of the ascent are propaideutical in nature. This is the case not only for arithmetic, geometry, harmonics, and astronomy, it is the case for dialectic as well. The movement in and through the forms is no more than a preparation for the highest level of philosophical insight, as we might infer from Plato's statement, in the *Parmenides*, that dialectic itself is no more than an exercise, a kind of mental gymnastics, that prepares the mind for possible reception of the highest revelation, without actually producing this revelation as its result (135b/c). The revelation itself unfolds from and discloses a source deeper than science, in part because it is the origin of science as of all else. This source is the beautiful. It is a real essence, not the abstract "beauty" to which Patterson has referred. It gives rise to conceptual discourse, but cannot be contained by any concept.

The sublime elevation of the Beautiful above the logical is indicated by the way it, the primal One, is yet the source of all difference. But because this relation of identity and difference can be dialectically resolved, it insufficiently expresses that sublimity. We come closer when, with Diotima, we recall that the Beautiful emerges "suddenly" (210e). It is not produced by the application of a method. We do not approach it, but it approaches us. We do not comprehend it intellectually, but intellectually gaze upon it. This serves to underscore the insufficiency of identifying the Good, the never fully disclosed essence of the Beautiful, with the "advantageous." What is advantageous is advantageous "for us." The Good is good "in itself." No enlightenment of the understanding can illuminate the mystery of its inner essence. If it discloses itself, it does so only from itself.

It is not the advantageous, but the source of "redemption." We turn towards it only when we realize the depth of our need, the horror of our collective residence in Hades. Eros mediates between the divine and the human. We discover the necessity of his mediation only when we suffer the poverty of a world which the gods have abandoned. Through our passionate encounter with other human beings, we are led into an encounter with the soul, not our own soul, but a soul that is "other," a soul that limits and modifies our autonomous quest for "advantages." In such a soul we can indeed discern the virtues and reason that provide it with measure. It bears the imprint not only of the social and political order that nurtured it, but of the entire cosmos itself. Our discovery of goodness in the other will bring us finally to that which is the source of all measure, the Beautiful itself. The "measure" to which I refer is not reflected solely in the limitations that constitute reason and morality, but in those sharper and infinitely more diverse limitations that constitute materiality itself. The measure is the measure of the depth of goodness that is the Good. It is a measure the Good sets for itself, that, under the guise of the Beautiful, it might actually appear. What is important is limitation as such, which always bears within it the stamp of the unique, even if internally, as in the rational idea, it comprehends something universal. Consider the beautiful soul which was Socrates. His beauty was an expression of his utter authenticity, not a sign of how successfully he internalized the mores of his society. When Socrates came late to dinner, he was — by the standards of his day as of ours — an almost unpardonably rude guest. Yet his rudeness was pardoned, because it was recognized as a function of that special calling whereby Socrates was elevated above, not assimilated to, the city of which he was a member. Or consider not a beautiful soul but a very particular face, the face of one you find strikingly beautiful. Its beauty is not simply a function of a rational order, but an expression of a remarkable uniqueness and fullness that separates it from everything that surrounds it. In the beauty of that face, all else disappears. We are delivered into the miracle of pure presence, into the sanctuary of the Divine.

College of the Holy Cross

Bacon, Helen. 1989: "Plato and the Greek Literary Tradition." Presidential Address delivered to the American Philological Association, December, 1989 (unpublished).

Irwin, Terence. 1977: *Plato's Moral Theory: The Early and Middle Dialogues* (Oxford at the Clarendon Press).

Kruger, Gerhard. 1973: *Einsicht und Leidenschaft: Das Wessen des platonischen Denkens* (Frankfurt).

Moravcsic, J.M.E. 1971: "Reason and Eros in the 'Ascent' Passage in the *Symposium*." In *Essays in Ancient Greek Philosophy*, eds. J. Anton and G. Kustas, pp. 285-302 (Suny Press)

Nehamas, Alexander and Paul Woodruff. 1989: *Plato's Symnposium. Translated with Introduction and Notes* (Hackett).

Nightingale, Andrea. 1991: "The Folly of Praise: Plato and the Encomiastic Genre." (Unpublished ms.).

Patterson, Richard. 1982: "The Platonic Art of Comedy and Tragedy." *Philosophy and Literature*, 6, pp. 76-93.

Patterson, Richard. 1987: "Plato on Philosophic Character." *Journal of the History of Philosophy*, 25, no. 3, pp. 325-350.

Price, A. W. 1989: *Love and Friendship in Plato and Aristotle* (Oxford at the Clarendon Press).

Rosen, Stanley, 1987: *Plato's Symposium* (London and New Haven).

Schmidt-Berger, Ute, ed., 1985: *Platon: Das Trinkgelage* (Frankfurt).

Colloquium 7
Aristotle on Substance, Essence and Biological Kinds
David Charles

I. INTRODUCTION

In this paper, my aim is to sketch an account (in some places, no doubt, somewhat controversial) of Aristotle's views on the discovery of essential definitions in the *Analytics*. Then I will examine how far, and how successfully, he attempted to approach issues concerning substances and biological kinds using the same or a similar, framework. I will suggest that he did attempt an approach of this general kind in the case of substances (such as men, sheep *etc*) in parts of the *Metaphysics*, but that his biological investigations did not provide the material to allow him to carry through this programme successfully without substantial modification. Finally, I will argue that the problems he encountered in his biological works stemmed from the nature of the subject-matter (as he investigated it), and could not be easily resolved within his conceptual framework.

II. THE *ANALYTICS* MODEL (INTRODUCTION)

The opening lines of *Post. An.* B.10 suggest an account of scientific enquiry which involves three stages:

Stage I: this stage is achieved when one knows an account of what a name or name-like expression signifies;

Stage II: this stage is achieved when one knows that what is signified by the name or name-like expression exists;

Stage III: this stage is achieved when one knows the essence of the object or kind signified by the

227

name or name-like expression.
Thus Aristotle writes:

"Since a definition is said to be an account given in reply to the "What is ___?" question, it is clear that one sort will be an account given in reply to the question "What is it that a name or name-like expression signifies?" An example of such a question is "What is it that 'triangle' signifies?" When we grasp that what (it is that) is signified exists, we seek the answer to the "Why?" question. It is difficult to understand in this way (*viz* through gaining an answer to the "Why?" question) things which we do not know to exist" (93b29-33).

If Aristotle does adopt a three-stage account of scientific inquiry, several questions become pressing.

(a)   What information is needed at stage (I) as a necessary preliminary to a discovery of the existence and essence of the kind involved?

(b)   What information is required at stage (II) in order to possess sufficient information to know that the object or kind exists?

(c)   What is the connection between the type of information acquired at stages (I) and (II) and the complete definition of (eg) thunder discovered at the conclusion of scientific investigation into its essence? (i.e. between pre- and post- explanatory accounts of 'thunder').

These questions raise, in an acute form, several even more fundamental issues. How is it, in Aristotle's theory, that one obtains at stage (I) information which is—on occasion—about kinds, even when one does not know that these kinds exist or even that they are genuine kinds (with their own essences)? How is it that what is discovered to exist at stage (II)—on the basis of this information—can be, on occasion, kinds with given essences? That is, how is it that stages (I) and (II) are connected, at least in some cases successfully, with the final stage of enquiry?

In this paper, my focus is on part of question (c). How are essences discovered in the *Analytics* account?

III. ESSENTIAL DEFINITIONS: THE METHOD OF DIVISION AND ITS PROBLEMS

In *Post. Analytics* B, chapters 8-10 are Aristotle's attempts to answer the difficulties raised in B. 3-7. These have focused on (a) what a definition is, and (b) whether there is a definition and demonstration of what a thing is (93a1-3, 90a35ff). In discussing (b), Aristotle raises the more specific difficulty of whether one can know the same thing in the same respect by definition and by demonstration (90b1-3), and does focus some attention on this issue. But that his interests are wider is clear in his aporetic conclusion to B.7:

"It is evident that definition and demonstration are not the same, and that definition and demonstration are not of the same thing; and in addition that definition neither demonstrates nor proves anything, and that you cannot be aware of what a thing is either by definition or demonstration" (92b35ff).

This range of interests is further evident in his more positive conclusion to B.10 (94a14-19), which refers in turn to accounts of definition, demonstration and their interconnection offered in the previous two chapters.

Aristotle's critical discussion in B. 4-6 focuses on what are described as *general deduction* and *deduction by division*, and introduces a range of arguments relevant to several of Aristotle's general concerns. In doing this, the chapters introduce some of Aristotle's background assumptions concerning the search for, and nature of, definitions and thus set targets which his own positive account in B. 8-10 should achieve. In this paper, I will concentrate chiefly on his discussion of the method of deduction by division in B.5 and 6, but similar assumptions are also to be found in his discussion of *general deduction* (B. 4, 6).

In *Post. An.* B.5, and briefly in B.6, Aristotle raises the issue of whether the method of *division* can yield a way of establishing definitions. In *Pr. An.* I.31 he had given examples of this method as follows:

Being animal $\Phi°$ all men

David Charles

<u>Being mortal or immortal Φ° all animals</u>
Being mortal or immortal Φ° all men.[1]

One of Aristotle's criticisms in *Pr. An.* (46b2-10) is repeated in *Post. An.* 91b23-25. In division, Aristotle notes, one cannot prove that:

All men are mortal.

This is merely assumed, as the most that division can establish is a disjunctive conclusion:

All men are either mortal or immortal.

But this is not of the right form to be a *definition*. Thus, Aristotle comments:

"A statement of this kind is not a definition, so that even if this statement were demonstrated by division, the *definition* would not turn out to be a deduction" (92a2-4).

Further, earlier in B.5 Aristotle has noted that even when the method of division *assumes* that man is mortal, it offers us no ground for the claim that mortality constitutes the essence of man.

"For what prevents all this being true of a man, yet not making it clear what a man is or what it is to be a man" (91b24-5)?

Finally, the method of division does not give us a way of establishing what should and what should not be included in the *definition* of man's essence.

"What prevents you from positing something additional, or from abstracting something, or from passing over something in the essence" (91b26-27)?

The method of division (as discussed in *Post. An.* B.5) fails to give us an acceptable route to know what it is to be a man, because it fails to isolate what is relevant to the definition of man. An adequate method, Aristotle assumes, should enable us to establish which properties are relevant to the definition of man, or constitute part of man's essence.

These points show that the method of division (as discussed as

1. I intend "Φ" to mean belong, and "Φ'" to mean belongs necessarily.

a mode of *deduction* in B.5) fails to provide an acceptable route to know what is relevant to the definition of man, or is part of man's essence. Further, they indicate that Aristotle is operating in this chapter with an assumption about one *desideratum* for an acceptable method of discovering definitions:

[Epistemic Assumption]: An acceptable method (which connects definitions with deductions) should establish that a given statement constitutes the *definition* of what it is to be defined (or expresses what is essential to what is defined).[2]

The method of division is criticized on a second ground in these chapters; it fails to account for the *unity of definition*. Aristotle make this point in two related ways. In B.5 he notes that even if (*per impossibile*) the method yielded conclusions of the form:

(1) All men are animals

and

(2) All animals are footed

the method would not itself *establish* that

(3) All men are footed animals.

For the method of division cannot from assumptions (1) and (2) establish (3) (91b15-21). This too would be assumed. Equally, he argues in B.6 (92a30-4), if man was defined by the divider as follows:

Man is animal, footed, two-footed

one would have no reason to accept that what was defined was a genuine unity rather than an accidental one like:

2. Aristotle had pressed a similar line of argument in discussing the method of general deduction in B.4 and B. 6. There he notes (91a30-3, b8-12, 93a12-13) that if one is using in one's deduction a premiss which expresses a definitional connection, one is already presupposing a grasp on what is a definition of F. But this point is only a criticism if the proponent of the method of general deduction is aiming to give some method to establish that a given (arbitrary) statement is a definition of F (without already assuming some other definition of F). The method of general deduction fails this test as clearly as does the method of division. Aristotle must assume that his apodeictic method in B. 8 can perform this task better.

Man is musical, grammarian.
Further, if cutting across varying divisions, one defined man as follows:

Man is two-footed, wingless, mortal (92a1),
one would also lack a reason for taking this to be a genuine unity.

These criticisms might provoke a (somewhat obvious) response from a defender of the method of division. If one could establish by his method:
°[man is mortal]
and

°[man is footed]
one would have good grounds for the conclusion
°[man is footed and mortal].

It seems too demanding to require (he might say) that the method of division by itself establish that *all differentiae* belong to *man* by the principle of division alone. It would be enough if it could prove that individual differentiae belonged to man; for one then could use the *agglomerative principle* to establish that

°[man is F and G]
Thus, if the method of division were able to establish
°[man is mortal]
and
°[man is 2-footed],
one could easily establish that
°[man is 2-footed and mortal]
in a way which showed that *being footed* and *mortal* was not an accidental unity (unlike musical and grammarian). It would indeed be *necessary* that what is mortal was 2-footed, and this would follow from the individual necessities *and* the principle of agglomeration.

This response, however, would be inadequate in Aristotle's view because the agglomerative principle gives us no insight into why

°[man is 2-footed and mortal]

is true: *i.e.* into why the two individual modal claims

    ° [man is 2-footed]

and

    ° [man is mortal]

are both true of one and same thing. One wants to show why both

    ° [man is 2-footed]

and

    ° [man is mortal]

are true in a way which reveals that it is no accident that both are true of the same thing. And this will apply to *any* differentiae term, no matter how basic, which the divider may use:

    man is animal, 2-footed, featherless, terrestrial.

Aristotle is assuming (if his criticism of the method of division is to be cogent) that in grasping an *adequate* definition one will find why a given set of properties are all true of the same thing. That is, one needs to show why man is at one and the same time necessarily *both* 2-footed *and* terrestrial. Such explanations will presumably advert to some property of the kind. If so, one arrives at a more determinate version of the Unity Condition which Aristotle is assuming:

Unity Condition: in grasping a definition one
                  needs to be able to explain why the
                  kind defined is a unity: *i.e.* to show that
                  it possesses necessarily certain proper-
                  ties in virtue of some basic property it
                  necessarily possesses.

Underlying both the Unity and Epistemic assumptions appears to be the following view of the type of property being sought in a definition. It should be explanatorily basic, explain why the kind has the other properties it has (necessarily), and be constitutive of what the kind is. In *Analytics* B. 8-10, Aristotle is concerned to outline an account which allows us to come to know in the case of given kinds what these properties are. This was the goal he needed to meet if he was to avoid his own criticisms of the alternative methods proposed in B. 3-6. So how is this done? Did he, in fact, in B. 8-10 and subsequently succeed in meeting the challenges implicit in his earlier discussions?

IV. ESSENTIAL DEFINITIONS: DEMONSTRATION AND UNITY

In *Post. An.* B.8. three syllogisms are discussed (93a30-93b14). The first, and possibly the third, exemplify the discovery of an answer to the "Why?" question. In these two syllogisms, the middle term (eg "the earth coming in between," "fire being quenched") specifies the efficient cause of

(1) eclipse belonging to the moon
and
(3) noise belonging to the clouds.[3]
So the answer to the "Why?" question is determined by giving *the* efficient cause.

This addresses the requirements outlined in the previous section directly. They demanded that an acceptable method for coming to know definitions should give us good grounds for the belief that:

[a] certain properties are explanatorily basic properties,
and
[b] these properties explain why the kind/phenomenon is a unity.

In the case of thunder, fire being quenched is explanatorily more basic than noise being in the clouds. For it is the former which is the efficient cause of the latter, and not *vice versa*. And this asymmetry is captured by syllogism [3]. By contrast, if the syllogism had been a general deduction of the form:

3. In the latter case, Aristotle uses *noise* and *thunder* interchangeably (93b9-11). This suggests a general procedure. If the account of what a term signifies is of the form:
"A" signifies BC
it is possible to substitute A for B. Thus, given that
"thunder" signifies a given kind of noise in the clouds (93a22-4)
one can in demonstration substitute *thunder* for *a kind of noise*. It is the same to explain why thunder occurs in the clouds as to explain why a given kind of noise occurs in the clouds. The answer in both cases refers to the cause: (eg) fire being quenched in the clouds.

Noise in the clouds belongs to all fire extinguishing
<u>Fire extinguishing belongs to all thunder</u>
Noise in the clouds belongs to all thunder

the middle term would not be the efficient cause of noise in the clouds belonging to thunder. But, if so, why treat the second premiss as *prior* to the conclusions? Remove the order of causation, and there is no ground for taking this premiss or the conclusion as prior. There is no way of establishing, in this case, the *order* of definition independently of the *order* of efficient causation.

What is the *basic* cause in this account? It is grasped when one has an immediate proposition (93a35-6). But what makes a proposition *immediate*?

In the case in point, one reaches an *immediate proposition* when there is no further cause which explains the connection between

(1) *eclipse* and the *earth screening* (93a30-6),

or

(2) *noise* and *fire being extinguished*.

If there is a further cause, one proceeds further in investigation until one reaches it (93b12-14). Immediate propositions constitute bed-rock from an explanatory viewpoint. When one has reached them, there is nothing futher to explain about the connection between the two relevant items specified. There is a direct, unmediated, causal connection between the items involved. There is no further middle term to be invoked which explains their connection.

In the examples in B.8, the referent of the middle term (which is immediately connected with (eg) noise) explains why noise occurs in the clouds. It will also explain other necessary properties of *thunder*: why noise is accompanied by lightning (for example), or, why thunder is noisy. For these will obtain because of fire being quenched—which gives off noise, lightning, and is in the clouds (as these are necessary for the quenching). In this way, *one* efficient cause explains all the other necessary properties of thunder. Thus, one would have discovered the *same* basic cause whichever of the relevant necessary properties had been the starting-point of one's enquiry. And this basic cause would be one and the same efficient cause in these cases.

This model provides a way of satisfying the Unity Condition. The necessary properties of thunder: noise, being in the clouds, being accompanied by lightning *etc* form a unity because there is one efficient cause which explains the presence of these phenomena: fire being quenched. It is *because* of fire being quenched that there is noise in the clouds, noise accompanied by lightning etc. The unity which eluded the methods of division and general deduction was this: they offered no explanation of why the following properties were all true of man:

> footed, two-footed, animal: 92b30
> featherless, footed, two-footed, mortal animal: 92a1

As Aristotle put it: "Why is *man* a unity, and not an accidental unity like *musical grammarian*" (92a31-3)? "At each stage, one can ask the question 'Why'" (92a1-3)?[4]

The causal model provides a way of answering this question in cases where the cause is distinct: there is one (eg efficient) cause, and this is what explains the presence of all the other *necessary* properties of the kind. If a property is not explained in this way, it is not a necessary property. By contrast, there is no one cause which explains why something is *both* musical *and* grammarian. What explains one fails to explain the other. And so this is an accidental unity unlike *thunder* or *eclipse*.

This model rests on there being *one* (eg efficient) cause which is explanatorily basic. As such, it rests on individuation conditions for one (eg efficient) cause. And Aristotle fails to spell these out in the *Analytics*. Still less does he say what counts as one teleological cause. However, the role of such causes is clear: they should provide the means for one to come to know that the kind

---

4. In 92a1, the *differentiae* are drawn from different division trees. This problem (of how to unite *differentiae* in different trees) is untouched by noting (as Aristotle does in *Meta.Z.12*) that in each separate division tree there is no need to represent intermediate stages. The *Analytics* discussion, in this respect, is closer to the real problems of biology than that in *Meta.Z.12*. (For a contrasting view, see Mary Louise Gill's comments.)

possesses other necessary properties. So they could not be given merely by stating a *list* of necessary properties (eg 92a1, b30). What is required is that they be ordered in a way which traces their source back to some *one* basic explanatory cause.[5]

The development of this model is important in Aristotle's progress in the *Analytics*—even if it is not fully worked out there. For without it, he had no way of satisfying the Unity Condition which he had used in his criticism of other proposals in B. 5-6. But in that case he would have no basis for rejecting their proposals. It was essential for his purposes that the method of demonstration provided a way of establishing the unity of the kinds such as thunder, eclipse or man. And it would do this if the middle term specified *one thing* which was the basic efficient or teleological cause. Thus, his method would be successful in establishing proper unities provided that there was—for each kind—just *one* such cause which was specified in the basic middle term in the relevant demonstrations.[6]

V. THE RANGE OF ARISTOTLE'S PROPOSAL IN *ANALYTICS* B. 8-10

At the beginning of B. 8 Aristotle distinguishes several types of cases: in one set,

[I] the cause is the same as the effect,

while in another

[II] the cause is different from the effect.

Aristotle then divides [II] further:

[IIa] the cause is different , and the effect is demonstrable/demonstrated.

5. It should be noted (in the light of Mary Louise Gill's comments) that the relevant cause must be *one* cause, and in this way (but no other) be simple. The cause may be complex in certain respects: *fire being quenched in way A in location B* may be one efficient cause as well as the simpler *fire being quenched.*

6. This method seems to be at work also in B. 17-18 in discussing scientific explanation: cf esp. 99b3-4. The requirement that one find causes (eg) for trees, qua trees, shedding their leaves (98b36-8) which are necessary and sufficient for this to occur in trees (as such) leads one to search for commensurate universals which are (a) explanatorily basic, (b) coextensive with trees and (c) fulfil the unity condition.

[IIb] the cause is different, and the effect is non-demon
strable/demonstrated.

The division between [I] and [II] corresponds to the division
between B. 9, which focuses on cases where the cause is the
same (93b21-2), and B.8, which focuses on cases where the cause
is different (93b19, cf. 93a7-8). The distinction between [IIa] and
[IIb] is not so significant or so clearly marked by Aristotle. It
may correspond to the division between examples where the
cause is immediate, and those where a further middle term is
required to explain the relevant causal connection (93b12-13). In
the latter, one does not have a demonstration because one has
not as yet found an immediate proposition. In the former, one
has a demonstration with an immediate proposition as its basis.
In the context of B. 8, [IIa] is the crucial set of cases. [IIb] seem to
be interim steps towards immediate propositions covered by
[IIa]. So it is on [IIa] that Aristotle focuses in this chapter.

His conclusion shows this:

"Without a demonstration you cannot become aware of what
a thing is (in cases where the cause is something else), yet
there is no demonstration of it (as indeed we said in the
aporetic discussion (in B. 3-7))" (93a18-20).

In section IV, I have attempted to show how this method works
in the case of [IIa]. However, in B. 8, Aristotle says little about
the scope of cases where the cause is different. He gives examples: *thunder, eclipse* (in 93a29-b14), but does not state the limits
of this class. Indeed, in 93a23-24, he cites as examples *man* and
the soul, but does not say whether they exemplify class [I] or [II].
In B. 8 Aristotle focuses on efficient causal examples; but is the
method of B.8 confined to cases where the effect is a substances-
attribute combination, and the cause an efficient one?

Aristotle, as always, proceeds cautiously. But in B. 9 he indicates to some extent the range of cases he is considering in B. 8
and B. 9. This chapter runs as follows:

"(1) Of some things there is something else that is the cause,
of other things there is not. (2) It is clear then of these things
some are immediate and starting-points with respect to their

essences; in these cases it is necessary to hypothesize their existence and what they are, or to make it apparent in some other way (which is what the arithmetician does—for he hypothesizes both what the unit is and that it is). (3). But of those things which have a middle term, and for which there is separable cause of their being the reality they are, one can—as we said—make them clear through a demonstration, but not by demonstrating what they are" (93b21-28).

Sentence (2) refers to the cases where the *cause* is not different in sentence (1). In (2), Aristotle transfers this to the case where the *what it is* is not different, and the objects are immediate or starting-points with respect to the *what it is*. In these examples, the thing and its essence will be identical, as the unit and the essence of the unit are identical. The grammatical subject, however, is the thing (*viz* the unit) and not its essence; for it is its existence that is hypothesized and which "has" an essence (93b23, 24-5). Further, it is objects not essences which are referred to in the sentences in apposition (*viz* (3) and (1)). So in sentence (2), Aristotle is referring (in subject place) to things which have essences, and marking off a category where the thing and the essence are not separated or distinct.

Sentence (3), by contrast, is concerned with objects or kinds where there is a middle term—that is, where there is a cause separate from the object/kind of its being the object or kind it is. In this sentence, "*ousia*" refers to the substance or kind, and not to the essence of the kind. For it is the latter which is the cause of the substance (or kind) being the substance (or kind it is). *Ousia* is used in this way in *Post. An.* B. 2. Thus, there the middle term is sought for the existence of "*ousia*" such as man, earth, sun or triangle (90a8-10). And what is sought is the answer to the "Why?" question which gives the essence (90a13-15). If so, in B. 2 *substance* and *essence* are treated as separable, and the latter can be placed in a middle term with respect of the former, *Ousiai*, elsewhere, are exemplified by man (83b2-6) and other particular *species* (73b7). The standard meaning of *ousiai* in the *Analytics* is, it appears, substance or kind, and not the essence of substances or kinds. Thus, if, for example, man and

239

David Charles

the essence of man are different (*Meta.* 1043b2-3), man would be placed within the class of entities (IIa): cases where the cause was different from the composite which is caused to be as it is. By contrast, soul and the essence of soul are identical and would be placed in category (I) (cf. 1043b1-2).

If this is correct, Aristotle in B. 9 is suggesting that the method of demonstration can be extended to cover not only the efficient causes of certain attributes belonging to substances, but also any case where the substance or kind and its essence are distinct. It would apply not only to the examples discussed in B. 8, but also to any further cases where there is a middle term which specifies the essence which is separable from the substance, whose essence it is. These cases should be separated from those where the substance and its essence are the same. For in such cases, there will not be a separate middle term (or cause), as they will be *immediate* with respect to their essences.

In B. 9, Aristotle does not attempt to determine which type of entities fall into category [I]: *i.e.* are identical with their essences, and which are not. But it seems clear that some cases of substances (*ousiai*) will fall into category (IIa). For these are the reference class of the phrase "where there is a separate cause of their being the *ousia* they are" (93b26-7).

In the *Analytics*, however, Aristotle proceeded no further with this interesting suggestion. If he pursued it further, this will be in his discussion of substances and kinds in the central books of the *Metaphysics* and the biological works. In the remainder of this paper, my aim is to examine the extent to which Aristotle applied this *Analytics* model for discovering the essences of some substances in certain sections of these works. My provisional conclusion will be that the *Analytics model* plays an important and illuminating role in Aristotle's discussion of composite substances in parts of the *Metaphysics*, but that he did not succeed in applying it in his account of animal kinds in the biological works (although there is some evidence that he attempted to do so). This conclusion is provisional because both sets of texts to be discussed raise a wide variety of relevant specific issues which lie outside the scope of a single paper, and because there

240

are other important texts which need to be analyzed before a more considered verdict can be reached on the issues at stake. In this paper (in effect) I am attempting only to propose that a given conjecture is *prima facie* plausible and worth further detailed investigation. The conjecture is the following:

Aristotle attempted to apply the *Analytics* model of substance and kind investigation in his discussion of substances in the *Metaphysics* and of animal kinds in the biological works.

VI. SUBSTANCES, ESSENCES AND EXPLANATION

The *Analytics* is invoked several times in *Meta. Z.* in discussing definition and unity (1037b8-9, 10-15). But references to it are especially frequent in Z. 17—where Aristotle is investigating the role of *ousia* or essence as cause (1041a9-10). Here he uses his favorite *Analytics* examples of *thunder* and *eclipse* to illustrate his approach to composite substances (1041b9-11; where these are contrasted with simple substances).

Thus, he writes of seeking the essence by asking the "why?" question:

"The question is : given something of something, why does it belong? That it belongs has to be clear; if it does not, nothing is sought. Take, for example the question:

'Why does it thunder?'

This is equivalent to
'Why does noise occur in the clouds?'
In this way, the object of inquiry is *something of something else.* And similarly,

'Why are these (eg bricks and stones) a house?'

Thus it is evident that the cause is being sought. This is the essence, to speak abstractly. In some cases, it is the final cause—as in the case of houses or beds; in others, it is the efficient cause. For this is the relevant cause"(1041a23-30).

In the case of thunder—something which comes into being—the efficient cause gives the essence; fire being quenched

241

David Charles

(as we know from the *Analytics*). And on this basis we can construct a full definition:

> thunder=noise in the clouds caused by fire being
> quenched.

This full definition (as we learn in *Post. An.* 94a1-7) follows the
pattern of the explanatory syllogism:

> noise Φ° fire being quenched
> fire being quenched Φ° those clouds (clouds in k)
> noise Φ° these clouds.

In the full definition of thunder, there are other elements beyond
the efficient cause: eg *noise in the clouds*. These are parts of the
definition in the *Analytics*, but are not the answer to the "Why?"
question.

So what is the analogue in the case of houses (to take the first
to be discussed in in Z. 17)?[7] Aristotle (as ever) proceeds cautiously by asking the question:

"why are these bricks or stones a house" (1041a27, b6-7)
and answering

"because what it is to be a house belongs to them" (1041b6-7).
He also notes that the general form of the relevant question is:
"why is the matter some definite thing" (1041b7-8),
and that the general form of the answer refers to the essence of
the thing. But while these passages reinforce Aristotle's insistence on the interconnection between the essence and the cause
(in the case of houses, the final cause), they do not spell out how
the crucial *terms* in the required explanatory syllogism are to be
understood:

house (A) Φ° what it is to be a house (B)

---

7. In her initial comments, Mary Louise Gill understood this sentence to suggest that (in my view) *both* matter *and* form are parts of the *essence* of composite
substances. That this was not my intention should be clear from (c) above.
"Matter-form" sentences represent the essence solely because the form-specify-
ing part of such sentences specifies the essence. Matter may, nonetheless, be
included in Aristotle's full definition of composite substances, but need not for
that reason be part of their essence (if this is restricted to the answer to the
"Why?" question: *Post. An.* 90a15, of *Meta.* 1041a28-30. In parallel, (e.g.) *clouds*
may appear in the full definition of *thunder*, but will not be part of its essence (if
this is restricted to the efficient cause).

242

what it is to be a house (B) Φ° these bricks (C)
house (A) Φ° these bricks (C)

In particular, it does not tell us how *house* is to be understood. Is this the compound, *house*, or some feature of these bricks (eg being arranged in a given way)? Or is it the same as *what it is to be a house*, which itself in some way involves the final cause (1041a29)? The approach in Z. 17 is left at a high degree of abstraction, precisely because it fails to specify an interpretation of either *house* or *what it is to be a house*. From the *Analytics* perspective, one would expect *house* to be present in such a syllogism if it is to provide an answer to the question: what is the cause of it being the reality (*ousia*) it is (93b26ff). Indeed, in the *Analytics* both *eclipse* and *thunder* appear in the demonstrations used to articulate their respective essences (*Post. An.* 93a30, b9). However, in the *Analytics* Aristotle does introduce a permissible substitution for thunder: *viz.* noise, which indicates how *thunder* is to be understood in the relevant syllogism. But in *Meta.* Z. 17 he gives no indication of how *man* or *house* is to be understood in the question:

"what makes this matter a house/man?"

In H. 2, some progress is made on this point. Aristotle introduces possible *differentiae* to distinguish types of matter (1042b9-11). These include position, composition, amongst a range of others (1042b25ff). In the case of house the relevant *differentia* is:

"bricks and stones arranged thus" (1043a7-8),

while Aristotle further notes that in some cases we may add the final cause as well (1043a8-9), which is in this case to be a covering for possessions and bodies (1043a16-18, 32-3). From these materials, we have the basis for the relevant full definition of *house*:

house = bricks etc arranged thus as a covering for possessions and bodies.

Amongst these differentiae, some will be causally more basic—the cause of each thing being what it is (1043a1-3).[8] In the present case, being a possessions-covering plays this role. It is because a house is a possessions-coverer that its bricks are arranged in given ways (*viz* with a roof *etc*). Further, it is

8. These will be the cause of the matter possessing the other *differentiae* (of each thing being what it is) as the final cause of the bricks being arranged thus (1043a8-10).

David Charles

because a house is a possessions-coverer that *bricks* are required; for bricks have the relevant capacities to be a possessions-coverer; being water-resistant, unmoved by the wind *etc.*

This definition of a house can be related (by the *Post. An.* B. 10 method: 94a1ff) to a syllogism of the form

      Being arranged thus Φ° possessions-coverer
      <u>Being a possession-coverer Φ° these bricks</u>
      Being arranged thus Φ° these bricks.

In this syllogism, *being arranged thus* replaces *house* in just the same way as *noise* replaced *thunder* in the *Analytics* B. 8 syllogism (93b9-12). In the *Analytics*, the question:

      why does thunder belong to these clouds?

is thus replaced by

      why does noise belong to these clouds?

In the *Metaphysics*, the question

      why does *house* belong to these bricks (1041b6)?

can be similarly replaced by

      why does being arranged in a given way belong to these bricks (1043a7-8)?

In both cases, the answer is discussed by isolating a causally basic phenomenon, in the first case an efficient, in the second a teleological cause (as predicted in 1041a29-31; see also 1044b1). In both, there is an immediate causal connection in the major premiss. It is because the bricks are used as a possessions-coverer that they are arranged thus. No further intermediate cause is being sought.

But what of the minor premisses? In the *Analytics*, Aristotle says very little about the connection in the the premiss:

      Being a quenching of fire Φ° these clouds.

Presumably, there can be no intermediate cause (or the process would not be complete). But Aristotle says little about the nature of the connection involved. In *Metaphysics* H. 2, he makes an interesting suggestion on precisely this point. In the case of the house-syllogism, the minor-premiss gives a form-matter predication:

      Being a possession-covering Φ° these bricks,

where the bricks are the matter with the relevant potentiality

(1043a15-16). Indeed, he seeks to extend the application of this model of predication further to cover examples like:

Calmness Φ° the sea (in certain conditions?),

as the sea is represented as *matter* to the relevant *form* or *actuality* (1043a23-24). Similarly with *air* in another case (1043a23). Thus, both the sea and air may be considered *as* matter (1043a25), even though they may not *be* matter in the strictest sense.

So how is the matter-form predication to be understood in the case of *the house*? It appears that this too is an *immediate preposition*, since the bricks themselves are potentially possessions-coverers. There is no further cause of what is potentially F being actually F (once we remove the efficient cause) because the relevant (teleological) cause (being a possessions-coverer) gives the essence of both (1045a30-3). What it is to be a brick is to be (potentially) a possessions-coverer. One teleological cause fixes the nature of both potentiality and actuality, and there is no further cause (of the appropriate type) required to explain their interconnection. In this case, the minor premiss is also an immediate proposition.

In the example of thunder, clouds may be regarded as like matter (1043a25), but the analogy is not strict as clouds are not essentially potentially locations for fire being quenched. Rather they are the immediate patient of the relevant change: the subject of the change (cf. 1044b9-12). Here again there is nothing intermediate between the change and the subject, although the relevant interconnection is not as strong as in the stricter cases of matter-form predications.[9]

In the case of *man* Aristotle is even less forthcoming about the terms in the relevant explanatory syllogism in Z. 17 or H. 2. What it is to be a man appears to be identified with the soul (of a given kind) in 1043b4-5, but in H. 2 and 3 Aristotle is very reticent about stating the differentiae used to mark out man (or, for

9. Aristotle is operating with a variety of cases of matter-form predication in this chapter. The basic case is that of substances (1043a4-7). Quasi-substances (like houses) are the next (analogous) case: 1043a5. Examples of calm (1043a24-25) are even less central, and Aristotle notes elsewhere that they differ in certain respects from matter-form° predications (1044b7-10).

that matter, foot: 1042b31). He does not specify what feature of man's shape (*morphe*) or activity (*energeia*) is to play the role of *arranged thus* in the house syllogism. so while we can construct a syllogism of the form:

A Φ° soul of kind k (B)

soul of kind k Φ° body of sort S (C)

A Φ° body of sort S

we do not know how to replace A with a term for *man*. If Aristotle followed the house-example, we would expect that a differentiae of *man* would take the A-place and would itself be explained by the requirements of being a soul of given kind. The candidates offered would be (e.g.) two-footed if a shape (1043b11, 1045a20), or if an activity, perhaps walking in a given way. But Aristotle is fairly unexplicit about the *differentia*, and is proceeding at a consistently abstract level (1044b16ff). If he had followed the first model, being 2-*footed* would replace *man* in the question:

why is this body a man?

as *arranged thus* replaces *house* in the question:

why are these bricks *a house*?

On this account, the answer to the "why?" question would be given by reference to the soul of the man as the teleologically basic cause. The soul represents what it is to be a man, as fire being quenched represents what it is to be thunder. However, as the full definition of *thunder* runs:

noise in the clouds caused by fire being quenched,

so the full definition of *man* will read

biped animal with soul of kind k.

There will be elements in the *definition* in both cases beyond the explanatorily basic phenomenon. In both, the unity of the definition is underwritten by there being one phenomenon which explains why noise/biped belongs to clouds/animal in the favoured way. Further, in the case of substances this phenomenon will additionally explain why the animal or its matter is as it is, because it is an actuality which requires the presence of this matter as potentiality. The presence of one strongly unifying explanatory factor underwrites the condition of a unified substance.

In this syllogism, *A* (eg being a biped) belongs to a soul of a given kind because it is a teleological consequence of there being such a soul. Further, it is an immediate consequence—with no additional teleological causal link. In the second premiss, the soul belongs to the body in an *immediate* way also. No further explanation of this connection is required because the soul is the actuality of the body's capacity. This is because the body's capacity is the one required if the soul is to function properly. Hence, there is no further cause required to articulate this connection. In both premisses, *A* and *C* are determined by what is required if the soul is to function properly.

If this is correct[10], the unity of the composite substance depends on there being a basic actuality/form which belongs immediately to the relevant matter, with the following features:

[a]   it should be linked *immediately* to the relevant
        matter in such a way as to explain why the matter is as
        it is; (minor premiss)

[b]   it should explain why the matter is possessed of other
        non-basic, but necessary, properties (eg being a biped...)
        (major premiss);

[c]   it should constitute the essence of the composite sub-
        stance;

[d]   its unity should be basic or self-evident.

For if the *soul* lacked this type of unity, one would not be able to use it to underwrite the unity of the kind. One would lack one basic teleological cause to guarantee the unity of man as one basic efficient cause guarantees the unity of thunder. Aristotle, in these passages, seems to assume that there is this degree of unity in the basic teleological cause: the soul. The "matter-form" basic sentences are, in this view, the immediate propositions which represent the essence of the composite substance.[11]

On this account, Aristotle introduces several additional moves in the *Metaphysics* to supplement the *Analytics* model. In the

10. I have argued for this view in more detail in Charles (forthcoming.).

11. In her initial comments, Mary Louise Gill asked for further specification of how the explanatory model works in the *Metaphysics*: e.g. what are the relevant

David Charles

Metaphysics, the basic structure of explanation is teleological while in the *Analytics* efficient causation, in general, predominates. Further, Aristotle introduces new notions to carry through the project: matter and form, potentiality and actuality. The *form* is the teleologically basic phenomenon and this explains why the matter is as it is (in the composite substance) and why it possesses other non-basic, but teleologically necessary, features.

But these differences should not obscure the two basic points of similarity between the two discussions. The first is that explanatorily basic immediate propositions have a central role in both. In the *Metaphysics*, Aristotle is searching (on this view) for a phenomenon which is capable of being linked immediately (without further explanatory connection) *both* to matter *and* to other necessary properties (being 2-footed). This is the role played (in Aristotle's account) first by *form* and most perspicuously by *actuality*. For the basic *actuality* is what is linked perspicuously and immediately to matter considered as *potentiality*, and that explains the other necessary features of the kind. On this view *potentiality* and *actuality*, when applied to the case of substances, provide the ontology required to make clear how *matter* and *form* can be united so as to share a common teleological goal of the relevant type. When this occurs, one has a unified composite substance. And this is because in such a case there is one teleologically basic phenomenon immediately linked to the matter in a teleologically immediate proposition.

The teleologically basic phenomenon has a further role to play. In the case of thunder, one essential efficient cause explains the presence of the other necessary properties. This might be presented in the following diagram (eg).

---

syllogisms and what is the full definition of *man*. I had initially left these issues unresolved in this paper (as I focused principally on the unity issue), but Professor Gill's questions prompted me to set out my views in somewhat more detail. In this section, I draw on material originally developed in graduate seminars in Oxford in 1989. I am grateful to Mary Louise Gill for helpful comments on these issues.

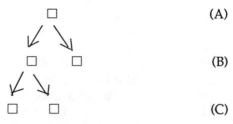

(A)

(B)

(C)

At base level (A), there is *one essential cause* which explains the presence and nature of a set of derivative necessary, but not essential, properties (B—C)—either directly *or* indirectly. The unity of the kind is underwritten in this way. Failure to meet this condition results in an accidental unity. If there were more than one basic cause discovered, *either* there would be one essential cause yet to be discovered which explained their presence *or* one would not be concerned with a unified phenomenon. (The case would be like pride, if divided into two types: *Post. An.* 97b23-26.)

In the case of *man*, the essential cause would be teleological, and express the essential activity of man—his/her soul. This would explain why (eg) being "two footed" *or* "featherless" belonged to an animal of this type—as these were required if the soul is to function in the appropriate way. But the basic condition is that there be *one* essential teleologically defined cause which plays this role. If there were not, *man* would be in danger of collapse into an accidental unity (like musical grammarian). There would at very least be no other resources in these chapters of the *Metaphysics* to prevent this.

This basic model may work for some simple physico-chemical natural kinds such as water or gold. Perhaps these do possess *one* unified basic property which explains the other necessary properties they possess. In one fashionable modern view, this would be H_2O or a given atomic number. But Aristotle was concerned to apply his structure to all *natural kinds*, including his favoured "task domain" of biology. The issue there is more acute, and gives his researches into biological explanation their especial interest for him (and for us).

249

VIII. PROBLEMS IN THE BEAUTIFUL PICTURE

In *Parts of Animals* I. 4, Aristotle is concerned with deciding which of two methods to follow in describing the properties of genera and species. One method consists in studying each indivisible species separately (644a29-644b1). Aristotle rejects this on the basis that it is "long-winded," making one describe the same attribute time and time again as they are common attributes of many species. He continues:

"So perhaps the right procedure is this: (a) so far as concerns the attributes of those groups (*genera*) which gave been correctly marked off by common usage—*groups which possess one common nature apiece and contain in themselves species not far removed from one another (I mean birds, fishes and any other group which though it lacks a name yet contains species generically similar)*—to describe the common attributes of the group all together; and (b) with regard to those animals which are not covered by this, to describe the attributes of each by themselves; eg those of man, and of any other such species" (644b1-9).

The passage contains the following thought. Certain genera have been correctly marked out by common usage: those that (i) possess one *common nature*, and (ii) contain species not far removed from one another. It appears that—in this passage—one such genus will be established if and only if it contains (i) a distinctive *common nature* and (ii) species not far removed from one another.

What then counts as a *common nature* (of the relevant type), and under what conditions are species not far removed from one another? In the *History of Animals*, Aristotle marks out seven main groups (genera) of animals: birds, fishes, cetacea (all of these are blooded), hard-shelled fish, soft-shelled animals, "softies" (types of calamary) and insects (490b7-14)—where the last four are bloodless. How did Aristotle arrive at this classification? Why did he exclude certain other candidates as genera or great genera (490b15-491a6)?

Aristotle's earlier discussion in *Hist. Anim.* I. 1-5 has laid the foundation for these claims. Birds have been marked out as feathered fliers (490a6-7, 12-13), fish as gilled, finned and footless swimmers (489b22-6). Cetacea are also swimmers, but lack gills and instead have a blow-hole (489b2). Insects are fliers with membraneous wings (490a9-11) and by contrast with other fliers are bloodless. The "softies" (*cephalopods*) are swimmers, possessed of feet and fins (490a1-3). The soft-shelled animals (*crustacea*) and all capable of locomotion (478b16-18)—whether by swimming or walking, while many types of hard-shelled animals (*testacea*) are stationary (478b15), and take in neither water nor air (487a25-6).

Aristotle, in this way, provided some justification for treating these *genera* as correctly marked out by common usage. This has been done by showing how these kinds exhibit genuine differences in the following respects:
  (a) *type of locomotion*: walking, flying, swimming
  (b) *method of breathing*: with lungs, gills, blow-holes
  (c) *method of eating*: where the animals find their food
  (487a22-7)
In some of these cases, modes of locomotion are the basic ingredients. Fliers are divided according to their method for doing so (feathers, membraneous wings). In others, modes of breathing are basic (gills, blow-holes *etc*). But each is marked out using basic divisions within the life functions (locomotion, breathing, eating *etc*). It is these affections and actions that provide the basis for Aristotle's classification at this point (cf. *Part. An.* 645b35ff). To have a common nature is to have a distinctive way of fulfilling at least some of the basic life-functions.

This claim becomes clearer when Aristotle considers cases of groupings which fail to yield *great genera*. *Wingless quadruped* is briefly canvassed as a possibility in 490b19-20, but not used elsewhere as a genus. By contrast, viviparous quadruped and oviparous quadruped are intoduced and retained as relevant genera, although neither are great genera. Why is this? Aristotle notes that wingless quadrupeds would divide into the viviparous and oviparous (490b20-1). These are nameless

David Charles

groups, but so are the immediate sub-divisions within the genera of viviparous quadruped (490b32-3). The explanation seems rather to be that if one had a genus such as wingless quadruped, the species within this genus would not be very similar (*Part. An.* 644b4-5) in a certain crucial respect: method of reproduction. And from this difference, other important differences follow—with respect to hair and horns (490b21-3).

In this example, Aristotle is relying on two ideas. If one has a *genus*, the species which comprise it should perform basic life functions in a basically similar way (eg reproduction). Further difference in mode of reproduction is sufficient to show that there are different genera in the case of quadrupeds. Both show that on the basis of a unified *common* nature—in which shared ways of performing certain basic functions are of central importance (locomotion and reproduction, in this case). In the case of a unified genus there is a distinctive way of moving, reproducing, feeding and breathing. Difference with respect of one of these life functions undermines the unity of the genus. The idea of a *common nature* rests on the thought of there being one organized collection of methods of moving, reproducing, feeding and breathing. A theory of what constitutes a common nature is at work in selecting the great genera in I. 6, and in de-selecting other possible candidates.

Armed with this view of *common nature*, Aristotle has good grounds for marking out great genera in I. 6. Once he has done this, he is able to mark out differing sub-kinds in a structured way. Fish are gilled, finned swimmers (489b24-5). He is then able to use these differentiae of fish to divide the genus further:
  (a) 4- finned vs 2-finned vs no-finned: 504b27-35
  (b) covered vs non-covered gills: 505a1-2
  (c) single vs double gills: 505a8-10
  (d) few vs many gills: 505a10-12
and thus to separate several major species within the genus of fish such as selachia (504b36), muraena (504b34), cf. 489b24-6), eels (504b27-30 cf. 489b24-6), as well as other smaller species (such as mullet, parrot-wrasse, perch, rainbow-wrasse, carp, dog-fish, sword-fish, tape-fish, fishing-frog—all discussed in *Hist. Anim.* II. 13.

All fish have other features in common also (in Aristotle's account). All are blooded (505b2-3), all have a bladder (506b4)—although this may be differently placed in different fish (*Hist. Anim.* II. 15). All have a gut of a given type—a feature they share with birds (508b14), although they differ from one another in the number they possess (508b15-25). Aristotle uses these differentiae to mark out varieties of fish (at a fairly specific level: eg angel-fish, skate, pipe-fish, bogy, burbet *etc*). But these are all varieties of *fish* because they are carrying out similar functions (nutrition of a given type) in similar ways, and all possess the differentiae of fish (they are either gilled or finned swimmers).

Through employing these intuitions about "common nature," Aristotle is able to vindicate the popular assumption that fish are *one* genus of animal—with similarity in function and in structural features related to those functions. Against this background, he is able mark out major differences between fish in other respects: some, the scaly fish, are oviparous, others viviparous (505b2-4)—for instance, the selachia. Indeed, he defines the *selachia* as footless creatures which have gills and are viviparous (511a5-7). Selachia have distinctive sexual differentiae (538a29), bone structure, and reproduce in a distinctive manner (540b5ff, 564b15ff). Thus, Aristotle is relying on the importance of the soul-function of reproduction to distinguish lower-level types of fish—where all are varieties of *fish* because all either breathe or move in the way distinctive of fish. There is a determinate enough *common nature* of this type to unify the class. Indeed, what it is to have a common nature is to have one organized mode of performing certain of these basic soul functions.

This pattern of argument suggests that Aristotle in the *Hist. Animalium* is beginning with a set of beliefs about what possessing a *common nature* consists in: being an animal with an organized set of soul-functions involving (typically) locomotion, breathing, reproducing and eating. To establish that a great genus exists involves establishing that there is an organized and distinctive set of soul-functions of this type, where one can see further species as differentiated (in large part) by their differing ways of performing the same set of soul-functions. To establish that a species of genus exists is to establish that there is a nature which performs the set of soul functions of the genus in a sufficiently distinctive manner. In both cases, one is grasping that there is a *common nature* involved, even if one has not fully grasped what that nature is: what all the precise soul-functions involved are.

This material in the *Historia Animalium* suggests the following picture. A *common nature* is a collection of distinctive ways of performing certain basic soul functions: moving, breathing, reproducing. More specific common natures within the "tribe of fish" emerge through considering further distinctive ways of performing these or other soul functions. But the problem is this: it is unclear how the set of soul functions themselves form an organized unity, rather than an accidental one. What is it that separates:

> moving in way A, reproducing in way B, breathing in way C

from

> musical, grammarian.

In the *Analytics* model this was answered by finding one property which explained why (eg) fish moved in way A, reproduced in way B, breathed in way C. For this underwrote the unity of the kind in question. The difficulty is to see how *this solution* is to work for a common nature thus understood.

This problem was already in the offing in Aristotle's critical discussion of division of a type in the *Parts of Animals* I. His criticisms hinge on two points.

(a) Division by itself does not show what is properly taken as a *genus*. If we divide in certain ways, then we mistakenly cut across genuine natural kinds (642b10-20), divide by essential accidents not by things that are in the essence (64327-32) or divide by the wrong things/features (643a35-b6). In these cases division leads to inaccurate results because it does not rest on a genuine account of what naturally belong to the *genus* or *essence* of a phenomena or kind in question. But if so, an account of the genus and essential properties is presupposed, and not established by division.

(b) Correct division must be by multiple, simultaneous differentiae (642b21, 643b9), where relevant differentiae are applied to the genus simultaneously.

For our purposes the second is the crucial point: division by multiple, simultaneous, differentiae essentially involves introducing a *variety* of different soul-functions (as in the discussion of a common nature). And this raises the issue of how the kind is to be unified in an appropriate way.

There are points of similarity between the discussion of the existence of kinds in the *Historia Animalium* and in the *Analytics*.[12] But is there a similar route to uncover their essences and underwrite their unity? Let us focus again on the case of fish. These are by nature swimmers within the genus of blooded animals. Can one explain their other features in terms of these properties?

On occasion, Aristotle moves in this direction. Thus, he writes:

"since fishes have a swimming nature as is stated in the account of their essence. . . they have no separate limbs. . . they have fins. . . " (*Part. Anim.* 695a18-24),

and alludes in this passage to their being essentially blooded animals (695a20-1). The hope would then be that one can explain other shared features of fish in terms of this essential unitary feature. Some further features may follow from this requirement. Qua swimmers, fish live in water and so need gills (rather than lungs) to cool their internal heat (*Part. Anim.* 696b2, *de Respir.* 476a11) and to eat quickly with little mastication to prevent ingesting too much water with their food (*Part. Anim.* 660b11ff, 675a6ff), and so have small tongues. Perhaps too their habitat qua swimmers explains why they have fluid eyes so that they can see long distances under

12. I have discussed this issue in greater detail in Charles 1990. For interesting critical remarks on this paper, see Lennox 1990.

water and avoid the effects of the water around them on their eyes (*Part. Anim.* 658a1-3).

However, other features of fish do not sustain this picture. Aristotle thought that fish tended to have their mouths underneath their bodies to prevent them over-eating and to avoid death from this cause (*Part. Anim.* 696b28-35). But fish are gluttonous because their equipment for reducing food is defective (675a20). And this in turn is not further explained in terms of what is needed for them to be successful swimmers. So their mode of feeding does not follow from their mode of locomotion (in this particular detail).

Similarly with fish-reproduction. Aristotle notes that they produce many eggs, because it is impossible for a large number to reach perfection as many are destroyed (*Gen. Anim.* 751a28-31; 755a25-30). This is a consequence of the nature of their habitat, and does not follow directly from the fact that they are essentially swimmers. (After all, the water could be as safe for them as for (eg) dolphins.) Similarly, in the eggs they produce the white is not distinct because they are small and "abound in cold and earthy matter" (*Gen. Anim.* 751b19-22). But there is no attempt to link these features to fishes' essential natures as swimmers. Nor, similarly, with the distinctive breeding patterns of *selachia* (*Gen. Anim.* 754a25ff), which follow from the size and roughness of their head and bodies and not from their essential natures.

The problem is that these differing teleological and causal explanations do not have a common starting point in one basic property which explains the rest (as in the *Analytics* model). Often they begin with claims about how feeding and reproducing are to work when one has certain other properties or lives in environments of certain sorts. And these do not trace back to the essential unifying property of swimming. Some begin from this starting point, others from facts about habitat, still others from facts about the matter of the fish. Not all begin with the essence of the fish.

Aristotle appears to recognize this problem himself in his introductory discussion in *Part. Anim.* I. 1. There he writes:

> "The best way of putting the matter would be to say that because the essence of man is what it is, therefore, a man has these parts... If we cannot do this, then the nearest to it must be done: *viz* there cannot be a man at all otherwise than with them, or that is well that a man should have them." (640a34-b1).

The first type of teleological explanation is what one would look to on the *Analytics* model: a unitary essence which explains the other properties in question. But this Aristotle sees will not always be possible. The next best thing is to argue that certain things are required for men to survive even if they cannot be shown to follow from man's essence. Such things might follow from what is required in this habitat or given man's matter (physical nature—made from certain materials). But to acknowledge this diversity of possible teleological explanations is to accept that not all the ones available will fit into the *Analytics* model (tree-diagram above).

It appears that in the Biological works, Aristotle is confronted with a problem for his *Analytics* style of explanation when combined with preference for teleological explanation and his robust (anti-Platonic) epistemology. In the *Analytics*, he developed a way of proving the unity of kinds via his favoured tree-diagram model. In the *Metaphysics*, he extended this model by taking teleology as the basic form of explanation for kinds and substances, and developing the matter/form structure to make these explanations perspicuous. But he now needed to find one unitary basic teleological property in the biological case to sustain these claims in the real world of biological natural kinds. Unfortunately, real life turned out differently from how it should have, if it had lived up to the *Analytics/Metaphysics* account. Aristotle could, of course, have saved his picture by invoking a specific unknown property (eg *the basic soul* of the fish) to explain the presence of the other relevant properties in the tree-diagram model. But this would have been to give up on the common-sense epistemology which underlies his account of significance, and anyway to reject the complex picture of the soul he had developed in *de Anima*. In the biological domain, it appears that Aristotle could not hold consistently his teleological model of explanation, his favored tree model for establishing the unity of kinds and his preferred (anti-Platonic) epistemological theory. So, more radically, he lacked a way of establishing the proper unity of the *common natures* biology discovers.

IX. POSSIBLE RESOLUTIONS OF THE DIFFICULTY

There are two problems at issue here.

[A] How to establish the *unity of the relevant teleological cause*—if for a given common nature this consists in a variety of distinct soul functions?

[B] How to establish what is essential for a *common nature* and what is not? Which of the features which fish need to have if they are to survive are *essential*?

The problem in [B] is this. There are, it seems, a variety of features concerning size, weight, habitat, reproduction which must be true if fish are to survive. But Aristotle wishes to hold that only some of these are *essential* (part of the essence), and to disallow others even in cases where the latter are not themselves explained by the essential ones. Problem [B] serves to undermine one plausible thought: to take as essential *all* properties which a common nature needs to survive, and to unify *the* teleological cause in this way. For Aristotle believes that not everything that fits this prescription is essential. Indeed, if one took the line suggested, his distinction between what is essential and what is merely necessary would itself be threatened.[13]

What possible resolutions of this problem are open to Aristotle? Several suggest themselves.

[1] Unify *the teleological cause* by taking one soul-function as

13. *Professor Gill's own proposal appears to be a version of this idea, and so subject to this objection. My criticism could be avoided if one could explain how some (but not all) of the soul functions necessary for survival are "integrated" so as to make one form,* or alternatively show that Aristotle could determine what counts as *one* form independently of what counts as *one* efficient or *one* teleological cause. To take the latter opinion is to reject *au fond* the *Analytics* picture in which what counts as *one* form is constrained by these explanatoriy considerations.

explanatorily basic—determining the nature of the rest.

[2] Unify *the teleological cause* by taking as the teleological cause *everything* that is necessary for the fish to flourish as a fish in its environment and exclude as merely necessary anything that is required only for its survival and not for its flourishing.

[3] Unify the teleological cause by taking as basic the idea of *one common nature* shared by all fish which consists (eg) in a given way of moving, breathing, reproducing *etc* which they all must have.

We considered [1] in the case of fish above, and saw that it was unsatisfactory. It appears unsatisfactory also in the case of man. It would require that human perception or human nutrition was different from that of all other animals in ways that could be explained by our (greater) rationality. But this does not seem to be Aristotle's perspective (eg *N.E.* VI. 2: 1139a24-8). If it is not, what holds together the nutritive, perceptual and rational soul in one human being?

One might suggest, in answer to this question, that human reproduction is the distinctive soul-function which is the sole efficient cause of the unified human being, and that this provides a unifying soul-function which explains why humans have the other capacities they possess. But this, too, seems inadequate. Aristotle proceeds from the nature of man to the process of his formation in his preferred account (*Part. Anim.* 640b1-4), and not vice versa. Further, how is one to distinguish between essential and necessary elements in what is transferred in reproduction (in Aristotle's account) without a prior grasp of what is being created—the unified human being?

Option [2] is, perhaps, more attractive taking, as it does, what is essential to be everything that is necessary for an animal's well-being or flourishing (and not merely for its survival). And this might suggest a way of separating certain elements as essential among the teleological *explanation*. However, there is reason to doubt whether Aristotle could have availed himself of it. In *de Anima* several basic perceptual soul-functions are regarded as necessary for survival rather than for flourishing (*de Anima* 435b19-21, 434b22-7), and there is no indication that they are any the less essential for the *soul* in question. These remarks must also apply to soul-functions such as breathing or reproducing. Indeed, in the biological perspective of *Part. Anim.* and *Gen. Anim.* well-being is less the focus of attention than survival. And, no doubt, this is why Aristotle does not employ this "way out" in *Part. Anim.* 640a33-7. But even if Aristotle had favored this solution, identifying flourishing for sheep or men with what is distinctive of men or sheep, he would have needed—if he had held to the *Analytics* model—to show how one can explain the other necessary properties of man in terms of this basic one.

The third option is the most radical because it involves taking as basic the notion of a *common nature* as a unified way of performing given soul functions, and giving up the attempt to underwrite its unity in the *Analytics* model. This would mark a major change in Aristotle's viewpoint. If he had adopted this in the *Analytics*, he could have said that

     biped animal

was a clear case of a *common nature*, while

     musical grammarian

was not, without needing to defend the first claim by finding a basic property which explains why biped belongs to animal. One could take at face value one's own, and other people's intuitions about what common natures are without any requirement that they be legitimized by scientific practice. The locus of authority now lies with common beliefs rather than scientific knowledge. This would suggest a clear way in which biology would be *dialectical*, and the *Analytics* model of science would not.

There are no definite signs that Aristotle steadfastly adopted this option. In his discussion of "the great genera" in *Part. Anim.* I. 4 he reconciles himself to standard beliefs provided that they are correct. Nor is it surprising that he did not opt wholeheartedly for this viewpoint. Had he done so, biological kinds would have been indeterminate at the point where common sense did not speak with one voice or with authority. Thus, the kind *"fish"* would be indeterminate if people did not agree that it was essential that they reproduced or breathed in given ways. And the term "fish" would be indeterminate (as they used it) if they lacked the resources to determine what was, and what was not, part of the common nature (eg Would artificially-produced fish be fish?). There would, it appears, be too many kinds of fish depending on which soul-functions were taken as constitutive of the common nature and which not.

The difficulty is not merely that Aristotle's biology is incomplete and not fully worked out. It is rather that in developing his biological theory, he produced questions about the nature and unity of biological kinds which he did not have the resources in place to answer. Biological kinds outran the possibilities of the simple, beautiful, picture he had developed in the *Analytics*, and called into question some of his basic assumptions about unity and definition. The study of biology, then as now, offers major challenges to a view of natural kinds developed to analyze physico-chemical kinds or ones with essential, unitary, efficient causes. Perhaps, this problem is as acute for us as it was for Aristotle; but that is another story.[14]

Oriel College, Oxford

14. An earlier version of this paper was read at the Boston Area Colloquium in Classical Philosophy in March 1991, and at the Los Angeles Colloquium in Classical Philosophy in April 1991. I gained greatly from the written comments of Mary Louise Gill, and have attempted to clarify some of the issues she raised. I also gained from the comments of an anonymous referee. In addition, I have been helped by discussion of these questions with Jim Bogen, Kei Chiba, John Cooper, David Depew, Montgomery Furth, Allen Gotthelf, Frank Lewis, Jim Lennox and Martha Nussbaum.

Commentary on Charles

Mary Louise Gill

The Boston Area Colloquium publishes revised versions of papers and commentaries that were previously orally presented. The point of printing the commentary, as well as the paper, is presumably to reproduce, to some extent, the dynamics and dialogue of the original occasion. Since both speakers can revise their papers prior to publication, the main speaker has the opportunity to respond to criticisms. But if the speaker incorporates suggestions and reconstructs arguments so as to answer objections, the commentator may be compelled, not simply to make revisions, but to start again virtually from scratch. My previous comments focused on part of David Charles's paper, the application of the *Analytics* to the *Metaphysics*. Since the section of his paper on the *Metaphysics* has been substantially reworked, I shall not here rehearse objections that no longer clearly apply. Instead I shall treat a topic I did not address on that occasion, the relationship between the *Analytics* and the biology.

David Charles has argued that in the *Posterior Analytics* Aristotle develops a method for establishing the definition of a substance or kind. Crucial to the method is that it enables the investigator to explain why the substance or kind defined is a unity. In the *Analytics*, according to Charles, Aristotle defends a procedure by which he can isolate a single basic property (an efficient cause) that explains why an object has the other properties it necessarily has. This basic property is constitutive of what the entity is. Charles then argues that Aristotle successfully applied this method, with important supplements to the theory (in particular, use of teleological causes, matter and form, and potentiality and actuality), in his investigation of substance in the *Metaphysics*, but was unable to apply it satisfactorily in his biological investigations, because of the nature and complexity of his subject-matter.

I am troubled that the method of the *Analytics* fails in Aristotle's biological practice. On Charles's view, for the method to succeed in this context, it should enable the investigator to explain all the necessary features of a particular biological kind as directly or indirectly caused by *one* essential feature. Explanation of this sort is what Charles calls "his [Aristotle's] favoured tree-diagram model" (p. 257) (for the tree diagram, see p.249). But the method fails, according to Charles, because the necessary features of biological kinds cannot all be explained in this way. Although the mode of locomotion, for example, can explain some of the necessary features of fish, other necessary features, such as mode of feeding, do not follow from it (p. 255-56). If there is no single explanatory feature that establishes the unity of a kind, what is it that distinguishes a list of differentiae—e.g., moving in way A, reproducing in way B, breathing in way C—from an accidental unity like musical, grammarian (p. 254)?

One can diagnose the failure in various ways. According to Charles:

> The difficulty is not merely that Aristotle's biology is incomplete and not fully worked out. It is rather that in developing his biological theory, he produced questions about the nature and unity of biological kinds which he did not have the resources in place to answer. Biological kinds outran the possibilities of the simple, beautiful, picture he had developed in the *Analytics*, and called into question some of his basic assumptions about unity and definition (p. 261).

Charles suggests that Aristotle's biology is to a large extent dialectical. Instead of satisfying the demands of science outlined in the *Analytics*, it derives authority from people's intuitions about the common natures of various classes of animals (p. 260).

Another diagnosis of the problem is worth considering. It could be that what Charles calls the "simple, beautiful, picture" of the *Analytics*, though an extremely interesting proposal, is not one proposed or assumed by Aristotle in the *Analytics*.

Charles argues that Aristotle's criticisms of division in *APo.* B.5 and 6 "introduce some of Aristotle's background assumptions concerning the search for, and nature of, definitions and thus set targets which his own positive account in B.8-10 should achieve" (p. 229). There are various reasons why the method of division cannot satisfactorily establish definitions, one of which is that it fails to account for the unity of definition (p. 231). The method of division cannot show why the various differentiae necessarily apply to the same thing—that is, why this combination differs from an accidental unity like musical, grammarian. At the end of his discussion in B.6, Aristotle criticizes division as follows:

> Why will man be a two-footed, footed, animal rather than animal and footed? For from the assumptions there is no necessity that what is predicated is a unity, but it might be like the case in which the same man is musical and grammatical (92a29-33).

Charles thinks that Aristotle's objection shows that he assumes the following *Unity Condition*:

> In grasping a definition one needs to be able to explain why the kind defined is a unity: i.e., to show that it possesses necessarily certain properties in virtue of some basic property it necessarily possesses (p. 233).

The passage quoted above from B.6 does apparently indicate that Aristotle finds the method of division wanting because it fails to show that the differentiae are unified. But Charles's explication of the Unity Condition goes well beyond what is warranted by the text. Aristotle does not say how an adequate method will establish unity, but indicates only that it should.

Does Aristotle say anything about unity in his constructive account in B.8-10? I find only one passage, which treats the unity of accounts:

> And an account is a unity in two ways, either by connection, like the *Iliad*, or by exhibiting one thing of one thing non-accidentally (B.10, 93b35-37).

But this passage does not reveal the thesis that Charles attributes to Aristotle.

Charles's reason for attributing the explicated Unity Condition to Aristotle seems not to be based on any explicit claims about unity in the text. His reason seems rather to be that the Unity Condition, as explicated, provides Aristotle with a means to meet the challenge about unity implicit in his criticisms of procedures like division, and also makes plausible sense of his constructive account in B.8-10. The method outlined in these chapters establishes definitions through demonstrations, as illustrated in *APo.* B.8 by thunder and eclipse. Charles contends that the syllogisms reveal one basic feature (an efficient cause) that explains why thunder and eclipse have whatever other necessary properties they have. Because the assumption makes considerable sense of the text, this is a strong argument in favor it. But the fact that, on the same assumption, the collection of differentiae that constitute a biological kind turn out to be virtually on a par with musical, grammarian is, I think, a strong argument against it. Is Charles's proposal the only possible one, or are there other readings of Aristotle's constructive account in the *Analytics*, which would reveal it as consistent with his research in biology?

Aristotle often simplifies a case to clarify a theoretical point. His use of artificial examples to clarify natural kinds is an obvious instance. Another interesting instance is *Met.* Z.12, where he treats division, which he regards in a more positive light than he did in the *Analytics*. In Z.12 Aristotle asks why man is one thing, if we define him as "biped animal." How does the combination *biped animal* differ from the combination *white man*? "White man" describes an accidental unity: the subject man partakes of the property whiteness. Aristotle claims that the genus animal does not partake of its differentiating features (1037b18-21). The relationship between a genus and its differentiae is not a relationship between a subject and its accidental or essential properties. The genus is a determinable kind which its differentiae determine—the genus is that common character shared by its various differentiated species. Aristotle contends that if the investigator performs his divisions correctly, always taking a differentia of a differentia (e.g., two-footed as a differentia of footed), the definition of an object will be the last differentia alone (1038a19-20). We need not define man as two-footed *and* footed *and* animal, because the higher differentiae and the genus add no information that is not contained in the last differentia alone.

This solution turns out to be too simple, of course. In *Parts of Animals*, where Aristotle treats division again, he rejects as inadequate the method of dichotomy, which marks off a species under a single line of division. The investigator, he says, must divide by many differentiae at once (*PA* I.3, 643b12-644a12).

Does the discrepancy between *Met.* Z.12 and *Parts of Animals* indicate that the former is a preliminary discussion, superseded by that in *Parts of Animals*, which relies on actual biological practice? Perhaps. But one might alternatively argue that Aristotle simplified his discussion in *Met.* Z.12 because his aim was to explain the unity of genus and differentia, not to explain how one must actually proceed in investigating the zoological world. If this suggestion is correct, then the insights of Z.12 may still be applicable, with the modification that the definition specify not one but a set of final differentiae.

Posterior Analytics B.8-10 focuses on very simple examples, thunder and eclipse. For these cases Aristotle can specify a single explanatory feature—in the case of thunder, fire being quenched. The examples are well-chosen precisely because they are so simple. A syllogism, with three terms, can reveal what thunder is by specifying its cause. The important point that Aristotle makes by means of these examples is that the nature of a thing is determined by its cause. But he need not be making the further point that Charles attributes to him, that the cause must be a single feature. What prevents the cause from being complex? The outcome Aristotle wants to avoid, as indicated in the passage quoted earlier from *APo*. B.6, is a list of differentiae that have only an accidental connection, like musical, grammarian.

The differentiating features of a particular kind of soul are not such an accidental assortment. We know from *De Anima* B.3 that there are various levels of soul, and that the higher levels presuppose the lower, but not vice versa. Thus some organisms have only nutritive capacities, and so their differentiae are restricted to those of nutritive soul, such as modes of reproduction and nutrition. Other creatures have perceptive souls. Of these, some have only touch, while others have higher perceptive faculties in addition to touch. And some perceptive organisms also have a means of locomotion. Some creatures, finally, have reason in addition to the lower faculties (414b32-415a13). The soul-functions, far from being a random collection of features, constitute an integrated hierarchical system, in which the higher functions depend for their existence on the presence of the lower. Although this passage claims an ontological dependence of higher faculties on lower, it does not suggest that any one function explains the others. This nonreducibility is consistent with David Charles's findings in Aristotle's biology: there is no single explanatorily basic function. On the alternative proposal that I am suggesting, the organism's various necessary features, for instance, its nutritive, reproductive, and locomotive organs, are explained by different soul functions that together make up its distinctive form.

On this view Aristotle's biology can be regarded as consistent with the model of science in the *Analytics*. The model of science in the *Analytics* should not be taken as prescribing that the investigator uncover a single basic feature that explains all of an object's other necessary properties. The model should rather be understood as prescribing that the investigator locate a unified cause—a cause that, in the case of animals, will itself be highly complex.[1]

University of Pittsburgh

1. My thoughts on the relationship between the *Analytics* and Aristotle's biology were stimulated by some of the questions raised by the audience at David Charles's presentation for the Boston Area Colloquium at Harvard.

CHARLES/GILL BIBLIOGRAPHY

Charles, D. "Matter and Form: Unity, Persistence and Identity."
Forthcoming in Scaltsas, Charles and Gill, edd.
_____. 1990: "Aristotle on Meaning, Natural Kinds and Natural
History." In *Biologie, Logique et Metaphysique chez Aristotle*,
Devereux, Pellegrin, edd. Edituris du CNRS, Paris 1990.
Lennox, J.G. 1990: Comments on Aristotle on Meaning, Natural Kinds
and Natural History. In *Biologie, Logique et Metaphysique chez
Aristotle*, Devereux, Pellegrin, edd. Editurris du CNRS, Paris
1990.

CRITICAL BIBLIOGRAPHY

Colloquium 8

Philodemus Resartus: Progress in Reconstructing the Philosophical Papyri From Herculaneum[1]

Richard Janko

For the study of ancient philosophy, the discovery of a library of some 800 rolls of papyrus containing otherwise unknown Hellenistic texts might have been expected to be an event of dramatic significance — the classical equivalent of finding the Dead Sea Scrolls. Such a discovery did of course take place, on the bay of Naples at Herculaneum between 1752 and 1754. It is our sole extensive library from the classical world, and one whose contents should at least stimulate, if not slake, the current thirst for more knowledge about Hellenistic thought. Yet, for a variety of reasons, its cardinal importance for the study of ancient philosophy has yet to be fully appreciated; and, as I shall argue below, a recent papyrological advance promises greatly to facilitate the reconstruction of many of the works contained in it. The library in question is of course that found at the sumptuous "Villa of the Papyri," of which the J. Paul Getty Museum in Malibu is a reconstruction. This villa was once the property of

1. This article, which represents work in progress, has grown out of a seminar delivered in the *BACAP* series at Wellesley College, and also at Columbia University and UCLA. I am grateful to the National Humanities Centre, North Carolina, and to the Mellon Foundation, for the Fellowship which enabled me to work on this material in Fall 1990; to Professor Marcello Gigante, for permission to study papyri of the *On Poems* in Naples in 1986 and 1991; to Mary W. Barringer, George Garrett and Helen Janko, for word-processing assistance; to the Research Council of the Academic Senate, UCLA, for financial support; to the Institute for Advanced Study and the Ecole Normale Supérieure, for use of the libraries where this article was drafted; and to Elizabeth Asmis, David Blank, Daniel Delattre, Marcello Gigante, Michele Hannoosh, Cecilia Mangoni, Dirk Obbink, James Porter, Costantina Romeo and Paul Vander Waerdt, for stimulating discussions of this material.

Richard Janko

L. Calpurnius Piso Caesoninus, known to history as the father-in-law of Julius Caesar but to philosophy as the patron of the Epicurean Philodemus of Gadara (ca. 110-35 B.C.). Philodemus apparently lived at the Villa, which became a major centre for the transmission of Epicurean and other Hellenistic philosophy to Augustan Rome.[2] He was well acquainted with Cicero,[3] and his school included Vergil's friend Siro and the poets Plotius Tucca, Varius Rufus, Quintilius Varus and Vergil himself, to whom Philodemus addressed one of his treatises.[4] Whether Horace attended is unknown but not improbable.[5] The Villa's importance as a centre for Latin poetry is shown by the recent discovery of texts of Lucretius and now of Ennius.[6]

Epicurus' aversion to poetry was notorious in antiquity;[7] yet his follower Philodemus was himself a prolific and accomplished epigrammatist.[8] Philodemus also theorized about what he practised; his teaching probably influenced the Roman poets whom he taught.[9] His interest in literary theory, shared with

2. For recent surveys of Philodemus' life and work see E. Asmis 1990a; T. Dorandi 1990; M. Gigante 1990. For bibliography the essential work is M. Gigante 1979, updated by M. Capasso 1989.

3. Cicero, writing in 45 B.C., mentions 'our friends ... Siro and Philodemus, excellent and very learned men' (*De Finibus* II 119). In 59 B.C., when conducting a lawsuit against Piso, he had necessarily adopted a less friendly attitude, which does, nonetheless, match his own personal aversion to Epicureanism: see M. Gigante 1983, pp. 35-53.

4. Siro was a friend of Philodemus and teacher of Vergil (Donatus, *Life of Vergil* 79); see further *PHerc.* 312 and M. Gigante 1984, pp. 71-7. Philodemus addressed his *On Virtues and Vices* to these four Roman poets, since their names have now been read in *PHerc. Paris.* 2 frag. 279a (see M. Gigante and M. Capasso 1989). Vergil's name is also restored in *PHerc.* 253 frag. 12 and *PHerc.* 1082 col. xi.

5. Horace quotes an epigram of Philodemus at *Sermones* I 2.120.

6. See K. Kleve 1989 (fragments of books I, III and V of the *De Rerum Natura*); id.,1990 (fragments of book VI of the *Annales*).

7. For an account of Epicurus' position on poetry, and a convincing explanation of how Philodemus' stance relates to it, see E. Asmis 1991, esp. pp. 3-17; see also D.C. Innes 1989, pp. 215-19.

8. About thirty of Philodemus' epigrams survive in the *Greek Anthology* (see A.S.F. Gow and D.L. Page 1968, I pp. 351-69). To these can now be added a list, found in Egypt, of the first lines of over 100 more (*POxy.* 3724, published by P. Parsons 1987). See further M. Gigante 1989.

9. See J.I.M. Tait 1941; G. Barra 1973; id. 1977-8.

and perhaps derived from his predecessor Demetrius Laco,[10] resulted in three substantial works of aesthetics: the *On Music* (in four books) on the function of music and poetry in society; the *On Poems* (in five books) on poetry and the good poet; and the *On Rhetoric* (in seven or eight books), on rhetoric and, in effect, artistic prose in general.

I will focus below on Philodemus' *On Music*[11] and *On Poems*,[12] which happen to interest me most; yet the developments on which I shall report have the potential to transform our understanding of much of the philosophical library from Herculaneum, including Stoic as well as Epicurean treatises. I will need to go into some technical details about ancient books, but this is unavoidable if I am to show how fundamentally our knowledge of Hellenistic philosophy, literary theory and linguistics may be altered by the progress of papyrology.

The Herculaneum library has suffered neglect for a number of reasons, most of them bad. The rolls of papyrus were preserved by being carbonized during the eruption of Vesuvius in A.D. 79. The texts were found at five different locations within the Villa. Some were scattered by the violence of the eruption, others were still in their wooden pigeon-holes (the ancient equivalent of bookshelves), and others were in the boxes used to store and transport sets of volumes (apparently there was an attempt to move the library to safety).[13] However, from the first the discovery fell victim to chaos and confusion: we do not usually know which papyri were found together, nor exactly where each came from. We must remember that the excavators of Herculaneum were pioneers of archaeology, just as the first people to open the texts were the pioneers of papyrology; it would be unjust to blame them for the difficulties we must now surmount in recon-

10. See now C. Romeo 1988.

11. See G.M. Rispoli 1969; A.J. Neubecker 1986; D. Delattre 1989. For a survey of recent work see F. Longo Auricchio 1983, esp. pp. 562-4.

12. For a survey of recent work see F. Longo Auricchio, *art. cit.* to which should be added C. Mangoni; J. Porter; E. Asmis 1990; N.A. Greenberg 1955 (1990); R. Janko 1991.

13. See F. Longo Auricchio and M. Capasso 1987.

structing the only extensive ancient library that has survived.

The charred rolls resembled logs in appearance, but were soon found to contain writing. After a number of failed attempts, the following method was adopted for opening them. Each roll to be opened was incised with a knife down either side, and the parts outside were peeled off. These formed concave surfaces like the bark of a tree, with writing visible on the insides (only the interior surface was used for writing); hence such a fragment from the outside was called a *scorza* ("bark"). The interior of the papyrus-roll, the narrow cylinder left after the removal of the *scorze*, was called the *midollo* ("marrow"). The *midolli*, being less badly burned, still retained some of their elasticity; accordingly the celebrated Father Piaggio was able to devise a method for unrolling these as continous texts, using the machines one of which is still on display in the Archaeological Museum at Naples. The *midolli* turned out to contain the ends of the treatises, often with a subscription giving the author, title and length of the work.[14] The continuous, if damaged, texts from the *midolli*, up to forty columns in length, are still extant; although substantial, they never represent more than about a quarter of the text originally contained in each book-roll, some 150 to 200 columns long.[15] The breakthrough I shall describe below does not affect texts derived only from the *midolli*, but rather those derived from the *scorze* or outer layers. Since the *scorze* had been cut down either side with a knife, they could not be unrolled to obtain continuous text: rather, they would yield in an ideal case a set of alternating fragments, one from one side of the papyrus-roll, the next from the other, each fragment containing a single column of writing (the writing was, as universally in antiquity, arranged in narrow columns at right angles to the length of the roll, and not along its length, as medieval representations might lead us to assume). However, the circumstances of their open-

14. For examples see G. Cavallo 1983, Plates XXIX, XLI, XLIII, LII.

15. On the average length of the book-rolls see G Cavallo 1983, 16. Book V of the *On Poems* was so long that one copy of it was divided between two rolls (*PHerc.* 1538); another copy (*PHerc.* 1425) was probably 245-269 cols. in length (R. Janko 1991, n. 346).

ing were far from ideal, and the results were much more complicated than one might wish.

First, the *scorze* derived from opposite sides of the same roll
were not kept together, but were assigned different and often
widely separated numbers in the inventory of Herculaneum
papyri; thus *PHerc.* 460 and *PHerc.* 1073 belong to the same roll.
The fact that the two or more sets of *scorze* and a single *midollo*
formed, respectively, the outer layers and the core of a single
papyrus-roll was forgotten. Hence, for a roll to be completely
reconstructed, one must first try to match up the outsides and
insides of the same roll, if all three survive (some were
destroyed in vain attempts to open them).

Second, the layers of the *scorze* could not simply be separated,
lifted off and preserved in the correct order, like layers of burnt
newspaper. What normally happened was that the first layer of
writing (layer A) which was visible on the concave interior of
the *scorza* was copied down by a paid draughtsman (a 'disegna-
tore'). This layer of writing was then lifted or scraped away to
expose the layer underneath (layer B). Layer A was often
destroyed in the process (occasionally pieces survive). Layer B
was then transcribed, and was then peeled away to expose layer
C beneath it, which was then transcribed and removed to expose
layer D, and so on. This process of transcription and destruction
(called 'scorzatura') would continue until the final layer was
reached, when no further layers could be separated. The end
result of the process was generally a set of numbered drawings
('disegni') and a single, sad-looking *scorza*, the bottommost layer
of writing, usually a mass of jumbled letters melted into each
other during the incineration of the outer layers of the
papyrus.[16]

Such, as far as we can establish it, was the procedure employed
for opening the Herculaneum papyri. Editors of the texts preserved in the *scorze* alone faced such serious difficulties that over
two centuries elapsed before appropriate techniques of reconstruction could be devised. These difficulties were the following.

16. On the *scorzatura* see F. Sbordone 1983a, pp. 199-200.

275

Richard Janko

1. The original papyri were and are very difficult to transcribe. The ink is grey to black, and the papyri are grey to black too (they are sometimes dark brown towards the middle of the roll, where the carbonization was less complete). The difference is that the ink is matt, whereas the papyrus is shiny, if one tilts it in the light. Neither infra-red nor ultra-violet photography has as yet been found to help, especially as the papyri are heavily buckled; painstaking study of the original, preferably with a binocular microscope, is our sole recourse.

2. The nineteenth-century transcriptions of the papyri (the *disegni*) are not always accurate. Obviously, where the originals still exist in the Officina dei Papiri in the Biblioteca Nazionale in Naples, these must be our primary source; but these have often decayed since the rolls were opened, because the papyri are very brittle. Hence the two series of *disegni*, one (*O*) kept in the Bodleian Library at Oxford, the other (*N*) in the Biblioteca Nazionale in Naples, are important witnesses to the original text. They were drawn by skilled artists, generally ignorant of Greek, but were checked by a Neapolitan philologist before each layer of writing was removed. Thus they often contain elementary errors of transcription, such as a good textual critic can often correct, but hardly ever serious errors or falsifications.[17]

3. Like all ancient texts, the papyri have no distinction between capital and small letters, no divisions between words, few accents and only minimal and unreliable punctuation. They are often carelessly written, containing scribal errors varying from the obvious to the totally incorrigible, such as the omission of entire phrases or sentences by haplography.[18]

17. On some falsifications, however, see M. Capasso 1986. These are rare, and most of the mistranscriptions are accidental. For example, in *On Poems* Treatise D frag. 16 Nardelli (= *PHerc.* 1081 *disegno* 29), the text of lines 5-8 should be emended to read [τὰ τοῦ] Σώφρονος καὶ τὰ [τῶν] ἄλλων μιμογρ[άφων] ἐνίοτε (*scripsi*: ΕΙΠΟΤΕ *N*, εἴ ποτε *edd.*) ποήμα[τα λέ]γεται. The usual text with εἴ ποτε makes no sense: Philodemus is in fact alluding to Aristotle's view that the mimes of Sophron could be classified as poems (*Poetics* 1.1447b10, *On Poets* frag. 72 Rose, with R. Janko 1991, Section V.1, with nn. 248-9).

18. Sometimes such omissions can be restored from parallel passages: thus in Parallel 3B below the *disegno* has [τὸ γὰρ λυ]ποῦν πολ[λάκις ἡμᾶς δ]ιὰ τὸν

4. The sequence of the fragments, when they derive from *scorze*, often makes no sense at all. Editors would usually arrange the pieces in a completely arbitrary order according to apparent associations or repetitions of ideas, or alleged coherence (this sometimes led them to emend the papyri, in order to create joins where there are none). This method is followed, for example, in the editions of the *On Music 'III'* by J. Kemke[19] or *On Poems* by F. Sbordone[20] and M.L. Nardelli;[21] yet it never gave the works as a whole any satisfactory structure. An alternative would be to follow the numeration of the *disegni*, as was done in Nardelli's publication of *PHerc.* 1581,[22] yet this too yielded no continuous sense. Thus this author's wife, after reading translations of the fragments of *PHerc.* 1581 arranged in Nardelli's order, observed that they might as well be backwards for all the sense they made. She was closer to the truth than either of us guessed at the time.

5. The style and argumentation of Philodemus in particular have often seemed obscure and contorted, for several reasons:

(i) Philodemus tends to use long periods, where the loss of any part of the sentence makes the whole difficult to reconstruct and understand, particularly where the sequence of the fragments is still undetermined. He can also be very concise and elliptical.

(ii) The vocabulary used by Hellenistic critics, grammarians and philosophers is large, complex, specialized, often multivalent and still poorly known. Moreover the prose of the later second and first centuries B.C. is still largely lost to us, the most notable exception being pseudo-Longinus, *On the Sublime*, a notoriously difficult work. Just after Philodemus' time, the Atticist movement imposed norms derived from the 'pure' Attic of the fifth and fourth centuries B.C.; this has rendered the

---

"λω[τόν]", but from the similar passage in Parallel 3A(i) I have restored [τὸ γὰρ ⟨οἰκειοῦν ἢ⟩ λυ]ποῦν πολ[λάκις ἡμᾶς δ]ιὰ τὸν ⟨ἦχον, ὡς τὸν⟩ "λω[τόν]".

19. J. Kemke 1884. For stern criticism of the early attempts to reassemble the fragments see O. Luschnat 1953.

20. F. Sbordone 1976. This contains the Treatises A, B and C discussed below.

21. M.L. Nardelli 1983. This contains Treatises D and E.

22. M.L. Nardelli 1978.

Richard Janko

Greek prose of the early Imperial period much more familar to most Hellenists than is the Greek of the late Roman Republic.[23] Philodemus' prose is closer to the spoken vernacular. A better understanding and more thorough exploitation of the Herculaneum papyri will contribute much to the lexicography and history of the Greek language,[24] as well as elucidate the development of technical, literary-critical, grammatical and philosophical terminology during this crucial period.

(iii) Philodemus' method of argument often consists of the refutation of the doctrines of his opponents, whose words may be quoted in direct or in indirect speech, inverted, taken out of context or reduced to absurdity. Such quotations can be hard to recognise. Their presence is not always signalled by punctuation in the papyri, nor indeed is it always marked by editors of texts, particularly for lack of a suitable typographic convention to indicate partial or adapted quotations (the use of spaced letters is in fact perfect for this purpose). Moreover, an undetected citation, often given in a long phrase marked by the article τό with the accusative and infinitive construction, can completely throw off balance all attempts to reconstruct the syntax of the sentence in which it appears.

(iv) Past editors of Herculaneum papyri have often failed to supply any translation of the text which they restore; this failure has tended to obscure how often their supplements are erroneous.

The result of all these problems has been not, as one might have hoped, the realisation that the Herculaneum papyri are one of the most challenging and exciting treasure-troves of classical philology and ancient philosophy, but a general neglect of this area even by precisely those scholars to whom it has most to offer. The inattention of the philologists is a scandal. If we had diverted but one tenth of the effort lavished on reexplicating the pre-Socratics or Plato to the Herculaneum papyri, we would

23. Cf. W.R. Roberts 1907, pp. 186-93; F. Donadi 1991, pp. 76-84.

24. The still fundamental study of W. Croenert 1903 (1963) needs updating in the light of recent work.

have gained much. Instead, two further problems have exacerbated the neglect. The first, surprising to relate, is a continuing prejudice against Epicureanism, which has its roots in the hostility of Cicero, Plutarch, and the Fathers of the early Church, since Epicurus' denial that the gods involved themselves in the world represented the closest approach to atheism available in antiquity. In his *In Pisonem*, Cicero contrived to damn Philodemus as a Greek and a poet; his praise of the elegance of Philodemus' epigrams would be, to a traditionally anti-Greek and anti-intellectual audience of Roman jurors, sufficient condemnation in itself.[25] Such prejudice still finds its echo among philosophers and philologists alike; we have all read Cicero and Plutarch long before we have even heard of Demetrius Laco or Philodemus. Only a handful of the greatest scholars in the evolution of ancient philosophy as a discipline — such giants as Gomperz, Usener, Croenert or Diels — worked on these materials, and thereby gave the field academic respectability. The brambles are always thickest in untended ground!

The second obstacle has been the location of the materials in Naples, which, despite its prominence as the terminus of the Grand Tour, has since tended to fall off the edge of the touristic map, displaced by Rome and Pompeii. Yet the city remains as colourful and lively as it ever was, and well worth an extended visit. For the ancient philosopher, moreover, the salient fact to note is the new spirit of international cooperation fostered in recent years by Professor Marcello Gigante, who founded the highly successful journal *Cronache Ercolanesi* in 1969, along with the Centro Internazionale per lo Studio dei Papiri Ercolanesi. The renewed efflorescence in Philodemean studies has resulted in a plethora of publications on Epicureanism and the Herculaneum papyri, including many greatly improved texts published in the fine series *La Scuola di Epicuro* and in *Cronache Ercolanesi*. This renewed attention to the library of Philodemus is directly responsible for the technical advances recently achieved in reconstructing the philosophical treatises from Herculaneum.

25. See above, n. 3.

Richard Janko

The revolutionary breakthrough to which I refer concerns the ordering of the *scorze*. It will be recalled that these were the outer parts of the papyri, which were cut lengthwise with a knife in order to open the roll. Each *scorza* had writing on its concave inner surface, which was transcribed and then removed in order to reach the layer of writing beneath; the process of transcription and destruction continued until no further layers of writing could be separated. This procedure yielded each time a set of drawings (*disegni*), numbered in sequence, starting from the first layer (layer A) which the draughtsman encountered. The drawing of layer A would be numbered 1, that of Layer B beneath it would be numbered 2, and so on. As remarked above, the resultant series of drawings yielded no continuous sense. In the mid-1980s, two scholars reconstructing different texts (both working from *disegni* of the *scorze*) discovered independently the solution to the puzzle: Dirk Obbink of Columbia University, working on the *On Piety*,[26] and Daniel Delattre of the CNRS, working on the *On Music*.[27] Their central insight is as brilliant as it is devastatingly simple. Ancient book-rolls were normally read from the outside in: the reader began at the outside of the roll, and continued until he reached the middle. The middle of the roll contained the end of the work, with a *subscriptio* indicating its author, its title and often its length. It accords with this that the *midolli* from Herculaneum preserve the ends of treatises. It must follow that the *scorze* contain earlier portions, less close to the end. Furthermore, the numeration assigned to the *disegni* by the nineteenth-century draughtsmen has to be retained — but usually in reverse! The first layer which the draughtsman encountered and drew, layer A (= *disegno* 1), is actually the layer closest to the *end* of the work. The second layer, layer B (= *disegno* 2), was one circumference further back towards the beginning; the third layer, layer C (= *disegno* 3) would be yet earlier in the text, and so on. One's intial impression that these parts of Philodemus' treatises made no sense is confirmed, but the fault is ours, not his: we had been reading much of his work backwards! Occasionally, however, the

26. Obbink 1986, pp. 24-43.

27. Delattre 1989.

sequence of *disegno*-numbers should not be reversed. This occurs when a set of *scorze* was detached, where the fragments came away starting from the outside.[28]

The insight basic to the Delattre/Obbink method is simple enough, but a few more steps are necessary before one can proceed to the full reconstruction of a Herculaneum text. It is not enough to reverse the order of a given set of *disegni*, because these represent only one side of the papyrus-roll; each set of *scorze* must be reunited with its missing Other Half, like Aristophanes' humans in the *Symposium*. G. Cavallo's excellent study[29] of the scribal hands is of great assistance in helping one to decide which papyri can belong to the same roll, and which cannot. So is careful attention to the number of lines per column. If one can find the missing Other Half, the two series of *disegni* must usually be *interleaved in reverse order* in order to obtain a coherent text. Even so, there are certain to be gaps in the continuity of the treatise, for several reasons:

1. It is extremely difficult to identify the missing Other Half, although this may well be lurking somewhere among the extremely numerous papyri which have not been unrolled or fully studied. Several different sets of *scorze* may in fact belong to one and the same roll.

2. There may be gaps in a given series of *scorze*, because superimposed layers may have stuck together and failed to separate during the process of transcription, resulting in a lacuna of at least one column (the number of columns missing depends on the circumference of the roll at that point).

3. Naturally, the vertical columns of writing cannot always be relied upon to coincide exactly with the vertical incisions made down the sides of the papyrus-roll in order to open it. Frequently, the knife will have cut away the left half of one column and the right half of the next, leaving intact in the middle of the *scorza* the blank space between the two columns. In such

28. An example of this is *PHerc.* 225, of *On Music* IV (see Delattre 1989, p. 66).
29. G. Cavallo 1983.

Richard Janko

cases, it is important to determine how the draughtsman react-
ed. Often, it was not thought worthwhile to draw columns with
only a few letters left in each line. This is a pity, since the
chances of a successful reconstruction of these works are greatly
increased when such fragments survive, since they offer the
hope of joining the left and right halves of the same column,
thereby linking different sets of *scorze* with different inventory-
numbers. Sometimes, however, when a single *scorza* contained
fragments of two columns, the draughtsmen did draw both. But
it was not their method to make a single drawing showing the
columns' relation to each other; instead, they would produce
separate drawings of the left- and right-hand columns. They
would sometimes indicate the relationship between them by
numbering them "A" and "B" (e.g. 15A to the left, 15B to the
right, or *vice versa*); but often they would not indicate it at all,
but would number the drawings 14 and 15 (or 15 and 14) as if
they represented successive layers of writing, when in fact they
do not. A proof of this is provided by the surviving fragment 5
of *PHerc.* 460, containing parts of two columns of *On Poems*
Treatise B. As Sbordone[30] realised when he published a photo-
graph of this fragment, the right-hand column corresponds to
PHerc. 460 *disegno* 5 lines 2-10 (= fr. 4 col. i Sbordone). However,
he did not see that the left-hand column has line-ends which
match *disegno* 4 lines 7-10 (= fr. 28 Sbordone), and that the two
disegni are therefore adjacent (= cols. 57*-58* in my provisional
numeration).[31] The identification of such cases does not usually
pose a serious problem. They can be recognized from study of
the outlines of the *disegni*, whence one can establish which is the
left-hand column and which is the right-hand; often one can
conjecture or prove verbal continuity between two such
columns. Thus *PHerc.* 460 *disegni* 23 and 24 form a single *scorza*,
joined by the word διδάσκειν; yet these are numbered frags. 30
and 19 in Sbordone's edition!

30. Sbordone 1976, Tav. 20.

31. Sbordone's failure to compare the surviving fragments with the *disegni* also
led him to miss the identity of *PHerc.* 460 frag. 3 with the lower part of *disegno*
28.

Let me now illustrate with examples the power and efficacy of this method, as well as its limitations. First, C. Mangoni[32] in her study of *PHerc.* 228, from Philodemus' *On Poems*, already noted that the order of the *scorze*, if reversed, yielded a series of quotations first from Crates and then from Zeno of Sidon, parallel to those in columns xxiii-xxiv, xxvi and xxvii-xxx of *On Poems* V, where Philodemus refutes the same doctrines in the same order. However, the parallelism is not complete, since *PHerc.* 228 consists of disconnected *scorze* from one side of the papyrus; the other side of it has, to date, not been identified.[33] The same situation obtains in *PHerc.* 1581, a text of extraordinary significance for Aristotelian catharsis. This, when published from *scorze* by Nardelli[34] in 1978, yielded little coherent sense; yet, when the order of the fragments was reversed, it became clear that Nardelli's frag. I summarised arguments preserved in fragments II-VII, only to advance to a new point.[35] Here internal evidence, rather than the external confirmation afforded by a parallel set of arguments, supports the reversal of the sequence of fragments. So does their state of preservation: frags. 1 and 2 are the best preserved of the series, which suggests that they come from the interior of the roll, whereas the rest, more badly damaged, must have been closer to the exterior, which was more badly burned. Moreover, the curvature of the fragments, which still survive, suggests that they derive from a part of the roll where its circumference was large.

But the most effective demonstration of the promise of this method comes from cases where both halves of the same papyrus-roll have been identified and put together. Whereas ordinary papyrology rarely yields texts of great length, at least nowadays, the Delattre/Obbink method allows us to reconstruct texts many columns long. The most striking case is Delattre's

32. C. Mangoni 1989.

33. For a tentative proposal that *PHerc.* 228 forms part of the same roll as the "scorze" *PHerc.* 403, 407, and 1581 and the "midollo" *PHerc.* 1425, and therefore derives from *On Poems* Book V, of which *PHerc.* 1425 contains the closing portion and title, see R. Janko 1991, Section VI.

34. M.L. Nardelli 1978.

35. See R. Janko, loc. cit. (n. 33); id., 1987, 61, 187-9; and id., 1992a, pp. 345-7.

reconstruction of 109 columns of Philodemus' *On Music* IV, from a number of papyri with different inventory-numbers.[36] By inverting and interleaving the order of various sets of *disegni*, Delattre has been able to show that the alleged Books I, III and IV of the *On Music* all in fact belong to a single roll 154 columns in length; it follows that they all belong to Book IV, of which the *midollo* preserves the closing title. His reconstruction is all the more secure because he was able to confirm it from internal evidence. He has shown that, like Cicero in the *De Natura Deorum*, Philodemus followed the procedure of, first, summarising the opinions of his opponent (in this case, Diogenes of Babylon, the successor of Chrysippus as head of the Stoa), and then refuting these same opinions, point by point, in the same sequence. Delattre discovered a series of twenty-six parallels between the summary of Diogenes' arguments, which occupied at least cols. 2* to 39* in the reconstructed text, and Philodemus' refutation of these same arguments in cols. 57* to 146. Delattre has succeeded in finding joins between all of the papyri assigned to the *On Music*, except for *PHerc.* 411, 1576 and 1583; and, in the case of *PHerc.* 411 and 1583, I have proposed that these papyri too can be shown to join down the middle of a column.[37] The enlarged *On Music* IV yields a major new text on ancient music, enabling us to reconstruct *in extenso* a work (called *On Music*) of Diogenes of Babylon.[38] Diogenes turns out to be a pivotal figure in the development of Stoic theory in this field, as he was in grammar, linguistics and political thought, since in each case he borrowed and adapted the insights of Aristotle to strengthen the approach of his predecessors.[39] Moreover, Philodemus quotes such earlier authorities as Damon, Plato, Democritus, Heraclides Ponticus, Aristoxenus, Dicaearchus, Chamaeleon, Theophrastus

36. Delattre 1989.

37. R. Janko 1992b.

38. Philodemus' work deals with the social and educational funtions of music and poetry rather than with technical aspects of music *stricto sensu*. It has been unjustly ignored in the secondary literature, e.g. in A. Barker's new collection of translations into English of works on ancient music, which purports to be comprehensive (Barker 1989). On its importance for Philodemus' literary theory see E. Asmis, loc. cit. (n. 7).

39. See R. Janko 1992b, esp. n. 21.

and Cleanthes — a reminder of his value as a source for earlier philosophers' views. What is also significant is Philodemus' distinctively Epicurean response to earlier, especially Stoic, aesthetics — that the purpose of art, in music, poetry and prose, is above all to convey pleasure; any moral improvement which such art-forms produce in their audience is purely incidental. But this topic must be pursued elsewhere.[40]

The Delattre/Obbink technique has also been applied to Philodemus' *On Poems*. A number of separate sets of *disegni* of *scorze* from the *On Poems* were published (following A. Hausrath and others) in 1976 and 1983 by F. Sbordone and M.L. Nardelli.[41] They identified five distinct Treatises, all from the *On Poems*, which they numbered A to E. The subject-matter of A, B and C was recognizably similar; the handwriting of A (*PHerc.* 994) is the same as that of C (*PHerc.* 1676), while that of B is the same as D. Treatise A is a *midollo*, which preserves the end of a text and its final colophon but has lost the closing title; the other Treatises all derive from *scorze*. Now C. Romeo, by applying Delattre's method, has reconstructed C and A as part of a single roll.[42] Her new edition of Treatises A and C (incorporating the previously unpublished *PHerc.* 1677) is well advanced. Working independently, I reconstructed part of Treatise C, finding some of the same joins between fragments; but most of my own work has been on Treatise B, although this also bears on Treatise A, as we shall see.

Sbordone described the problems involved in reconstructing Treatise B as grave and in part, insoluble.[43] The work consists of *scorze* only.[44] One half of the roll is composed of *PHerc.* 1073, opened and drawn in 1824 by C. Malesci. Apart from the series of 19 *disegni*, there survives only the final *scorza*, which is unpublished. That this was originally the bottom, i.e. outermost, layer

40. See above, n. 7.

41 Above, nn. 20-21.

42. Personal communication (Naples, June 1991). That Treatises C and A form a single roll was first proposed by M.L. Nardelli 1979; cf. F. Sbordone 1983, p. 10.

43. Sbordone 1983a, p. 161.

44. For descriptions of the *disegni*, see F. Sbordone 1976, pp.xiii-xviii.

of this set of *scorze* is proved by the fact that parts of lines 9*f. and 20*f. of *disegno* 18, my col. 8* (the last of the series to depict the lower halves of the columns), are still legible on the *scorza*, to which they obviously continued to adhere when the rest of that layer of writing was lifted off. The other half of the roll is contained in *PHerc.* 460, a series of 31 *disegni* drawn by G.B. Casanova in 1822; five original fragments also survive. These fragments mainly derive from the outside of the roll. Frag. 1 corresponds to *disegno* 29 (my col. 9*), frag. 3 to *disegno* 28 (my col. 12*) and frag. 2 to *disegno* 27 (my col. 14*). Casanova never drew frag. 4, which is in poor condition. But frag. 5 contains parts of *disegni* 4 (on the left) and *disegno* 5 (on the right), together with the blank space between the two columns; hence, as we saw, *disegni* 4 and 5 depict the same single *scorza* (my cols. 57*-58*). Frag. 5 is the least burnt of the five fragments, being only dark brown instead of black; this confirms the hypothesis that it was closest to the centre of the roll, i.e. the end of the treatise, whereas the others derive from the outside. The surviving fragments and *disegni* of *PHerc.* 460 and 1073 together contain some 54 columns of text, with an average of 26 lines per column.

The two papyri were first edited by A. Hausrath,[45] who discovered that a quotation of Euripides (*Ion* 237-40) begins at the bottom of 460/19 (shorthand for *PHerc.* 460 *disegno* 19) and continues at the top of 1073/10 (my cols. 28*-29*). Another feature uniting them is that these are the only Herculaneum papyri known to use accents[46]— aptly enough, since the aesthetic effects of Greek accents constitute one of the topics discussed in the treatise. The accents only appear frequently in my cols. 26*-29*.

To apply the Delattre/Obbink method to Treatise B, I used the following techniques, which anyone with a good knowledge of Greek can apply: it is easy to get used to the handwriting of the *disegni*. These procedures only became possible because of recent technological progress, i.e. the invention of transparent adhesive tape and of photocopying machines; one can imagine a not very distant future when the images of the *disegni* can be

45. A. Hausrath 1889.
46. W. Croenert, 1903 (1963), pp. 8-9. See below, n. 72.

manipulated more efficiently by being scanned into a computer. First, I made photocopies of the *disegni* to the correct scale, and transcribed them as accurately as possible. Following Delattre, I find it essential to number the lines correctly, assigning provisional line-numbers (using an asterisk, e.g. 15*) where the vertical placing of the fragment is uncertain (Sbordone had often erred in this). When the top of the piece has perished, one counts from the bottom, assuming that the column contained the same number of lines as the average in the adjacent columns. An analogous procedure should be used to estimate how many letters are lost at the end of each line: the scribe of Treatise B regularly wrote an average of 18 letters per line, if we count the wide letters mu and omega as two letters and the narrow iota as half a letter. It is important to count the letters, tedious as this procedure may sound, because one can thereby eliminate or improve upon supplements that are too long or too short. I entered the line numbers onto my photocopies, and added, in ink of different colours, the numbers of the respective series of *disegni* to which the fragments belong.

The next stage is to spread out the *disegni* on a very large table in sequence, forwards or backwards as required, remaining alert for cases where the draughtsman drew adjacent columns of the same layer of writing as successive *disegni*. This phenomenon is common in *PHerc.* 460, as is proved by *disegni* 4 and 5, which are proved to be adjacent columns by the survival of frag. 5 of the original, containing parts of both; yet none of the *disegni* deriving from *PHerc.* 1073 reflect this phenomenon. Evidently, when the papyrus-roll was opened longitudinally, one side (*PHerc.* 460) was wider and hence better preserved than the other (*PHerc.* 1073). By studying the shapes of the papyri, and by superimposing them in front of a translucent electric lampshade, one can recognise the outline of the successive layers of the *scorze* (the silhouette of those of *PHerc.* 460 often resembled a map of France). By this method, I found many joins between successive columns of *PHerc.* 460 which had not been even remotely associated by previous editors. Other joins in the same set of *disegni* are rare, unless the upper and lower parts of the same column have been drawn separately. Successive layers of writing cannot join, unless (as occasionally happens) a fragment of one layer has become stuck to a preceding or following layer (these are called 'sovraposti' and 'sottoposti'). Thus I was able to unite a small scrap (drawn with 460/14, my col. 40*) with 460/19 (my col. 28*), yielding a new fragment of the lyric poet Timotheus. Such detached fragments are recognizably in the wrong place, simply because they make no sense where they were drawn. Occasionally a detached fragment of the same series has fallen out from the edge and been drawn out of sequence, e.g. Treatise D frag. 44 Nardelli (see below).

Joins between different sets of *disegni* are rarer but more important. Such joins offer the best hope of reconstructing the whole papyrus, since they permit one to establish fixed link-points as pivots around which the different sets of *disegni* can be interleaved in approximately alternating order. This is essential to the next step in the process of reconstruction — to solidify the relation between the two halves of the papyrus. There are three kinds of joins between different series:

(i) In some cases, the papyrus-roll was fractured horizontally as well as vertically. The upper and lower parts of the same side may have been drawn as members of the same set of *scorze*, or as different sets. In such a situation there could be as many as four sets of *disegni* derived from a single roll; a single circumference that contained four columns might therefore be represented by as many as eight different drawings. Such sets of *scorze* are obviously much harder to reassemble, since at least one line of writing tends to be lost at the horizontal break; it is therefore hard to prove that *disegni* belong to the same column, and such reconstructions must often remain speculative. Part of Treatise D seems to be in this state. For example, I tentatively reassemble a sequence of three columns as follows (the fragment-numbers are Nardelli's):

(a) The first column is frag. 7 col. i (*PHerc.* 1074/23).

(b) The second column is made up of frag. 15 (*PHerc.* 1081/27, the upper half of the column) and frag. 50 (1081/28, the lower half of the column), with a line or two lost in between the two fragments.

(c) The upper part of the third column is made up of frag. 7 col. ii (1081/25, the upper left side of the column), which joins perfectly with the small detached frag. 44 (1081/4), its upper right edge, which must have fallen out and been drawn out of sequence; the lower part may consist of frag. 24 (1081/26), but the gap between the upper and lower sections of the column makes this hard to verify. In any case, the 'join' identified by Nardelli between frag. 7 cols. i and ii appears to be illusory.

(ii) When two different sets of *scorze* comprise the two opposite halves of a single roll, and the vertical fracture coincides with a break between columns, the sense may simply run on from the bottom of the column in one *scorza* to the top of the column in another *scorza*, from a different set of *disegni*. Such joins have most productive value when (as not infrequently happens) the bottom of the first column and the top of the next are perfectly preserved. It is also important if the sense at such potential junctures excludes a join, since one may have to adjust one's reconstruction as a result. As in the other cases, the join can best be confirmed if it comprises a quotation or *doxa* known from elsewhere, e.g. Euripides' *Ion* lines 237-40 unites *PHerc*. 460/19 and 1073/10.

(iii) The third and rarest type of join between different sets of *disegni* is when two different series comprise the two halves of a complete papyrus-roll, and the right edge of one *scorza* forms a single column when joined with the left edge of a *scorza* from the other series. Such joins are hard to find, but, once found, constitute a powerful proof that the two sets of *scorze* derive from the same roll.

The next step, after systematically testing all the fragments for joins, is to arrange them in the best order. This is the order which (i) allows for all the confirmed joins and non-joins, (ii) makes the best sense, (iii) adheres scrupulously to the *disegno-*numbers, (iv) aims at the minimum number of columns and (v)

Richard Janko

allows for missing columns if the joins indicate that the *disegni* of one series are more numerous than those of the other. Philodemus' method of summarising his opponents' doctrines, and then refuting them in the same order, offers opportunities for finding repetitions of ideas that can be useful in confirming this reconstruction; so do internal cross-references within the work. One needs physically to reconstruct the papyrus, calculating its circumference (this diminishes towards the centre). The columns must then be assigned a provisional numeration, for which Delattre uses an asterisk, e.g. 5*. This numeration can be added both to the photocopies of the *disegni* and to the transcription and translation. Following the example of Delattre and Romeo, I have found it useful, in preserving the provisional order of the photocopies of the *disegni*, to put them into bound folders with many transparent plastic page-size pockets (such as business-men use for the display of documents), taped if necessary to a sheet of paper to hold them in place; the result is as if one has cut up the papyrus-roll and pasted the resulting sheets, containing perhaps three columns each, into a bound book-shaped codex.

Continued work on the transcription and translation will of course lead to alterations in the provisional order of the columns, although on the whole my initial results, based purely on the Delattre/Obbink method, have so far turned out to hold firm. At this point, and not before, one can to start to consider the philosophical implications of the new text which one has reconstructed. One useful technique, if one feels confused by the numerous brackets and dotted letters necessary for a scholarly text, is to produce by computer a text with these lectional signs removed, and with the lines run together, so far as is possible, into continous Greek like any other philosophical text. This facilitates the recognition of parallel passages, the finding of supplements, searching the text by computer and the comprehension of the argument, although such a text must obviously be used only for private, heuristic purposes.

Let me now exemplify the reconstruction of *On Poems* Treatise

B. The Delattre/Obbink method yielded the following order of fragments, with joins and a series of parallels in Treatise A as noted below. Those quoted later are in bold type:

col. no.	papyrus/ *disegno* no.	Sbordone's frag. no.	comment
21*	460/23	30	left half of *scorza*
22*	460/24	19	right half of *scorza*
23*	1073/12	32	opposite; cf. **Tr. A col. a 7-14**
24*	460/21	29	left; cf. Tr. A col. a 27-b 4, b 19-c l
25*	460/22	7 col. i	right; cf. **Tr. A col. b 23,**
			col. d 25-e 8
26*	1073/11	7 col. ii	opposite side of roll
27*	460/20	12	left; cf. Tr. A col. e 16, f
28*	460/19	5 col. i	right half of *scorza*, with *sottoposto*
	+frag. of 14		
29*	1073/10	5 col. ii	opposite; join with 28* (quotation)
30*	460/17	11 col. ii	left ; cf. Tr. A col. iv 19-20, xiv 22-3
31*	460/18	3	right half of *scorza*
32*	1073/9	23 col. i	opposite; cf. Tr. A col. xiv 20-3
33*	460/not drawn	—	[opposite side of roll — lost]
34*	1073/8	4 col. ii +38	opposite side of roll
35*	460/16	10 col ii	opposite side of roll

36*	1073/7	9 col. ii + 8 col. ii	opposite side of roll
37*	460/15	23 col. ii	opposite; cf. **Tr. A cols. v 5-17, 22-6, vi 5-7**
38*	1073/6	23 col. iii	opposite; cf. **Tr. A col. v 22-6**
39*	460/not drawn	—	[left half of *scorza* — lost]
40*	460/14	6 col. i	right; cf. Tr. A cols ix 24-x 7 (both on Homer, *Iliad* 5.838)[47]
41*	1073/5	6 col. ii	opposite; cf. Tr. A col. x 23-6
42*	460/not drawn	—	[left half of *scorza* — lost]
43*	460/13	2	right half of *scorza*; on *Od.* 11.207
44*	1073/4	31	opposite of roll; on *Od.* 11.207
45*	460/12	13	left; cf. Tr. A col. xi 20-xii 1 (both on Homer, *Iliad* 21.260-1)
46*	460/11	16	right half of *scorza*
47*	1073/not drawn	—	[opposite side of roll — lost]
48*	460/9	26 col. i	opposite; ref. back to col. 37*; cf. Tr. A cols. xvi 13, 24, xviii 18
49*	1073/3+460/10	26 col. ii+ 15	opposite; cf. Tr. A col. xvii 11-12

My provisional column-numeration runs from 1* to 64*, but this sample should give an adequate idea of the method of reconstruction. Note that, although Sbordone identified a num-

47. On this parallel, and the text of Treatise A at this point, see M.L. Nardelli 1982.

ber of joins between columns, his ordering of the fragments on the basis of supposed similarities of content bears little relation to their true sequence, and that sometimes he had united columns which are in fact widely separated.[48]

It is not always certain how many columns are lost, since three columns are, at this point in the roll, only approximately equal to one circumference; the breaks between columns shift to the left by about the width of two letters, or 0.1 column-widths, in the successive *scorze* 460/21 and 460/20, but by the width of four letters in the later pairs 460/15-460/14 and 460/12-460/9.[49] This accords with the expected diminution of the circumference towards two column-widths as we approach somewhat closer to the centre of the roll; but this part of the Treatise is obviously fairly near the outside, i.e. the beginning of the whole text. The apparent reference back to col. 37* in col. 48* also accords with the reconstruction. The parallels with Treatise A, some of which have long been recognized,[50] provide another valuable check on the sequence obtained by studying the *disegno*-numbers and the shapes of the fragments. The order of columns in Treatise A is secure, since this is a *midollo* deriving from the centre of the roll, and was unwound continuously on one of Father Piaggio's machines, except for a break between the two series of columns designated by letters of the alphabet w-z and a-f, and another before the series of columns designated by the Roman numerals which run to the end of the text.

Let me now set out four examples of the parallels, rendered as accessible to philosophers as possible by the use of continuous Greek in a normalised transcription, and the addition of a translation. This is not the place to present a full scholarly text, preserving the layout of the papyrus and with a proper *apparatus criticus*; such a text is indispensable for any rigorous and philo-

48. In the list of six such joins offered by Sbordone 1983a, pp. 34-5, only three survive scrutiny.

49. Such a shift was already noted by Sbordone 1983a, p. 163.

50. See A. Hausrath 1889, pp. 220ff.; T. Gomperz 1890, pp. 1-8; F. Sbordone 1983, pp. 36-8, p. 93, pp. 96-7, pp. 162-3, p. 170, pp. 172-7; M.L. Nardelli 1982; N. Greenberg 1955 (1990), pp. 238-44.

Richard Janko

logically sound work on the text, but cannot be provided until I have time to produce it. Moreover, the text of Treatise A will be considerably improved by the labours of Romeo. But that of Treatise B is new, as is the order of its fragments. The present text is meant only to indicate the interest of the reconstruction, and to argue for the method employed. Square brackets denote lost letters; angle-brackets indicate letters supplied by modern editors; braces signify letters deleted by modern editors, and lower half-brackets delimit letters lost in the papyrus but certain because they are supplied from quotations elsewhere. Where a letter is still extant on one or both *disegni*, but is no longer extant in the surviving papyrus-fragments because of their continuing disintegration, it is printed without square brackets.

Parallel 1A (Treatise A, col. a 5-16 Sbordone)

. . . καὶ ἀπαι[τεῖ οὐ] τῶι ἀποδιδόναι "[τ]ῆς ἡδείας φωνῆς", ἀλλὰ τῶ⟨ι⟩ "μηδὲν ἡμᾶς ἄν[ε]υ τῶν φωνηέντων φθέγγεσθαι". [τ]ὸ δὲ "κἀν τούτοις μη[δὲ]ν ἧττ[ον αὐ]τοὺς [.... ἀ]περείδε[σθ]αι ἂν α[ὐτῆι τ]ῆι ῥή[σει τῶ]ν γρ[αμμ]άτων", γενναίως [τινὰ] τέρψιν ἀκούσεως ἀνίστησιν.[51]

" . . . and he requires this not by explaining (his phrase) 'the pleasant sound', but by (explaining his phrase) 'we utter nothing without vowels'. But (in saying) 'in these too they would be supported no less . . . by the utterance of the letters itself', he generously posits some pleasure in hearing . . .''

Parallel 1B (Treatise B, col. 23*.1-8 = *PHerc.* 1073/12)

. . . ἀποδοῦναι περιαληθές", φησιν, "ὅτι οὐδὲν δυνάμεθα φθέγξασθαι χωρὶς τῶν φωνηέντων· ἐν [γὰρ τού]τοις οὐδὲν ἀπερεί[δεται], ἀλλ' αὐτὸς ὁ ἦχος· ἂν [δέ τι] καὶ ἄλλο τῶν γραμμάτων προσλάβωμεν, ...[52]

51. The parallel was noted by A. Hausrath 1889, pp. 226, 243; cf. T. Gomperz 1890, pp. 14-15. The text is Sbordone's, checked against the *disegni* but not the original.

52. The text is that of Hausrath and Sbordone. Gomperz proposed ἀλλ' ⟨ἢ⟩ αὐτὸς (1890, p. 15).

" . . . to explain the truth," he says, " because we cannot utter anything without using vowels; for nothing is supported by these except the sound itself. But if we add any other of the letters, . . ."

Parallel 2A (Treatise A, cols. a 25-b 9 Sbordone)

. . . τὸ δὲ "[τ]ὰ μὲν αὐτῶν εὐηχεῖσ[θα]ι ⟨κατὰ⟩ τὰ {γράμματα} προσλαμβανόμ[ενα] γράμμα[τ]α, πάλιν δ' [ἀποτιθέμενα] ἐπὶ τῶν ὀνομά[των ἢ] τῶ[ν] ῥημάτων καὶ τῶν ἄ[λ]λων μερῶν τοῦ λόγου καὶ τῶν παρακειμένων αὐτοῖς συμβεβηκότων", πάντα πλὴν τούτου διδόσθω{ι}, τό γε ⁵³ . . .

" But as for (his claim that) 'some of them sound good <according to> the letters added or conversely removed with regard to nouns, verbs, the other parts of speech and the incidental elements that attach to them', let it all be granted except for (his claim) that . . ."

Parallel 2B (Treatise B, col. 24*.2-10 = PHerc. 460/21)

. . . τὰ προσλ]αμβανό[μενα γρά]μματα καὶ ἀπο[τιθέμενα] ἐπὶ τὰ ὀνόματ[α καὶ ῥήματα] προβαίνον[τες c. 7 κα]ὶ τὴν διά[λεκτον κατα]λαμβά[ν c. 9] τάς τε πρ[οθέσεις καὶ τοὺς] συνδέσ[μους . . .⁵⁴

" . . . letters that are added and removed, advancing to nouns and verbs . . . and understand speech . . . both prepositions and conjunctions . . ."

Parallel 3A(i) (Treatise A, col. b 16-c 1 Sbordone)

. . . τὰ [δ'] ἀπὸ τούτ[ο]υ φανερῶς οὐ φιλαλη[θ]εῖν [ν]ομίζομεν, καὶ πρῶτον τὸ "τὰς τῶν αὐτῶν ⟨ῥημάτων⟩ πολλάκι θέσεις οἰ[κει]οῦν ἢ λυπεῖν διὰ τὸν ἦχον, ὡς τὸν **λωτὸν** καὶ τοὺς

53. I have supplied ⟨κατὰ⟩, otherwise largely following the text of J. Porter 1989, p. 152, who reads εὐηχεῖσ[θα]ι, τὰ ⟨δὲ μή, κατὰ τὰ⟩ προσλαμβανόμ[ενα] γράμμα[τ]α, πάλιν [c. 10], etc. But ἀποτιθέμενα is Sbordone's supplement.

54. ἀπο[τιθέμενα is my supplement (ἀπὸ [τούτων Gomperz). The 'prepositions and conjunctions' reflect the 'other parts of speech' in Parallel 2A.

Richard Janko

Λωτοφάγους δὶς τεθὲν ἄλυπον εἶναι δ[ι]ὰ τ[ὸ] τ[ο]ὔνομα κατὰ
τὸν ἦχον ἡδὺ τῆι ἀκοῆ[ι] ὠρ[θ]οεπῆ[σ]θ[αι . . .⁵⁵

" But we consider untrue his statements from this point on,
and firstly (his claim) that 'the repeated use of the same
words suits or pains (the ear) on account of their sound, as
the words "lotus" and "lotus-eaters" (sc. at *Odyssey* 9.91-7)
used twice are painless, because of the fact that the noun has
been correctly formed to be pleasant in its sound for the hearing'."

Parallel 3A(ii) (Treatise A, cols. d 25-e 8 Sbordone)

. . . κα]ὶ εἴπερ ἄρα ψυχαγωγίαν ἐ[δ]ύνα[το c. 22 τῆι τῶν]
Λωτοφάγων, ὡς καὶ [αὐτῆι] τῆι τοῦ **Νειρέως**, ἐπειδὴ τὸ
π[ρ]οσηνῶ[ς] δὶς τεθὲν ἀεὶ καὶ πολλάκι λεγό[μεν]ον εὐφρ[α]ίνει . . .⁵⁶

"If after all he (sc. Homer) was able (to create?) entertainment
(*one line lost* . . . by the repetition) of the word 'lotus-eaters'
(sc. at *Odyssey* 9.91-7), as by that of 'Nireus' (sc. at *Iliad* 2.671-
3), since what is soothing when used twice gives pleasure
when it is uttered continually or often . . ."

Parallel 3B (Treatise B, cols. 24*.21-25*.7= *PHerc.* 460/21-22)

. . . τὰς τῶͺν αὐτῶν [ῥημάτων] ͺποͺλλάκι θέσεις ͺοίͺ[κει]ͺοῦν ἢ
λυͺπεῖν διὰ τὸν ͺῆχονͺ. [τὸ γὰρ (οἰκειοῦν ἢ) λυ]ποῦν πολ[λάκις
ἡμᾶς δ]ιὰ τὸν ⟨ἦχον, ὡς τὸν⟩ **λω**[τόν, δι' οὐδὲ]ν ἕτερον [τέρπειν
ἢ] διὰ τὸ τῶι [ῥήματι μά]λα ἡδὺ προσ[πίπτειν εἰς] τὴν ἀκ[οήν
linearum vii fragmenta] καὶ τὸν **λω**[**τὸν** ἀρέσ]κειν δὶς
τεθέντα.⁵⁷

(He claims that) " . . . repeated uses of the same [words] suit
or pain (the ear) on account of the sound. For what <suits

55. Again I follow Porter's text (1989, p. 152), checked against the *disegni*, but I
hesitantly supply ⟨ῥημάτων⟩ and conjecture δὶς τεθὲν for Porter's δὴ μηδὲν (ἂν
μηδὲν Sbordone); I suspect that the scribe wrongly wrote διατιθὲν, as in Parallel
3A(ii).

56. This is Sbordone's text, checked against the *disegni* (the papyrus has
διατιθὲν corrected to δὶς τεθέν).

57. This is my own text (some supplements are from Gomperz).

or> pains us often on account of the <sound, like the word> 'lotus' (sc. at *Odyssey* 9.91-7.), arouses delight for no other reason than because the very pleasant element in the word impinges on the hearing . . . (*parts of seven lines*) and the word 'lotus' pleases when used twice . . ."

Parallel 4A(i) (Treatise A, cols. iv 26-v 19 Sbordone)

. . . ὥστε, τοῦ λεγομένου βουληθεὶς ὑπόδειγμα παραθεῖναι, περισπώμενο[ς ὑ]πὸ διανοήμα[τος] αὐ[τὸς] κατεχώρισεν, οὐχ ἡμε[ῖς]. "οἷον γάρ", φησιν, "καὶ ὅταν Σοφοκλῆς εἴπηι·

ναῦται δ' ἐμηρύσ{σ}αντο νηὸς ἰσχάδα.

φιειρόμεθα γὰρ ἐφ' ὃ βούλεται καὶ ὁ ποιητής, οὐ[δ'] ιἐπιὶ τὸν καρπόν, [κ]αίπερ ἴσ{σ}ως γενιοιμένης τινὸς πληγιῆςι πρὸς τὴν ιἀκοήιν, ιἐιν ἧιι μᾶλιλον ἄν τις ἐξεδέιξαιτο τὸν καριπόν. τι[ὸ] δ' αὐτὸ καὶ ἐπ' ἄλλων συμβαίνει{ν} πλειόνων." ὡς καὶ ἐπὶ τῶν ἄλλων τοιοῦτο συμβαίνειν ὑπολαμβάνομε[ν], παραθεωρητέον δ' ἅμα καὶ τὸ φύρειν ὁμοῦ διάνοιαν ἀκοῆι, λέγοντα "κα[ὶ] γίνεσθαί τινα πληγὴν πρὸς τὴν ἀκοήν, ἐν ἧι μᾶλλον ἄν τις ἐξεδέξατο τὸν καρπόν". [58]

"So, when he (sc. my opponent) wanted to provide an example of what is meant, he was himself 'distracted by the sense' in offering it, not we. For he says 'e.g. too, when Sophocles (frag. 761) said:

"The sailors raised the fig-iron (sc. anchor) of the ship."

For we are brought to what the poet too intends, and not to the fruit, although perhaps some blow impinges upon one's hearing, in which one might rather have expected the fruit. The same thing happens in most other cases'. Although we understand that something similar happens in the other cases too, one must at the same time observe that he (sc. my oppo-

58. So Sbordone's text, verified against the *disegni*, except that he supplies περισπώμενο[ν.

Richard Janko

nent) mixes up sound and sense, when he says 'although some blow impinges upon one's hearing, in which one might rather have expected the fruit'."

Parallel 4A(ii) (Treatise A, col. vi 4-18 Sbordone)

. . . βαρβαριζόντων ἕτερος [αὐ]τῶν, τοῦ μὲν ἡδέως [ἡ]μᾶς ἀκούειν, τοῦ δὲ τἀναντ[ί]α, κἂν "διὰ μηδὲν ἕτερον ἢ διὰ τὸν ἦχον γίνηται καὶ ἐͅπὶͅ τῆς ᾀηδόνος καὶ τῶν ἄλλων ὀρνέων", πῶς ἀ[πο]δεικτικόν ἐστι τοῦ "τὸν ἐκ τῆς ἀρθρώσεως ἦχον ἀπ[ο]τελεῖν τινα χάριν, περισ[π]ᾶσθαι δ' ὑπ' ͺἄͺλͺιͺλͺͺωνͺ τιͺνῶνͺ"; λέ[γει γ]ὰρ ἐπὶ [τ]ῶν βαρβαριζόν[τ]ων ὑπ[ὸ] τοῦ διὰ τὴν ἄρ[θρ]ωσ[ιν ἦχ]ου τὴν ἡδονὴν ἔξω χεῖν καὶ τὴν [ἀλ]λοτριότη[τ]α συμβαί[ν]ειν. 59

... the other of them speaking barbarously, we hear the first with pleasure, the other with the opposite feeling; even if (his claim is true that) 'it (sc. pleasure?) comes about for no other reason than because of the sound, in the case of both the nightingale and the other birds', how is this demonstrative of (his claim) that 'the sound which results from the articulation affords a certain delight, but it is distracted by some other factors'? For he says that 'in the case of speakers of barbarous language the pleasure is nullified (?) by the sound which arises from the articulation, and alienation occurs'."

Parallel 4B (Treatise B, col. 37*.1-38*.2 = PHerc. 460/15 + 1073/6)

. . . ἀρθρώ]σεως [δὲ ψεύ]δετ' ἀναλ[όγως, λέγων] "ἕτερον δι' [αὐτῆς εἶναι] τὸν ἦχον, ὅ[περ γίνεται] ἐπὶ τῆς ᾀῃδόνος καὶͅ [ἐ]πὶ τῶν ἄλλων ὀρνέων. οὕτω τοίνυν καὶ ἐπὶ τῶν ἑλληνιζόντων ὁ μὲν ἦχος ἀποτελεῖ τὸ ἴδιον κατὰ τὴν δ[ι]ά[νοιαν]" (ἢ δεινὸν ἂν εἴη [τὰ ἴ]δια τὸν ἑλληνισμὸν ἀποστερεῖσθαι;), "περισπᾶται δ' ἴσως ὑπὸ ἄλλων ͺτͺινῶν, οἷον ͺὅταͺν ἐπὶ τοῦ [πλευσι]διᾶν Σοφοκλῆς ͺεͺἴͺπͺηͺ·

ναῦτα⟨ι⟩ δ' ἐμηρύͺσανͺτο νηὸͅς ἰσχͺιάδα.

59. So the text of Sbordone and of G.M. Rispoli 1981, pp. 173-4. I have checked it against the disegni.

298

φερόμεθα γὰιρ ἐφ' ὃ βοιύλεται καὶ ὁ πιοητιής, οὐ[δ'] ἐπὶ τιὸν
κιαρπόν, [κ]ιαίπιερ ἴσως γενομένιης τιινὸς πληγῆς πρὸς τιὴν
ἀικοήν, ἐν ἧι μᾶλλον ἄν τις ἐξεδέξατο τὸν καριπιόν. τ[ὸ] ιδ'ι
αὐτὸ καὶ ⟨ἐ⟩π' ἄλλων συμβαίνει πλειόνων."⁶⁰

" . . . (but regarding) articulation (his claim) is false analogously, when he says that 'the sound is different on account
of it, as happens in the case of the nightingale and the other
birds. So, therefore, in the case of people speaking pure
Greek too, the sound creates what is characteristic in terms of
the sense' (wouldn't it be dreadful for pure Greek to be
deprived of its characteristics!), 'but it (sc. the mind?) is perhaps distracted by some other factors, e.g. when Sophocles
(frag. 761) says regarding setting sail:

The sailors raised the fig-iron (sc. anchor) of the ship.

For we are brought to what the poet too intends, and not to
the fruit, although perhaps some blow impinges upon one's
hearing, in which one might rather have expected the fruit.
The same thing happens in most other cases'."

I can give here only a preliminary account of the argument of
these passages. First, the identity of Philodemus' opponent is
unstated; elsewhere in Treatise B he quotes Andromenides (cols.
61*-62*, = 1073/1 + 460/2, = frag. 25 cols. ii-iii Shordone) and
possibly Crates (col. 61*). Each has been proposed as
Philodemus' adversary here.[61] However, a certain Pausimachus
ὁ κριτικός appears in Treatise A; his name occurs in cols. w, y
and e, and it is likely that his ideas are the topic throughout cols.
w-e. In fact we can show that Philodemus' opponent in cols.
24*-25* is this same Pausimachus, who is otherwise completely
unknown.[62] In Treatise A cols. e 23-f 1, just after the discussion

60. I follow here the text of G.M. Rispoli 1981, p. 174. But I hesitantly accept
Sbordone's supplement δ[ι]ά[νοιαν] rather than Rispoli's proposal δ[ι]ά[λεκτον],
because of the parallel in cols. 48*-9* below.

61. By Jensen and Sbordone respectively (see Rispoli 1981, p. 179 n. 19).

62. C. Romeo (1988, pp. 60-2) shows that, contrary to a proposal of Croenert, he
probably does not appear in Book II col. viii of the On Poetry of Philodemus' predecessor and possibly teacher, Demetrius Laco.

Richard Janko

of how Homer used the words 'lotus-eaters' and 'Nireus' repeatedly, Philodemus continues from col. d his discussion of
Homer's harsh-sounding phrase ῥῆξε σάκος, 'smashed the
shield', with the sentence [ἂν δ]ὲ φῆι "παρατεθέν[των ἀκ]οῆι",
ταὐτὸν ἐνό[μισε Πα]υσίμαχος εἶναι τὸ πρὸ[ς ἀ]κοὴν ἡδὺ καὶ τὸ
χαλεπῶς κα[ὶ] μετ' ὀ[χλήσ]εως ἐκ[φερό]με[νον], i.e. " but if he says
'juxtaposed to the hearing', Pausimachus considered what is
pleasant to hear identical with what is pronounced with difficulty and annoyance'. Pausimachus is Philodemus' adversary in
Treatise B for at least cols. 22*-27*, since the discussion there of
repeated and cacophonous words is linked with the sibilant letters sigma and xei, which also appear in this part of Treatise A.
Philodemus began to review Pausimachus' discussion of sound
in col. 22*.22-7, because he there says of his opponent νῦν δέ,
περὶ τῶν ἤχων μ[έλλ]ων διαλέξεσθαι, τὴν [μὲ]ν χάριν τὴν ἄλογόν
π[αρ]ὰ τοῖς αὐτοῖς ἀνατιθεὶς [διδάσ]κει, i.e. 'now, being about to
discuss sounds, ascribing irrational delight to the same sources,
he teaches . . .

In fact Pausimachus' teaching began earlier and ends later. In
col. 15* (= 1073/15, = frag. 11 col. i Sbordone) he praises
Homer's phrases ἁλὸς ἔξω and τείχεος ἐκτός for their sound, noting that they would be less good if they were altered. The same
phrases reappear in col. 35*, where the critic argues that Homer
avoided saying ἁλὸς ἐκτός and τείχεος ἔξω because he did not
want successive words to be accented in the same manner. If
this is the same critic, Pausimachus' ideas occupy at least cols.
15* to 35*. Incidentally, this must be one of the earliest surviving
discussions of Greek accentuation, and the only one to consider
its aesthetic aspects. It is couched in almost unique terminology:
in τείχεος ἐκτός the first πτῶσις (ending) is said to be 'relaxed' or
unaccented (ἀνίεσθαι),[63] the second the opposite, 'tensed'
(ἐπιτετάσθαι). The discussion of nightingales and the relation
between sound and sense (my parallel 4B) follows only two
columns later (cols. 37*-38*), immediately after a Pausimachean-
sounding disquisition on iota, eta and words combining stops

63. For ἡ ἀνειμένη τάσις as the grave accent see the Scholia to Dionysius Thrax,
p. 130 Hilgard.

300

Philodemus Resartus

and liquids like πλάκα and κατακλάζου[σα] (col. 36*). Now a mention of lambda, alpha and kappa, and another discussion of πλάκα and similar words (κλάδοι, γλαυκῶπις), recur in cols. 54*-55* (= 1073/2 + 460/6, = frags. 8 col. ii and 9 col. ii Sbordone), after another mention of the nightingale (cols. 48*-49*, = 460/9 + 1073/3, = frag. 26 cols. i-ii Sbordone). This all suggests that the review of Pausimachus' doctrines in fact extends as far as col. 61*, where the presence of the names of Crates and Andromenides indicates that Philodemus turns his attention to the theories of others.

Pausimachus' designation as a κριτικός suggests that he was an associate of Crates, with Stoic leanings.[64] His Stoic inclinations appear both in his terminology and his theory of language. This is best seen in what appears to be Philodemus' critique of his reference to nightingales (cols. 48*-49*):

. . . ἡ δ]ιάνοια οὐ βλέ[πεται καὶ] καταλείπετα[ι τὸ ἀνακ]ινοῦν κατὰ τ[ὸν ἦχο]ν. δεινὸν δ', ὡς ἐλέγετο, εἰ παρὰ τὸ τὴν διά[ν]οιαν βλέπεσθαι ἀποστερηθήσεται ὁ ἦχος [το]ῦ ἰδίου. θεωρητέον [τοί]νυν καὶ ἐπὶ τῶν ἐ[πῶν] οὐ τὸν ἦχον αὐτὸν [χωρὶς ὑ]ποτεταγμένων [τοὺς ἀκο]ύσαντας γοητεύ[ειν ποιημά]των. ὅταν δέ [τις τά]δε μεί[ξηι, ἐ]πικρ[ατ]εῖ ἡμῶν εἰς [τὴ]ν ἐπι[π]ρέπειαν ἀνακινῶν. ὅτι δ' ἀρχηγὸν ἡ φωνὴ καὶ ἐκ τῶν ὀρνέων ἔστιν ἰδεῖν· καὶ γὰρ ἐπ' ἐκείνων χωρὶς τοῦ ἐκπίπτοντος ἤχου ἀποτελεῖταί τις καὶ ἔναρθρος φωνή, καθάπερ καὶ ἐπὶ τῆ[ς ἀη]δ[όν]ος φέρεται. τὴν δ' ὑπο[τεταγ]μένην ἔνν[οιαν ἀ]φῶμεν νῦν. οὐδ[ὲ γὰρ ὁ] σίττακος οἶδεν ε[ἰ τρα]γωιδίας λέγει στί[χον, ἀλ]λ' ὅμως ἀποτελεῖ[ται] τοὺς ἤχους, οὕτω[ς ὡς] ὁ ἄνθρωπος.[65]

" . . . the sense is not evident, and that which arouses us through the sound remains. It would be dreadful, as was said (sc. in col. 37*), if, because of the fact that the sense is evident,

64. So already C. Romeo 1988, p. 61.

65. This is my own text, with some supplements from Gomperz. ἐ[πῶν] and [τοὺς ἀκο]ύσαντας γοητεύ[ειν are bold conjectures on my part: in the latter case the *disegno* has]XEANTACOCHTEI[.

301

Richard Janko

the sound is deprived of its characteristic. Therefore one must observe that, regarding epic verses too, it is not the sound itself, divorced from the underlying meanings, that enchants those who listen to poems; but when someone mixes (both) these things, he dominates us by arousing us to the proper response. One can see from the case of birds too that the word is a principal element. For, in their case, a kind even of articulated word is produced, divorced from the sound which pours forth, just as is held to be true of the nightingale. Let us now leave aside the (question of the) underlying intent. For a parrot does not know whether it is speaking a line from a tragedy, but it produces the sounds all the same, just as a person does."

Despite the difficulties which this unfamiliar Greek, replete with strange technical terms, presents to the translator, the philosophically alert reader will have noticed that this striking passage, like Parallel 4A(ii) above, leads directly to the nucleus of Stoic linguistic theory.[66] To what extent is 'articulation' essential to intelligent speech? Do not birds like nightingales and parrots produce articulated speech, yet do not understand it at all? The key to this argument lies in Sextus Empiricus, *adv. Math.* viii 275 (= *SVF* ii 135, 223):

ἄνθρωπος οὐ τῶι προφορικῶι λόγωι διαφέρει τῶν ἄλλων ζώιων (καὶ γὰρ κόρακες καὶ ψίττακοι καὶ κίτται ἐνάρθρους προφέρονται φωνάς), ἀλλὰ τῶι ἐνδιαθέτωι.

" A human being differs from other animals by using not speech which is pronounced (for crows, parrots and jays can pronounce articulated words), but speech which is internalised."[67]

This is from Diogenes of Babylon, fifth scholarch of the Stoa, who, as W. Ax has recently demonstrated, developed Aristotle's biology of language in order to improve on the ideas of his predecessors Cleanthes and Chrysippus.[68] Ax has made a fine and

66. So G.M. Rispoli 1981, who, however, misses the parallel in Sextus.
67. On the concepts in this passage see G. Watson 1988, p. 50.
68. W. Ax 1986.

exhaustive study of ideas of sound, voice and speech in antiquity, while apparently remaining unaware that a major dated source for early Stoic linguistics was already published (albeit badly), viz. Philodemus' *On Poems*. For our purposes, however, Ax's study is all the more useful, since he has been able to show independently that the terminology used here by Pausimachus was developed by Diogenes of Babylon, whose importance for the history of linguistics must not be underrated. Thus Pausimachus' term for 'articulation', ἄρθρωσις, has replaced the term διάρθρωσις used until Aristotle's time, and ἔναρθρος has replaced διηρθρωμένος or the like.[69] Similarly, Aristotle was extremely insistent that the word ψόφος be used for 'noise' and φωνή be reserved for 'voice'; yet the use of φωνή to mean 'sound', (musical) 'note' or even 'word', already known in Plato, became even more prevalent after Aristotle. Moreover the word ἦχος, first found in Theophrastus and the spurious works of Aristotle, is characteristically Hellenistic.[70]

I wish to close by considering how Treatise B relates to Treatise A. In the case of *On Music* IV, Delattre has proved that Philodemus first set out his adversary's views, and then refuted them in the same sequence; in the course of this, he was able to show that the *scorze* forming the alleged Books 'I' and 'III' of the *On Music* all belong in fact to the same roll as the *midollo* which comprises Book IV, and which is identified as such by a closing title. Is the relationship between Treatises A and B similar, in that the *scorze* comprising Treatise B form the outer sections of the *midollo* which comprises Treatise A, wherein Philodemus refutes the arguments of his adversaries which he had set out earlier in the same Book?[71] In fact this cannot be so, and the situation is more complicated.

(i) The handwriting of Treatise A is distinctive, in that the epsilon and the sigma are both very narrow characters, with the

69. See Ax 1986, pp. 98-100, pp. 127-9, p. 150.

70. See R. Janko 1991, commentary on *PHerc.* 207 col. viii 3.

71. So M.L. Nardelli 1982. For earlier explanations see F. Sbordone 1983a, pp. 162-3.

Richard Janko

curves of the letters almost reduced to vertical bars. This same
script is faithfully reflected in the *disegni* of Treatise C, *scorze*
which have been shown by Romeo to form the earlier sections
of Treatise A. But the script in the surviving fragments and *disegni* of Treatise B is quite different, with a normal epsilon and
sigma, and is identical to that of Treatise D, which likewise consists of *scorze*.[72] It follows that Treatise B is either a different
copy of a different portion of the same Book of the *On Poems*, or
comes from an entirely different Book.

(ii) In a summary of an adversary's doctrines, we do not expect
to find polemic by Philodemus on anything like the scale found
in Treatise A. Nonetheless, there is still some polemic in Treatise
B, albeit on a reduced scale. Since it is unlikely that Philodemus
is quoting polemic offered by his opponent or opponents, it
seems that he polemicized twice against the same material, but
that Treatise B is largely summary with some polemic, whereas
Treatise A is a detailed polemic.[73] Such repetition seems at first
sight implausible, but in fact we know that Philodemus discussed euphony at least twice in the *On Poems*, in Book I and
then in Book II. In Treatise A (col. xxxi 4-10 Sbordone), after discussing harsh juxtapositions of vowels and consonants,
Philodemus continues:

οὐ μὴν [οὐδ', ὡς προ]επέδ[ει]ξα ἐν τῶι πρώτωι περὶ [ε]ὑφ[ωνί]ας
ἐπακολ[ούθων γραμμά]των [κα]ὶ ὁμ[ο]ίων, κι[ν]ῆσαί τι δύναται
τῶν ἐπιλελογισ[μ]ένων.[74]

" Nor indeed, as I showed previously in Book I on the euphony of sequential letters and the like, can any of the considerations which he advanced move us."

---

72. There are also ten rather extensive surviving papyrus-fragments, which I
have seen in Naples; these are not mentioned in the edition of M.L. Nardelli
1983. *PHerc.* 1074/7 line 9 has an accent (cf. above, n. 46).

73. So G.M. Rispoli 1981, pp. 176 n. 8.

74. I follow Sbordone's text here, but propose οὐ μὴν [οὐδ' for οὐ μὴν ἀ[λλ':
that a negative is needed was seen by D.M. Schenkeveld 1968, p. 204, p. 213.

Evidently Treatise A is not Book I, but refers back to another discussion of euphony. Unless Philodemus discussed euphony
more than twice, which does indeed seem implausible, Treatise
B must be a probable candidate to be identified as Book I. The
following passage from Book V (col. xxvi 7-18) suggests that
Treatise A in fact represents Book II:

τὰ δὲ περὶ τῶν στοιχείων, ἐν ο[ἷς] τὴν κρί[σ]ιν εἶναί φησι (sc. ὁ
Κράτης) τῶν σπου[δ]α[ίων] ποιημάτων, τίνος αὐτῶι καὶ πόσης
ἡδονῆς γέμε[ι π]αρεστακότες ἐν τ[ῶ]ι δευτέρωι τῶν ὑπομνημάτων,
διὰ τὸ καὶ περὶ ποιήματος εἶναι κοινῶς, ἀποδοκιμά[ζομ]εν παλιλ-
λογε[ῖ]ν.[75]

"But as for his remarks on the letters, in which he (sc. Crates)
claims that the judgement of good verse resides, we have
shown him in the second of our treatises (since it is also about
the verse in general) what kind of and how much pleasure
they contain, and we decline to repeat it."

Philodemus apparently repeated his discussions of euphony
because they were incorporated in different Books which dealt
with different aspects of literary theory; that is, he looked at the
topic from different angles. If this argument is correct, then
Treatise B is part of *On Poems* Book I, and Treatise A is the end of
Book II. But the full publication of the newly reconstructed text
of *On Poems* Book I must await another occasion; this brief
account of work in progress can give only glimpses of its interest. My real purpose here has of course been to sketch the
extraordinary potential of the new papyrological advances for
reconstructing many more rolls from the philosophical library
from Herculaneum. The Herculean task of sewing its remnants
back together will be at once frustrating, exacting and exciting;
but at least we can now see how to begin. There is much work
to be done.

University of California, Los Angeles

75. So Jensen's text, soon to be replaced by the edition of C. Mangoni (forthcoming in the series *La Scuola di Epicuro*).

305

Asmis, E. 1990a. "Philodemus' Epicureanism." *Aufstieg und Niedergang der römischen Welt* II 36.4, pp. 2369-2408.
Asmis, E. 1990b. "The Poetic Theory of the Stoic 'Aristo'." *Apeiron* 23, pp. 147-201.
Asmis, E. 1991. "Philodemus' Poetic Theory and *On the Good King According to Homer*." *Classical Antiquity* 10, pp. 1-45.
Ax, W. 1986. *Laut, Stimme und Sprache* (Göttingen).
Barker, A, 1989. *Ancient Musical Writings*. 2 vols. (Cambridge).
Barra, G. 1973. "Filodemo di Gadara e le lettere latine." *Vichiana* 2, pp. 247-60.
Barra, G. 1977-78. "Osservazioni sulla poetica di Filodemo e di Lucrezio." *Annali della Facoltà di Lettere e Filosofia di Napoli* 20, pp. 87-104.
Capasso, M. 1986. *Cronache Ercolanesi* 16, pp. 149-53.
Capasso, M. 1989. "Primo supplemento al *Catalogo dei Papiri Ercolanesi*." *Cronache Ercolanesi* 19, pp. 193-265.
Cavallo, G. 1983. *Libri Scritture Scribi a Ercolano. Cronache Ercolanesi* Suppl. I (Naples).
Croenert, W. 1903. *Memoria Graeca Herculanensis* (Leipzig), (repr. Hildesheim 1963).
Delattre, D. 1989. "Philodème, *De la musique*: livre IV, colonnes 40* à 109*." *Cronache Ercolanesi* 19, pp. 49-143.
Donadi, F. 1991. *Pseudo-Longino, "Del Sublime"* (Milan).
Dorandi, T. 1990. "Filodemo: gli orientamenti della ricerca attuale." *Aufstieg und Niedergang der römischen Welt* II 36.4, pp. 2328-68.
Gigante, M., edd., 1979. *Catalogo dei Papiri Ercolanesi.* (Naples).
Gigante, M. 1983. *Ricerche Filodemee*, ed. 2 (Naples).
Gigante, M. 1984. *Virgilio e la Campania.* (Naples).
Gigante, M. and Capasso, M. 1989 "Il ritorno di Virgilio a Ercolano." *Studi italiani di filologia classica* 7, pp. 3-6.
Gigante, M. 1989. "Filodemo tra poesia a prosa." *Studi italiani di filologia classica* 7, pp. 129-51.
Gigante, M. 1990. *Filodemo in Italia.* (ed. 2, Florence; English translation forthcoming, Ann Arbor 1992).
Gomperz, T. 1890. "Philodem und die ästhetischen Schriften der Herculanischen Bibliothek." *Sitzungsberichte der Akademie der Wissenschaften in Wien*, Phil. Hist. Cl. 123, pp. 1-88.
Gow, A.S.F. and Page, D.L. 1968. *The Garland of Philip* . (Cambridge).
Greenberg, N.A. 1955. *The Poetic Theory of Philodemus* . (Diss. Harvard University; published New York and London, 1990).

Bibliography

Hausrath, A. 1889. "Philodemi Περὶ ποιημάτων libri secundi quae videntur fragmenta." *Jahrbucher fur classische Philologie* Suppl. 17, pp. 213-76.

Innes, D.C. 1989. "Philodemus." In G.A. Kennedy, ed., 1989. *The Cambridge History of Literary Criticism. I: Classical Criticism.* (Cambridge), pp. 215-19.

Janko, R. 1987. *Aristotle: Poetics* (Indianapolis).

Janko, R. 1991. "Philodemus' *On Poems* and Aristotle's *On Poets.*" *Cronache Ercolanesi* 21.

Janko, R. 1992b. "A first join between *PHerc.* 411 + 1583 (Philodemus, *On Music* IV)." *Cronache Ercolanesi* 22.

Janko, R. 1992a. "From Catharsis to the Aristotelian mean." In A. Rorty 1992, pp. 339-56.

Kemke, J. 1884. *Philodemi de Musica librorum quae exstant* (Leipzig).

Kleve, K. 1989. "Lucretius in Herculaneum." *Cronache Ercolanesi* 19, pp. 5-27).

Kleve, K. 1990. "Ennius in Herculaneum." *Cronache Ercolanesi* 20, pp. 5-16).

Longo Auricchio, F. 1983. "Filodemo: La *Retorica* e la *Musica.*" In *Syzetesis: Studi sull'epicureismo greco e romano offerti a Marcello Gigante,* II pp. 553-65 (Naples).

Longo Auricchio, F,. and Capasso, M. 1987. "I rotoli della villa ercolanese: dislocazione e ritrovamento." *Cronache Ercolanesi* 17, pp. 37-47.

Luschnat, O. 1953. *Zum Text von Philodems Schrift "De Musica"* (Berlin).

Mangoni, C. 1988. "Prosa e poesia nel V libro della Poetica di Filodemo." *Cronache Ercolanesi* 18, pp. 127-38.

Mangoni, C. 1989. "Il *PHerc.* 228." *Cronache Ercolanesi* 19, pp. 179-86.

Nardelli, M.L. 1978. "La catarsi poetica nel *PHerc.* 1581." *Cronache Ercolanesi* 8, pp. 96-103.

Nardelli, M.L. 1979. "Papiri della 'Poetica' di Filodemo." *Cronache Ercolanesi* 9, pp. 137-40.

Nardelli, M.L. 1982. "*PHerc.* 994, col. x." *Cronache Ercolanesi* 12, pp. 135-6.

Nardelli, M.L. 1983. *Due trattati filodemei 'Sulla poetica'* (Περὶ ποιημάτων). In F. Sbordone 1983b.

Neubecker, AJ. 1986. *Philodem Über die Musik. Viertes Buch..* La Scuola di Epicuro IV (Naples).

Obbink, D. 1986. *Philodemus: De Pietate I.* (Diss. Stanford University, unpublished).

Parsons, P. 1987. *The Oxyrhynchus Papyri* LIV (Oxford).
Porter, J. 1989. "Philodemus on material difference." *Cronache Ercolanesi* 19, pp. 149-78.
Rispoli, G.M. 1969. "Il primo libro del *Peri Mousikês* di Filodemo." In F. Sbordone 1969, pp. 25-286.
Rispoli, G.M. 1981. "Suono ed articolazione nella teoria epicurea del linguaggio." *Proceedings of the XVIth. International Congress of Papyrology*, edd. R.S. Bagnall *et al.* , pp. 173-81 (Chico).
Roberts, W.R. 1907. *Longinus: On the Sublime* (Cambridge).
Romeo, C. 1988. *Demetrio Lacone: La Poesia*. La Scuola di Epicuro IX (Naples).
Rorty, A., edd., 1992. edd. *Essays on Aristotle's Poetics* (Princeton).
Sbordone, F., edd., 1969. *Ricerche sui Papiri Ercolanesi* I (Naples).
Sbordone, F., edd., 1976. *Ricerche sui Papiri Ercolanesi* II (Naples).
Sbordone, F. 1983a. *Sui Papiri della "Poetica" di Filodemo*. (Naples).
Sbordone, F. edd., 1983b. *Richerche sui Papiri Ercolanesi: IV* (Naples).
Schenkeveld, D.M. 1968. "οἱ κριτικοί in Philodemus." *Mnemosyne* 21, pp. 176-215.
Tait, J.I.M. 1941. *Philodemus' Influence on the Latin Poets* (Diss. Bryn Mawr).
Watson, G. 1988. *Phantasia in Classical Thought* (Galway).

About Our Contributors

Elizabeth Asmis is Associate Professor of Classics at the University of Chicago. She was educated at the University of Toronto and Yale University. She is the author of *Epicurus' Scientific Method* (Cornell University Press, 1984), and several articles on Presocratic, Stoic, Epicurean, and Platonic philosophy. She is currently preparing a book on Hellenistic Theories of Poetry.

Harold W. Attridge is Professor of Theology and Dean of the College of Arts and Letters at the University of Notre Dame. He was educated at Boston College and Cambridge University, where he read Classics and Philosophy, and at Harvard University where he studied Christian origins. He has taught at Southern Methodist University and at the University of Notre Dame. His publications include critical editions of several of the Gnostic tractates from the Nag Hammadi collection, as well as a commentary on the *Epistle to the Hebrews*.

David Charles is a Fellow of Oriel College, Oxford. He read Philosophy and Ancient History at Oxford University, where he received B.A., B.Phil. and D.Phil. degrees. He is the author of *Aristotle's Philosophy of Action* (London, 1984), and co-editor with Kathleen Lennon of *Reduction, Explanation and Realism* (Oxford, 1992). Presently, he is finishing a book about *Aristotle on Meaning and Natural Kinds*.

311

About Our Contributors

John J. Cleary is Associate Professor of Philosophy at Boston College, and lecturer in Philosophy at Maynooth College (Ireland). He received his B.A. and M.A. from University College, Dublin, and his Ph.D. from Boston University in 1982. He has written on ancient philosophy and on ethics, including *Aristotle on the Many Senses of Priority* (1988) and *Aristotle and Mathematics* (forthcoming).

Mary Louise Gill is Associate Professor of Classics and Philosophy, and Director of the Graduate Program in Classics, Philosophy, and Ancient Science at the University of Pittsburgh. She was educated at Barnard College and Cambridge University. She is the author of *Aristotle on Substance: The Paradox of Unity* (Princeton, 1989) and of a number of articles on Plato and Aristotle. She is Co-Editor of the journal *Ancient Philosophy*, and is currently coediting two collections of papers: *Unity and Identity of Aristotelian Substances* (with Theodore Scaltsas and David Charles), and *Self-Motion: From Aristotle to Newton* (with James G. Lennox).

Richard Janko, Professor of Classics at the University of California, Los Angeles, is the author of *Aristotle on Comedy* (Berkeley and London, 1984), *Aristotle: Poetics* (Indianapolis, 1987), *The Iliad: A Commentary. Volume IV: Books 13-16* (Cambridge, 1992), and articles on Philodemus' aesthetic works (*Cronache Ercolanesi*, 1991 onwards). He is currently reconstructing Philodemus' *On Poems*.

Richard Kraut is Professor of Philosophy at the University of Illinois at Chicago. He is the author of *Socrates and the State* (Princeton University Press), and *Aristotle on the Human Good* (Princeton University Press). He is co-editor of *Nature, Knowledge, and Virtue: Essays in Memory of Joan Kung* (Edmonton, Alberta: 1989), and editor of *The Cambridge Companion to Plato* (Cambridge University Press, forthcoming). He has published a number of articles on Plato and Aristotle, and is currently working on *Aristotle's Politics VII and VIII*, a translation with commentary (Oxford: Clarendon Press).

Joseph P. Lawrence is Associate Professor of Philosophy at Holy Cross College. He was educated at Washington University, Columbia University and the Universität Tübingen. He has published a variety of articles on both Greek and German metaphysics and the philosophy of art. He is the author of *Schellings Philosophie des ewigen Anfangs* (Konigshausen, 1989).

Jaap Mansfeld (b. 1936) is Professor of Ancient and Medieval Philosophy at the University of Utrecht, the Netherlands, where he received his education. His recent publications include *Die Vorsokratiker I—II* (Reclam, Stuttgart 1983-1986), *Studies in Later Greek Philosophy and Gnosticism* (Variorum: London 1989), *Studies in the Historiography of Greek philosophy* (Assen: Van Gorcum 1990), "Doxography and Dialectic: The Sitz im Leben of the Placita," in W.H. Haase (ed.), *Aufsteig und Niedergang der Romischen Welt* II Vol. 36.4 (De Gruyter: Berlin—New York 1990) pp. 3076-3229. A book on Hippolytus' *Elenchos* as a source for Greek philosophy is printing. He is currently working on two chapters in the *Cambridge History of Hellenistic Philosophy*, of which he is co-editor, and on a new edition of the fragments of the Early Stoics. He also is co-editor of the series Philosophia Antiqua (Brill: Leiden). He is a Fellow of the Royal Dutch Academy and of the Academia Europea, and has several times been chairman of the Philosophy Department.

Richard Patterson, Associate Professor of Philosophy at Emory University, was educated at Stanford University and the University of Pennsylvania. His publications include *Image and Reality in Plato's Metaphysics* and a number of articles on Plato and on Aristotle's modal syllogistic.

About Our Contributors

Pheme Perkins is Professor of Theology (New Testament) at Boston College. She has been president of the Catholic Biblical Association and of the New England Region of the American Academy of Religion. Currently she serves as Editor of the Society of Biblical Literature Dissertation Series in New Testament. Professor Perkins has written fourteen books including *The Gnostic Dialogue, Resurrection,* and *Jesus as Teacher* as well as some sixty articles in scholarly and popular journals. Her current work, *Gnosticism and the New Testament,* will be published by Fortress Press. Professor Perkins received her A.B. from St. John's College in Annapolis and her M.A. and Ph.D. degrees in New Testament and Christian Origins from Harvard University.

Christopher Rowe is Professor of Ancient Philosophy and Greek at the University of Bristol. He was educated at Trinity College, Cambridge, and has taught in Bristol since 1968. He has published on Homer, Hesiod, Plato, and Aristotle, including *The Eudemian and Nicomachean Ethics: A Study in the Development of Aristotle's Thought, Plato,* and a translation of Plato's *Phaedrus,* with commentary. He is currently completing a commentary on the *Phaedo* for Cambridge University Press.

David N. Sedley is presently Reader in Ancient Philosophy at the University of Cambridge. He was educated at Trinity College, Oxford, and at University College, London. He has published essays on a broad range of topics in ancient philosophy and is co-author (with A.A. Long) of *The Hellenistic Philosophers* (1987). Since 1986 he has served as editor of the *The Classical Quarterly.* Presently he is working on an edition of the Anonymous *Theaetetus* commentary.

the Department of Classics at Fordham University. He was educated at the City College of New York and Columbia University. He is the author of *The Fragments of Anaxagoras* (Meisenheim 1981) and several articles on Greek poetry and philosophy and the relationship between the two. He is currently preparing an edition with commentary of the epigrams of Philodemos.

Thomas M.Tuozzo studied philosophy and classics at Yale University and received his Ph.D. in 1987. He is currently Assistant Professor of Philosophy at the University of Kansas. He has published on Aristotelian ethics and moral psychology and is currently working on the moral psychology of the later Plato.

General Index

General Index

General Index

Index of Passages

Index of Passages

83b2-6: 239
90a8-10: 239
90a13-15: 239
90a35ff.: 239
91a30-33: 231
91b8-12: 231 fr.
91b15-21: 231
91b23-25: 229
91b26-27: 229
92a1: 232, 236 fr., 237
92a2-4: 230
92a30-34: 231, 236 fr., 243
92b30: 230, 237
92b35ff.: 229, 243
93a1-3: 229
93a7-8: 238
93a12-13: 231 fr.
93a18-20: 238
93a22-24: 234 fr.
93a30-36: 235
93b9-11: 243
93b12-14: 235, 238
93b19: 238
93b21-22: 238
93b21ff.: 239, 240
93b29-33: 228
93b35-37: 259
94a1-7: 236, 244
94a14-19: 229
97b23-26: 249
98b36-38: 237 fr.
99b3-4: 237 fr.
Prior Analytics
46b2-10: 230
Aristoxenus
frr. 18-19 Wehrli: 187n
Arius Didymus
Fr. 21 Diels : 116n
Fr. 38 Diels : 116n
ap. Stob. II, *Ecl. Eth.* (ed. Wachsmuth)
p. 60.21 ; 120n
p. 61.11-12 : 120n
p. 62.17 ff: 117n
p. 62.24-63.1 : 117n
Athenaeus
Deipnosophistai
187c: 64n
513a-c: 66n
588a: 68n
Augustine
Confessiones
7.4: 113n
7.9: 1n
8.2: 1n
De civitate Dei
10.23: 25n
XIV xvi.28: 112n
De Trinitate
IX-XI: 108n
XI ii.5: 131-32n
XI vi.10: 131-32n
XI vi.12: 131-32n
XI viii.15: 131-32n

Calcidius
In Tim. (ed. Waszink)
220, p. 232.22-233.2: 139-40n;
pp. 140-41n
220, p. 233.16 ff. : 139-40n;
pp. 140-41n
236 ff., p. 248 ff.: 139-40n
Cicero
Brutus
131: 97
De Divinatione
I 118 ff.: 110n
I 120: 110n
II, 37: 110n
De Fato
9: 117-18n
23: 120n
23-25: 117-18n
De finibus (On Ends)
1.25-26: 74n, 76n
1.71-72: 74-75
II 199: 272n
De Natura Deorum
III 92 : 110n
In Pisonem
70: 94
Luc. (= *Ac. pr. II*)
122: 139-40n
124: 139-40n
Tusc.
I 20: 139-40n
IV 11-32: 123-24n
IV 12: 123-24n
Clemens Alexandrinus
Stromateis (ed. Pott)
II, p. 466 (SVF III, 433): 116n
3.2.5,2-9,3: 13n
4.89.6-4.90.1: 18
Colossians, Epistle to
1:15: 19n
Corinthians I
8:6: 33
Corinthians, Second Epistle to
4:4: 19n
Demetrius Laco
De Poësi
II col. viii: 299n
Diogenes Laertius
Lives of the Philosophers
1.63: 98n
7 55 : 136n
7 116 : 123-24n
7 138 : 139-40n
7 157 : 115n
7 158: 116n
8 29 = Vorsokr. I p. 450.4: 139-40n
8 31 = Vorsokr. I p. 450.22: 139-40n
10.1: 98n
10.6: 68, 76-77
10.13: 73
10.26: 100n
10.120: 69n, 72, 73n

10.121: 71-74, 90-91
10.136: 95n
10.137: 67n
10.138: 98n
Donatus
Vita Vergilii
68: 97n
79: 272n
Ennius
Annales
VI: 272n
Epictetus
Diatr.
II 23.8ff.: 123-24n
Epicurus
Letter to Menoeceus
132: 73
Vatican Saying
45: 76
KD
29 Scol.: 100n
Fragmenta, ed. Usener
2: 95n
56: 102
164: 101
Erasistratus
Fragmenta (ed. Garofalo)
Fr. 36: 139-40n
Fr. 39: 140n
Fr. 200: 139-40n
Euripides
Ion
237-40: 286, 289
Eusebius
Praeparatio evangelica
11.17.11-18: 12n
11.18.22-23: 11n
11.22.3-5: 11n
Fronto
De Eloquentia, ed. van den Hart
p. 13: 97
Galenus
Compendium Timaei Platonis (edd. Kraus and Walzer)
p. 55.18-22: 139-40n
De Nervorum Dissectione (ed. Kühn, vol. II)
p. 831.2: 131-32n
De Affectuum Dignotione (ed. Marquardt, vol. I)
3 ff.: 134n
3, p. 5.14 ff.: 135n
4, p. 15.15-16: 122n
4-5: 134n
5, p. 20.12-4: 122n
5-6, p. 20.11-21.10: 134n
De Anim. Mor.
4: 134n
De Foetuum Formatione (ed. Kühn, vol. IV)
4, p. 674: 138n
De Morib. (ed. Kraus)
p. xxvi: p35; 137n
p. xxvii-xxviii: 134n

322

Index of Passages

273, 283, 285-305
Tractatus 'A': 285, 291-92, 293, 300, 303-305
Tractatus 'A', col. a: 294, 295
Tractatus 'A', col. b: 295
Tractatus 'A', col. d: 295, 296
Tractatus 'A', col. e: 299, 299
Tractatus 'A', col. f: 299
Tractatus 'A', col. iv-v: 296-97
Tractatus 'A', col. vi: 297-98
Tractatus 'A', col. xxxi: 304
Tractatus 'B': 285, 286-305 et vide PHerc. 460, 1073
Tractatus 'C': 285, 303
Tractatus 'D': 276, 285, 288, 289, 290, 303
Tractatus 'E': 285
V: 268, 283
V col. xxvi: 304
De Ir.
  cols. xxxi.24 ff.: 117-18n
  cols. xxxiii.25 ff.: 117-18n
De Lib. Dic. (ed. Olivieri)
  Fr. 52 : 134n
  Fr. 87: 134n
De Oecon. (ed. Jensen)
  col. vii, p 23.6-7 : 134n
De Virtutibus et Vitiis
  272n.
Epigrams
  17: 98
  23: 102-103
Palatine Anthology
  11.44: 90
On the Good King according to Homer
  Col. 25.20: 88n
  col. 43.16-19 Dorandi: 87n
On Music 4
  IV: 277, 280, 284-95, 303
  IV, col.37.38-39: 95
  col.5.25-37 Neubecker: 80
  col. 6.5-18: 81
  col. 13.16-24: 84
  col. 14.7-13: 81
  col. 15.1-23: 83n, 84
  col. 16.17-21: 88
  col. 17.2-13: 89
  col. 20.7-17: 84
  col. 26.1-7: 84
  col. 26.9-14: 83n
  col. 28.16-35: 83
  col. 37.8-39: 89
  col. 38.12-30: 89-90
On Piety
  280
  fr. 37 Gomperz: 87n
  fr. 48: 81
  fr. 63: 87n
  fr. 95: 87n
  fr. 145: 87n
On Poems 5, 67
  col. 1.10-18 Jensen: 81
  col. 26.19-23: 82n

col. 28.26-32: 83
col. 29.9-17: 82n
col. 29.17-19: 85
col. 29.33-36: 83
On Rhetoric
  v. 1, p. 262 Sudhaus: 85
ap. PHerc
  225: 281
PHerc
228: 283
253: 272n
312: 272
403: 283n
407: 283n
411: 284
460: 275, 291-92, 293-305
460, fr. 2: 286
460, fr. 4-5: 282, 286, 287
460, fr. 6: 300
460, fr. 9: 300, 301
460, fr. 14: 288
460, fr. 15: 298, 301
460, fr. 16: 300
460, fr. 19: 286, 288, 293
460, fr. 21: 295, 296
460, fr. 22: 296
460, fr. 23: 283
460, fr. 24: 283, 300
460, fr. 27: 286
460, fr. 28: 282n., 286
460, fr. 29: 286
994: 285
1012: 68n, 80n
1073: 275, 286, 291-92, 294-305
1073, fr. 1: 299
1073, fr. 2: 300
1073, fr. 3: 300, 301
1073, fr. 6: 298
1073, fr. 7: 300
1073, fr. 10: 286, 289
1073, fr. 12: 294
1073, fr. 15: 300
1073, fr. 18: 286
1074: 283, 303n
1081, fr. 4: 288, 289, 290
1081, fr. 25-8: 289
1081, fr. 29: 276n
1082: 272n
1425: 274n, 283n
1538: 274n
1576: 284
1581: 277, 283
1583: 284
1676: 285
1677: 285
PHerc. Paris
  2: 272n
ap. POxy.
  3274: 272n
Plato
Apology: 202
Charmides
  154e: 198-99

154e4: 198-99
154e8-155a1: 198-99
155d-e: 197f.; 197-98n
156e-157a: 199
159a: 199
Cratylus
  403a-404b: 137n
  438C: 20
  439A: 19
  439B: 20
Euthyphro:
  205-6
Gorgias
  462a-465e: 205-6
Lysis:
  197n
Meno
  86a-b: 173
Leges
  I 644e: 117-18n
  I 644e2: 117-18n
Phaedo
  59a: 167
  59d: 167
  61d-63a: 168-69
  61de: 186
  61d7: 167n
  63b-69e: 166-70
  65a3: 171
  66e5-6: 171
  69e-70b: 170
  70b2-4: 154, 173
  71d6ff.: 171
  71c6-9: 171
  71e11: 171
  72d: 190n
  72d4-5: 171
  72e: 173
  73a2-3: 160
  75c-d: 167
  75d1-3: 174
  77a-b: 173
  77b: 185
  77c1-d5: 160
  77d-e: 170
  77e: 188
  77b5-7: 172
  78b4-84b8: 163-66, 178
  76d7-8: 174
  77c1-2: 175
  77e-78a: 175
  78d: 161, 174
  84c6-7: 164
  85b10-d10: 167n
  85c-d: 164n, 175, 187n
  85e3-86b5: 175
  86b-d: 167n
  87a: 177
  88a: 177
  88b5-6: 177
  88c: 161, 176
  88c-d: 160, 177
  89c3-4: 177
  90e-91c: 170

Index of Passages